'*Enemy Images* provides a comprehensive overview of our history of socially constructing an enemy Other, documenting how and why we marshal racist stereotypes and scapegoating rhetoric to inflame emotions and spur aggression. A much-needed primer to help make sense of the dehumanizing propaganda so prevalent in contemporary geo-political conflicts.'

Erin Steuter, *Mount Allison University, author of* At War with Metaphor: Media, Propaganda, and Racism in the War on Terror

'A must-read for anyone who wishes to understand and analyse enemy images. This impressively multidisciplinary book is a treasure trove and great source of inspiration for all students and scholars of peace and conflict in all their forms.'

Leena Malkki, *University of Helsinki, director of the Centre for European Studies at the University of Helsinki and co-editor of* The Routledge Handbook on Radicalisation and Countering Radicalisation

T0388492

ENEMY IMAGES

This book offers a detailed understanding of 'enemy images', which are used in political rhetoric to dehumanize adversaries for various purposes, such as to legitimate violent conflicts.

Applying theoretical models to a strong catalogue of historical and recent examples – from blood libel narratives in medieval manuscripts to state-sponsored children's board games in Nazi Germany and social media posts about the wars in Gaza and Ukraine – the book identifies how 'enemy images' have led to the development of dominant socio-political paradigms by providing justifications for and reinforcements of violent conflicts both within and between societies. In doing so, the work offers an up-to-date, accessible, and authoritative overview of how to identify, analyse, and counteract energy images – which will be key to fostering social environments of reconciliation and peacebuilding for the future.

This book will be of much interest to students and scholars of peace and conflict studies, International Relations, history, political sociology, and communication studies.

Kristian Steiner is Associate Professor in Peace and Conflict Studies at Malmö University, Sweden. He has authored numerous articles in peace and conflict studies and political science. His research revolves around the usage of religious language to justify violence. He co-edited *Expressions of Radicalization: Global Politics, Processes and Practices* (with Andreas Önnerfors, 2018).

Andreas Jahrehorn Önnerfors is Full Professor in Intellectual History and works as a project manager at Fojo Media Institute at Linnaeus University, Sweden. He has specialized in contemporary radicalization, populist mobilization, and conspiratorial meaning-making. In 2021, he co-edited *Europe: Continent of Conspiracies. Conspiracy Theories in and about Europe* with André Krouwel.

ENEMY IMAGES

Emergence, Consequences and Counteraction

Kristian Steiner with Andreas Jahrehorn Önnerfors

Routledge
Taylor & Francis Group

LONDON AND NEW YORK

Designed cover image: Getty / Vernon Lewis Gallery/Stocktrek Images

First published 2025
by Routledge
4 Park Square, Milton Park, Abingdon, Oxon OX14 4RN

and by Routledge
605 Third Avenue, New York, NY 10158

Routledge is an imprint of the Taylor & Francis Group, an informa business

© 2025 Kristian Steiner and Andreas Jahrehorn Önnerfors

British Library Cataloguing-in-Publication Data
A catalogue record for this book is available from the British Library

Library of Congress Cataloging-in-Publication Data
Names: Steiner, Kristian, author. | Önnerfors, Andreas, 1971– author.
Title: Enemy images : emergence, consequences and counteraction /
Kristian Steiner with Andreas Jahrehorn Önnerfors.
Description: Abingdon, Oxon ; New York : Routledge, 2025. |
Includes bibliographical references and index.
Identifiers: LCCN 2024026724 (print) | LCCN 2024026725 (ebook) |
Subjects: LCSH: Propaganda. | Propaganda–Psychological aspects. |
Enemies in art. | Hostility (Psychology)
Classification: LCC HM1231 .S847 2024 (print) | LCC HM1231 (ebook) |
DDC 303.3/75–dc23/eng/20240625
LC record available at https://lccn.loc.gov/2024026724
LC ebook record available at https://lccn.loc.gov/2024026725

ISBN: 978-1-032-24636-9 (hbk)
ISBN: 978-1-032-24635-2 (pbk)
ISBN: 978-1-003-27957-0 (ebk)

DOI: 10.4324/9781003279570

Typeset in Times New Roman
by Newgen Publishing UK

CONTENTS

ILLUSTRATIONS

Figures

Tables

Boxes

PREFACE

This book is the result of many years of teaching peace and conflict studies. It all started when I was commissioned to give a course called 'Enemy Images'. I soon realized there was no suitable or comprehensive textbook in the field. My teaching, therefore, rested on a patchwork of different academic texts, and the idea was born to write a textbook that discussed themes of relevance to enemy images in a pedagogical and systematic way. After many years of teaching and reading in the field, I felt ready to systematize my knowledge and plan a textbook. I soon realized that the quality of the book would be better if I had an experienced researcher with complementary skills by my side. I therefore contacted my friend and colleague Professor Andreas Jahrehorn Önnerfors, now active at Linnaeus University, Sweden, who has for many years researched conspiracy theories, their causes and effects, and how to counteract them. We became a perfect match. I am the main author and have written about 80% of the book – specifically, the bulk of Chapters 1–6, with Professor Önnerfors constructively reviewing and criticizing my drafts, and contributing additional shorter text sections. In the case of Chapter 7, these roles were reversed.

Enemy images are powerful ingredients of political rhetoric. In their most simple function, they establish powerful narratives where an out-group is depicted as an existential threat, and an unbridgeable divide between 'us' and 'them' fuelled by fear is created. Once these frames of perceiving the other are established, enemy images also serve to condone or endorse violence in its different forms, both indirect (structural) and direct (physical). Enemy images are thus central ingredients in violent conflicts and warfare both within and between societies, and counteracting them is key to the processes of reconciliation and peacebuilding. Understanding and unpacking war rhetoric has long been a central theme in social science, at least since 1927 when Harold D. Lasswell first published his pathbreaking book

Propaganda Technique in the World War, possibly for even longer. The impact and prevalence of such rhetoric increased as an effect of modernisation and the dawn of mass communication.

This book has seven main themes. First, we define what enemy images are, discussing some of their main consequences and why we should study them. Second, we elaborate with two different ideal–typical enemy images, enabling the reader to identify and unpack hostile rhetoric. Third, the book deals with persuasion, and the different strategies undertaken to make enemy images generally accepted. Fourth, we discuss acceptance, and why people tend to buy into a rhetoric tainted by hostility against 'them'. In connection with this, we explain the social and political conditions that seem to facilitate acceptance of enemy images, and whether certain individuals are more likely to credit them. Fifth, we reflect on which groups tend to be repeatedly targeted, i.e. depicted as an enemy. Sixth, we discuss what we can do to counteract enemy images. Lastly, we discuss how successive media revolutions have affected the formation of enemy images and how these have been expressed through media over time. In our endeavour to discuss these themes, we offer readers (both inside and outside academia) perspectives, concepts, theories, and explanations from a plurality of academic fields, most importantly from international relations, social psychology, cognition studies, and communication studies. We also provide the reader with contemporary and historical examples and illustrations of enemy images, thereby delivering an overview not found in other publications. For the first time, a book will bring a proper understanding of enemy images to the forefront of academic teaching.

Kristian Steiner

ACKNOWLEDGEMENTS

We would like to extend our thanks to the editors and editorial assistants at Routledge: without your patience and guidance, this book would not be published. We also want to thank our peer reviewers for their valuable and constructive criticism, and our language editor, David Ronder. We would like to express our gratitude, too, to our research interns, Charles Hagstedt, Mariam Bonson, and Attila Fodor for their superb assistance. Thanks are likewise due to colleagues who, in various seminar and conference contexts, have reviewed different parts of our manuscript. These include Professor Jan Ångström, Swedish Defence University, Dr. Caroline Adolfsson, Malmö University, Sweden, and Associate Professor Ralph Sundberg, Swedish Defence University. Moreover, we would like to express our gratitude to our colleagues at the Department of Global Political Studies at Malmö University, Sweden, and at Fojo Media Institute at Linnaeus University, Sweden. Lastly, in writing this book, we took quite a lot of inspiration from the students in peace and conflict studies at Malmö University. They and their contributions to our class discussions have been very much in mind throughout the whole process. We therefore dedicate this book to them.

HOW TO READ THIS BOOK

In the Preface, Kristian Steiner briefly presents the seven themes that this book addresses. Discussing them requires consulting a wide array of theories, methods, and approaches from social sciences and humanities.

As will emerge later, neither the term 'enemy images' nor the themes of this book are commonly discussed in scholarship, so the authors have taken an eclectic approach in gathering and drawing insights from various disciplines. Most of the scholarly literature consulted has not been produced to explain enemy images or shed light on the themes presented here but stems from areas of inquiry such as psychological and social–psychological explanations of violence and prejudice, propaganda and communication studies, research on cognition, media history, and so on. With the risk of some overlaps, these approaches are used several times with the aim of providing insights across different themes. The same approach or theory can be used to increase the reader's understanding of why enemy images are produced and accepted, and how they can be countered. For instance, an approach such as the Elaboration Likelihood Model (ELM, see below) explains why humans tend to process information at two speeds: a) quick and intuitive, and b) slow and reflective. The ELM is referred to both when explaining the susceptibility to enemy images and what needs to be done to counter them. Such theories and many other approaches are thus discussed in more than one chapter and with more than one purpose.

The book also discusses several historical examples. The Holocaust and its scholarly treatment cannot be underestimated in this regard. But the Rwandan genocide (see Chapters 2, 6, and 7) and other historical atrocities are also addressed. The ambition is to present well-documented cases that can serve as the starting point for investigations about past, current, and future instances where enemy images are constructed, accepted, and countered. While working on this book, the full-scale Russian invasion of Ukraine was unleashed in 2022. The warfare, its rhetoric, and information influence campaigns have – with the risk of a short expiry date – offered plenty of opportunities to draw from a very contemporary example, which we see as both an opportunity and a challenge for future analyses. Media products are discussed in several chapters and there are some parallels between Chapters 2, 3, and 7 in this regard. The main difference is that Chapters 2 and 3 use propaganda posters, printed outlets, theatre plays, or speeches as exemplifications of persuasive propaganda and manipulation techniques, whereas Chapter 7 is focused on the development of certain types of media and how they shape and transmit their content over time.

To enhance the readability of the subsequent chapters, we would like to explain how they should be read. First, considering what we have said, each chapter brings together different approaches to each question we aim to discuss. Some of the leading theories and theorists we have consulted are explained further in *boxes*, which can be read as stand-alone pieces supporting the main text and the narrative of each chapter. Our argument is also supported by a wealth of images, figures, and tables illustrating and summarizing chapter content. Together with parts of the main text highlighted with bullet points or presented as lists, these should be studied with particular attention. Chapter *summaries* aim to discuss the inferences that can be made from the line of reasoning. Each chapter has a few *study questions*, where we encourage readers to deepen different aspects of the content. *Potential essay or thesis suggestions* are intended to inspire readers to develop certain subjects further, and *suggested further reading* aims to recommend titles or resources we found worthwhile for exploring certain perspectives more deeply. Naturally, the *references* to each chapter serve the same purpose.

Many theories, experiments, and explanations in social sciences and the humanities have their own name and even acronyms. Since we deploy these terms across the book with different purposes, and in order to provide a useful overview, we have listed them in alphabetical order, with a short explainer, the chapter(s) they are mentioned in, and further information in Table 0.1.

TABLE 0.1 List of major theories, models, and approaches referred to in this book

Name and typical traits	Short explainer	Chapter(s)	More information
Authoritarian personality theory (APT) 'F-scale'	Explains why societies with strong leaders maintaining order are accepted and obeyed	4	• Theodor Adorno • biography in Box 4.5 • F-scale variables in Box 4.5
Cobweb model of international relations (IR)	Suggests frequent ties and connections between different forms of communities on a global scale	6	• John Burton
Cognitive consistency theory (CCT)	Information is more likely to be accepted when it is consistent with previously held beliefs	3, 4	
Cognitive dissonance theory (CDT)	Explains conflicting cognitive states and attitudes influencing behaviour	3, 4	• Leon Festinger • biography in Box 4.3
Cognitive factors: • cognitive bias • illusory correlation	Factors that explain why information is processed in a way that promotes the acceptance of enemy images or the ascription of collective blame	4, 5	
Continued influence effect (CIE)	Explains how false information tends to 'stick' even if countered or corrected	6	
Counternarratives	Types of narratives undermining a dominant narrative through various strategies	6	
Cross-categorization and out-group theory	Explains that collective categorization can occur across multiple categories due to membership of two or more groups	5	
Elaboration likelihood model (ELM)	Explains cognitive shortcuts and preferences in two modes: a) quick and intuitive, and b) slow and reflective	3, 4, 6	
Healing of victims and perpetrators	Approaches explaining how group divisions can be overcome after traumatic events	6	• Erwin Staub • biography in Box 6.1
Human needs	Human needs are structured as a pyramid ranging from physiological to abstract and explain human behaviour	3, 4	• A.H. Maslow • biography in Box 4.1
Ideological model of scapegoating	Explains that scapegoating is a collective process creating a common understanding of collective misfortunes and shifting blame onto other groups	5	• Peter Glick

(Continued)

Stanford prison experiment (SPE)	Institutionalized settings of punishment encourage dehumanization	1	• Philip Zimbardo
'Sphere of deviance'	Explains how crises and wars establish three zones of journalistic coverage: a) consensus, b) legitimate controversy, and c) deviance	2, 3, 7	• Daniel Hallin
Social identity theory (SIT) (alienation and othering)	Denotes a person's sense of group belonging and explains intergroup behaviour	1, 2	• Henri Tajfel and John Turner
Social dominance orientation (SDO)	Explains that societies are based on stable group-based hierarchies (three categories: gender, age, and arbitrary)	4	• Sidanius and Pratto • SDO-scale with 14 items (c. 4)
Relative gratification theory (RGT)	Explains that out-group hostility and stigmatization can occur even if needs are abundantly satisfied	4, 6	
Relative deprivation theory (RDT)	Explains that satisfaction is not related to objective circumstances but is perceived in relation to other people or groups	4	
Realist group conflict theory (RGCT) 'Robbers Cave experiment'	Explains that when resources are limited and groups compete, resentment, prejudice, and discrimination are likely	4, 6	• Muzafer Sherif • biography in Box 4.4
Obedience to authority	Obedience to authority is a necessary ingredient in social life	1	• Stanley Milgram • biography in Box 1.1
Moral disengagement theory (MDT)	Explains moral disengagement from norms and behaviour in certain contexts	1, 4, 6	• Albert Bandura • biography in Box 1.3
Lingua Tertii Imperii (The Language of the Third Reich, LTI)	Refers to authoritarian regimes using language to impose repressive patterns of thought	3	• Viktor Klemperer • biography in Box 3.1
Intergroup contact theory (ICT)	Suggests that negative perceptions of out-groups are reduced when contacts and interactions are increased	6	• Gordon Allport

TABLE 0.1 (Continued)

Name and typical traits	Short explainer	Chapter(s)	More information
Stereotype content model (SCM) 'warmth and competence'	Explains that stereotyping builds on dynamic attributions where the content of stereotypes can be both negative and positive	5	• Fiske, Cuddy, Glick and Xu
System justification theory (SJT)	Explains why the role of status in societies with unequal distribution of resources and positions leads to the justification of societal arrangements	5	• Jost and Banaji
Theories of prejudice	Explains the willingness to accept intergroup prejudice (e.g. the razor experiment) as a way of reducing cognitive complexity	4	• Gordon W. Allport • biography in Box 4.2

1

WHY STUDY ENEMY IMAGES?

An introduction

CHAPTER OBJECTIVES

- To introduce the concept of enemy images
- To offer a concise overview of some important consequences of enemy images
- To describe a variety of strategies and conditions that make people obey and participate in organized violence

Introduction

Warfare and other hostile policies must be prepared carefully. In addition to military planning, the domestic population must be provided with an explanatory narrative claiming that the war is legitimate, rational, necessary, and even moral. And the need for justification has probably increased after the Industrial Revolution since wars have 'become more pervasive, brutal – and therefore more ethically problematic' (Fox and Welch, 2012: 7). Enemy images, the focus of this book, are an essential element in the formation of cognitive foundations and worldviews by which war and violent conflict are justified and rationalized.

Enemy images are potent components of political rhetoric that seek to denigrate or dehumanize collective adversaries for a wide range of purposes, most commonly to legitimize violent conflicts and mobilize a population. In their most simple function, they establish powerful imaginings of existential antagonisms, an unbridgeable divide between 'us' and 'them' fuelled by fear. Once these frames of perceiving the absolute other are established, enemy images serve to condone

DOI: 10.4324/9781003279570-1

or endorse violence in its different forms, whether structural, cultural, or direct (physical) (see Galtung, 1969 and 1990). Enemy images are thus central in violent conflicts and warfare both within and between societies, and counteracting them is key to processes of reconciliation and peacebuilding. A comprehensive definition is offered further below.

This book is an introduction to the study of enemy images. In our understanding, neither 'enemies' nor 'images' are stable categories. They are not set once and for all but are subject to complex processes of construction in diverging contexts over time. For instance, after the Napoleonic Wars, France was portrayed as an existential archenemy of Germany. The foundation of the German Empire in 1871 was celebrated in the Hall of Mirrors in Versailles to humiliate the French. Likewise, the Armistice of 11 November 1918 following the defeat of Germany in the First World War was signed in a simple railroad carriage in Compiègne. Just over three decades later, the European Coal and Steel Community was founded to entangle West German and French economies and thus achieve durable peace and stability. Today, Germany and France are united in official friendship. The emergence of toxic enemy images about France was embedded within the development of exclusionary nationalism in which ideas of ethnic purity necessitated existential adversaries (Fiebig-von Hase, 1997: 19–24). By contrast, concepts about European peace and unity facilitate the disarming of enmity constructs.

In other words, who an enemy is, how this enemy is perceived, and how this perception is expressed are not fixed at any point in time, but relative to the community's self-definition and the purpose for which such a perception of an absolute antagonist develops explanatory power.

The distinction between the enemy and 'us' and 'our' ally is central to understanding the dynamics of human conflict, making the images invoked to describe these relationships of significant interest in peace and conflict studies and related areas of enquiry. In the subsequent chapters, we will address rhetorical strategies, the emergence, acceptance, consequences, and potential counteraction of enemy images, uniting approaches from sociology, international relations, intellectual history, social psychology, cognition studies, and communication studies.

Chapter overview

In the first part, we define what an enemy image is and relate it to similar concepts. In the second part, we discuss the consequences enemy images have, the things they do to individuals and communities. That is why they are used and why we analyse them in this book. Although enemy images are indeed essential in mobilizing people to participate in war, they are not the only tool in this endeavour. Therefore, in the third part, we will discuss other strategies and conditions that influence behaviour and make people participate in organized violence.

Defining enemy image

'Enemy image' constitutes the core concept in this volume and needs a careful definition. In this volume, we define an enemy image as

- a cognitive construct of the collective other as an imminent, real, serious (but not invincible), and possibly growing threat to 'our' most vital interests, with the purpose of mobilizing and desensitizing an in-group, and legitimizing (often violent) responses against a threatening out-group.

For us, these intergroup relationships are at the heart of understanding the (rhetorical and practical) dynamics of enemy images. As Vuorinen has argued (2012), the enemy image underscores that a threat is imminent and neither theoretical nor distant. The threat is here and now and must be dealt with urgently. Likewise, it does not concern marginal or unimportant assets, values, or interests. On the contrary, an enemy image represents the other as an urgent threat towards 'our' most valued and essential assets and sometimes it is a matter of 'our' survival (Luostarinen, 1989: 125). Vital interests tend to vary depending on for instance culture, economy, and geostrategic position, but they often relate to democracy, territory, sovereignty, freedom, life, or welfare.

An enemy image has at least three, often interrelated, purposes: (1) to mobilize and (2) to desensitize an in-group and (3) to make a response (often violent) against a threatening out-group appear legitimate. To be successful in the attempts to mobilize a population to take part in (usually violent) actions against the enemy, the cause of those actions must appear just and legitimate. It is also easier to mobilize a population to take part in violence against the enemy if the population is desensitized so that it can inflict harm on the enemy without feelings of remorse and pain. To achieve this, the enemy image usually portrays the enemy as either deindividuated (deprived of individuality and turned into an anonymous figure in a group) or dehumanized (turned into something evil and/or subhuman).

In addition, it is also important that the enemy and the threat are *not* understood as invincible. Harold Dwight Lasswell (1902–1978) was a prominent American political scientist and communication theorist writing seminal works on war propaganda. As a 25-year-old, he published his thesis titled *Propaganda Technique in World War I* (1927), in which he laid down the foundations of studying communication as a tool of modern conflict. Lasswell noted that 'the fighting spirit of a nation feeds upon the conviction that it has a fighting chance to win' and that 'the will to win is intimately related to the chance to win' (Lasswell, 1927: 102 and 118).

A legitimate response must be constructed carefully and understood as reasonable in relation to the construct of the threat. In other words, 'the social design of a security problem conditions and legitimates the kind of means used to stop it' (Balzacq, 2011: 1). A legitimate response against a threatening out-group requires at least three things: the response must have a legitimate *objective*, its *means* must be legitimate, and the *costs* involved must be perceived as acceptable.

The most common way to make the objectives appear legitimate is to describe the war as one of defence. Before the First World War, the so-called *Einkreisungstheorie*, the notion that Germany was encircled and threatened, was widespread in the country. The reason for this was that neighbouring France and Russia, and later also Great Britain, had entered an increasingly strong alliance that the German leadership felt was directed against their country (Carroll, 1938: 485). Partly because of this perception, Kaiser Wilhelm II could claim in his 'balcony speech' at the outset of the First World War that 'the sword has been forced into our hands' (Lasswell, 1927: 56). 'Our' violent aggression was thus styled as the inevitable consequence of imperative causes.

Whereas Wilhelm II justified war as the inevitable consequence of a threat against the German nation, other objectives could also be constructed in line with international norms such as democracy, security, and human rights. Humanitarian interventions with reference to the 'Responsibility to Protect' (R2P) principle are of course just one of the varieties of justifications for war and were even invoked by the Russian regime during the invasion of Ukraine in 2022.

Secondly, to be legitimate, the means – often violent – must appear as measured and well-considered in relation to the threat. Brutality, violence against civilians, and unnecessary violence are hard to justify. In an interview some years ago, with Messianic Jewish[1] leaders in Israel, conducted by Kristian Steiner and Anders Lundberg, one Messianic leader defended Israel's bombings of civilians in Gaza in a previous war. The Messianic leader, an ardent supporter of Israel and its policies, tried to put the blame on the victims.

> There is no room for manoeuvre. They are using the mosques, they are using schools they are using hospitals, they are using civilian homes. To shoot from. There is no … whatever you do it is a lose-lose situation, for them and for us. Because we hold ourselves from retaliating, and eventually you have to put a stop to it, so it is a scenario every few years, there's a big operation in Gaza, a lot of people are getting killed on both sides, you know, and they would do it again. How to fight? This is not a tank against tanks or airplanes against airplanes or soldier against soldier.
>
> *(Steiner and Lundberg, 2018: 159)*

To make the violent response appear legitimate, the costs involved must also be justifiable. In addition to the loss of human lives, a political leader must consider financial costs and 'our' potential loss of status/reputation in the eyes of the world.

The concept of enemy image bears a resemblance to other concepts used in peace and conflict studies or other relevant academic fields. One such concept is *war propaganda*. The main difference between the two concepts is that propaganda in war is directed as much to the *enemy population* and sometimes other foreign audiences, as to the in-group. In relation to the enemy, war propaganda has an inverse purpose compared with an enemy image. It tries to demoralize the enemy and spread defeatism. It tries to communicate to the enemy that their goals are morally illegitimate, their means inhumane, and that the costs of their policy will be substantial. Or as Lasswell (1927: 164) puts it: 'your case is hopeless. Your blood is spilt in vain'. And if possible, it will attempt to depict 'us', 'their' targets, as worthy humans. All in all, an enemy image in this volume is understood as a construct of the out-group directed to the in-group. War propaganda, on the other hand, refers to communication to two audiences: the in-group and the out-group (see Box 3.1 for a more elaborate discussion).

Enemy images also share characteristics with the social psychological concept of *prejudice*. Just like an enemy image, prejudice represents the other as inferior in some respects (see Chapter 2), but unlike the enemy image, not necessarily a threat. In an enemy image, you might admit that the out-group is in some limited ways superior to yours (maybe more powerful), but the concluding verdict is that the out-group remains inferior (usually morally). One could say that the enemy is 'perceived as low in status but as having high power to affect the in-group prominently' (Sternberg and Sternberg, 2008: 98). In any case, what seems to be a feature common to enemy images and prejudice is the goal of enhancing the self-esteem of the in-group (and its individual members) by describing the out-group as inferior and the in-group as superior in relevant and important respects.

Thirdly, an enemy image also has similarities with a *stereotype*. Stereotypes tend to describe out-groups with rigid characterizations and strong generalizations; they tend to be fixed and oversimplified. Although stereotypes have potentially harmful effects and the term is often understood as negative, they facilitate processing of the stimuli produced by the five senses, enabling rapid and smooth perception (for a more elaborate discussion, see Chapter 4). According to John F. Dovidio et al.,

> more recent research emphasizes the functional and dynamic aspects of stereotypes as simplifying a complex environment. Stereotypes are cognitive schemas used by social perceivers to process information about others.
>
> *(Dovidio, Hewstone, Glick, and Esses, 2010: 7)*

'Schemas' are understood to 'work as a set of lenses, which filter and organize … information according to the prevailing set of the individual's established values, goals, and preferences' (Fiebig-von Hase, 1997: 8). Still, stereotypes are not always helpful. Sometimes they lead to misperception and erroneous decision-making (see below). And normatively they are problematic since they tend to make people believe that an individual belonging to a certain group 'automatically … represents traits and characteristics perceived to apply to the group as a whole' (Petersson, 2009: 460). Since enemy images resemble stereotypes, they also enable rapid and smooth perception but, on the other hand, also lead to problematic decisions caused by flawed perception.

An enemy image, lastly, is also related to *othering* (Brons, 2015). Othering is primarily a sociological concept (in social identity theory) describing a process where a group is identified that does not follow the norms of the in-group or deviates from it in other important aspects. Behind the process of othering (or the characterization of external groups) lies the idea of self-categorization, the knowledge of social membership of a particular group, and its emotional meaning. According to David and Bar-Tal (2009: 361–366), collective identity shares six generic features:

- A sense of a common fate
- The perception of the uniqueness of the collective and its distinction from other collectives
- Coordinated activity of the collective's members
- The commonality of beliefs, attitudes, norms, and values
- Concern for the welfare of the collective and mobilization and sacrifice for its sake
- Continuity and consecutiveness in the dimension of time

Furthermore, collective identity revolves around the meaning-making content of these features such as territory, culture and language, collective memory, and shared societal beliefs. Differentiation and demarcation against other collectives are deeply inscribed in these processes of identity formation.

The difference between an enemy image and 'othering' is that the other is depicted as an outsider and different but not necessarily as a threat. Othering is a very common phenomenon, perhaps even unavoidable, and occurs in group formation processes where there is a need to define 'them' to define 'us'. A Swedish 'us' is, at least partly, constructed in relation to significant out-groups such as Danes, Finns, and Norwegians. Without 'them', it would be hard to develop a consistent self-definition. One effect of othering, self-definition, and group formation is divisions between 'us' and 'them' as well as inclusion and exclusion. And, as stated, an enemy image is a construct of 'them', but a very potent version, since 'they', being external to 'us', also constitutes a threat. The elements of collective identity are easy to manipulate in the construction of fear directed towards the significant collective other. Therefore,

> the existence of an enemy has many obvious advantages to those in power. For example: An enemy image may strengthen integration within a given group and moderate internal conflicts; it may help to bring the rank and file behind the group leaders; it may be used (scapegoat) to explain any injustices within the group.
>
> *(Luostarinen, 1989: 127)*

And in the wake of this process, prejudice, stereotypes, and sometimes enemy images are likely to develop. So, all enemies are others, but not all others are

TABLE 1.1 Categories of others

		Resemblance	
		Similar to 'us'	*Different from 'us'*
Attitude to out-group	Friend	1. Benign out-group. Potential friend, ally, and role model.	2. Exotic out-group that is either inferior (a group we pity) or superior (a group we adore).
	Foe	3. Benign enemy whose behaviour and violence could have been 'ours' since 'we' regard them as similar to us.	4. Malign enemy is constructed as different from us, often as inferior. Legitimizes violence.

necessarily enemies. This means that othering processes can form various types of 'others', some quite innocent, others toxic. In Table 1.1, we have constructed four different categories of other. In the first category, they are seen as friends who accordingly do not constitute a threat. But in addition, 'they' are also regarded as similar to 'us'. This kind of out-group is usually perceived as the most benign. Within this category, out-groups can occasionally also be seen as potential assets, allies, and even role models. It is also hard to develop prejudiced constructs of 'them'.

The second category is more complex. Here, too, the out-group is seen as a friend but understood as different from 'us'. And this is potentially very problematic. Within this category, the other tends to be constructed not only as different but also as inferior. Colonial or paternalistic attitudes can grow out of this kind of othering. Prejudices might develop, and there is a risk that 'we' see such out-groups as exotic. Bo Petersson puts it very succinctly:

> And although the exotic might appear rather positive on the surface, it should be kept in mind that it too represents the immature and the irresponsible that … needs to be taken care of by …. persons who know better.
>
> *(Petersson, 2006: 48)*

This category includes constructs not only of the other as inferior but also of groups that are constructed as superior. Philosemitism – respect or admiration for the Jewish people – is one example. Philosemitism could, in addition to admiration of Jewish history, culture, and religion, involve ideas that Jews are superior. For instance, within the cognitive framework of Christian Zionism (a Christian belief in an eschatological purpose of the foundation of Israel as a state), Jews are often depicted as superior, sometimes by referring to the number of Jewish Nobel Prize laureates (Steiner, 2013: 57).

Still, this is on the right of the table, and the belief that groups are fundamentally different from 'us' is risky, even if on the surface the group is admired. In our view constructs of the other that combine *difference* and superiority are treacherous, since 'it is only a short journey from making claims about a group's natural *superiority* to making claims about a group's natural *inferiority*' (Jones, 2002: 31). Thomas C. Wilson claims that philosemitic 'benign stereotypes of Jews are widespread, but whether they are genuinely complimentary remains unresolved' (Wilson, 1996: 465). He argues that such 'benign Jewish stereotypes are far more common than corresponding blatantly anti-Semitic images' (1996: 465) before concluding that 'there is no evidence that benign stereotypes are genuinely complimentary but strong indications that they are subtle expressions of underlying prejudice' (Wilson, 1996: 465). Antisemites and philosemites seem thus to share underlying attitudes. Jean-Paul Sartre had already discovered this during the Second World War, stating that

> the anti-Semite readily admits that the Jew is intelligent and hard-working; he will even confess himself inferior in these respects. This confession costs him nothing...the more virtues the Jew has the more dangerous he will be.
>
> *(Sartre, [1944] 1995: 22)*

The point we want to make is that the right column in Table 1.1 is very unstable. Positive exoticism can very easily turn into patronizing colonial attitudes, or even worse, transform philosemitism into antisemitism or blatant enemy images (Category 4). The distance is short 'between banal prejudice, on the one hand, and fully fledged ... enemy images, on the other' (Petersson, 2009: 464).

In Categories 3 and 4, we are dealing with 'others' who are foes and constitute a threat. Category 3 could be understood as a benign enemy construct. This construct would not deny the threats and existing violence committed by the enemy. However, since the enemy in this category still resembles 'us', they are never deprived of their humanity, and this resemblance could potentially make us reflect on 'their' violent behaviour. Could 'their' violence be committed by 'us' in a similar situation? Ergo, this construct of the enemy could lead to soul-searching and potentially inhibit a spiral of violence since 'harming a person who seems so much like oneself is very difficult because it arouses feelings of repentance and pain' (Sternberg and Sternberg, 2008: 45). The concept and the distinction between benign and malign enemy image will be further developed in Chapter 2 (see Table 2.3).

The fourth and final category displays a 'threatening other' that is understood as very different from 'us', and often also as inferior in at least some important aspects. This implies that we cannot identify with the enemy and there is a risk that 'they' (being constructed as radically different from us) are dehumanized and rejected. We define this kind of enemy image as malign, partly because it is likely to desensitize the in-group and to legitimize and normalize violence against the out-group. Possibly, this kind of enemy image, portraying the other not only as a threat but also as different (most commonly as inferior), could enhance group cohesion and the in-group's sense of superiority. And for these reasons, this kind of construct is politically useful.

Consequences of enemy images

Enemy images, particularly malign ones and those with a dominant discursive position in society, have significant and far-reaching consequences: they impact individuals, collectives, and intergroup relationships.[2] They are not only of academic interest. Some consequences are desired and calculated by political or other leaders. Other consequences are unforeseen by the same leaders, and some are even undesired.

The literature on the consequences of enemy images per se is limited. But since they share properties with war propaganda, prejudice, stereotypes, and othering, it makes sense to consult research in those areas as well. In this overview, we have categorized the consequences into four main themes. The first consequence on the cognitive level concerns *perception* and focuses on how enemy images impact attention, interpretation, and memorization. A second important consequence, on the normative level, concerns *values* and how enemy images impact morals, norms, and ethics. This means that enemy images could affect how one assesses, evaluates, and appreciates what is perceived. A third consequence, on the emotional level, concerns *emotions*, primarily directed towards the enemy. A last and overarching consequence, on the behavioural level, concerns how enemy images affect *behaviour*, including *public policies*. In the following section, we will discuss these four consequences more in detail.

Cognitive effects of enemy images

A fundamental point of departure in this section is the role of preconceptions in perception, attention, memory, interpretation, and expectations. Or as Robin Fox put it, 'for the most part we do not see first and then define, we define first and then see' (1992: 147). For instance, if we assume that an enemy has a certain innate 'nature', we will interpret everything the enemy does through the labels we have attached to it. When enemy images are adopted, they become a preconception, and they influence people's understanding of the enemy as well as what they expect from it in the future. Inspired by Silverstein and Flamenbaum (1989: 53), Oskamp (1965), and Douglas (1992), we have listed below eight important cognitive effects of enemy images, to be elaborated in the forthcoming sections. We believe that enemy images make us:

1 tend to remember enemies' threatening actions more readily than those of non-enemies
2 evaluate enemy actions as more hostile than similar ones performed by non-enemies

3 predict future hostile actions from enemies
4 exaggerate differences between groups and underestimate differences within groups
5 believe that situational pressures play a minor role in the hostile actions of enemies
6 believe that situational pressures play a major role in friendly actions by enemies
7 believe that friendly enemy actions may also be attributed to hostile motives, such as the desire to deceive or manipulate
8 judge the credibility of sources of statements attacking enemies less rigorously than they do those defending them.

First, it seems we tend to remember enemies' threatening actions more readily than those of non-enemies. Enemy images describe the other as a threat, and if people are fed with this notion for an extended time, it will form their preconceptions and beliefs and thereby affect what they perceive. It makes them more willing to accept information or stimuli that are consistent with the enemy image since they focus on things that are in accordance with what they already 'know'. This is like a vicious circle: once an enemy image is established, people will focus on stimuli that confirm their beliefs about that group. Another term that can be used to explain this process is 'confirmation bias' (see Chapter 4), a selective focus on information that confirms prior beliefs or values, frequently seen in online search behaviour and socializing in 'bubbles' where all information that seemingly contradicts individual or group beliefs is filtered out.

Moreover, enemy images affect not only perception but memory. Research indicates that stimuli that fit with one's established preconceptions are 'easier to remember, and later easier to retrieve' (Stangor, 2000: 14). And along the same lines, 'accusations against enemies will be more influential and more memorable than statements (made either by the enemies or by third parties) that deny enemy wrongdoing' (Silverstein and Flamenbaum, 1989: 53). Again, once a group has been defined as an enemy, there is a risk of this preconception distorting perception so that threatening actions will be more memorable than messages contradicting this image. This tendency has been empirically tested numerous times. For instance, in a study conducted by Brett Silverstein and Catherine Flamenbaum in 1987, American students were given a mock newspaper article to read. The two researchers

> had subjects read a selection dealing with international events that contained descriptions of hostile and peaceful actions ascribed to a target nation. Half of the subjects read a selection that supposedly dealt with recent relations between the Soviet Union and China. The other subjects read a selection that was identical except for the substitution of Australia for the Soviet Union.
>
> *(Silverstein and Flamenbaum, 1989: 54)*

Later, the students were asked what they remembered. There was a difference. The American students were more likely to recall Soviet 'actions in which military force was projected', except for the most severe military aggression (Silverstein and Flamenbaum, 1989: 55).

A second effect of enemy images is that we tend to evaluate the actions of enemies as more hostile than similar actions performed by non-enemies, meaning we might perceive an enemy's aggressive behaviour as more violent and hostile than identical behaviour by a friend or ally. In the 1960s, Stuart Oskamp performed several studies demonstrating that American students evaluated Soviet actions more negatively than they evaluated the same actions when performed by the United States. In one of the tests, two completely parallel 50-item questionnaires were constructed, asking how the students evaluated political and military actions. In one questionnaire, the actor was the United States; and in the other, the USSR. As predicted, there was a very strong differential evaluation of the actions depending on which country was being rated (Oskamp, 1965). The study found that American students evaluated Soviet actions more negatively than they did the same actions when performed by the United States.

> These results clearly show the double standard with which world affairs are often viewed. If the U.S.A. does something, warlike or peaceful, it is usually seen as mildly to moderately favorable, whereas if the U.S.S.R. does the same thing, it is viewed as mildly to moderately unfavorable. This double standard makes possible the mirror-image phenomenon.
>
> *(Oskamp, 1965: 46)*

In other words, 'actions of enemies that are attended to and remembered will be evaluated as more hostile than will similar actions performed by non-enemies' (Silverstein and Flamenbaum, 1989: 53). It seems as if the capacity to perceive nuances related to the enemy is impaired: 'once an actor is categorized as an enemy, it is assumed to possess the characteristics of the ideal-typical enemy and information that contradicts such an assessment is either ignored or given very little attention', as Blanton put it (1996: 26).

A *third* effect of an enemy image is that people tend to 'predict future hostile actions from enemies' (Silverstein and Flamenbaum, 1989: 53) since they expect their enemies, unlike 'us' and 'our' friends, to be static, unable to change or grow morally. If a group is labelled 'enemy', people will expect hostile actions from this group in the future (Zadny and Gerard, 1974: 34). The human brain expects behaviour that is consistent with their (enemy) images. This kind of preconception could also make future peace appear unattainable. In other words, if enemy images make people expect hostilities, they make it hard to imagine peace, build trust, or legitimize a future peace agreement.

A *fourth* effect of an enemy image is that it underlines the experience of in-group similarity. Faced with a potent enemy image, ethnic, social, and religious

TABLE 1.2 Explaining good and bad behaviour

| | | Actors' role | |
		Me and my friends	*The enemy*
Behaviour to be explained	Good behaviour	Good behaviour reveals 'our' true character, and situational pressure does not explain it.	Good behaviour is the effect of situational pressure and does not reveal 'their' true character.
	Bad behaviour	Bad behaviour is the unfortunate effect of situational pressure and does not reveal 'our' true character.	Bad behaviour reveals 'their' true character, and situational pressure explains it.

differences or conflicts within the in-group are downplayed or underestimated. One may 'think of the members of one's group, and...allies, as much "the same" as oneself', and 'minimize the significance of conflict to mythologize and rationalize "we" feelings and perceptions' (Stein, 1989: 481). The difference between 'us' and 'them', on the other hand, is emphasized and exaggerated. In that case, human commonalities are underestimated.

A *fifth* effect of an enemy image is that we tend to believe that situational pressures play a minor role in the hostile actions of enemies (Oppenheimer, 2006: 279). This simply means that when the enemy is doing something hostile or violent, 'they' are showing 'their' true colours, revealing who 'they' really are. The enemy did not do evil because 'they' had to; 'they' were not forced by the situation (see Table 1.2). These actions confirm what 'we' believe that 'we' know. Above, we referred to Oskamp and his discussion about double standards. One effect of double standards is that people judge the enemy's and 'our' bad behaviour in different ways (see Table 1.2). 'Their' bad behaviour reveals 'their' true character, whereas 'our' bad behaviour is an effect of the situation. 'We' were forced to be violent, for instance. 'We' had no choice. Somewhat related to this tendency is the trend to interpret indisputably good and bad behaviour differently, depending on who performs it. If 'we' are doing something good, this is described using 'broad trait terms' like 'we are generous and friendly' (Stangor, 2000: 14). 'Our' bad behaviour, on the other hand, is depicted as specific behaviour ('Bill hit someone'). And the logic is reversed when people describe the enemy.

As repeatedly stated, enemy images influence what people perceive, and people try to avoid changing their basic preconceptions. Still, sometimes the enemy unambiguously does good and engages in morally positive actions, i.e. something that contradicts the enemy image and preconceptions, thus challenging preconceptions. How can this be solved? According to Silverstein and Flamenbaum's *sixth* proposition above, people tend to believe that situational pressures play a major role in friendly actions by enemies. 'They' did good because 'they' had to (see Table 1.2). 'Their' good behaviour does not reveal who 'they' really are nor will it 'be seen as evidence that the enemy is conciliatory, while aggressive acts will be seen as evidence that the enemy is hostile' (Silverstein and Flamenbaum, 1989: 53). In the 1980s, during the Cold War, the Soviet leader Mikhail Gorbachev suggested substantial nuclear disarmament. The reaction from hawkish political commentators in the West was that the true and evil character of the Soviets had not changed. The reason for this disarmament initiative was financial. The Soviet Union had run out of money. They suggested nuclear disarmament because they had to. And again, if 'we' make a similar disarmament initiative, the true cause behind it is 'our' true character (cf. Blanton, 1996: 26 and Zur, 1991: 367).

The same logic and preconception will of course not apply to 'our' behaviour. Policymakers, Lindsey Shannon Blanton says, 'typically presume that the behavior of their own state is compelled by circumstance' (Blanton, 1996: 26), reflecting neither 'our' intent nor representing an outcome of 'our' character. Likewise, 'our' good behaviour reflects 'our' true inner character, and 'our' bad behaviour is an effect of unfortunate circumstances.

A *seventh* cognitive consequence of enemy images, and not dissimilar to the previous one, is that people tend to believe that the friendly actions of enemies may also be attributed to hostile motivations. The point is that people try not only to explain away good and peaceful behaviour as an effect of situational pressure (Oppenheimer, 2006: 279). Instead, they go one step further and believe that seemingly friendly actions have hostile motivations and are driven by a desire to deceive or manipulate (Silverstein and Flamenbaum, 1989: 53). As Petersson has stated, 'their' peaceful behaviour 'can conveniently be interpreted as affirming the cunning and conniving nature of the enemy' (Petersson 2009: 460). The enemy 'is even devious enough to try to manipulate us into believing in her/his good intentions, or so the argument might run' (Petersson, 2009: 460).

Lastly, an *eighth* cognitive effect of enemy images is that people judge the credibility of sources accusing enemies of violence and hostility less rigorously than they do those defending them. In other words, people are more likely to believe in information that confirms what they believe they know (the enemy image) than challenge it (Zur, 1991: 360). Also, this is related to the human tendency to maintain established preconceptions (the enemy image) and to interpret incoming stimuli in a way that is compatible with people's understanding of the world (this will be discussed more thoroughly in Chapter 4). The point is that people want to keep their established preconceptions – such as enemy images – intact and are searching for reasons to do so. If the information is the slightest bit ambiguous, then they will try to interpret it 'in ways that are consistent with existing stereotypes' (Stangor, 2000: 14). If people want to maintain an enemy image, 'there are always loopholes for reading the evidence right' (Douglas, 1992: 9).

Taken together, these eight cognitive effects of enemy images ultimately fuel conflicts and make them self-perpetuating. They make people blind to their enemy's longing for peace, and they have an impact on people's actions and behaviour, since 'action is based on the actor's image of reality' (Galtung and Holmboe Ruge, 1965: 64).

Normative effects of enemy images

Enemy images do more than just influence people's perceptions. When accepted, they do something to their normative system. Peacetime norms are, as a rule, supposed to uphold peace and prevent violence. But in certain situations, norms change drastically, so that 'moral norms that normally would prevent hostility and violence may instead act as accelerators and moral justifications for harm-doing or moral exclusion' (Oppenheimer, 2006: 278). And enemy images, if they are spread and embraced, have this effect.

In this section, we have gathered and organized some of enemy images' most important normative effects that are discussed in academic literature. We believe that enemy images

1 legitimize wars
2 legitimize war crimes
3 legitimize structural violence
4 justify political priorities
5 increase social cohesion
6 legitimize political leaders.

In the following, we will discuss these normative effects in turn. First, enemy images impact people's norms, values, and attitudes so that both *specific wars* and *wars in general* appear *rational and legitimate*. As an effect of modernization, wars have become devastating. Since the Industrial Revolution, armies have possessed arsenals with a historically unique capacity for destruction. Possibly, therefore, wars are no longer considered a legitimate political tool. The resistance against them has become so great, 'that every war must appear to be a war of defence against a menacing, murderous aggressor' (Lasswell, 1927: 47). And this is a common notion among researchers of war rhetoric. To legitimize war, people must be made to believe that neither the population nor its leadership is to be blamed for it. An enemy image must be constructed where the enemy appears as the aggressor and 'we' as the victims. As Robert Ivie, Professor of Rhetoric and Public Culture, concisely puts it:

> A people strongly committed to the ideal of peace, but simultaneously faced with the reality of war, must believe that the fault for any such disruption of their ideal lies with others.
>
> *(Ivie, 1980: 280)*

The use of enemy images thus enables blame to be shifted from 'us' to the enemy, allowing 'us' to free ourselves from responsibility (Ivie, 1980: 280).

Another slightly different way to make war appear legitimate is through moral justification. Johan Galtung (1930–2024),[3] a prominent scholar in Scandinavian peace research, constructed three useful concepts of violence: direct (or physical), structural, and cultural (Galtung, 1969 and 1990). The concept of enemy image and Galtung's concept of cultural violence are related. He defines cultural violence as

> those aspects of culture, the symbolic sphere of our existence – exemplified by religion and ideology, language and art, empirical science and formal science (logic, mathematics) – that can be used to justify or legitimize direct or structural violence.
>
> *(Galtung, 1990: 291)*

And this is exactly one of the purposes of an enemy image – to change the values, norms, and ethics of the audience, so it perceives war as legitimate. Enemy images and cultural violence make 'direct and structural violence look, even feel, right – or at least not wrong' (Galtung, 1990: 291). So enemy images change values and norms to such an extent that violence and exploitation we would not tolerate in other situations now appear normal. Galtung continues:

> Just as political science is about two problems – the use of power and the legitimation of the use of power – violence studies are about two problems: the use of violence and the legitimation of that use.
>
> *(Galtung, 1990: 295)*

According to the social psychologist Albert Bandura (1925–2021, see Box 1.1), moral justification provides a war with legitimizing meaning, and a moral cause legitimizing it:

> In this new context of moral obligation, soldiers see themselves as fighting ruthless oppressors, protecting cherished values, honoring their country's obligations, preserving world peace, and saving humanity from subjugation. With commitment to the justness of the cause, killing becomes an act of heroism.
>
> *(Bandura, 2016: 49)*

Although Bandura never refers specifically to enemy images, it is clear that an image portraying 'them' as a threat to 'us' and 'our' legitimate interests provides moral justification.

A *second* effect of enemy images is that they might legitimize not only war, but also violations of international law – maybe even crimes against humanity. During an ongoing war, combatants must comply with *jus in bellum* (International Humanitarian Law, IHL). However, if 'we' portray 'them' as criminals, killers, rapists, murderers, and so on (see malign enemy image, Table 2.3), 'we' rhetorically legitimize violence that is not militarily strategically motivated; 'we' might make excessive force and war crimes acceptable. 'We' give 'them' what 'they', based on the enemy image, deserve. Howard Stein puts it pertinently:

> The implicit logic reads: 'Since the Russians disregard human life, therefore we may disregard theirs'. Their violence becomes a necessary precondition or releaser of ours.
>
> *(Stein, 1989: 493)*

In January 2003, President George W. Bush gave a speech to troops at Fort Hood, a United States Army post near Killeen in Texas, reflecting this very logic: 'They're nothing but a bunch of cold-blooded killers, and that's the way we're going to treat them' (Bush, 3 January 2003). In other words, the more horrible traits 'we' give 'our' enemy, the more horrendous violence against' them' seems acceptable, even appropriate and justified. The 'War on Terror' is an example of how IHL was derailed to denounce enemies of the United States as 'unlawful enemy combatants', frequently abducted to 'black sites' and exposed to harsh interrogation or torture such as waterboarding, with no recourse to legal remedies.

If we want to harm a group in this excessive way, 'we' cannot have anything in common with 'them' because recognizing commonalities will foster empathy. There is therefore a tendency that we consciously exaggerate (cultural, religious, or phenotypic) differences as a way of withdrawing affiliative feelings. 'We' must not allow ourselves to feel that we have much, if anything, in common with the enemy (Stein, 1989: 481). So when portraying the enemy as very different, norms, values, and attitudes towards the group are changed. In some cases,

> once cast in the role of an enemy or a scapegoat, the targeted category comes to be regarded as impure, indeed as filth and excrements that should be flushed out and gotten rid of by society as soon as possible. The sooner the better; or otherwise the health of the majority is held to be in jeopardy.
>
> *(Petersson, 2009: 460)*

Not all enemy images go this far. But in some cases, when the enemy is dehumanized, characterized as filth and vermin, their mere existence constitutes a threat. In this case, 'their' existence is questioned, and mass killing and genocide are not unthinkable. The American historian Richard Hofstadter puts it succinctly:

> Since the enemy is thought of as being totally evil and totally unappeasable, he must be totally eliminated – if not from the world, at least from the theatre of operations to which the paranoid directs his attention.
>
> *(Hofstadter, 1964: 82)*

Moreover, if 'our' army is guilty of horrible human rights violations, there seems to be a need to describe the enemy as primitive (Gilly, 2016) or depict it as so horrible that disproportionate violence is justified. In other words, the crueller 'our' army is, the more horrible the enemy that needs to be constructed. There must be a correspondence between 'our' violence and cruelty and the image of the enemy.

Images of enemies, especially explicitly dehumanizing ones, can have effects beyond wars and war crimes. Colonial powers have historically used enemy images to legitimize slavery, exploitation, and land theft. By dehumanizing and demonizing colonized peoples, these powers could justify their actions and maintain control (Fanon, 1961). By extension, orientalist discourses, as Edward Said (1978) has argued, construct narratives of 'barbaric' and 'pre-modern' cultures to assert the superiority of Western civilization and justify imperialist endeavours.

Thirdly, it seems that enemy images can also *legitimize structural violence*. As mentioned above, Johan Galtung developed the concept of 'violence' in identifying three distinct forms of it: direct and physical, structural, and cultural. Over the years, the concept 'structural' has received several definitions but could refer to situations where social structures and institutions harm people by preventing them from meeting their basic needs and achieving the quality of life that would otherwise be possible (Lee, 2019). On a macro level, neo-imperialistic economic exchange between the Global South and North could worsen structural violence in the south and enrich the north (Galtung, 1971). Our point is that enemy images can also make structural violence – for instance exploitation and neo-imperialism – appear normal. One strategy is to use a market economy narrative.

In a market economy narrative, exploitation does not exist because economic exchange takes place in a free market where participants voluntarily sell or buy goods and services. The prices reflect supply and demand. The fact that many products from the Global South are valued low is not an expression of exploitation, but of neutral market forces. This narrative conceals the fact that market participants have completely different power resources. Weaker players sell their labour or products at under-priced levels as they have no alternative.

This tendency to develop a language concealing exploitation can be explained through justification theory. According to this social psychology theory, when people occupy a dominant position in society, they translate their advantage into flattering stereotypes of themselves and derogatory ones of less successful groups, mobilizing beliefs to justify their superior social position (Yzerbyt, 2010: 151). So instead of admitting that 'we' benefit from a socioeconomic structure and that it is this structure that has made 'us' wealthy or given 'us' a dominant position, they might argue that 'we' are more hardworking, capable, and organized. An example of an ideology that justifies social inequalities and oppression is racial supremacism. This ideology is rhetorically powerful because, in addition to describing 'us' as superior to 'them', it describes 'them' as a threat to the existing order and power structure (Bonilla-Silva, 2006).

Similar rhetoric can develop between collectives such as states. The states in the Global North might claim that their favoured position is the effect of 'our' national characteristics giving 'us' the capacity to produce high-tech products that are in high demand. It has supposedly nothing to do with an exploitative economic system benefiting 'us'. Moreover, people in the Global North are likely to develop derogatory stereotypes of less successful nations in the Global South. If actors in the south start questioning these socioeconomic structures, enemy images could develop. In that case 'they' would not only be seen as inferior but could also be portrayed as a threat to 'our' vital economic interests.

Fourthly, large-scale wars are an economic burden, even for great powers. In war, states must make major economic reprioritizations, and here is where enemy images come in. They can be used to justify political choices where the political leadership prioritizes military rearmament over social investments, and to make a population ignore domestic problems (Frank and Melville, 1988: 203). The Finnish information scientist Heikki Luostarinen puts it very well: 'enemy images are functional for purposes of justifying political choices (guns instead of butter) ... and for diverting people's attention from other problems' (Luostarinen, 1989: 127). This logic is not only apparent in contemporary Russia, where the population is paying a bitter price, both economic and humanitarian, but also in the EU, where policies against terrorism threaten to limit personal freedom. In the EU, these policies have seen the adoption of sometimes draconic anti-terror laws undermining human rights and giving extraordinary surveillance rights to intelligence agencies. There is a fine line between effective terrorism countermeasures and the infringement of human rights and the rule of law.

Fifthly, enemy images can be used to increase social cohesion, for instance national unity (Frank and Melville, 1988: 203), especially in young nations (Luostarinen, 1989: 127). It is common knowledge that the presence of an out-group usually strengthens an in-group (Fiebig-von Hase, 1997: 15–19). Put another way, to construct an 'us', a corresponding 'them' is required (see Chapter 2). And when you compare your group with the out-group, yours is usually better, at least in important aspects (see Chapter 2, Table 2.1). So, the out-group is essential in defining who 'we' are, who belongs to 'us', and what 'we' are like. In an enemy image, the other is portrayed as a particularly potent out-group. 'They' are not only described as different; 'they' have the capacity and the intention to harm 'us'. Such an image of 'them' turns 'us' into a highly relevant in-group. In this case, 'we' are facing a similar threat or fate, 'we' have a common destiny, and my survival is dependent on 'my' group's survival (Luostarinen, 1989: 127). Facing a common enemy, 'our' group provides safety and is likely to become highly relevant. This group (in the modern world, usually the nation-state) will appear important to its individual members, more so than other groups they belong to. The group providing safety could become their primary identity. But there is also a risk that the 'hysteria about the outer threat' is used to create an oppressive domestic situation characterized by artificial national unity, witch hunts, and other policies that suppress dissent (Frank and Melville, 1988: 203). In other words, if you do not buy the war rhetoric and clearly dissent, there is a risk that your position in the group is questioned; more about that in Chapter 4.

The *sixth* and final point is that enemy images legitimize not only wars and violence, but sometimes also political leaders. Since enemy images conjure up an imminent and serious threat, 'our' leaders, who claim to be those best suited to avert it, are likely to use the presence of the enemy and external threat as tools to increase their popular support and legitimacy (Luostarinen, 1989: 127).

Emotional effects of enemy images

To be a soldier, to maim and kill, is emotionally disturbing and harmful. Hardly any soldier can take part in war without experiencing post-traumatic stress disorder (PTSD). And in war, soldiers perform violent actions that they would never do in peacetime. Many feel a burden of guilt and self-loathing, and this is emotionally devastating (Bandura, 2016: 29). In this situation it is natural that soldiers or other participants in violence seek relief from guilt (Taillard and Giscoppa, 2013: 108) so that they can preserve a self-view as decent, self-respecting people. And enemy images can provide solace after participating in bloodshed.

Bandura (mentioned below) studied moral disengagement, namely how people can do harm (for instance taking part in war crimes) and 'still live with themselves', how they can maintain emotional wellbeing in such situations and avoid self-condemnation (Bandura, 2016). Usually, 'people refrain from behaving in ways that violate their moral standards because such conduct will bring self-condemnation. This restraint of negative self-sanction keeps one's conduct in line with one's moral standards' (Osofsky, Bandura, Zimbardo, 2005: 371). In some cases, we even act proactively, seeking to alleviate the suffering of fellow human beings (Bandura, 2016). This is how people normally function. They avoid doing things that violate their moral standards for reasons of self-preservation: immoral behaviour would lead to self-condemnation and similar burdensome emotions.

BOX 1.1   ALBERT BANDURA

Albert Bandura (1925–2021) was a Canadian-born American social psychologist and Professor of Psychology at Stanford University. The fourth most-frequently cited psychologist of all time (Haggbloom, 2002), he contributed to the field of education as well as multiple psychology fields – most prominently perhaps, social cognitive theory and moral disengagement theory (MDT), proving highly influential in the transition between behaviourism and cognitive psychology (MacCormick, 2021). He coined the term social cognitive theory and the theoretical construct of self-efficacy, devising the Bobo doll experiment in 1961. This experiment was a study in which adult researchers physically and verbally abused an inflatable clown doll called Bobo in front of preschool-age children, who then mimicked the adult's behaviour by attacking the Bobo doll in the same fashion (Bandura, Ross, and Ross, 1961: 578). The study thus demonstrated that children learn from watching others, suggesting that televised violence can teach and glamorize aggressive behaviour. The findings of the experiments upended the established behavioural doctrine that learning was a conditioned response to external punishments and rewards. The results also challenged the prevailing theory that watching violence on television alleviated aggressive impulses in children (Bandura, Ross, and Ross, 1961: 579).

More reading: Bandura, A., Ross, D., & Ross, S. A. (1961). Transmission of aggression through imitation of aggressive models. *The Journal of Abnormal and Social Psychology*, 63(3).

Bandura's research, however, focused on people acting in ways that *contradict* their moral standards. In other words, he explains the irregular and the surprising, when people's behaviour (i.e. killing and maiming in war) is *inconsistent* with their regular moral standards. In the bulleted list below, we have summarized how Bandura describes human strategies to circumvent normal moral standards (Bandura, 2016) and disengage from immoral behaviour, thereby avoiding 'self-sanctions' and self-condemnation (Bandura, 1986). Inspired by his theory, we will go on to discuss how enemy images can offer moral disengagement, adopting some of his arguments as a point of departure and organizing tool.

1 Behavioural locus
   • Moral justification
   • Palliative comparison
   • Euphemistic labelling
2 Agency locus
   • Displacement of responsibility
   • Diffusion of responsibility
3 Effects locus
   • Minimizing, ignoring, or misconstruing the consequences
4 Victim locus
   • Dehumanization
   • Attribution of blame

Bandura's theory thus has four loci. The *first* one, behaviour, claims that people sanctify harmful means by investing them in worthy social and moral purposes. In the *second* locus, agency, Bandura describes how 'people evade personal accountability for harmful conduct by displacing responsibility to others and by dispersing it widely so that no one bears responsibility' (Bandura, 2016: 3). This locus is not related to enemy images, but rather to Stanley Milgram's arguments below, and will therefore not be discussed here. The *third* locus concerns the outcome of one's actions, how 'perpetrators disregard, minimize, distort, or even dispute the injurious effects of their actions' in order to disengage morally (Bandura, 2016: 3). The *fourth* and last locus, which Bandura calls the victim locus, is where the perpetrators exclude those they maltreat from their humanity or claim that the victims are to blame since they brought it on themselves (Bandura, 2016). In our discussion about how enemy images can be used to disengage from violent behaviour, only two of these loci are relevant: the *first* and the *fourth*.

Let us start with the first locus, *behaviour*. We have already referred to Bandura and his discussion of *moral justification* for legitimate war and violence (2016) in the previous section, on the normative effects of enemy images. But moral justification can do more than legitimize wars. It can also make perpetrators feel good about themselves after killing and maiming. Moral justification is particularly common in radical contexts, where it is assumed that their ideas and visions will bring happiness, freedom, and harmony. Here violence is unavoidable and necessary to end future violence and humanity into a paradisiac future and is therefore justified or even sanctified. Since the violence was carried out for a higher purpose, its perpetrators of violence are freed from moral responsibility. In short, 'harmful behavior is turned into good behavior' (Bandura, 2016: 48). This logic is present in both secular and religious contexts.

Another way to retain a good self-image is through *palliative* (or advantageous) *comparison*. This could mean that 'we' compare 'our' behaviour to 'theirs' in a way that makes 'us' look comparatively good: 'Sure, we bombed Dresden, but look at what the Germans did'. Or as Bandura puts it:

> How the self and others view human behavior is colored by what it is compared against. Self-exoneration by advantageous comparison with more flagrant inhumanities is a third mechanism for cloaking behavior in an aura of benevolence.
>
> *(Bandura, 2016: 57)*

Another version of advantageous comparison is based on utilitarian logic. This strategy implies that unless 'we' do certain harm now, more harm will occur in the future, so 'our' 'injurious actions will prevent more human suffering than they cause' (Bandura, 2016: 58). According to this logic, the bombings of Hiroshima and Nagasaki were necessary because they shortened the war, and a prolonged conventional war would have caused more casualties. The bombings are described as morally justified since killing now will prevent more deaths in the future. Enemy images can support this kind of argument. If the enemy is depicted as evil and unlikely to change (see Richard Hofstadter's argument above and the discussion about malign enemy images in Chapter 2, Table 2.3), the most rational action is to go to war to end this evil. By eliminating the enemy (or at least its leadership), we are in fact saving lives.

Euphemistic labelling involves using words that gloss over something we regard as undesirable and making something negative less unpleasant. Words like 'death' or 'cancer' are often replaced with less scary euphemisms. And people tend to do the same when they know that they are violating their moral standards. This is a strategy to make the immorality of 'our' behaviour less egregious. Maybe people call the death of civilians in war 'collateral damage'. According to Bandura, people can replace killing with 'wasting'. In other words, sanitizing euphemistic language renders injurious conduct benign. Sometimes people use the passive voice since 'the agentless passive form is a linguistic device for creating the appearance that harmful acts are the work of nameless forces rather than of individuals' (Bandura, 2016: 54–55) – e.g. 'the target was eliminated' to cloak the deliberate killing of a human being.

Since enemy images tend not only to dehumanize but also to deindividuate the enemy, they can help people make the effects of their actions less visible. Deprived of their individual character, victims become indistinguishable within a crowd, a number in statistics (see Chapter 2 for a more elaborate discussion). Similarly, in his study of the American film industry's stereotypes of Native Americans, Martin Berny notices that the Natives' suffering is glossed over, that they rarely speak and are given little space in the story (Berny, 2020: 25–26).

According to Worchel and Andreoli, we tend to deindividuate both before and after the actor aggresses against the victim (Worchel and Andreoli, 1978: 550). The point is, since enemy images deindividuate enemy soldiers and civilians, they help people to gloss over the moral consequences of their actions. The process of turning fellow human beings into 'collateral damage' or 'military targets' is facilitated by deindividuation.

Let us now turn to the *fourth* locus, that of the *victim*. As we know by now, almost all of us are reluctant to harm fellow human beings – particularly when we 'perceive another as a sentient human being with the same basic needs as one's own' (Bandura, 2016: 84). And this is where dehumanizing enemy images kick in.

> Once entire classes of people are rendered less than human, their stigmatization, persecution, and exclusion from the most basic human rights becomes personally and socially acceptable. If the justifications are crafted skillfully, the degrading treatment can be made morally acceptable as well.
>
> *(Bandura, 2016: 84)*

And if people are reduced to mere creatures, we might think that 'they' are less sensitive than 'us', perhaps insensitive to maltreatment, that the only way to influence 'them' is through primitive methods (Bandura, Underwood, and Fromson, 1975: 255). That it is easier to maltreat groups that have been dehumanized is common knowledge. There are many personal testimonies, from both perpetrators and victims, verifying this effect. There is also a lot of research in this area. And again, dehumanizing enemy images can be used both to *prepare* soldiers for an upcoming order and to *console* them after committing war crimes (see the discussion about Christopher R. Browning's book *Ordinary Men* above).

The second theme in this locus concerns *attribution of blame*, which is another efficient means of seeking relief from guilt and avoiding self-condemnation. In this book, one part of our definition of an enemy image suggests that an enemy allegedly constitutes an imminent, real, serious (but not invincible), and possibly growing *threat* to 'our' most vital interests. This alleged threat can serve as an excellent pretext to blame the enemy for the violence that will or has befallen it. Since the enemy constitutes a threat, they are 'faulted for bringing maltreatment on themselves' (Bandura, 2016: 90). Ergo, 'we' are released from guilt, 'they' are morally responsible for 'our' acts of violence, and guilt is shifted.

Blame attribution can often be reinforced through group dynamics. Acts of violence are often committed in concert by a group – typically a group of soldiers. In addition to feeling less individual responsibility for actions performed in groups, the group can also 'provide exonerations for each other' (Bandura, 2016: 100). Since the group members have acted together on their shared beliefs, 'members do not have to concoct their own individual exonerations' (Bandura, 2016: 100). Together, the group (re)produces a guilt-releasing narrative and uses it for mutual emotional support.

Moreover, when a war breaks out, the course of events that proceeds with the hostilities is often not entirely clear ('the fog of war'). It is not always possible to point out the culprit beyond any doubt. And this gives room for interpretation and the possibility to shift blame:

> One can select from the chain of events a defensive act by one's adversaries and portray it as the initiating provocation. One then blames the adversaries for bringing suffering on themselves by their instigative belligerent behavior. Hence, they deserve to be punished.
>
> *(Bandura, 2016: 90)*

Here the aggressor can free himself from responsibility or feelings of guilt since the victims are allegedly responsible for 'our' acts of violence; 'they started it'. And most importantly, enemy images contribute to this blame-shifting narrative, since with an enemy, 'they' are always seen as a serious threat to 'us' and 'our' vital interests.

Behavioural effects of enemy images

A last overarching consequence of enemy images concerns their impact on behaviour. This section might be slightly repetitive since some of the consequences of enemy images on perception, values, and emotions are also of relevance here. The literature we reviewed indicates that enemy images have at least five important behavioural effects, influencing

1 soldiers' willingness to kill
2 leaders' decision-making
3 public behaviour and conduct
4 target groups' behaviour and conduct
5 future willingness to make and accept peace.

A *first* behavioural effect of an enemy image and a starting point in this book is that enemy images can in some cases increase soldiers' propensity to use violence against the enemy. We have already established, when discussing the definition of an enemy image, that the purpose of the enemy image is to mobilize and desensitize 'us' so that participation in violence against the enemy can take place without feelings of remorse or pain. One type of enemy image that can be particularly effective is atrocity propaganda, where the enemy is accused of cruel and shocking acts (Morrow, 2018: 49).

Although political leaders want to increase soldiers' propensity to use violence on the battlefield, this is not always guaranteed. In a now classic study from 1947, US combat historian Samuel Lyman Atwood Marshall conducted several interviews with American soldiers from the Second World War, analysing their actions on the battlefield. He argued that they underperformed and that at most 25% of them fired their weapons (Marshall, [1947] 2000: 50 and 54), concluding that 'what we need in battle is more and better fire' (Marshall, [1947] 2000: 23). Our conclusion is that despite a clear enemy and enemy image, the willingness to shoot was quite low. And when Marshall wants to correct this 'problem', he does not discuss war propaganda or enemy images as appropriate means.

Spontaneously, we might suppose that enemy images are used by political leaders to influence soldiers and the masses, serving as instruments in the hands of manipulative leaders. And this is often true. However, it is not uncommon for decision-makers themselves to believe in their own enemy images and prove 'captives of their own beliefs and expectations' (Blanton, 1996: 26). This means that leaders, too, are affected by their own enemy images. And this is a *second* behavioural effect of enemy images. Leaders seek cognitive consistency and will perceive information and stimuli in a manner consistent with their enemy image (Blanton, 1996). They also run the risk of having such unnuanced and inflexible enemy images that 'perceptions and facts are blurred' (Dodge, 2012: 466). In stressful international conflicts, decision-makers who have spread enemy images in various contexts could end up with an 'unchallenged and highly rigid belief system' that makes them deny 'new discordant information' (Dodge, 2012: 466). And there is an imminent risk that such decision-makers do 'not respond to the "objective" facts of the situation … but to their "image" of the situation' (Boulding,

1959: 120). As Fiebig-von Hase states, 'during the Cold War, decision-making in foreign policy' became an area of research since 'enemy perception played an important role in this context' (1997: 9). A main concern was that 'leading statesmen might be influenced by a distorted or misperceived enemy image and thereby make inadequate conclusions about the intention of their adversary'. In other words, cognitive and perceptual biases threaten to enter the decision-making process and in the worst case, 'hostile relationships produce mirror images' where each of the conflicting parties constructs 'diabolical images of the adversary' (Fiebig-von Hase, 1997: 11).

Third, discourses, particularly those that become dominant in a society, can also influence social norms and behaviour in general. This is a fundamental idea within post-structuralism (Fairclough, 2003: 73). And this comes as no surprise. It is easier to harm individuals belonging to a dehumanized group since dehumanizing enemy images tend to portray the other as beings without the same emotional and physical needs as 'ours'. And 'the more one dehumanizes the out-group, the less they deserve the humane treatment enjoined by universal norms, and hence the greater the aggression' (Struch and Schwartz, 1989: 365). If dominant dehumanizing and deindividuating enemy images impact cognition, norms, and emotions (as we have said above), it is almost a matter of course that they also impact *public behaviour and conduct* in relation to the enemy and catalyse violence. The enemy is believed to understand only one language: violence. That is allegedly the only way to deal with 'them'. If this is how 'we' perceive the enemy, there is a risk that people will cling to this understanding no matter what.

> If the enemy resists the effort to apply force, our side must double its efforts. If, on the other side, the enemy seeks conciliation or compromise, this is a sign that force is having effect.
>
> *(Frank and Melville, 1988: 202)*

In armed conflicts, people, usually soldiers, regularly gain power – sometimes unsupervised – over individuals belonging to the enemy. It could be Israeli soldiers at checkpoints in the West Bank. It could be prison guards. Bandura, whom we mentioned above, also states that when

> people are given punitive power, they treat dehumanized individuals more harshly than those who are personalized or are invested with human qualities.
>
> *(Bandura, 2016: 85)*

We have seen countless examples of abuse by people in a position of power. There are numerous testimonies of how German Jews were treated in the 1930s. We have seen it in former Yugoslavia in the 1990s, in Cambodia in the 1970s, and in Rwanda in the 1990s. Yet another horrible example is the abuses by the US military at the Abu Ghraib prison in Iraq in 2003.

However, norms can also influence the behaviour of civilians far from battlegrounds. The American author and scholar of religion, Nathan Lean, discusses in his book *The Islamophobia Industry* how negative attitudes towards Muslims spread among ordinary American citizens after the terrorist attack of September 11 (Lean, 2017: 3). And the FBI reported a drastic increase in the number of hate crimes against Muslims in the same period (Lean, 2017: 3). That Americans' feelings were upset right after this terrorist attack is perhaps unsurprising. But Lean argues that the hatred of Muslims has continued for more than 15 years after the terror attack in 2001 and that this was partly 'the product of a tight-knit and interconnected confederation of right-wing fear merchants' (Lean, 2017: 14). In the wake of this rhetoric, crime targeting Muslim and Arab communities also followed (Lean, 2017: 7). Lean goes so far as to claim that the hate rhetoric was so toxic that violence became the only logical conclusion (Lean, 2017: 17).

A *fourth* behavioural effect of an enemy image is that it can also impact target groups' behaviour and conduct. The intended audience of an enemy image is the in-group, often your own nation. However, enemy images can sometimes spill over and influence the enemy, particularly if they share the same territory.

Imagine that you belong to the enemy, a group that is always portrayed as violent, less intelligent, lazy, or criminal. That is how your group has always been represented. In such a case, there is a risk that members of your group will act in accordance with those expectations and stereotypes. Enemy images and other forms of dominant stereotypes might 'cause the stereotyped individual to behaviorally confirm the perceiver's stereotype' (Snyder, Decker Tanke, and Berscheid, 1977: 658). Such stereotypes could affect performance in school or choices in life (Steele and Aronson, 1995: 797–798). This effect can be called 'behavioural confirmation effects', 'self-fulfilling prophecies', (Stangor, 2000: 14), or 'stereotype threat' (Steele and Aronson, 1995: 797).

A *fifth* consequence of enemy images is that they might delegitimize future peace. During the war, it is not uncommon for the belligerent parties to cast their enemies as dehumanized, demonic, bestial, and incorrigible, making it hard to imagine peace, and thus hard to legitimize a future peace agreement. Any attempt to build future peace is undermined.

Explaining participation in organized violence

A core theme in peace and conflict studies is war, and a central conundrum in this field is why people, often willingly, take part in this kind of violence. Enemy images are *one* important tool, but not the only one, explaining participation. After the Second World War, when its horrors and those of the Holocaust were revealed, several research projects were initiated to understand the violent potential residing in people. A variety of explanations for participation in violence were offered by, among others, Theodor W. Adorno (1903–1969), Muzafer Sherif[4] (1906–1988), Stanley Milgram (1933–1984), Christopher R. Browning (b. 1944), and Philip

Zimbardo (b. 1933). At the risk of oversimplification, the explanations can be divided into two broad categories: one focusing on personality types, and the other on context and socio-political structures.

The German philosopher Theodor W. Adorno (for a more extensive discussion, see Chapter 4, section *The authoritarian personality*), along with his co-researchers, Else Frenkel-Brunswik and Daniel Levinson Nevitt, conducted research in Germany directly after the end of the Second World War, and in 1950 they published the book *The Authoritarian Personality*. These researchers were appalled by the Holocaust, but unlike the other researchers mentioned above, Adorno and his colleagues were not primarily interested in contexts fostering obedience to participation in violence but rather focused on the role of *personality*. They tried to identify the authoritarian personality, 'the authoritarian type of man' who 'seems to combine the ideas and skills which are typical of a highly industrialized society with irrational or anti-rational beliefs' (Adorno et al., 1950: ix). Their focus was authoritarianism, and why a 'potentially fascistic individual' is particularly open to authoritarian political ideas and solutions (Adorno et al., 1950: 1). In their study they developed various scales, the F scale measuring anti-democratic personality profile being the best remembered (Adorno et al., 1950: 224). Their theory is based on a Freudian explanatory model that underlined the effects of punitive parenting and harsh application of rules (Adorno et al., 1950: 683).

The other category of researchers tended to focus more on people with no known extreme attitudes and an ordinary upbringing, and how, given the right circumstances, such people are motivated to participate in violent actions. The American social psychologist Stanley Milgram (see Box 1.2) published the results of his research in a seminal paper, *Behavioral Study of Obedience* (1963), and in a well-known book, *Obedience to Authority* (1974). In these works, he claimed that obedience is necessary in society, constituting a 'basic element in the structure of social life' (Milgram, 1963: 371). But obedience is also potentially destructive. It can make people perform acts conflicting with their personal conscience (like taking part in war or in other forms of violent acts). The Holocaust, for instance, could only be carried out 'if a very large number of persons obeyed orders' (Milgram, 1963: 371).

> This is, perhaps, the most fundamental lesson of our study: ordinary people, simply doing their jobs, and without any particular hostility on their part, can become agents in a terrible destructive process.
>
> *(Milgram, 1974: 6)*

Milgram's famous social psychology experiments conducted at Yale University in the 1960s found that the research participants/subjects (40 males, aged 20–50) with different occupations and levels of education obeyed an authority figure who instructed them to harm (administer electric shocks) to a fake learner (Milgram, 1963: 371–372). The research participants were told, among other things, that 'we know very little about the effects of punishment on learning' and that Milgram wanted to know 'what effect punishment will have on learning in this situation' (Milgram, 1963: 372). With a few exceptions, the subjects 'were convinced of the reality of the experimental situation'. Believing that they were taking part in a learning experiment, they administered painful and harmful shocks to another person (Milgram, 1963: 375). Although some research participants disapproved of distributing shocks and others called it 'stupid and senseless', the majority complied with the instructions they were given (Milgram, 1963: 376). Milgram claimed that 26 of his 40 research participants administered shocks they believed to be potentially lethal, although with emotional strain.

The key question remains: what made the research participants obey? Milgram concludes that there is a 'tendency to obey those whom we perceive to be legitimate authorities' (Milgram, 1963: 378). But that is not his only conclusion. Other factors seem to interplay with legitimate authority. People appear to be persuaded to harm when placed in a hierarchical structure and when the order is given by an authority figure. According to Milgram, this behaviour is also facilitated if the individual believes that they are anonymous, not responsible for their behaviour (the authority figure takes responsibility, Milgram, 1974: xii, 7), and if they cannot see the victim's suffering (Milgram, 1974: 32).

BOX 1.2   STANLEY MILGRAM'S 'OBEDIENCE TO AUTHORITY' EXPERIMENTS

The experiments began in July 1963, in the basement laboratory of Linsly-Chittenden Hall at Yale University, three months after the trial of SS-Obersturmbannführer Adolf Eichmann in Jerusalem. Their purpose was to examine how far ordinary people (men) would go in obeying instructions if it involved harming another person, out of interest in how easily one can be influenced to commit atrocities, such as the Germans did in the Second World War (Milgram, 1963: 371). The subjects of the experiment were 40 males between the ages of 20 and 50, drawn from New Haven and the surrounding communities. Subjects were recruited by a newspaper advertisement and direct mail solicitation. Those who responded to the appeal believed they were to participate in a study of memory and learning at Yale University and included postal clerks, high school teachers, salesmen, engineers, and labourers. Subjects ranged in educational level from one who had not finished elementary school to holders of doctorates and other professional degrees. In his 1963 article, Milgram writes that it was conducted with one naive subject and one victim (an accomplice) performing in each experiment (Milgram, 1963: 371).

A pretext had been devised to justify the administration of electric shocks by the subject, who drew slips of paper from a hat to determine who would be the teacher and who would be the learner in the experiment. The draw was rigged so that 'the naive subject' (research participant) was always the teacher and the accomplice always the learner. After the draw, the participants were taken to an adjacent room and the learner strapped into an 'electric chair' apparatus. To enhance credibility, the experimenter declared, in response to a question by the learner: 'Although the shocks can be extremely painful, they cause no permanent tissue damage' (Milgram, 1963: 373). After the learner had memorized a list of words, the teacher tested him by saying a word and asking him to recall its pair from a list of four possible choices; as instructed by the conductor of the experiment, he administered an electric shock for every mistake, increasing the shock level each time. There were 30 switches on the shock generator marked from 15 volts, slight shock, to 450, danger – severe shock (Milgram, 1963: 4). Overall, 65% of the 'teachers' continued to the highest level of 450 volts, and all continued to at least 300 volts (Milgram, 1963: 376).

Read more: Milgram, S. (1963). Behavioral Study of Obedience. *The Journal of Abnormal and Social Psychology* 67(4).

A few years after Milgram's experiment, American psychologist Philip Zimbardo carried out a famous study together with two other colleagues: the Stanford prison experiment (SPE, see Box 1.3). The research results were originally published in 1973 in the lesser-known *Naval Research* journal (Haney, Banks, and Zimbardo, 1973b), and later in more reputable ones. This research has been discussed, criticized, and reconsidered in many subsequent texts. Influenced by Milgram, Zimbardo and his colleagues created a mock prison and, using newspaper ads, recruited volunteers (all male) to participate in the 'prison simulation in exchange for payment' (Haney, Banks, and Zimbardo, 1973a: 73). The research participants were randomly assigned to be either 'guards' or 'prisoners' (Haney, Banks, and Zimbardo, 1973a: 71–74). They had been selected by an extensive intensive interview process to achieve a prison 'entirely populated by individuals who are undifferentiated in all essential dimensions from the rest of society' (Haney, Banks, and Zimbardo, 1973a: 71). The guards were given uniforms, wooden batons, reflecting sunglasses, and a whistle. The prisoners were given identical prisoner clothing (Haney, Banks, and Zimbardo, 1973a: 72).

Just like Milgram's, Zimbardo's experiment indicates that context matters more than personality–attitude dispositions: the mock prison impacts 'the affective states of both guards and prisoners as well as upon the interpersonal processes taking place between and within those role-groups' (Haney, Banks, and Zimbardo, 1973a: 80). The participants assigned to be guards embraced their roles and used their power position to enforce authoritarian measures and in some cases abuse the 'prisoners'. And the 'prisoners expressed intentions to do harm to others more frequently' (Haney, Banks, and Zimbardo, 1973a: 80). As O'Toole (1997) has pointed out, the experiment demonstrated the ease with which ordinary people could be led to engage in anti-social acts by putting them in situations where they felt anonymous or could perceive others in ways that made them less than human – as enemies or objects.

BOX 1.3 PHILIP ZIMBARDO'S STANFORD PRISON EXPERIMENT

In August 1971, Philip Zimbardo conducted the now notorious and controversial SPE in the basement of Stanford University's psychology building. In his 1973b article about the study, Zimbardo writes that the environment created was that of a 'mock' prison which physically constrained the prisoners in barred cells and psychologically conveyed the sense of imprisonment to all participants (Haney, Banks, and Zimbardo, 1973a: 71). His intention was thus to not create a literal simulation of an American prison, but rather a functional representation of one. The participants in the experiment were 24 male college students and/ or college-aged men living in Palo Alto, predominantly white and middle class, apparently healthy and psychologically stable. Though originally planned for two weeks, the study was shut down after just six days due to concerns raised by non-participants about the increasingly brutal and dehumanizing behaviour exhibited by the guards, such as forcing the prisoners to do push-ups, clean out toilets with their bare hands, and simulate sodomy (Zimbardo, 2008: 171). Zimbardo himself, acting as the prison superintendent, was not inclined to end the experiment at first, as he, much like the guards, was consumed by his role. The SPE has in later years fallen under a lot of scrutiny and criticism due to its unethical nature. Its scientific validity has been discredited and its methods described as 'deeply flawed' (Reicher, Haslam, and Van Bavel, 2018: 5). In 2018, Zimbardo published a book titled *The Lucifer Effect: Understanding How Good People Turn Evil*, in which he compared the SPE with the abuse of power by US prison guards in the infamous Abu Ghraib prison in Baghdad.

Read more:

Haney, C., Banks, C., and Zimbardo, P. (1973a) Interpersonal dynamics in a simulated prison. *International Journal of Criminology and Penology*. Stanford University.
Zimbardo, P. (2008) *The Lucifer Effect*. New York: Random House Publishing.
Zur, O. (1991) The love of hating: The psychology of enmity. *History of European Ideas* 13(4).

Milgram's research and results have inspired many researchers, including those outside social psychology. One of them is Christopher R. Browning, an American historian and Holocaust specialist who tried to understand why 'ordinary men' take part in violence. In 1992, Browning published *Ordinary Men: Reserve Police Battalion 101 and the Final Solution in Poland*, a book on a paramilitary group of 500 slightly older soldiers from Hamburg. Browning selected this group for scrutiny since he had reasons to believe that they were *not* fanatical Nazis but ordinary middle-aged men from the working- and lower-middle classes in Hamburg, a city where Nazism was not particularly strong (Browning, 1992: 164–165). Still, these men were responsible for mass shootings and roundups of Jewish people for deportation to Nazi death camps in 1942 (Browning, 1992: 121). Only 10–20% of them did not become killers, according to Browning (1992: 159). And at the mass murder in Józefów, only 'a mere dozen men out of nearly 500 had responded instinctively to Major Trapp's offer to step forward and excuse themselves from the impending mass murder' (Browning, 1992: 71). But the question remains: why did 'ordinary men' take part in this violence? After refuting or at least downgrading various explanatory models, Browning turns to Milgram for answers. Browning's general argument is that most people are susceptible to the pressure of a group setting. If you refused to take part in the mass killing, you could be accused of leaving the dirty work to your comrades (Browning, 1992: 184). And of course, the police battalion was, just like the rest of society, 'immersed in a deluge of racist and anti-Semitic propaganda' (Browning, 1992: 184). These two factors, propaganda (cognitive factors) and group pressure (socio-psychological factors), could be the most important ones.

Another researcher inspired by Milgram's research is anthropologist and genocide expert Alexander Laban Hinton (b. 1963) who in 2005 published a seminal book on the genocidal Democratic Kampuchea regime.[5] During its years in power from April 1975 to January 1979, the Maoist-inspired Khmer Rouge regime killed 1.5–2 million people, nearly a quarter of Cambodia's population. In his research on this genocide, Hinton worked for about a decade collecting data and travelling through the country. In addition to a traditional anthropological method (living with Cambodians and participating in their daily lives), he recorded testimonials, gathered a variety of documents, and conducted interviews with journalists, human rights workers, politicians, and acquaintances. His research focused on one parent question: why did you kill (Hinton, 2005)? The answers he received echo what we have heard so many times before: I was just following orders (Hinton, 2005: 277) – an answer that absolves the perpetrators and is unsatisfying for victims. Hinton sees that obedience in the Cambodian context, just as in Nazi Germany, plays a role.

> This is exactly how perpetrators like Lor, Pauk, and Eichmann wish to portray themselves – as passive subjects whose murderous deeds were ultimately the responsibility of others – when they explain that they were 'only following orders'.
>
> *(Hinton, 2005: 278)*

Still, obedience cannot explain all the cruelty exhibited by the perpetrators. Some perpetrators often brutalized their victims in ways that exceeded the orders. Hinton concludes that violence on this scale is the combined effect of a few processes, an important one being socioeconomic or political upheaval and power vacuum. This can

> upset the status quo, destabilize previous understandings and people's sense of well-being, contribute to unemployment and hunger, intensify group divisions, force people to take sides, undermine social structures that promote cohesion and solidarity, and create a sense of threat and danger.
>
> *(Hinton, 2005: 282)*

In addition to that, Hinton also underlines the importance of scapegoating or an ideology dehumanizing 'them' (what we call an enemy image). And this ideology must make sense to ordinary men, it must be 'localized' to make it appeal to followers (Hinton, 2005: 287). Abstract Marxist–Leninist ideas would simply not work in the Cambodian countryside. Instead, as Hinton underlines, structural transformations of society were implemented that 'manufacture the differences they have envisioned' (Hinton, 2005: 285). In simple terms, a world is created where normal rules do not apply (a ghetto, a concentration camp) but where the new ideology rules. Lastly, the reason why people kill probably changes over time. According to Hinton, and here he refers to Milgram, people probably experience more psychosocial dissonance the first time they kill. After numerous killings, they begin to engage in a 'cognitive shift' by dehumanising their victims, displacing responsibility, and 'morally justifying what they have done' (Hinton, 2005: 288).

The last researcher we would like to mention in this context is the Polish-British sociologist Zygmunt Bauman (1925–2017), who published an article (1988) and a book (1989) on the Holocaust that have become contemporary classics. The focus of these works does not concern participation in organized violence, but rather the relationship between modernity and the Holocaust. We believe, though, that these texts can still shed some light on the issue that concerns us, participation in organized violence.

Bauman challenges some basic tenets within sociology. Traditionally, sociology has seen the Holocaust as an effect of barbarism and an unfinished civilizing process (Bauman, 1989: 13). The Holocaust is also seen as a deviation from an otherwise healthy modern society (Bauman, 1988: 475). Bauman, on the other hand, argues that 'it was the rational world of modern civilisation that made the Holocaust thinkable' (Bauman, 1989: 13). It was this world, with its technological and organizational achievements, that made it possible. It was the possibilities of bureaucratized industrial society that enabled it. And, Bauman underlines, 'none of the societal conditions which made Auschwitz possible has truly disappeared' (Bauman, 1988: 479), while concluding that modernity cannot carry the entire burden of the Holocaust; he sees it as a necessary but not sufficient condition (Bauman, 1988: 480–481).

In these two texts, Bauman emphasizes one aspect of modernity that has possibly been neglected in previous academic thinking – the role of modern bureaucracy:

> the mass murder on unprecedented scale depended on the availability of well developed and firmly entrenched skills and habits of meticulous and precise division of labour, maintaining a smooth flow of command and information, or impersonal, well synchronized coordination of autonomous yet complementary actions.
>
> *(Bauman 1988: 482)*

Once Adolf Hitler had defined the goal of making Nazi Germany's territories *judenfrei* (emptied of Jews, literally 'Jew-free'), and since forced deportation was not possible, a bureaucratic structure implemented Holocaust as a strategy to make Germany *judenfrei*.

> The most shattering of lessons deriving from the analysis of the 'twisted road to Auschwitz' is that – in the last resort – the choice of physical extermination as the right means to the task of 'getting rid' of the Jews was a product of routine bureaucratic procedures: means-ends calculus, budget balancing, universal rule application.
>
> *(Bauman, 1988: 484)*

Ergo, the Holocaust was the outcome of a rational modern bureaucracy, impossible without it. Bauman also underlines that the bureaucracy implementing this killing was not staffed by abnormal people. On the contrary, and this is in line with Milgram, Zimbardo, and Browning as above, not more than ten per cent of the bureaucrats could be considered abnormal, sadistic, or fanatical (Bauman, 1988: 486).

But how can Bauman's understanding of the bureaucracy help us to understand participation in organized violence? Well, when Bauman, inspired by the German sociologist Max Weber, describes the essence of bureaucracy, he is repeating the dynamic discussed previously. *Firstly*, the bureaucracy is hierarchical with a clear chain of command. For it to function, obedience must permeate its structures. The ideal bureaucrat obeys the commands of superiors and sacrifices self-interests (Bauman, 1988: 488 and 1989: 21). The readiness to make such sacrifices is seen as a virtue. The civil servant's own morals are irrelevant; 'discipline is substituted for moral responsibility'. And the civil servant's moral misgivings about certain decisions are 'counterbalanced by the superior's insistence that he and he alone bears the responsibility for his subordinates' actions' (Bauman, 1989: 22).

A *second* essential characteristic of bureaucracy is its ability to conceal the moral character of actions (Bauman, 1988: 490), and here Bauman refers to Milgram's research. They both identify distance and invisibility as factors inhibiting compassion. Many civil servants, particularly those making crucial decisions, are detached from the moral consequences of their decisions. The complexity and scale of the bureaucracy render the actions invisible to the different actors. Bauman here refers to Holocaust scholar Raul Hilberg (1926–2007), who says that

> it must be kept in mind that most of the participants [of genocide] did not fire rifles at Jewish children or pour gas into gas chambers... Most bureaucrats composed memoranda, drew up blueprints, talked on the telephone, and participated in conferences. They could destroy a whole people by sitting at their desk.
>
> *(Hilberg, 1983, vol. 3, p. 1024, cited in Bauman, 1989: 24)*

The decision-makers did not have to do the dirty work and could keep the killing at a distance. They could not see the end product (genocide) of their daily routines as obedient civil servants.

> The increase in the physical and/or psychic distance between the act and its consequences achieves more than the suspension of moral inhibition; it quashes the moral significance of the act and thereby preempts all conflict between personal standards of moral decency and immorality of the social consequences of the act.
>
> *(Bauman, 1988: 492)*

Even for the *Einsatzgruppen*, who directly killed their victims, 'efforts were made to keep the weapons at a longest possible distance from the ditches into which the murdered were to fall' (Bauman, 1998: 492). And the killers did not have to see their victims die in the gas chambers. Bauman calls this technique to keep victims at a distance 'moral sleeping pills' (Bauman, 1998: 493).

Lastly, Bauman underlines that the bureaucracy implementing the genocide also dehumanized the victims (Bauman, 1998: 493). This did not necessarily mean that the German Holocaust bureaucracy created an enemy image, as we define it below, but merely dehumanized them, describing them as non-humans with no human rights. All in all, the modern bureaucracy is the structure that enables ordinary people to become participants in genocide without losing their minds or feeling personally responsible.

Let us summarize. Enemy images are not the only tool to make people participate in organized violence. What the clinical as much as the historical studies suggest is that participation in organized violence is not mainly facilitated by individuals' psychological profiles but by structural settings and specific contexts. Authority and obedience, peer pressure, and physical distance also enable participation in violence.

Overview

In this chapter we have thus introduced the topic and explained the book's approach to the study of the concept of enemy images. Strategies that make people obey and participate in organized violence have been described briefly. This introductory chapter also addresses some of the consequences that result from enemy images. In the subsequent chapters, we will address rhetorical strategies, the emergence, acceptance, consequences, and potential counteraction of enemy images, uniting approaches from sociology, international relations, intellectual history, social psychology, cognition studies, and communication studies as follows.

Chapter 2 constructs two different ideal–typical enemy images – one we call malign and the other benign. The former focuses on what constitutes a 'successful' ideal-type enemy image. The latter is constructed to give an alternative view of enemy images, showing one which does not legitimize violence to the same extent. These ideal types can be used as analytical instruments in the studies of enemy images.

Chapter 3 is concerned with the persuasive power of enemy images to explain how messages are formulated to persuade an audience. This chapter also provides an analytical framework to illustrate the construction of a persuasive system of indoctrination.

Chapter 4 explains the general human tendency to accept enemy images, mainly drawing on social psychology and cognition theory. It also discusses whether certain contexts, situations, and personality traits make us more willing to accept enemy images.

In Chapter 5 the targets of enemy images become a topic, dealing with the fact that not all out-groups are equally likely to become targets of an enemy image. This part of the book will explain how and why some groups are more likely to be selected as objects of hate.

Chapter 6 examines an important question: how to counteract enemy images?

And the last chapter (7) explains how enemy images are expressed and communicated through different forms of medialization, providing an overview of how enemy images are conveyed to a wide range of target audiences with different forms of expressions. Moreover, several classical examples of how different kinds of medialization communicate enemy images are given, with guidance on how to analyse similar content.

Study questions

- Every nation has out-groups, and some of them are considered to be enemies. Starting from what you know about your own nation and the rhetoric used within it, try to find examples of out-groups for each category of Table 1.1.
- In addition to legitimizing acts of war, what other consequences can hate speech and enemy images have?

Potential essay or thesis suggestion

- Read the studies on participation in organized violence presented above, especially the method and theory of the studies. Choose a historical case of genocide where you have access to original sources about the course of events at the individual or grassroots level. Create your own analytical and methodological framework, and apply it to the original sources.

Recommended further reading

Bauman, Z. (1989) *Modernity and the Holocaust*. Cambridge: Polity Press.
In this ground-breaking book, Zygmunt Bauman describes how modernity is *not* the cure for the Holocaust but a necessary condition for it. The book has become a contemporary classic because of its unique perspectives on and analysis of the Holocaust.

Hinton, A. (2005) *Why Did They Kill? Cambodia in the Shadow of Genocide*. Berkeley, CA: University of California Press.
This book and the study it is based on are a must for students with an interest in genocide and mass killing. In addition to its analysis of a violent time in history, the book's anthropological method, as well as its data and results, are both interesting and relevant for peace researchers and other social scientists.

Welch, D. and Fox, J. (eds.) (2012) *Justifying War, Propaganda, Politics and the Modern Age*. Basingstoke: Palgrave Macmillan.
This edited volume provides an excellent overview of how wars in the modern age have been justified in different political, economic, and cultural contexts.

Notes

1   Messianic Judaism is a religious movement espousing a largely evangelical theology while adhering to Jewish cultural heritage, including the observance and celebration of life-cycle events, the Sabbath, and the Jewish feasts. The movement is small and has suffered persecution in Israel (Steiner and Lundberg, 2018: 147).

2   This book deals exclusively with enemy images and this section discusses their consequences. However, we are painfully aware that stereotypes, prejudices and othering also had – and still have – enormous consequences. Ideas of white supremacy still affect our society: politically, socially, and economically. According to Onika June Winston, the idea that people of Black African ancestry were 'racially inferior stock for domination' was reproduced to legitimize slavery in the evolving capitalist system (Winston, 2021: 36). And white supremacy, even after the abolition of slavery in the nineteenth century, not only condoned apartheid but continues to condone the economic marginalization of people of Black African ancestry (Winston, 2021: 36).

3   Professor Johan Galtung was a leading figure in Scandinavian peace research and perhaps even its founder. Unfortunately, in recent years his reputation has been tarnished by a series of antisemitic statements. As early as 2012, his invitation to speak at a peace research conference at the University of Gothenburg was withdrawn. The organizers gave three main reasons: Galtung's suggestion that Anders Behring Breivik's terror attack on Utøya had a connection to Israel; statements about the alleged veracity of the

Protocols of the Elders of Zion, an antisemitic forgery peddling conspiracy theories; and statements about Jewish control over the international media (Vergara and Leman, 14 June 2012).

4   Muzafer Sherif's work is discussed in Chapter 4.

5   From 1975 until 1979, Cambodia was ruled by the dictatorship of Pol Pot and the Communist Party of Kampuchea. During those years, Cambodia was called Kampuchea or Democratic Kampuchea.

Bibliography

Adorno, T., Frenkel-Brunswik, E., Levinson, D. and Sanford, N. (1950) *The Authoritarian Personality*. New York, NY: Harper & Brothers.

Balzacq, T. (2011) *Preface, Securitization Theory. How Security Problems Emerge and Dissolve*. London, New York, NY: Routledge.

Bandura, A. (1986) *Social Foundations of Thought and Action: A Social Cognitive Theory*. Upper Saddle River, NJ: Pearson Education, Inc.

Bandura, A. (2016) *Moral Disengagement, How People Do Harm and Live with Them-Selves*. New York, NY: Worth Publishers.

Bandura, A., Ross, D. and Ross, S. A. (1961) Transmission of aggression through imitation of aggressive models. *The Journal of Abnormal and Social Psychology* 63(3): 575–582. https://doi.org/10.1037/h0045925

Bandura, A., Underwood, B. and Fromson, M. (1975) Disinhibition of aggression through diffusion of responsibility and dehumanization of victims. *Journal of Research in Personality* 9(4): 253–269. https://doi.org/10.1016/0092-6566(75)90001-X

Bauman, Z. (1988) Sociology after the Holocaust. *The British Journal of Sociology* 39(4): 469–497. https://doi.org/10.2307/590497

Bauman, Z. (1989) *Modernity and the Holocaust*. Cambridge: Polity Press.

Bauman, Z. (1998) Allosemitism: Premodern, Modern, Postmodern. In Cheyette B. and Marcus L. (eds.) *Modernity, Culture and 'the Jew'* (pp. 143–156). Cambridge: Polity Press.

Berny, M. (2020) The Hollywood Indian Stereotype: The Cinematic Othering and Assimilation of Native Americans at the Turn of the 20th Century. In Maillet, J. and Dudouyt, C. (eds.) *Creating the Enemy. Angles, New Perspectives on the Anglophone World* (Issue 10, pp. 1–26). https://doi.org/10.4000/angles.331

Blanton, S. L. (1996) Images in conflict: The case of Ronald Reagan and El Salvador. *International Studies Quarterly* 40(1): 23–44. https://doi.org/10.2307/2600930

Bonilla-Silva, E. (2006) *Racism without Racists: Color-Blind Racism and the Persistence of Racial Inequality in the United States*. Lanham, MD: Rowman & Littlefield.

Boulding, K. (1959) National images and international systems. *The Journal of Conflict Resolution* 3(2): 120–131. https://doi.org/10.1177/002200275900300020

Brons, L. (2015) Othering, an analysis. *Transcience: A Journal of Global Studies* 6 (1): 69–90. https://philpapers.org/archive/BROOAA-4.pdf, accessed 8 November 2022.

Browning, C. (1992) *Ordinary Men, Reserve Police Battalion 101 and the Final Solution in Poland*. New York, NY; London: Harper Collins.

Bush, G. (2003, January 3) *President Rallies Troops at Fort Hood*. [Speech] Texas: Fort Hood. https://georgewbush-whitehouse.archives.gov/news/releases/2003/01/20030103. html, accessed 16 October 2023.

Carroll, E. M. (1938) *Germany and the Great Powers 1866–1914: A Study in Public Opinion and Foreign Policy*. New York, NY: Prentice-Hall.

David, O. and Bar-Tal, D. (2009) A sociopsychological conception of collective identity: The case of national identity as an example. *Personality and Social Psychology Review* 13(4): 354–379.

Dodge, T. (2012) Enemy images, coercive socio-engineering and civil war in Iraq. *International Peacekeeping* 19(4): 461–477. https://doi.org/10.1080/13533312. 2012.709756

Douglas, M. (1992) *Risk and Blame: Essays in Cultural Theory* (1st ed.). London, New York, NY: Routledge. https://doi.org/10.4324/9780203430866

Dovidio, J., Hewstone, M., Glick, P. and Esses, V. (2010) Prejudice, Stereotyping and Discrimination: Theoretical and Empirical Overview. In Dovidio, J., Hewstone, M., Glick, P. and Esses, V. M. (eds.) *The SAGE Handbook of Prejudice, Stereotyping and Discrimination* (pp. 3–28). SAGE Publications Ltd. https://doi.org/10.4135/9781446200 919.n1

Fairclough, N. (2003) *Analyzing Discourse*. London: Routledge.

Fanon, F. (1961) *The Wretched of the Earth*. New York, NY: Grove Press.

Fiebig-von Hase, R. (1997) Introduction. In Fiebig-von Hase, R. and Lemkuhl, U. (eds.) *Enemy Images in American History* (pp. 1–40). Providence, RI; Oxford, NY: Berghahn.

Fox, J. and Welch, D. (2012) Justifying War: Propaganda, Politics and the Modern Age. In Welch, D. and Fox, J. (eds.) *Justifying War, Propaganda, Politics and the Modern Age* (pp.1–22). Basingstoke: Palgrave Macmillan.

Fox, R. (1992) Prejudice and the Unfinished Mind: A New Look at an Old Failing. *Psychology Inquiry* 3(2): 137–152. https://doi.org/10.1207/s15327965pli0302_12

Frank, J. and Melville, A. (1988) The Image of the Enemy and the Process of Change. In Gromyko, A. and Hellman, M. (eds.) *Breakthrough: Emerging New Thinking, Soviet and Western Scholars Issue a Challenge to Build a World Beyond War* (pp. 198–207). New York, NY: Walker and Company.

Galtung, J. (1969) Violence, peace, and peace research. *Journal of Peace Research* 6(3): 167–191. https://doi.org/10.1177/002234336900600301

Galtung, J. (1971) A structural theory of imperialism. *Journal of Peace Research* 8(2): 81–117. https://doi.org/10.1177/002234337100800201

Galtung, J. (1990) Cultural violence. *Journal of Peace Research* 27(3): 291–305. https://doi.org/10.1177/0022343390027003005

Galtung, J. and Holmboe Ruge, M. (1965) The structure of foreign news. *Journal of Peace Research* 2(1): 64–90.

Gilly, P. (2016) *Konsten att sälja ett krig, Propaganda från Cato till Nato* [The Art of Selling War: Propaganda from Cato to NATO]. Stockholm: Verbal förlag.

Haggbloom S. (2002) The 100 most eminent psychologists of the 20th century. *Review of General Psychology* 6(2): 139–152. https://doi.org/10.1037/1089-2680.6.2.139

Haney, C., Banks, C. and Zimbardo, P. (1973a) Interpersonal dynamics in a simulated prison. *International Journal of Criminology and Penology* 1: 69–73. https://purl.stanf ord.edu/fb081wn8980

Haney, C., Banks, C. and Zimbardo, P. (1973b) A study of prisoners and guards in a simulated prison. *Naval Research Reviews* September 1–17.

Hinton, A. (2005) *Why Did They Kill? Cambodia in the Shadow of Genocide*. Berkeley, CA: University of California Press.

Hofstadter, R. (1964) The paranoid style in American politics. *Harper's Magazine* November.

Ivie, R. (1980) Images of savagery in American justifications for war. *Communication Monographs* 47(4): 279–294. https://doi.org/10.1080/03637758009376037

Jones, M. (2002) *Social Psychology of Prejudice.* Upper Saddle River, NJ: Prentice Hall.

Kaiser Wilhelm II, op cit. Lasswell, H. D. (1927) *Propaganda Technique in World War I.* Cambridge MA: The MIT Press.

Lasswell, H. (1927) *Propaganda Technique in World War I.* Cambridge, MA: The MIT Press.

Lean, N. (2017) *The Islamophobia Industry, How the Right Manufactures Hatred of Muslims,* 2nd ed. London: Pluto Press.

Lee, B. (2019) *Violence: An Interdisciplinary Approach to Causes, Consequences, and Cures.* Oxford: John Wiley & Sons, Inc.

Luostarinen, H. (1989) Finnish Russophobia: The story of an enemy image. *Journal of Peace Research* 26(2): 123–137. https://doi.org/10.1177/0022343389026002002

MacCormick, H. (2021) Stanford psychology professor Albert Bandura has died. *Stanford News.* https://news.stanford.edu/2021/07/30/psychology-professor-albert-bandura-dead-95/, accessed 16 October 2023.

Marshall, S. L. A. ([1947] 2000) *Men against Fire: The Problem of Battle Command.* Norman, OK: University of Oklahoma Press.

Milgram, S. (1963) Behavioral study of obedience. *The Journal of Abnormal and Social Psychology* 67(4): 371–378. https://doi.org/10.1037/h0040525

Milgram, S. (1974) *Obedience to Authority: An Experimental View.* London: Tavistock Publications.

Morrow, P. (2018) A theory of atrocity propaganda. *Humanity: An International Journal of Human Rights, Humanitarianism, and Development* 9(1): 45–62. https://doi.org/10.1353/hum.2018.0002

Oppenheimer, L. (2006) The development of enemy images: A theoretical contribution. *Peace and Conflict, Journal of Peace Psychology* 12(3): 269–292. https://doi.org/10.1207/s15327949pac1203_4

Oskamp, S. (1965) Attitudes towards U.S. and Russian actions: A double standard. *Psychological Report* 16(1): 43–46. https://doi-org.proxy.mau.se/10.2466/pr0.1965.16.1.43

Osofsky, M., Bandura, A. and Zimbardo, P. G. (2005) The role of moral disengagement in the execution process. *Law and Human Behavior* 29(4): 371–393. https://doi.org/10.1007/s10979-005-4930-1

O'Toole, K. (1997) The Stanford Prison Experiment: Still powerful after all these years. *Stanford News.* https://news.stanford.edu/pr/97/970108prisonexp.html

Petersson, B. (2006) *Stories about Strangers: Swedish Media Constructions of Socio-Cultural Risk.* Lanham, MD: University Press of America.

Petersson, B. (2009) Hot conflict and everyday banality: Enemy images, scapegoats and stereotypes. *Development* 52(4): 460–465. https://doi.org/10.1057/dev.2009.59

Reicher, S., Haslam, A. S. and Van Bavel, J. (2018) Breaking free from Stanford. *Psychologist* 31(8): 4–5.

Said, E. W. (1978) *Orientalism.* New York, NY: Pantheon Books.

Sartre, J. ([1944] 1995) *Anti-Semite and Jew: An Exploration of the Etiology of Hate.* New York, NY: Schocken Books.

Silverstein, B. and Flamenbaum, C. (1989) Biases in the perception and cognition of the actions of enemies. *Journal of Social Issues* 45(2): 51–72. https://doi.org/10.1111/j.1540-4560.1989.tb01542.x

Snyder, M., Tanke, E. D. and Berscheid, E. (1977) Social perception and interpersonal behavior: On the self-fulfilling nature of social stereotypes. *Journal of Personality and Social Psychology* 35(9): 656–666. https://doi.org/10.1037/0022-3514.35.9.656

Stangor, C. (2000) *Stereotypes and Prejudice.* Philadelphia, PA: Psychology Press.

Steele, C. M. and Aronson, J. (1995) Stereotype threat and the intellectual test performance of African Americans. *Journal of Personality and Social Psychology* 69(5): 797–811. https://doi.org/10.1037/0022-3514.69.5.797

Stein, H. (1989) The indispensable enemy and American-Soviet relations. *Ethos* 17(4): 480–503. https://doi.org/10.1525/eth.1989.17.4.02a00040

Steiner, K. (2013) War and peace theology in German and Swedish Christian Zionism. *ID: International Dialogue, A Multidisciplinary Journal of World Affairs* 3: 38–76. www.unomaha.edu/college-of-arts-and-sciences/goldstein-center-for-human-rights/ID/3_steiner2013.pdf

Steiner, K. and Lundberg, A. (2018) Loving Violent Arabs: A Study of Radicalism within the Israeli Messianic Movement. In Önnerfors, A. and Steiner, K. (eds.) *Expressions of Radicalization: Global Politics, Processes and Practices* (pp. 147–180). London: Palgrave Macmillan.

Sternberg, R. and Sternberg, K. (2008) *The Nature of Hate.* Cambridge: Cambridge University Press.

Struch, N. and Schwartz, S. (1989) Intergroup aggression: Its predictors and distinctness from in-group bias. *Journal of Personality and Social Psychology* 56(3): 364–373. https://doi.org/10.1037/0022-3514.56.3.364

Taillard, M. and Giscoppa, H. (2013) *Psychology and Modern Warfare: Idea Management in Conflict and Competition.* New York, NY: Palgrave Macmillan US.

Vergara, D. and Leman, J. (2012) Galtung stoppas som talare på fredskonferens. [Galtung is stopped as a speaker at a peace conference] *Expo.* https://expo.se/2012/06/galtung-stoppas-som-talare-p%C3%A5-fredskonferens, accessed 16 October 2023.

Vuorinen, M. (2012) Introduction: Enemy Images as Inversions of the Self. In Vuorinen, M. (ed.) *Enemy Images in War Propaganda* (pp. 1–13). Newcastle upon Tyne: Cambridge Scholars Publishing.

Wilson, T. C. (1996) Compliments will get you nowhere: Benign stereotypes, prejudice and anti-semitism. *The Sociological Quarterly* 37(3): 465–479. www.jstor.org/stable/4121294

Winston, O. J. (2021) Why does the political economy of race and ethnicity matter? *SOAS Undergraduate Research Journal* 2(1): 34–42.

Worchel, S. and Andreoli, V. (1978) Facilitation of social interaction through deindividuation of the target. *Journal of Personality and Social Psychology* 36(5): 549–556. https://doi.org/10.1037/0022-3514.36.5.549

Yzerbyt, V. (2010) Motivational Processes. In Dovidio, J., Hewstone, M., Glick, P. and Esses, V. M. (2010) *The SAGE Handbook of Prejudice, Stereotyping and Discrimination* (pp. 146–162). SAGE Publications Ltd. https://dx.doi.org/10.4135/9781446200919

Zadny, J. and Gerard, H. (1974) Attributed intentions and informational selectivity. *Journal of Experimental Social Psychology* 10(1): 34–52. https://doi.org/10.1016/0022-1031(74)90055-9

Zimbardo, P. (2008) *The Lucifer Effect.* New York, NY: Random House Publishing.

Zur, O. (1991) The love of hating: The psychology of enmity. *History of European Ideas* 13(4): 345–369. https://doi.org/10.1016/0191-6599(91)90004-I

2

WHAT IS AN ENEMY IMAGE?

Concepts and ideal types

CHAPTER OBJECTIVES

- To offer two ideal types of enemy image
- To introduce readers to how ideal–typical enemy images can serve as an analytical instrument

Introduction

In Chapter 1, in defining an enemy image, we emphasized that the other is seen as a threat to 'us' and 'our' vital interests. In this chapter, we want to give the readers tools to identify and analyse enemy images. Specifically, we will construct two different ideal–typical enemy images. In the first of two sections, we elaborate on what constitutes a 'successful' ideal-type enemy image – in other words, an enemy image that has a maximal chance of being accepted by its intended audience and achieves desensitization, legitimization, and mobilization of an in-group to a maximum degree. In the second section, we construct an alternative and benign kind of enemy image that for analytical and normative reasons does not legitimize violence to the same extent.

The ideal–typical enemy image

Constructions of enemy images, regardless of time and space, seem to have a stable and recurring rhetorical structure. According to American psychologist Jerome D. Frank, enemy images are 'remarkably similar no matter who the conflicting parties are'. They 'mirror each other – that is each side attributes the same virtues

DOI: 10.4324/9781003279570-2

to itself and the same vices to the enemy' (Frank, 1980: 483). 'We' are trustworthy, peaceful, honourable, and even humanitarian. 'They' are just the opposite.

The method of constructing ideal types was created by German sociologist Max Weber (1864–1920). As British sociologist Anthony Giddens pointed out (1971), an ideal type is an abstract model, a mental image or conception that cannot be found empirically anywhere in reality. The ideal type is an elaborated and clear example but not necessarily a normative ideal. Let us imagine that we are constructing an ideal–typical democracy. This ideal type would be so elaborated and specific that no actual democracies in the entire world could ever possibly meet all its requirements although some democracies would come close and share many of its properties. One purpose of an ideal type is to see how much empirical cases resemble it and thus to use it as an analytical instrument, a benchmark against which to assess or evaluate reality. Based on the enemy image definition in Chapter 1, we propose that an enemy image as an ideal type has the following five elements:

1 Delimitation of 'us' from 'them'
2 Characterization of 'our' and 'their' essence
3 Depiction of 'their' threats to 'our' assets
4 Legitimization of actions to neutralize this threat
5 Mobilization of the in-group to take part in actions to neutralize this threat.

Guided by these five elements, we believe it is possible to compare the ideal type of enemy image to real-life expressions. Below, we will discuss these five elements systematically and comprehensively.

Delimitation of 'us' from 'them'

According to our ideal type, an enemy image first delimits or separates 'us' from 'them'.[1] In any rhetoric constructing an enemy image, the audience must know who 'we' are and who belongs to 'us'; who 'they' are and who belongs to 'them'. The dialectic between 'us' and 'them' is thus necessary for any narrative involving an enemy.

In an enemy image, the distinction between 'us' and 'them' does not have to run along national lines. Constructs of 'us' and a hostile 'them' can be based on a variety of principles. Still, since an enemy image includes a hostile out-group threatening 'us', not just any sort of othering is relevant. 'They' should be a group with the capacity and wish to threaten and harm 'us'. 'We' should be a group with a realistic capacity to provide safety. In European history after the introduction of the Westphalian system, the nation-state is the main political community providing overarching safety.

How a national 'we' is constructed can differ; its principles of inclusion and exclusion are not consistent. One principle is derived from the tenets of civic nations. In this form of nation, 'we' are not expected to have a common lineage or origin, but 'we' should share common values and national ideology. This way of defining 'us' developed during the Enlightenment and influenced French and American self-understanding. According to this definition, the nation is perceived as a group sharing common values and a common future, not a common origin. Writing about the situation in France after the Revolution in 1789, the Australian political philosopher Eugene Kamenka said:

> When the new rulers of France had to decide whether the Jews, too, were Frenchmen, they did not ask whether the Jews had taken part in a common heritage; they asked only whether the Jews could take part in the common work of the future.
>
> *(Kamenka, 1973: 10)*

Discussing immigration in his inaugural address in 2001, President George W. Bush Jr. borrowed from the same ideas:

> America has never been united by blood or birth, or soil. We are bound by ideals that move us beyond our backgrounds, lift us above our interests and teach us what it means to be citizens. Every child must be taught these principles. Every citizen must uphold them. And every immigrant, by embracing these ideals, makes our country more, not less, American.
>
> *(Bush, 20 January 2001)*

According to this principle, individuals who do not share the ideology and values of the French and American revolutions should be excluded. In the United States, being a communist, particularly during the Cold War, would lead to public rejection and persecution.

Although it is doubtful that these principles are consistently upheld in the daily life of civic nations, their way of constructing an 'us' is different from practice in ethnic nations, which is the antithesis of civic nations. In ethnic nations, an individual's ethnic and/or 'racial' background determines whether they belong to 'us'. In a hardcore version, the nation is understood as a people sharing a common genetic code and pedigree. Self-evidently, Nazi Germany's understanding of Germanness falls into this category. But more surprisingly, so did that of some Swedish Social Democrats regarding Swedishness. In 1933, the Social Democratic Minister of Education, Arthur Engberg, gave a speech on Swedish Flag Day at the open-air museum *Skansen*. It is known that he was an antisemite who had aired antisemitic sentiments until President Paul von Hindenburg appointed Adolf Hitler as Reichskanzler in January 1933 (Blomqvist, 2001: 84). But still in June 1933, Engberg persisted in an ethnonational understanding of the nation. In the speech, he discussed the importance of communities like family, the native district, and lastly the nation. His comparing of the nation to a family and calling it a 'national tribe' ('folkstam') clearly indicated that he saw 'us' as a group sharing blood ties.

> So, the second ring widens and grows into the third, to the nation, the country, the kingdom, the sibling circle, which our Swedish tribe constitutes.
>
> *(Engberg, 1934: 214)*[2]

Arthur Engberg was not the only one to delimit the Swedish 'us' in this way. There are numerous examples from that time. Rudolf Kjellén, a Swedish professor in political science at Uppsala University, had claimed in a speech as early as 1898 that blood ties affect how we read and understand history:

> How personally does not the development of our own people touch us? Don't we follow Gustav Vasa with a very particular interest ... A foreign history does not affect us in the same way, although it is just as exciting in itself, for it does not touch upon the strings of family love in our chests. Yes, there is some of our own blood in this history.
>
> *(Kjellén, [1898] 1906: 137)*[3]

In enemy images, the plot is often more complicated than a simple game of two parties between a clearly defined 'us' and 'them'. The researcher of enemy images must be aware of the presence of more than one 'us' and more than one 'them'. It is not uncommon for 'we' to refer to more than one object. Most frequently, a political leader using the pronoun 'we' in a conflict situation would be referring to the nation and maybe also to the government. But in many cases, even in the same communication, 'we' can refer to other objects. In a speech given by George W. Bush to the American people on 11 September 2001, the day of the terror attack on the World Trade Center, 'we' not only referred to the United States but also included its allies.

> America and our friends and allies join with all those who want peace and security in the world, and we stand together to win the war against terrorism.
>
> *(Bush, 11 September 2001)*

In a few cases, one can also find subgroups within the enemy that are not understood as an enemy. Sometimes, 'we' claim to save allied subgroups within the enemy. It could be the Christian minority among Arabs or allegedly oppressed women among Muslims. In these cases, an enemy image construct would identify subgroups among 'them' that are construed as part of or compatible with an extended 'us'.

Likewise, in enemy images, people can also encounter more than one enemy. Again, and most commonly, the enemy refers to external groups who represent the main threat, usually a hostile nation or its government. But it is not uncommon for enemy images also to include *internal* enemies, the traitors in our midst. And it is in this context that conspiracy theories are likely to appear. A famous and important example of a leader identifying internal enemies was Adolf Hitler. To him, the Jews primarily but not exclusively constituted the internal enemy. In addition to them, political parties on the left were seen as enemies. 'They' were the ones who sold out Germany to its external enemies at the end of the First World War, the so-called *Dolchstoßlegende* (stab-in-the-back myth). In his political manifesto *Mein Kampf,* Hitler says:

> Kaiser William II was the first German Emperor to hold out a conciliatory hand to the leaders of Marxism, without suspecting that scoundrels have no honor. While they still held the imperial hand in theirs, their other hand was reaching for the dagger.
>
> *(Hitler, [1925–1926] 1999: 206)*

In the current political situation in Europe, it is not unusual for immigrants, particularly Muslims, to be depicted as an internal threat to 'us' (Bergmann, 2021: 36–53). An entire book genre reproducing the idea of a Muslim threat has developed over the last two decades. A common denominator in this genre is that 'they' need an accomplice among 'us' to be successful in 'their' scheme. According to Bruce Bawer, an American journalist writing about Europe, 'the political, media, and academic establishment' are traitors, since 'they' allow the destruction of the West from within (Bawer, 2006: 41). There is in his view a leftist–Muslim alignment (Bawer, 2006: 101). The British journalist Melanie Phillips agrees. Referring to the situation in the United Kingdom, she claims that

> among Britain's governing class – its intelligentsia, its media, its politicians, its judiciary, its church and even its police – a broader and deeper cultural pathology has allowed and even encouraged Londonistan to develop.
>
> *(Phillips, 2006: 15)*

The government is doing nothing to stop the development, Phillips complains, but rather seeks to appease Muslims. Her use of the term 'appease' (Phillips, 2006: 22) of course recalls the failed British and French policy against Hitler in the 1930s.

But this rhetoric can be found not only in recently published books but also in the digital environment. Maxime Dafaure has found similar ideas in researching the current alt-right movement's online communication (2020). Here, the traitors are 'Cultural Marxists', liberals, and of course Jews (2020: 60–62). And the person who has most often been depicted as the epitome of treason is George Soros. According to Dafaure, the alt-right has an 'almost pathological obsession with George Soros, the Hungarian-American billionaire and long-time supporter of progressive causes' (2020: 62).

Characterization of 'our' and 'their' essence

The second element in an ideal–typical enemy image concerns 'our' and 'their' essential *character*, what 'we' and 'they' are like. The discussion of 'our' and 'their' essential characters can also be divided into elements or sub-elements, some of which have been mentioned before. We have found four relevant traits that will constitute sub-elements in the construction of our and their ideal–typical character:

1. 'We' are multifaceted, and 'they' are all the same
2. 'They' are completely different from 'us'
3. 'We' are dynamic, 'they' are static
4. 'We' are superior but vulnerable, 'they' are inferior but powerful.

'We' are multifaceted, and 'they' are all the same

The first thing we notice when an enemy image characterizes 'them' is that 'they' tend to be stereotyped, since 'we' tend to imply that 'they' are all the same. However, people tend to have double standards, so 'we' do not do the same for our group. By contrast, 'we' differentiate, recognizing that 'we' are multifaceted.

In a stereotyped group, the individual characteristics of its members are erased, meaning there is no difference between the group and its individual members. Sometimes 'we' do that by turning 'them' into statistics or an anonymous crowd without any distinguishable individuality. In Chapter 1, we discussed Zygmunt Bauman's research and how bureaucratic structure and the way the bureaucracy works helped to conceal the individuality of the victims. The bureaucrats only saw the deindividuated numbers and statistics.

Sometimes, photojournalism can be a non-verbal tool to portray 'them' as a group without distinguishable individuals. In North American and Western European media, it is not uncommon for Muslim women to be represented wearing burqas or niqabs so that their faces do not appear. Thereby 'they' become faceless symbols of a hostile religion. If you harm 'them', it is as though you are fighting a hostile religious system – Islam – and not a person or neighbour. Another version of deindividuation is to see 'them' as a crowd without any distinguishable individuals. It can be helpful to use a photo as an illustration. Below we see one from the First Intifada (1987–1993), where people are photographed from a distance, with individuals barely discernible. 'They' become a crowd representing violence and fanaticism (Figure 2.1). Photos like this are common in Western media.

'They' are completely different from 'us'

A second sub-element in the depiction of 'us' and 'them' is alienation. This implies that 'they' are completely different from 'us', and that 'we' have nothing in common with 'them'. Everywhere on the planet, parents love their children

FIGURE 2.1   Deindividuated violent crowd.

Intifada in Gaza Strip, 1987.

Source: National Library of Israel: Dan Hadani collection via wikimedia commons.

and children take care of their elderly parents. As a rule, humans also go through the same stages of development. They learn how to crawl, walk, and talk. And all children have dreams and aspirations; they all need love and safety. The point is that in enemy images, 'their' human traits are consciously concealed, implying that 'they' are completely different from 'us', as if 'we' have nothing in common with 'them'. So we can expect 'them', unlike 'us', not to love their children as 'we' love ours.

Alienation rarely happens explicitly. Very few propagandists would say that 'they' are not at all like 'us'. Instead, a propagandist might recurringly depict 'them' in situations or when doing things that 'we' cannot relate to, or which scare 'us'. This strategy is often used in the media. Newspapers, TV, and social media repeatedly publish alienating film clips or photos of 'them', making 'us' despise 'them'. Below is a photo illustrating this kind of depiction of Muslim men. They have their backs turned to the readers (Figure 2.2); they are not only deindividuated and stereotyped but also shown praying facing Mecca. This way of praying estranges the predominantly Christian or secular audiences in North America and Western Europe.

Treatment of children is symbolically charged, and maltreatment of children evokes strong negative emotions. If propaganda could convince 'us' that 'they' abuse 'their' children, that 'they' even use them on the battlefield, 'we' would

FIGURE 2.2 Deindividuated praying men.

Source: Emisakhan via wikimedia commons.

probably alienate 'them', it would prove once and for all that 'they' really are different from 'us'. And this is exactly what propaganda sometimes does.

To have an impact, propaganda must be accepted as true, and it does commonly contain a core of truth. It was true that Iran used children in the Iran–Iraq war 1980–1988. One of the forces of the Islamic Revolutionary Guard Corps was the Basij. When Iran was attacked by Iraq and the war started, hundreds of thousands volunteered for the Basij. Many were children, some as young as 12 but also old men (Riazaty, 2016: 249–256). The reason for these children enlisting is debated. Often both Iranian officials and Western scholars underline that the boys did not come from poor families and that

> boys ignored the dangers and enrolled for four principal reasons. The first was mysticism and religious devotion, which made martyrdom seem like a natural choice, colored by heroism and romanticism.
>
> *(Razoux, 2015: 347)*

Other scholars emphasize that children from poor backgrounds were more often recruited (Ahmadi, 2018). In any case, horrible abuse of children took place and was for some normalized. The regime took pride in photos like the one in

FIGURE 2.3   Iranian child soldier.

Source: Public domain via wikimedia commons.

Figure 2.3. But this abuse also became powerful ammunition in the propaganda war against Iran's Islamic regime.

Between 2015 and 2018, one of the authors (Steiner) visited Israel and the Palestinian areas with his colleague, sociologist of religion Anders Lundberg, where they conducted interviews with leaders of local Palestinian Evangelical Christians and (Jewish) Messianic congregations.[4] These two groups have a lot in common. They both represent a conservative Christian theology and both have an evangelical theological foundation. Still, alienation is common, particularly from the Messianic side. In an interview, a female leader of a Messianic congregation claimed that Muslim kids 'from the age of twelve, ... are being taught jihad in the school' (interview 18 October 2015). Likewise in an interview with a male leader of a Messianic congregation a few days later, the following dialogue took place:

Interviewee: You know Golda Meir; she said something very smart once. She said that 'We will only have peace with the Arabs when they learn to love their children more than they hate us.'

   Kristian Steiner: Do you think that she indicated that Arabs don't love their children?

   Interviewee: If they send them to explode ... 13-year-old girl stabs people in the street. Today a 15-year-old girl. It is not that ... today. She was captured eventually. Not killed. But captured. Her parents did not beg them to stay at home. No, they [said] 'go be a shahid, be a martyr'.

In both these cases, the horror of training child combatants makes it possible to portray 'them' as a group that is antithetical to 'us', to 'our' values and behaviour. Common human traits usually uniting 'us' and 'them' disappear, leaving 'us' to believe 'we' have nothing in common with 'them', not even love for our children.

The worst kind of alienation is dehumanization. Here, the group is not just alienated, differentiated, or deindividuated. When people are dehumanized, they become subhuman or in some cases even non-human. In Nazi antisemitic propaganda, Jews were often given grotesque features and said to have a large hooknose ('Jewish nose'), dark beady eyes, and drooping eyelids. But Jews did not only have a supposedly subhuman phenotype. Their inner moral qualities were also rendered inferior. 'They' could be defined as greedy and miserly, controlling the world politically and financially. Sometimes the Nazis deployed explicitly dehumanizing depictions of Jews, typically as parasites, vermin, and rats. And the natural solution for vermin is extermination.

Dehumanization has not only affected Jews but also many other groups such as people of Black African ancestry in both colonial and post-colonial times, Asians, and indigenous peoples. The list goes on and on. Figure 2.4 shows Russian racist propaganda from the early 1900s and is a picture of Tōgō Heihachirō, the admiral who led the Japanese fleet to victory in the Russo-Japanese War (1904–1905). Depicting him as a macaque (a monkey), it was originally the front cover of the Russian magazine *Budel'nik* in 1904 (no. 12).

A more recent case of blatant dehumanizing enemy images is the genocide of Tutsi in Rwanda in 1994. In the spring and summer of 1994, for approximately a hundred days, a planned campaign of mass murder took place (Hintjens, 1999; Kellow and Steeves, 1998; McCoy, 2009). The Rwandan genocide started after the downing of a plane carrying Rwanda's President Juvénal Habyarimana and Burundi's President Cyprien Ntaryamira. The day after, Rwanda's Prime Minister Agathe Uwilingiyimana, a moderate Hutu, was assassinated. Hutu extremists were responsible for both attacks. The genocide was organized by extremist elements within the Rwandan Hutu majority. These extremists killed more than 800,000 civilians, mainly Tutsi but also moderate Hutu. Before and during the genocide, the radio station Radio Télévision Libre des Milles Collines (RTLM) played an important role. Television and newspapers were of less importance. This radio station was successful in the Rwandan media market. Unlike Radio Rwanda, with its formal and old-fashioned style, RTLM appealed to a younger generation with popular music, satire, and irony. While the dehumanization of Tutsis was probably its most important contribution to the massacres, RTLM contributed to the genocide in more than one way. The Tutsi minority was repeatedly called 'cockroaches' who should be exterminated. But in addition to dehumanization, the station also sent coded messages that coordinated the killing. Transcripts of radio transmissions leading up to the genocide have been made available by the Montreal Institute for Genocide and Human Rights Studies (MIGS, 2022).

FIGURE 2.4 Admiral Tōgō Heihachirō as a macaque.

Source: Budel'nik, issue no. 12, 1904 via wikimedia commons.

'We' are dynamic, 'they' are static

A third sub-element in the representation of 'their' essential character is to claim that unlike 'us', 'they' never change but remain *unrepentant* and *static*. Of course, most people know that in the course of history, 'we' too have maimed and killed, perhaps even been responsible for mass killing. But the historiography of 'our' group is different. 'We' are supposedly dynamic: 'we' change, 'we' learn, 'we' confess 'our' historical sins. 'They', on the other hand, are incapable of change. The notion that some people (individuals or groups) are incapable of change is universal. Expressions like 'a leopard can't change its spots' appear in many languages. Yet, this idea is rarely expressed explicitly. Such a statement would appear vulgar and would be rejected.

However, different rhetorical strategies can be undertaken to make this point without saying it bluntly, and varying with the context. In the era when racism peaked as a respected analytical perspective, it was perfectly acceptable to claim that 'they' belong to an inferior race. If 'they' have a genetic heritage that makes 'them' violent, greedy, and insidious, these characteristics will never go away. In the Nazi era, one could argue that German education and culture could never fundamentally improve the genetically inferior Jew. Or, as illustrated in the German Nazi children's book *Der Giftpilz*, (*The Poisonous Mushroom*, Hiemer, 1938) not even a Christian sacrament like baptism could alter the fundamental racial character of 'the Jew'.

Today, in a post-Holocaust reality, this kind of explicit racism is much less acceptable. Instead, cultural racism, sometimes called neo-racism, has replaced it. Although culture and nature are supposedly antonyms, there are several similarities between traditional racism and neo-racism (see Steiner, 2010). The main dogmas of traditional racism can easily be translated into a neo-racist logic (Steiner, 2010: 44). Like racism, neo-racism claims that it is reasonable to divide mankind into distinct groups (cultures instead of races). And culture (norms, values, attitudes, behaviours) is transferred from one generation to the next, just like the previously supposed racial character. According to the Swedish professor of intellectual history, Michael Azar, contemporary neo-racists have replaced the old obsession with race and genetics with a similar preoccupation with culture, without anything changing in depth (Azar, 2006: 90). Among today's neo-racists, culture is generally portrayed as something static (Steiner, 2010: 45) – or rather, 'we' know that 'our' culture changes. 'We' are not the same as before. 'We' grow morally. But 'they' do not!

Let us return to the interviews Steiner and Lundberg conducted in Israel and the Palestinian areas. In October 2015, Steiner and Lundberg recorded the following exchange:

Steiner: Do you think Islam can reform?

Interviewee: I think in the heart of it, it cannot be reformed. There were periods when Islam was less ... was more lenient, more tolerant towards Westerners or other civilizations. As a whole, if you look at the history of Islam, the amount of wars and battles it has against Western civilizations and Christianity it is in the hundreds over 1400 years. It is not something new.

(Steiner and Lundberg, 2018: 158)

This way of viewing Muslims and Islam is not reserved for the Messianic believers in Israel. On the contrary, it dominates in several anti-Islam environments, including not only far-right groups but also among some academics and journalists who use this rhetoric in their writing. Bat Ye'Or, the frontal figure for the Eurabia literature,[5] states the following:

The universality of *jihad* was proclaimed from the beginnings of Islam. *Jihad* has been ordered not only against specific groups or for specific times, but like Muhammad's mission (Qur'an 34:28), it is a universal injunction that will endure until the only religion remaining is that of Allah (Qur'an 2:189). This ongoing striving 'in the path of Allah' triggers the process that Huntington called 'Islam's bloody borders' ... There are countless treatises on *jihad* written today by Muslim jurists and theologians. They reaffirm this standardized interpretation and conceptualization of international relations.

(Bat Ye'Or, 2005: 32, original italics)

'We' are superior but vulnerable, 'they' are inferior but powerful

The last sub-element in the construction of 'our' and 'their' essential character is the portrayal of 'us' as vulnerable despite 'our' alleged superiority, and 'their' power despite 'their' inferiority. It might appear surprising that the allegedly superior 'we' is seen as vulnerable, and the inferior 'they' as powerful. But these two contrasting images are common.

Before discussing this duality, we want to underline that the portrayal of 'our' superiority and 'their' inferiority is not always explicit, and this must be considered when researching enemy images. One must read implicit messages and capture what is said between the lines. Again, in Steiner's research on Swedish Islamophobic newspapers, it was apparent that they avoided sweepingly prejudicial value judgements like 'Muslims *are* violent' (thus risking illegality) and preferred instead less contestable claims like 'Muslims murder' (Steiner, 2015: 35–37).

We believe the rhetorical formula that 'we' are superior yet vulnerable whereas 'they' are inferior but powerful could be universal. At least, we have found it in various contexts in time and space, and different guises. Below, we have demonstrated this idea with seven examples (see Table 2.1) that we believe are relevant and enlightening.

The *first* example concerns the nation-state (see Table 2.1). In the era of nationalism, the *raison d'être* of the state was not only to be the primary safety provider but also the instrument of the nation, giving it freedom, self-determination, and sovereignty. After the collapse of European empires in 1918, several nations

TABLE 2.1 Superior and yet vulnerable

'We' are superior	and yet vulnerable.	'They' are inferior	and yet powerful.
1. 'Our' nation is peaceful, sovereign, and free, and 'we' do not spend too much money on the army,	but that makes 'our' state vulnerable.	'They' are violent, imperialistic, and militarized	and 'they' have a strong state.
2. 'We' have the best genetic code,	but 'our' genes are recessive.	'They' have inferior genes, making 'them' less advanced,	but 'their' inferior genes are dominant.
3. 'We' believe in the true God,	but 'we' are irresolute and wavering.	'They' are godless and lead a sinful life,	but 'their' values, and lifestyle are powerful temptations.
4. 'We' are democratic	but that makes 'our' decision-making slow and makes 'us' weak and ineffective.	'They' are undemocratic, ruthless, and violent,	and that makes 'them' powerful and efficient.
5. 'We' have a generous welfare system	but this system can easily be abused.	'They' are poor and lazy,	and that makes 'them' a burden to us.
6. 'We' use birth control and have few children and small families,	but that makes 'our' population older and its size stagnant.	'They' do not use birth control and have many children and large families,	and that makes 'their' population young and growing.
7. Groups such as women, homosexuals, Jews, and elderly live and prosper in 'our' society,	but these groups are frail and their safety among 'us' is frail.	'They' despise our women, homosexuals, Jews, and elderly,	and 'they' have a potential power over our frail groups.

achieved sovereignty. New nation-states emerged from the ruins of the collapsed empires. All these newborn nation-states claimed that their political and territorial demands were modest, peaceful, and in line with the guiding norms. Moreover, 'our' nation-state was not militarized but comparatively weak and vulnerable. Other states, however, made outrageous requests, demanding far more territory than acceptable. Ergo, 'they' were imperialist and therefore morally inferior. Empirically, these kinds of allegations were directed by the newly established Czechoslovak state at the German minority in Czechoslovakia, and vice versa. The German minority directed similar allegations at the Czechoslovak leadership. And both states saw themselves as militarily weak but their opponent as strong (Steiner, 1996: 62–89).

If we return to the utterly racist and divisive interwar era (see the *second* example in Table 2.1), we discover that voices from that time would not only claim 'our' racial and genetic superiority. 'Our' genes were also portrayed as recessive, and 'our' superior racial character therefore as vulnerable. And 'they' are allegedly racially inferior, yet 'their' genes are dominant and robust. If we combine, the offspring will have the character of the inferior parent, meaning 'they' constitute a threat to 'our' race and everything else that could entail.

In this period, a significant number of Swedish academics adopted explicit racist ideas. One of them was Kjell Kumlien (1903–1995), a historian at Stockholm University who claimed that humanity was divided into distinct 'races' with different qualities. It was his contention that the 'Aryan race' is a high-quality 'race' since it had founded 'peoples creating culture'[6] (Kumlien, 1934: 6). He continued that 'the Nordic race' constituted the 'purest remnant' of the superior Aryan race (Kumlien, 1934: 6). The factor that caused 'us' to be 'pure' and superior was according to him the Baltic Sea, which supposedly barred inferior groups with dominant genes from procreating with 'us' (Kumlien, 1934:16). Kumlien was of course not the only one who advocates ideas about Swedish racial superiority. Värner Rydén (1878–1930), a Social Democratic member of the Swedish parliament, wrote a Swedish elementary school textbook in 1923 titled *Medborgarkunskap* (Citizenship Knowledge). In it he follows Kumlien in portraying the Swedes as superior and purer thanks to the Baltic Sea. According to him, 'the Germanic national archetype, tall with blue or grey eyes, nowhere in our time occurs in a purer from than in the Nordic countries' (Rydén, 1923: 5–6).[7]

The idea that 'we' are frail despite 'our' superiority did not die out after the Second World War. It can also appear today in new versions. In religious contexts, among Conservative Muslims as well as Christians, the secular world with its values and lifestyle or competing religions is a powerful temptation to 'our' wavering souls (the *third* example).

Even contemporary democratic societies can produce rhetoric with the same logic (the *fourth* example). In this case, 'we' would describe 'ourselves' as democratic and morally superior to authoritarian political systems. And yet, 'our' democratic societies are, despite 'our' superiority, slow and ineffective decision-makers, and therefore ultimately weak. Likewise, democracies could be described as inherently vulnerable and weak since they do not control citizens as closely as dictatorships. Moreover, the fact that democracies also give their citizens the right to organize, travel, access, and spread information and/or propaganda makes the state defenceless against actors (including internal ones) with undemocratic ideals. 'They', undemocratic states, would be described as morally inferior, ruthless, and violent but that makes 'them' powerful, and efficient decision-makers. Merete Riisager, a member of the Danish parliament representing the Liberal Alliance, wrote an op-ed in 2014 applying this logic. However, in her case, it is not only democracy that makes Denmark vulnerable but also its size:

> Islamists are opposed to democracy, human rights, diversity, homosexuality, and personal freedom...
>
> Denmark is a democratic Lilliputian country formed by cooperatives, folk high school spirit and conversational culture. That is why we are also deeply foreign to the fact that there are forces in Denmark that are working hard to subjugate freedom and democracy. Nevertheless, this is what some of the extreme Islamist environments in Denmark are working on.
>
> *(Riisager, 29 May 2014)*[8]

Moreover, Western European welfare states, our *fifth* example, can be represented as vulnerable to 'their' abuse. Bruce Bawer, an American writer living in Norway quoted earlier, is known for his writing on immigration and criticism of Islam. Seeing Muslim immigration as a problem, he claims that Muslims in Denmark constitute a future burden to the welfare state. According to him,

> In Denmark, Muslims make up five percent of the population but receive 40 percent of welfare outlays. Statistics for other countries are comparable. The ease with which immigrants can rip off the system sometimes boggles the mind.
>
> *(Bawer, 2006: 30)*

Demographic development and birth rates, the *sixth* example, can also be seen in this light. The basic logic is that since 'we' are modern, 'we' use birth control and have few children and small families. Regrettably, that makes 'our' population older and population size stagnant. 'They', on the other hand, are underdeveloped, do not use birth control, and have many children and large families. This inferiority is also 'their' strength, at least in the long run. 'Their' population will be young, and growing, and might outnumber 'us'. This type of argumentation is peddled by various movements and individuals. One is French writer and politician Renaud Camus in his *Le Grand Remplacement* (The Great Replacement) from 2012. In this theory, he claims that immigrants from Africa and the Middle East are colonizing Europe and replacing the white population (Dafaure, 2020: 61). This development, Camus argues, is partly an effect of high birth rates among these immigrants and partly a consequence of the implicit policies of European leadership (see the discussion above on internal enemies).

The controversial Canadian right-wing writer Mark Steyn also makes this kind of demographic extrapolation. Steyn, who also adopted the concept of Eurabia, discusses demography on a global level in his book *America Alone: The End of the World as We Know It* (2006).

> Just to recap those bald statistics: in 1970, the developed (sic) nations had twice as big share of the global population as the Muslim world: 30 percent to 15 percent. By 2000, they were at parity: each had about 20 percent. And by 2020?
>
> *(Steyn, 2006: xxxi)*

Later in the same book, he discusses the low birth rate in Europe. In this case, he does not see Europe as advanced. Rather its low birth rate is a self-destructive tendency, a 'self-extinction' (Steyn, 2006: 3). But one thing is sure, the Muslim world is inferior:

> No Islamic nation could have flown to the moon or invented the Internet, simply because for a millennium the culture has suppressed the curiosity necessary for such a venture.
>
> *(Steyn, 2006: 17)*

According to Steyn, Europe is barren and doomed. Europe's self-extinction and its Muslim population growth have a dire consequence: 'Europe will be semi-Islamic in its politico-cultural character within a generation' (Steyn, 2006: 3).

In some cases, power relationships between 'us' and 'them' make it hard to convincingly portray 'us' as vulnerable. Currently, Islamists living in Europe cannot be understood as powerful. In those cases, and this is our *last* example, a slightly different strategy could be applied, where 'we' identify a subgroup among 'us' who can persuasively be described as 'our' vulnerable subgroup. Women, homosexuals, Jews, and elderly people could potentially be exploited for this purpose and convincingly portrayed as vulnerable targets to 'them'. Right-wing parties, which in other contexts do not support feminism, gay rights, or Jews, use these groups for their purpose, a phenomenon referred to as femo- or homo-nationalism.

An example of this is how refugees are described as rapists. In his study of the alt-right's use of memes, Maxime Dafaure demonstrates how in its online communication this movement describes refugees as dangerous to 'our' women and at times calls them 'rapefugees', thereby creating 'an association between refugees (believed to be almost exclusively Muslim) and sexual violence' (Dafaure, 2020: 49). Likewise, male refugees are perceived as a threat to women as 'they' possess a characteristic that makes 'them' dangerous despite 'their' alleged general inferiority; 'they' are overly masculine and laden with an unchecked sexuality (Dafaure, 2020: 50).

In an interpellation debate held in the *Riksdagen*, or Swedish parliament, on 1 March 2021, Tobias Andersson from the populist right-wing Sweden Democrats (SD) party presented a study on rape offenders in Sweden, claiming that

> One of the things found in the study was that 60 per cent of the rapes that led to convictions between 2000 and 2015 were committed by first- and second-generation immigrants.[9]

SD also instrumentalized the Jews in Sweden although this party has historically been antisemitic. In Malmö, Sweden's third largest city, the synagogue has experienced repeated vandalism from young men with predominantly Palestinian backgrounds. For some time, this was neglected and not taken seriously by leading politicians. SD, who now saw Palestinians as a more important enemy than Jews, portrayed the Jewish population in Malmö as a vulnerable part of 'us' intimidated by the 'them', 'extremist Muslims'. In a question written in January 2021 to the Swedish Green Party's Minister of Culture and Democracy, Amanda Lind, SD member Björn Söder firstly claimed that antisemitism was something 'largely imported through immigration to Sweden'[10] and secondly asked the minister what measures she would take to address the increasing and often imported antisemitism in Sweden. Yet another example of exploiting a vulnerable group among 'us' concerns the LGBTQ+ community. Bruce Bawer describes how 'gay bashing' is on the rise in Europe as an effect of Muslim immigration (Bawer, 2006: 39) – but covered up, he says, since researchers do not dare to touch the subject.

All these examples tie into the five thematic domains in the discursive construction of Muslim threats to Europe identified by Spanish sociologist Estrella Gualda: demography, politics, economy, religion, culture, and identity (Gualda, 2021: 55). In each of these five domains, Islamization is identified as an existential threat. Muslim fertility is a biopolitical weapon, our politics are influenced by Muslim radicalism, our economy is burdened by Muslim immigration, our religion is threatened by extinction, and our (secular) culture and identity will be destroyed by Islam. Arguably, nature forms yet another thematic domain: in the ecofascist reading, mass migration to Europe is also a threat to ecology, and the European habitat must be defended against invasive species.

Depiction of 'their' threats to 'our' assets

The third element in our ideal–typical enemy image is the portrayal of the enemy as an imminent, real, serious, and possibly growing *threat* to 'our' most vital *assets*. This discussion will be based on the rhetorical formula discussed in the previous section, where 'they' were portrayed as powerful despite 'their' inferiority. And again, it can appear contradictory that 'they', being inferior, not only have the *intention* but also the *capacity* to threaten 'us' (Sternberg and Sternberg, 2008: 98).

And yet, this contradiction and assessment of the enemy are important elements in enemy image constructs.

It is not self-evident what a vital asset is. Sometimes referred to as 'sacred values', depending on political priorities or culture, different groups might define it differently. But, as we indicated in Chapter 1, assets could be abstract values such as 'our' faith, democracy, freedom, sovereignty, lifestyle, or material assets like territory, physical safety, livelihood, and welfare. Something to note about this component is that 'their' capacity and intention to exploit 'our' weaknesses and threaten 'our' most valuable assets is the one that separates enemy images from other forms of othering. In other words, unlike most out-groups, enemies constitute a threat to 'us' and what 'we' hold dear.

In Table 2.2, we have added a fifth column to those in Table 2.1, where we express the *threat* that might arise from the conditions described in columns 1–4. Let us return to the examples we discussed above and start with the first row, based on nationalism. In this case, 'they', unlike 'us', are militarized and imperialistic, and thereby constitute a threat to our peace, sovereignty, and freedom.

The discussion of interwar racism is our second example. As we stated in the previous section, the Swedish race is portrayed as superior but its genes as recessive and therefore frail; and though 'they' (virtually all other groups) are inferior, by virtue of their dominant genes 'they' can still threaten 'us' (if 'we' procreate with 'them'). 'Their' inferior racial character would dominate in a common offspring. The British-German political philosopher Houston Stewart Chamberlain (1855–1927), a proponent of racist ideas, claimed that mixing 'us' with 'Mongolian elements' would lead to a decrease in brain size and intelligence:

> Over and above this came the considerable commixture with Mongolian elements, that, according to Buschan's research, resulted in a provable decrease in skull capacity, brain size and therefore also in cultural capabilities – in plain English, a stupefaction – of entire nations.
>
> *(Chamberlain, 1938b: 40–41)[11]*

Herman Lundborg (1868–1943), a Swedish 'racial physician', 'race biologist', and head of the State Institute of Racial Biology, confirmed the threats Chamberlain portrayed. If 'we' procreated with 'them', Lundborg feared, it would lead to a deteriorating culture, degeneration, loss of national character, lawlessness, and revolutions (Lundborg, 1920: 16). According to Lundborg, particularly dangerous is 'a mixture between three or more widely different peoples, such as Negroes, Indians and Indo-Europeans' (Lundborg, 1918: 4). This kind of 'racial degeneration' would, according to his thinking, lead to criminality and other social problems (Lundborg, 1918: 4).

Our assessment is that the two first propositions in Table 2.2 are not frequently employed in contemporary constructions of enemy images. However, we believe our third example could be relevant and reflect current political discourse. The idea

TABLE 2.2 'Their' exploitation of 'our' vulnerabilities

'We' are superior	and yet vulnerable.	'They' are inferior	and yet powerful	and constitute a threat.
1. 'Our' nation is peaceful, sovereign, and free, and 'we' do not spend too much money on the army,	but that makes 'our' state vulnerable.	'They' are violent, imperialistic, and militarized,	and 'they' have a strong state.	'They' constitute a threat to 'our' peace, sovereignty, and freedom.
2. 'We' have the best genetic code,	but 'our' genes are recessive.	'They' have inferior genes, making them less advanced,	but 'their' inferior genes are dominant.	'Their' genes will harm 'us' if we reproduce.
3. 'We' believe in the true God,	but 'we' are irresolute and wavering.	'They' are godless and lead a sinful life,	but 'their' values, and lifestyle are powerful temptations.	'Their' lifestyle will corrupt 'us' if 'we' are not separated.
4. 'We' are democratic,	but that makes 'our' decision-making slow and 'us' weak and ineffective.	'They' are undemocratic, ruthless, and violent,	and that makes 'them' powerful and efficient.	'They' can threaten 'us' and 'our' democracy.
5. 'We' have a generous welfare system,	but this system can easily be abused.	'They' are poor and lazy,	and that makes 'them' a burden to 'us'.	'They' threaten 'our' welfare system and undermine 'our' economy.
6. 'We' use birth control and have few children and small families,	but that makes 'our' population older and its size stagnant.	'They' do not use birth control and have many children and large families,	and that makes 'their' population young and growing.	'They' will in the end outnumber 'us', locally and globally.
7. Groups such as women, homosexuals, Jews, and the elderly live and prosper in 'our' society,	but these groups are frail and their safety among 'us' is frail.	'They' despise 'our' women, homosexuals, Jews, and elderly,	and 'they' have a potential power over 'our' frail groups.	'They' constitute a threat to the freedom of 'our', women, homosexuals, Jews, and elderly.

that 'our' faith is superior to 'theirs' is valid and maybe more relevant than ever in a multicultural society and globalized international system. It is believed that 'their' godless and sinful lifestyle invades 'our' public as well as private spheres, and has become a more powerful temptation than ever to 'our' wavering souls. 'Their' corrupting lifestyle constitutes a threat. 'We' might be led astray and lose 'our' faith in the true God.

In the previous section, we made the claim that democracies (the fourth example) can be portrayed as morally superior but at the same time as slow and inefficient at decision-making. 'Our' openness and freedom also make democratic societies more exposed. There is a risk that 'they', efficient and ruthless as 'they' are, exploit 'our' vulnerability and threaten 'our' democracy.

The same logic applies to 'our' welfare system (the fifth example). The welfare system is generous, but – and this is its main weakness – if too many poor (or lazy) people use it, 'they' will be a burden for 'us' and the system. 'We' are net contributors, the pillars of society. And a welfare system is possible because 'we' contribute. But the system can easily be abused because 'we' are naïve. Since 'they' are poor and lazy, 'they' threaten 'our' welfare system and possibly 'our' entire economy. This type of rhetoric was widely used by the alt-right and Donald Trump before the 2020 elections. In this case, people from South and Central America were not only depicted as lazy and a burden on the welfare system but also as 'bad hombres' in general associated with crime, drugs – and again, sexual violence (Dafaure, 2020: 52).

Demographic development, the sixth example, can also be seen as a threat, at least if we extrapolate and see the development in the long run. In that case, 'they' will outnumber 'us', locally and globally, potentially threatening 'us'.

The seventh and last example in Table 2.2 portrays 'them' as a threat to the freedom of 'our' women, homosexuals, Jews, and the elderly. It is probably hard to portray 'them' as a genuine threat to 'us', the majority. In that case, subgroups within 'us', who more convincingly could be described as vulnerable and facing a threat from 'them', will be exploited. These groups (women, children, homosexuals, Jews, and the elderly) might have been neglected for years by the majority but could now be exploited. It could be said that 'threats against "our" vulnerable groups are a threat to "us" all'.

Legitimization of actions to neutralize threats

Let us now go to the fourth element in our construct of an ideal–typical enemy image, the one that concerns *legitimacy*. To be more precise, to legitimize a violent response to an enemy's threat requires legitimization not only of the *cause* (protecting 'our' assets) but also the *means* used and *costs* involved.

It is important to underline that in this discussion, legitimacy is a relational concept which usually means that the ruled legitimize the rulers and their policies (Beetham, 1991: 15–17). In this context, it matters that the ruled perceive a violent response as morally right and proper (Steiner, 1996: 21). In the endeavour to gain legitimacy – to make the cause, the means, and the costs appear morally right and proper – there must be a convincing narrative. According to Thierry Balzacq, 'the social design of a security problem conditions and legitimates the kind of means used to stop it' (Balzacq, 2011: 1). In other words, the way 'we' describe the out-group, the assets that 'they' allegedly threaten, and the portrayal of the threat itself, constitute building blocks in a narrative legitimizing the measures and violence that 'we' use to stop it. Thus, the narrative legitimizes the remedy.

If we turn to Table 2.2, it is vital that 'our' sovereignty, race, religion, democracy, welfare system, vulnerable groups, etc. appear so important for the in-group that it believes in and legitimizes the cause to protect them. Losing one or some of those assets must appear fatal, with unpredictable consequences. Today, procreating with a person from another 'race' seems completely normal and innocent. For people immersed in the racist narrative we discussed previously, 'racial mixtures' would have grave consequences, not only for the offspring themselves but for society as a whole. In other words, it is vital in an enemy image that the assets 'we' legitimately try to rescue must be seen as very important by the in-group. Moreover, one way to strengthen the narrative that 'our' violence is legitimate is to claim that 'we have been attacked', making 'our' warfare an act of self-defence.

In a speech on 28 March 2011 at the National Defense University in Washington, DC, President Barack Obama tried to justify the US attack against Libya's leader Muammar Qaddafi. There was a clear emphasis on Qaddafi having started the insurgencies. The President not only underlined American values and his nation's advocacy for human freedom but also the fact that Libya's leader Muammar Qaddafi had opened the hostilities.

> For generations, the United States of America has played a unique role as an anchor of global security and as an advocate for human freedom. Mindful of the risks and costs of military action, we are naturally reluctant to use force to solve the world's many challenges. But when our interests and values are at stake, we have a responsibility to act. That's what happened in Libya over the course of these last six weeks.
> ...
> Faced with this opposition, Qaddafi began attacking his people.
>
> *(Obama, 28 March 2011)*

Another way to legitimize 'our' violence is to underline that 'their' actions gave 'us' no choice, as for instance expressed in Russian war rhetoric in 2022. Since 'we' are peaceful, 'our' first choice is not war and military violence. But 'their' immoral character and the imminence of 'their' threat forced 'us' to respond. In the interviews with Messianic believers in Israel mentioned above, Steiner and a Messianic interviewee discussed the many casualties in a recent war in the Gaza

Strip. There was no doubt that the violence killed many more Palestinians than Israelis. But according to the interviewee, Israel was not to be blamed. He said:

> There is no room for manoeuvre. They are using the mosques, they are using schools, they are using hospitals, they are using civilian homes. To shoot from... There is no ... whatever you do it is a lose-lose situation, for them and for us. Because we hold ourselves from retaliating, and eventually you have to put a stop to it, so it is a scenario every few years, there's a big operation in Gaza, a lot of people are getting killed on both sides, you know, and they would do it again. How to fight? This is not a tank against tanks or airplanes against airplanes or soldier against soldier.
>
> *(Steiner and Lundberg, 2018: 159)*

At the beginning of this section, we mentioned not only the cause and the means that must be legitimized but also the *costs* involved. The measures undertaken to safeguard 'our' assets have a price, not only for the enemy but also for 'us'. It might lead to loss of lives and to increasing poverty. The government must prioritize weaponry over nutrition and public services – guns rather than butter. And enemy images are useful in this regard, as they can divert people's attention from such consequences (Luostarinen, 1989: 127).

In a society where a narrative of being under siege prevails, there is a risk that people must pay with another currency: their freedom. In the name of security, the government will infringe upon fundamental democratic and human rights. This is a topic addressed by The Copenhagen School of Security Studies. Barry Buzan, Ole Wæver, and Jaap de Wilde (1998) describe how enemy images help to legitimize undemocratic policies and authoritarian tendencies. Policies to dismantle various threats might be seen as a 'special kind of politics or as above politics' (Buzan, Wæver, and de Wilde, 1998: 23) legitimizing undemocratic policies. Curfews and martial laws are legitimized since democracy or human rights weigh easily when superior core assets are jeopardized (Buzan, Wæver, and de Wilde, 1998: 23–25). When threats are narrated as existential, they legitimize measures and policies far beyond 'the established games of "normal" politics' (Stritzel, 2007: 360) in an aggravated 'state of exception' (Scheuerman, 2013).

As a closing remark in this discussion on legitimacy, we would like to underline that the narrative discussed not only legitimizes cause, means, and costs. An enemy image also simultaneously *delegitimizes any other means to solve the conflict*. Compromise or peace initiatives appear futile, and counternarratives inconsistent with an enemy image might be seen as irresponsible.

Mobilization of the in-group

The fifth element in our ideal–typical enemy image is the *mobilization* of the in-group to make sacrifices and take part in violent actions against the enemy to neutralize the threat 'they' constitute. As stated previously, these actions are costly, and the population might be paying a high price. Sons and daughters will be sacrificed on the battlefields. Public spending will go to guns instead of important public services. For political leaders, it is essential to make individuals overcome their self-interest and willingly make sacrifices for their group.

Mobilization through enemy images is not the only way to make people obey. An alternative strategy is strict discipline and hard punishment for refusal to obey orders or desertion. Another strategy to make people participate in the war effort is to improve the economic benefits for those in uniform. Decent food, accommodation, and payment usually improve morale. In his study of French nation-building, the Romanian-born American historian Eugen Weber (1925–2007) analysed the development of the French army. He saw a clear correlation between improving material conditions in the army and the willingness to participate in it (Weber, 1976: 299). Our point is that both carrot (economic benefits) and stick (discipline and punishment) strategies are expensive. If political leaders can mobilize a population using enemy images to make people overcome their self-interest and *willingly* make sacrifices for their group, this is by far the most cost-efficient method.

Some of the previously discussed elements of an enemy image also impact mobilization. If a population is convinced that it is fighting for a just cause or if it is made to believe that 'they' constitute a real threat to 'our' most important assets, it will be easier to mobilize. Successful dehumanization will also facilitate mobilization. In addition to that, we have identified a few more strategies to mobilize a population: *hope for victory*, *status*, and *meaning*. These will be discussed in the following paragraphs.

We know from the definition of an enemy image that the enemy allegedly poses a serious threat to 'our' most important assets. However, 'their' capacity to threaten and harm 'us' must never be perceived as overwhelming, because such a threat would lead to defeatism and fail to mobilize a population. The threat should appear serious enough to make people fight without portraying the enemy as invincible. Harold D. Lasswell realized as early as 1927 that mobilization is intimately related to *hope for victory*, or an 'illusion of victory', as Lasswell put it (1927: xxi) since 'the will to win is intimately related to the chance to win' (Lasswell, 1927: 118). And Lasswell continues:

> The fighting spirit of a nation feeds upon the conviction that it has a fighting chance to win. The enemy may be dangerous, obstructive, and satanic, but if he is sure to win, the moral of many elements in the nation will begin to waver and crumble.
>
> *(Lasswell, 1927: 102)*

The other mobilizing strategy is based on social psychological theories, particularly Abraham H. Maslow's theory of needs. According to Maslow (1943), whom we will discuss in more depth in Chapter 4, on top of basic physiological safety and social needs, people have a need for status (esteem need) and meaning. The basic idea is that people have various needs that dictate their behaviour. Two such needs are for high status and for meaning (a cause beyond the self). What is important here is that political leaders can manipulate those needs as mobilizing tools.

We discussed above how belonging to a high-status group can give the individual positive self-evaluation if they view their own group favourably over out-groups. But in addition to that, positive self-evaluation will also be enhanced if they have a *high-status position* within their own group and see themselves as a better group member than others belonging to the in-group (Hinton, 2000: 124). This implies that individuals do not *only* want to be included in a high-status group. They also want to separate from the crowd in the group to which they belong (Dawson, 2017: 8) and occupy a unique, visible, and glorious position within it. According to Cottee and Hayward, part of what makes extremist groups attractive is 'the scope they offer their members to define or remake themselves as heroic figures, belonging to an exalted elite' within a group (2011: 976). And making sacrifices for the protection of your own group, even to 'kill and die for each other' (Atran, 2010: xi), adds to your status.

Meaning is a third strategy to mobilize a population. If rulers can produce a convincing narrative, in which fighting on the battlefield and making other forms of major sacrifice for the nation is regarded as commendable (you are saving your group from a horrible fate), it is probably possible to mobilize young men or women and to give them incentives to make sacrifices. War, where you become the saviour of the group, might increase 'the social meaning' of the individual's life. 'It gives him a clear objective and enables him to participate in a meaningful collective project. He is involved in something important, together with the rest of the community' (Luostarinen, 1989: 126).

From an outsider's perspective, giving up your life in the service of the nation (or in some cases your religion) might be inconceivable. But to the individual within the group, such a life choice makes sense. Saving the nation from a hostile enemy probably gives them an experience of a purpose and a cause beyond the self, and the same goes for religion.

> In defending the sacred, one experiences something larger than him- or herself, a meaning that gloriously soars above and renders insignificant one's own often frivolous and banal personal concerns.
>
> *(Cottee and Hayward, 2011: 973)*

Being part of God's salvation history and fighting in defence of the sacred gives the individual a sense of an ultimate meaning (Cottee and Hayward, 2011: 975). It might bring 'an all-embracing narrative for understanding the world and how it works' (Cottee and Hayward, 2011: 973). Jihadists, in Lorne L. Dawson and Amarnath Amarasingam's research, 'felt the need for something more in their lives' (2017: 199), the 'feeling that one is an active participant in a cosmic battle to defend the sacred' (Cottee and Hayward, 2011: 973). And if a narrative like this becomes dominant within a group, it is a mobilizing instrument.

Benign and malign enemy images

As stated at the beginning of this chapter, in this second part of the chapter, we will construct an alternative enemy image. We do so for both methodological and normative reasons. In the first section, we will discuss why having two contrasting constructs of enemy images, one malign and one benign, is methodologically and normatively advantageous. In the second section, we will construct and contrast them.

Why contrasting enemy images?

An ideal–typical enemy image can be constructed as an analytical instrument. The purpose of ideal types is to enable assessment of the extent to which empirical cases resemble or differ from the ideal type. However, this method has a weakness which could influence the results of an analysis. The problem is that if a researcher carefully searches for the elements of an ideal–typical enemy image in an empirical case, they will most likely find them. There is therefore a risk of the researcher exaggerating the prevalence of those elements and thereby inflating the resemblance between the ideal type and the data. Even a careful and non-bellicose rhetoric would have *some* resemblance to an enemy image.

Imagine that the researcher, instead of constructing *one* ideal–typical enemy image, created *two* contrasting ones. One would be based on the ideal type we discussed in the previous section, which we will henceforth call a *malign* enemy image because of its destructive potential. Another, quite different enemy image, we will call a *benign* enemy image. A benign ideal type would never deny the violence that really occurred or threats that really existed but could only with great difficulty be used to escalate or protract a conflict. So, what is the methodological reason for constructing two contrasting enemy images? The idea is that if we formulate two contrasting constructs of enemy images, one malign and one benign, they can serve as two extreme positions on a scale. Between these two extreme positions, an analytical field opens, in which a researcher can place empirical cases. This allows the researcher to analyse the data in a more nuanced way and position/deploy the case in question within the field.

Constructing a benign ideal-type enemy image to contrast with the malign one also has a *normative* effect. In a threatening situation, enemy images *will* arise. People and elites alike will produce enemy images, portraying the agent of threat. This is an almost unavoidable process. However, not all enemy images are necessarily equally harmful. Not all of them must legitimate a violent response, nor mobilize a population to take part in organized violence. There is a moral obligation on the peace researcher and peacemaker to use a narrative in an ongoing conflict that does *not* contribute to an escalation or protraction. Remember Table 1.1, where (in Category 3) we discussed an enemy image that was not dehumanizing. On the contrary, it was a construct where the enemy was portrayed as like 'us'. Such a construct also underlines the fact that the enemy's behaviour and violence could have been 'ours' since 'we' are much alike. In an escalating conflict, a benign enemy image is of course useless for most political leaders who have a vested interest in mobilizing their people to go to war and make great sacrifices. But this fact does not release the peace researcher/builder from the responsibility to highlight other non-conflict-generating narratives. Further discussion of benign enemy images as an instrument of peace will take place in Chapter 6. In this chapter, our focus is on the analytical potential of having two contrasting enemy images.

Lastly, we must emphasize that we will not find any empirical examples of either completely malign or completely benign enemy images. Probably even as the peace-minded authors of this book, we would not create a completely benign enemy image of Russia in discussions about its attack on Ukraine in 2022. And conversely, even President Vladimir Putin would be unlikely to produce a completely malign enemy image of Ukraine. Both the benign and malign enemy images are thus completely *theoretical* ideal–typical constructs that together deepen our analysis. The benign enemy image, moreover, could challenge us and serve as an ethical guideline.

Two contrasting enemy images

In the first chapter, we underlined that the purpose of a (malign) enemy image is usually to legitimize violent responses, mobilize a population to take part in that violence, and desensitize it so that the exercise of violence against the enemy appears less emotionally burdensome. As already said, a *benign* enemy image construct has a very different purpose: to construct a narrative that, without denying violence and atrocities committed by the enemy, does not legitimize violence but contributes to future reconciliation, mobilizes peace work, and increases compassion for enemy suffering. The two contrasting enemy image constructs will therefore be very different. The aim of this section is to construct a benign enemy image and to contrast it to the malign one discussed above (see Table 2.3). But before embarking on this construction, it is legitimate to question whether such a benign image of an external threat can really be called an enemy image – i.e. whether the term 'benign enemy image' is not a contradiction in terms since such a benevolent image does not meet the requirements of an enemy image according to our definition. It neither legitimizes violence, mobilizes nor desensitizes the in-group. We have nevertheless chosen to use this expression because we thereby create a clear pair of concepts, malignant and benign enemy images. And as argued above, this pair constitutes two polar positions on a scale.

Firstly, we know that in malign enemy images, there is a clear demarcation between 'us' and 'them'. Ambiguous identities are unwanted and threatening.

It should be clear where one belongs. But not only that: in enemy images, the safety-providing group (in modern societies, often the nation-state) should be our overriding identity, even though we know that most people have *multiple* identities embracing class, gender, profession, native district, and religion. Music, football, and many other things can also generate subcultures and identities. And lastly, most people also belong to a family. But in the last analysis, according to the malign enemy image, people must have *one* overriding/superior identity, usually the nation, to which we owe our undivided loyalty.

A benign enemy image is different. Here, identities are less clear and distinct. They overlap. This kind of construct underlines that many of 'us' have – indeed should have – ties of loyalty crossing the separation between 'us' and 'them'. Thus, 'we' have multiple and competing identities and loyalties. Normatively, such crosscutting identities should be nurtured since they could have a peacebuilding effect. If 'we' have loved ones on the other side of the national border, it is probably harder to mobilize 'us' to wage war and kill 'them' (although we know that President Putin has been relatively successful in this). Building an international society with transnational loyalties could be seen as a peacebuilding strategy and will be discussed further in Chapter 6.

Again, a malign enemy image separates 'us' and 'them' clearly and distinctly. Ambiguities regarding identity, belonging, and loyalty are not welcome. However, the ideal–typical malign enemy image would *not* make a similar separation between the enemy's leaders and people in general. Constructs of the enemy tend to be homogeneous: 'they' are all the same. The character of bellicose leaders spills over and tends to forge the image of the entire group. President Putin's character becomes the Russian national character. A benign enemy image construct, on the other hand, would make clear separations between 'their' leaders and the population at large. Benign constructs aim at depicting people on the other side as different from their leaders but similar to 'us'.

A *second element* in an ideal–typical malign enemy image concerns 'our' and 'their' *character*, how 'we' and the enemy are portrayed. And as already established, in a (malign) enemy image the characterization of 'them' and 'us' first aims to desensitize 'us' so that 'we' can hurt 'them' without remorse. Further aims of characterization are to legitimize violence and make belonging to 'our' group attractive.

To achieve the first goal, a first strategy was to alienate or differentiate 'them', to make it appear as if 'we' have nothing in common with 'them'. 'They' do not even seem to have any normal human characteristics. A second strategy was deindividuation – stereotyping, lumping 'them' altogether – so one sees no nuances, no distinguishable individuals. 'They' are all the same. 'We', on the other hand, are multifaceted. A third strategy was to dehumanize 'them', to depict 'them' as subhuman or in some cases even non-human. Self-evidently a benign enemy image would never characterize 'them' and 'their' essence like this. In a benign enemy image, (see Table 1.1), the resemblance is emphasized, and 'we' realize that 'their' reprehensible and violent acts could also have been perpetrated by 'us' in the same circumstances. Likewise, a benign enemy image depicts 'them' as a multifaceted group where 'they' are individuated. And lastly, the enemy is of course humanized in every way.

In this context, we would like to mention the British series of documentaries *Born in the USSR*,[12] which is a convincing example of the humanization of 'them'. In this documentary, starting in 1990, director Sergei Miroshnichenko visited 18 young Soviet children/youths every seven years and filmed their lives (John, October 4, 2013). Our point is that Miroshnichenko, particularly in the first documentaries, managed by interviewing cute and innocent children to depict 'our' main and feared enemy, the USSR, as like 'us'; 'they' were individuated and humanized. Anyone in the West seeing the documentaries would realize that children in the USSR had dreams just like 'ours', played and giggled just like the kids 'we' know. In other words, this series made an important contribution to a benign image construct of the enemy.

Furthermore, a malign enemy image depicts 'us' as superior, thereby making 'our' group attractive in our own eyes. The group members would probably enjoy being part of this group and stay loyal to it since it enhances their self-esteem. As stated, this way of protecting the status of 'our' group, is not reserved for enemy images. It occurs in most forms of othering and identity formation. Depicting 'us' as an attractive high-status group is also compatible with a benign enemy image. A malign enemy image takes things further, depicting 'us' as delicate and vulnerable to 'them' despite 'our' superiority. The allegedly inferior enemy still has the capacity to harm and threaten 'us'. And this is incompatible with a benign enemy image construct. In a benign enemy image construct, it is essential to make a realistic depiction of 'our' vulnerabilities and 'their' strengths.

Our previous discussion of 'our' and 'their' character concerned 'their' inability, or unwillingness, to change and reform. Ascribing this kind of characteristic to the enemy is problematic because it can potentially represent current conflicts as natural and lasting, making a future peace unimaginable. It can also legitimize violence since leaders can claim that is the only language 'they' understand. A benign enemy image construct would describe things differently. Since this construct is rooted in the idea that all humans are virtually the same and share the human potential to change and grow, it will describe the enemy as equally dynamic and capable of change or repentance.

A third element in a malign enemy image is the presence of threats, the enemy's capacity as well as the intention to threaten 'our' most important interests. Since the international system remains anarchic and the enemy remains unrepentant and aggressive, 'we' can expect the threats and the conflict to remain.[13] The benign enemy image construct depicts threats differently. Firstly, alarmism should be avoided. From a peacebuilding perspective, it is counterproductive to exaggerate 'their' capacity to threaten 'us' and to speculate about 'their' present and future intentions. The threats that do exist should be represented neutrally and soberly, and extrapolations (see discussion above) avoided. It is also important to imagine peace, to outline a future that is different from the current state of affairs. The anarchic international system can be transformed. We are not doomed to live in an eternal zero-sum game. A future characterized by reconcilable interests and mutually beneficial cooperation is possible (see Chapter 6).

The fourth element in our ideal–typical enemy image is a legitimization of actions to neutralize the threat. In light of what has been said about the character of the enemy and threats directed towards 'us', in a malign enemy image it comes naturally to claim that violent measures against 'them' are legitimate, responsible, and necessary. And for the same reason, peace attempts and negotiations will both appear and be portrayed as illegitimate and even irresponsible. If it seems unlikely that 'they' will ever change, peacemakers come across as naïve. Perhaps 'we' are putting 'our' group in danger if 'we' come across as soft-spoken and willing for peace.

In a benign enemy image narrative, very different responses appear legitimate. Here, violent measures against 'them' could appear illegitimate and irresponsible. Maybe by conducting such policies, 'we' are missing out on chances to achieve peace and contributing to the continued spiral of violence. Blood will be shed in vain. Peace attempts and negotiations, on the other hand, will appear and be described as legitimate, responsible, and necessary.

The fifth element in our ideal–typical enemy image is mobilization. In a previous discussion, we concluded that a narrative that legitimizes violence ('our' cause is just, and 'they' threaten 'us') also contributes to mobilization, as does the belief that 'we' have a chance to win the war and be victorious. Another way to mobilize the in-group is to turn the soldiers (and others who contribute to the war effort) into heroes and an exalted elite, and to describe sacrifices for the group (its survival or cause) as something sacred.

The purpose of a benign enemy image is not to mobilize people to support and take part in organized violence. On the contrary, it is to make people think and reflect, and to cast sacrifices for peace in a sacred light. It therefore sticks to objective facts regarding 'our' cause and does not wade into moral evaluations. A benign enemy image, moreover, would not sweep bloodshed and other costs of war under the carpet and would involve realistic assessments of our chances of military victory. Not all soldiers are heroes, so they would not always be described as morally superior. And lastly, to be a peacemaker is risky. The peacemaker can be publicly ridiculed or ostracized. Such risk-taking and the sacrifices it can imply are to be portrayed as something sacred.

TABLE 2.3 Malign and benign enemy image constructs

	A malign enemy image	A benign enemy image
Delimitation of 'us' from 'them'	• Clear and distinct separations between 'us' and 'them' • One clear and overriding identity • One clear loyalty • Unclear separation between 'their' leaders and population	• Identities overlap. No clear distinctions between 'us' and 'them'. • Multiple competing identities • Clear separation between 'their' leaders and population
Characterization of 'our' and 'their' essence	• Alienation/differentiation: 'we' have nothing in common with 'them'. • 'They' are deindividuated, depicted as all the same. 'We' are multifaceted. • Dehumanization: 'they' are subhuman or non-human. • 'We' are vulnerable in spite of 'our' superiority. • Unlike 'us', 'they' are static and unrepentant, and never change.	• 'We' and 'they' are depicted as similar, sharing general human traits. • 'They' are individuated and multifaceted, just like 'us'. • 'They' are humanized. • Vulnerabilities are neither exaggerated nor exploited. • 'We' and 'they' are equally repentant, dynamic, and capable of change.
Depiction of 'their' threats to 'our' assets	• 'They' have the capacity and the intention to threaten 'our' most important interests. • The threat is imminent, real, serious, and possibly growing. • The threats and the conflicts will remain.	• 'Their' capacity will not be exaggerated – no speculation about their intentions. • Realistic depictions of the threat. Avoids extrapolations. • Depicts a future where peace is possible.
Legitimization of actions to neutralize this threat	• Violent measures against 'them' will appear and be depicted as legitimate, responsible, and necessary. • Peace attempts and negotiations will appear and be depicted as illegitimate and irresponsible.	• Violent measures against 'them' will appear and be depicted as illegitimate and irresponsible. • Peace attempts and negotiations will appear and be understood as legitimate, responsible, and necessary.
Mobilization of 'us' to take part in actions to neutralize this threat	• 'Our' cause is just, and the enemy threatens 'us'. • Exaggerates 'our' chances to win and underestimates the costs. • 'Our' soldiers are heroes and an exalted elite. • Sacrifices for the group and its safety are sacred.	• Sticks to objective facts and does not wade into moral evaluations of 'our' cause. • Realistic assessments of 'our' chances of military victory and the costs it entails. • Soldiers are not described as morally superior. • Sacrifices for peace are sacred.

Summary

In the first section of this chapter, we presented an ideal–typical malign enemy image, discussing its five constitutive elements in detail: (a) the delimitation of 'us' versus 'them', (b) the characterization of 'our' and 'their' essence, (c) 'their' threats to 'our' assets, (d) the legitimization of actions to neutralize this threat, and lastly (e) the mobilization of 'us' to take part in violent actions against the enemy. In the second section, we introduced another kind of ideal–typical enemy image, the benign one, and by contrasting the two enemy images presented a more complex and complete analytical instrument, enabling a more nuanced analysis. In this instrument, the two contrasting ideal–typical enemy images constitute opposite poles on a scale that helps us to assess and analyse rhetoric in a nuanced way.

In the chapter, we underlined that the traditional malign enemy image is of a kind that legitimizes organized violence. One essential trait of the malign enemy image is that 'we' are portrayed as superior but vulnerable, and 'they' as inferior but powerful and therefore a threat. This threat needs to be serious enough to mobilize a population to participate in violence, without portraying the enemy as invincible.

The benign enemy image, on the other hand, is conceived as an alternative that legitimizes peace. Enemy images will inevitably emerge in threatening situations like war. By constructing a benign enemy image, we introduced a normative guideline, helping us to talk about the enemy and the conflict in a way that will neither escalate the conflict nor legitimize violence. On the contrary, a benign enemy image should support reconciliation, peace, and compassion.

Study question

- Imagine that you have a professional or other role in Ukraine during the war starting in 2022, where you can influence the values and opinions of those around you. Maybe you are a teacher, football coach in a local team, journalist, priest, politician, or something similar. In this role, you are expected to participate in the work of strengthening morale in the country. How would you handle the situation?

Potential essay or thesis suggestion

- Select a conflict situation where different elites (see Figure 3.4) have produced and disseminated political messages in support of a war effort. Choose elites who have produced messages in a language you are proficient in. Select primary sources. Formulate an analytical framework based on the discussion in this chapter or use the contrasting ideal types (see Table 2.3). Apply the analytical framework to this material.

Recommended further reading

Kruglanski, A. W., Bélanger, J. J. and Gunaratna, R. (2019) *The Three Pillars of Radicalization: Needs, Narratives, and Networks*. Oxford: Oxford University Press.
In this accessible and timely book, the authors review major theories of radicalization and incorporate them into a unifying theoretical framework. According to the authors, radicalization rests on three pillars: needs, narratives, and networks. The section on narratives is particularly relevant for those who have an interest in enemy images and how they provide a licence to kill.

Notes

1 This passage is based on a dualism, the belief that there is an 'us' and a 'them'. Of course, we recognize that there are other positions such as neutrality. Still, for those who produce and disperse enemy images, neutral positions are unwelcome. They wish to create a Manichean world of 'us' and 'them'. Dichotomies are their goal. The purpose of this section is to present an analytical instrument to analyse their language and dualistic image of the world.
2 'Så vidgas den andra ringen och växer ut till den tredje, till nationen, landet, riket, den syskonkrets, som vår svenska folkstam utgör'.
3 Rudolf Kjellén gave the speech 'The nationality idea' in 1898, and it was subsequently published as a pamphlet in 1906.

> Huru personligt berör oss icke vårt eget folks utveckling i hävderna! Med vilket alldeles särskilt intresse följa vi ej Gustaf Vasa då han röjde det väg i egoismens vildmarker, Gustaf II Adolf då han på den vägen förde det ut till världshistorisk gärning, Karl XII då han betäckte dess reträtt tillbaka till hemmet och för dess ära gav sitt stora liv! Så verkar aldrig på oss en främmande historia, om än lika spännande i sig själv; ty den tangerar icke släktkärlekens strängar i vårt bröst. Ja. det ligger något av vårt eget blod i denna historia.

4 The Messianic group and its theology were introduced in Chapter 1.
5 A literary genre that emerged after the Cold War is so-called Eurabia literature. The term was originally the name of a newsletter and was made famous by the author Gisèle Littman, who writes under the pseudonym Bat Ye'Or. For Bat Ye'Or, Eurabia is a close political alliance between the states of Europe and the states of the Arab world, the result of a conspiracy between a political and academic elite in the two regions. This alliance will be built through the mass immigration of Muslims and Arabs to Europe, which forever changes the demographic composition there. In addition, Europe is forced by dependence on oil into obedience and submission to the Arab world (Steiner, 2010: 58; Malm, 2009: 17–66; Bergmann, 2021: 36–53).
6 'verkligt kulturskapande folk'.
7 'den germanska folktypen med dess resliga växt, dess ljusa hår, dess breda, höga panna och dess blå eller grå ögon ingenstädes i vår tid förekomma renare än i de nordiska länder…'
8

> Islamister er modstandere af demokrati, menneskerettigheder, mangfoldighed, homoseksualitet og personlig frihed. …
> Danmark er et demokratisk lilleputland rundet af andelsforeninger, højskoleånd og samtale-kultur. Derfor er det os også dybt fremmed, at der er kræfter i Danmark,

der arbejder målrettet på at betvinge friheden og demokratiet. Ikke desto mindre er det, hvad nogle af de ekstreme islamistiske miljøer i Danmark arbejder på.

9 'En av de saker man kom fram till i studien var att 60 procent av de våldtäkter som ledde till fällande dom mellan 2000 och 2015 begicks av första och andra generationens invandrare'.

10 'Antisemitismen är till stor del importerad genom invandring till Sverige'.

11 This book was originally published in German in 1905. The quote is from the 8th edition. 'Dazu dann die Starke Vermischung mit mongolischen Elementen, welche nach Buschan's Untersuchungen eine nachweisbare Abnahme der Schädelkapazität, der Hirngröße und somit auch der Kulturfähigkeit – kurz, auf deutsch, eine Verdummung – ganzer Völkerschaften herbeigeführt hat' (Chamberlain, 1938a: 40–41).

12 There were four documentaries in the series, filming the children at different ages. The films were called *Born in the USSR: 7 Up* (1991); *Born in the USSR: 14 Up* (1998); *Born in the USSR: 21 Up* (2005); and *Born in the USSR: 28* Up (2012).

13 This book concerns enemy images. That means it focuses on actors, not structure. In traditional international relations theories, such as realism, it is not only the character of the enemy that legitimizes our armament and preparedness for violent conflicts but just as much the anarchic character of the international system. To include the systemic level in our book would take things too far.

Bibliography

Ahmadi, S. R. (2018) "In my eyes he was a man": Poor and working-class boy soldiers in the Iran-Iraq war. *Journal of Middle East Women's Studies* 4(2): 174–192. https://doi.org/10.1215/15525864-6680218

Andersson, T. (2021, March 1) *Andelen invandrare bland de som begår våldtäkt* [The Proportion of Immigrants among Those Who Commit Rape] Interpellation 2020/21:517. Sveriges Riksdag. https://data.riksdagen.se/dokument/H810517.html, accessed 15 February 2024.

Atran, S. (2010) *Talking to the Enemy: Violent Extremism, Sacred Values, and What It Means to Be Human*. London: Allen Lane.

Azar, M. (2006) *Den koloniala bumerangen, Från schibbolet till körkort i svenskhet* [The Colonial Boomerang. From the Shibboleth to Driving License in Swedish]. Eslöv: Brutus Östlings bokförlag Symposium.

Balzacq, T. (2011) *Preface, Securitization Theory. How Security Problems Emerge and Dissolve*. London and New York, NY: Routledge.

Bawer, B. (2006) *While Europe Slept, How Radical Islam Is Destroying the West from Within*. New York, NY: Broadway Books.

Beetham, D. (1991) *The Legitimation of Power*. Basingstoke: Macmillan.

Bergmann, E. (2021) The Eurabia Conspiracy. In Önnerfors, A. and Krouwel, A. (eds.) *Europe: Continent of Conspiracies. Conspiracy Theories in and about Europe* (pp. 36–53). London: Routledge.

Blomqvist, H. (2001) *Socialdemokrat och antisemit? Den dolda historien om Arthur Engberg* [Social Democrat and Antisemite? The Hidden Story of Arthur Engberg]. Stockholm: Carlssons Bokförlag.

Bush, G. (2001, January 20) *Inaugural Address*. [Speech] Washington, DC. www.presidency.ucsb.edu/node/211268, accessed 16 October 2023.

Bush, G. (2001, September 11) *Address to the Nation on the Terrorist Attacks*. [Speech] Washington, DC. www.presidency.ucsb.edu/node/216451, accessed 16 October 2023.

Buzan, B., Wæver, O. and de Wilde, J. (1998) *Security, A New Framework for Analysis*. Boulder, CO: Lynne Rienner Publishing.

Chamberlain, H. (1938a) *Arische Weltanschauung* (8th ed.). München: F. Bruckmann A.-G.

Chamberlain, H. (1938b) *Aryan World-view* (8th ed.). München: F. Bruckmann A.-G.

Cottee, S. and Hayward, K. (2011) Terrorist (e)motives: The existential attractions of terrorism. *Studies in Conflict and Terrorism* 34(12): 963–986. https://doi.org/10.1080/1057610X.2011.621116

Dafaure, M. (2020) The "Great Meme War:" The Alt-Right and Its Multifarious Enemies Maxime Dafaure. In Maillet, J. and Dudouyt, C. (eds.) *Creating the Enemy. Angles, New Perspectives on the Anglophone World* 10. https://journals.openedition.org/angles/279

Dawson, L. (2017) *Sketch of a Social Ecology Model for Explaining Homegrown Terrorist Radicalisation*. The Hague: International Centre for Counter-Terrorism. http://dx.doi.org/10.19165/2017.1.01

Dawson, L. L. and Amarasingam, A. (2017) Talking to foreign fighters: Insights into the motivations for Hijrah to Syria and Iraq. *Studies in Conflict & Terrorism* 40(3): 191–210. https://doi.org/10.1080/1057610X.2016.1274216

Engberg, A. (1934) *Tre tal på Skansen, De tre ringarna* [Three Speeches at Skansen, The Three Rings.] In Lindblom A., Berg G. and Svensson S. (eds.) *Fataburen: Nordiska museets och skansens årsbok* (pp. 209–215). Stockholm: Nordiska museet.

Frank, J. (1980) The nuclear arms race-sociopsychological aspects. *American Journal of Public Health* 70(9): 950–952. https://doi.org/10.2105/ajph.70.9.950

Giddens, A. (1971) *Capitalism and Modern Social Theory. An Analysis of the Writings of Marx, Durkheim and Max Weber*. Cambridge: Cambridge University Press.

Gualda, E. (2021) Metaphors of Invasion: Imagining Europe as Endangered by Islamisation. In Önnerfors, A. and Krouwel, A. (eds.) *Europe: Continent of Conspiracies. Conspiracy Theories in and about Europe* (pp. 54–75). London: Routledge.

Hiemer, E. (1938) *Der Gilftpilz: Ein Stürmerbuch für Jung und Alt/ Der Gilftpilz: Erzählungen*. Nürnberg: Der Stürmerverlag.

Hintjens, H. (1999) Explaining the 1994 genocide in Rwanda. *The Journal of Modern African Studies* 37(2): 241–286. www.jstor.org/stable/161847

Hinton, P. (2000) *Stereotypes, Cognition and Culture*. New York, NY: Psychology Press.

Hitler, A. ([1925–26] 1999) *Mein Kampf*. New York, NY: A Mariner Book, Houghton Mifflin Company.

John, A. (2013, October 4) Russia brings another edition to the 7Up trend. *The Atlantic*. www.theatlantic.com/culture/archive/2013/10/russia-brings-another-edition-7up-trend/310290/, accessed 16 October 2023.

Kamenka, E. (1973) *Nationalism: The Nature and Evolution of an Idea*. Canberra: Australian National University Press.

Kellow, C. and Steeves, H. (1998) The role of radio in the Rwandan genocide. *Journal of Communication* 48(3): 107–128. https://doi.org/10.1111/j.1460-2466.1998.tb02762.x

Kjellén, R. ([1898] 1906) Nationalitetsidén [The Idea of Nationality] In Kjellén, R. (ed.) *Nationell samling: politiska och etiska fragment* (pp. 130–161). [National Collection: Political and Ethical Fragments] Stockholm: Geber.

Kruglanski, A., Bélanger, J. and Gunaratna, R. (2019) *The Three Pillars of Radicalization, Needs, Narratives, and Networks*. Oxford: Oxford University Press.

Kumlien, K. (1934) *Arierdöme och judendom: En raspsykologisk och rashistorisk studie* [Aryanism and Judaism: A Racial Psychological and Racial Historical Study] Stockholm: Svea rikes förlag.

Lasswell, H. (1927) *Propaganda Technique in World War I.* Cambridge, MA: The MIT Press.

Lundborg, H. (1918) *Biologiska och kulturella verkningar av rasblandningar och släktgiften* [Biological and Cultural Effects of Racial Mixing and Inbreeding] Uppsala: Almqvist & Wiksell.

Lundborg, H. (1920) *En svensk bondesläkts historia sedd i rasbiologisk belysning* [The History of a Swedish Peasant Family Seen in Racial Biological Light]. Stockholm: PA Norstedt & Sons.

Luostarinen, H. (1989) Finnish Russophobia: The story of an enemy image. *Journal of Peace Research* 26(2): 123–137. https://doi.org/10.1177/0022343389026002002

Malm, A. (2009) *Hatet mot muslimer.* Stockholm: Bokförlaget Atlas.

Maslow, A. H. (1943) A theory of human motivation. *Psychological Review* 50(4): 370–396. https://doi.org/10.1037/h0054346

McCoy, J. (2009) Making violence ordinary: Radio, music and the Rwandan genocide. *African Music* 8(3): 85–96. www.jstor.org/stable/20788929

Miroshnichenko, S. (1991–2012) *Born in the USSR.* [Series] Gosteleradio USSR. www.imdb.com/title/tt4505410/episodes/?ref_=tt_ep_epl, accessed 16 October 2023.

Montreal Institute for Genocide and Human Rights Studies (2022) *Rwanda Radio Transcripts.* no date of publication. www.concordia.ca/research/migs/resources/rwanda-radio-transcripts.html, accessed 16 October 2023.

Obama, B. (2011, March 28) *Remarks by the President in Address to the Nation on Libya.* [Speech] Washington, DC. https://obamawhitehouse.archives.gov/photos-and-video/video/2011/03/28/president-obama-s-speech-libya#transcript, accessed 16 October 2023.

Phillips, M. (2006) *Londonistan: How Britain Is Creating a Terror State Within.* New York, NY: Encounter Books.

Razoux, P. (2015) *The Iran Iraq War.* Cambridge, MA: The Belknap Press of Harvard University Press.

Riazaty, M. (2016) *Khomeini's Warriors: Foundation of Iran's Regime, Its Guardians, Allies around the World, War Analysis, and Strategies.* Bloomington, IN: Xlibris.

Riisager, M. (2014, May 29) Islamisme er en trussel mod friheden. [Islamism is a threat to freedom] Debate article. *Berlingske.* www.berlingske.dk/politik/islamisme-er-en-trussel-mod-friheden, accessed 16 October 2023.

Rydén, V. (1923) *Medborgarkunskap för fortsättnings- och andra ungdomsskolor* [Civic Knowledge for Secondary and Other Junior High Schools]. Stockholm: P. A. Nordstedt & Söners Förlag.

Scheuerman, W. (2013) States of Emergency. In Meierhenrich J. and Simons O. (eds.) *The Oxford Handbook of Carl Schmitt.* https://doi.org/10.1093/oxfordhb/9780199916931.013.017

Söder, B. (2021, January 29) *Antisemitismen i Sverige* [Antisemitism in Sweden] Written question 2020/21:1547. Riksdagen. www.riksdagen.se/sv/dokument-lagar/dokument/skriftlig-fraga/antisemitismen-i-sverige_H8111547, accessed 16 October 2023.

Steiner, K. (1996) *Strategies for International Legitimacy: A Comparative Study of Elite Behavior In ethnic Conflicts.* Diss. Lund: Lund University Press.

Steiner, K. (2010) *"Vem är min nästa?", Bilden av islam och muslimer i den kristna nyhetstidningen Världen idag* ["Who Is My Neighbour?", The Image of Islam and Muslims in the Christian Newspaper The World today] Uppsala: Swedish Science Press.

Steiner, K. (2015) Images of Muslims and Islam in Swedish Christian and secular news discourse. *Media, War & Conflict* 8(1): 20–45. https://doi.org/10.1177/175063521 4531107

Sternberg, R. and Sternberg, K. (2008) *The Nature of Hate.* Cambridge: Cambridge UP.

Steyn, M. (2006) *America Alone: The End of the World As We Know It.* Washington, DC: Regnery Publishing, Inc.

Stritzel, H. (2007) Towards a theory of securitization: Copenhagen and beyond. *European Journal of International Relations* 13(3): 357–383. https://doi.org/10.1177/135406610 7080128

Weber, E. (1976) *Peasants into Frenchmen: The Modernization of Rural France*, 1870–1914. Redwood City, CA: Stanford University Press.

Ye'or, B. (2005) *Eurabia, The Euro-Arab Axis.* Madison, NJ: Fairleigh Dickinson University Press.

3
HOW TO MAKE ENEMY IMAGES PERSUASIVE

Senders, messages, and discursive consistency

CHAPTER OBJECTIVES

- To describe the characteristics of persuasive senders
- To describe the characteristics of persuasive messages
- To describe the characteristics of an effective propaganda machinery

Introduction

As long as people have lived in groups, their leaders have produced messages intended to persuade and unite the group under their rule. This comes as no surprise since 'a search for the keys to persuasion is surely among the most basic of human desires' (Perloff, 2003: 33), and how to produce persuasive propaganda has 'been a matter of extensive study for millennia' (Taillard and Giscoppa, 2013: 6). The interest in the power of persuasive messages has not diminished over time. Books, articles, and lately online guides on how to persuade and communicate convincing strategic messages to target audiences proliferate. Strategic communication has emerged as a field where organizations (from civil society to corporations to state actors) intentionally seek to advance the impact of their specific mission or narrative. It is studied at the intersection of public relations, advertising, rhetoric, propaganda, and media studies (Hallahan et al., 2007: 3–35). The goal of strategic communication is more about influencing the general perception of different actors than accounting for factual actions. A prominent case that revealed a gap between the stated mission and reality in so-called corporate social responsibility (CSR) is a globally established Swedish clothing brand. Its strategic communication was about its purported leading role in sustainable fashion in responsibly recycling excess clothes returned by customers. In reality, most of these goods ended up on a

DOI: 10.4324/9781003279570-3

dump in Africa (Lindberg and Wennman, 2023), aggravating an ecological crisis in a vulnerable ecosystem. A more serious example is how governments use strategic communication as a tool to legitimize their actions in international relations either in soft politics like diplomacy or hard politics like military campaigns. In Chapter 7, we will address how strategic narratives are used to plant worldviews that can serve as rationalizations of enemy images, in which meaning-making divisions between friends and foes are expressed.

With modernity and industrialization, 'the sheer number of persuasive communications has grown exponentially' (Perloff, 2003: 5). Messages have also become increasingly impersonal and institutionalized, faster, and probably more differentiated and complex (Perloff, 2003: 5–6). In this chapter, we use Richard M. Perloff's definition of persuasion, defined as

> a symbolic process in which communicators try to convince other people to change their attitudes or behavior regarding an issue through the transmission of a message, in an atmosphere of free choice.
>
> *(Perloff, 2003: 8)*

In this kind of communication, the sender of a message intends 'to change another individual's attitude' (Perloff, 2003: 9). Persuasion might involve propaganda (Jowett and O'Donnell, 2015: 269) but not coercion (Perloff, 2003: 9). This means that persuasion takes place in an atmosphere of (at least basic) free choice. Moreover, persuasion takes time; it is a slow process (Perloff, 2003: 9). In this sense, persuasion differs from propaganda, which unidirectionally imposes a message and does not allow leeway for any freedom of interpretation or ambiguity about its truth value or value judgements.

Research on persuasion not only has a long tradition but is also extensive and diversified. It involves all forms of persuasion – political, commercial, secular, and religious – as well as taking place in both the private and the public sphere. It involves both empirical and normative statements. It is rooted in various academic disciplines and has produced numerous theories.

The scope of this chapter is limited. It is only concerned with how to persuade an audience into *accepting enemy images* and describes relevant research in no more than broad outlines. It is divided into three sections, where *firstly* we discuss persuasive communicators/senders/ messengers; *secondly*, how to make messages (enemy images) persuasive; and *thirdly* how to construct a persuasive system of informational influence and indoctrination. In the previous chapters, we discussed the desired *outcome* of an enemy image (to legitimize organized violence and desensitize and mobilize a population). While the focus of this chapter is on persuasion, some of the ideas presented will resemble arguments in Chapter 2, since some rhetorical techniques can be used both to legitimize, mobilize, and desensitize and to persuade. There are also several overlaps with Chapter 7, in which the media with which enemy images are expressed is covered extensively.

Here, we use these as examples for our argument about how enemy images are made persuasive, whereas in the later chapter they will be discussed in their own right, as modes of dissemination.

The discussion in this chapter is inspired by dominant approaches in the field – the cognitive response approach to persuasion and the elaboration likelihood model (ELM). According to the ELM, humans process information through two channels: (a) one quick and intuitive (superficial and prone to cognitive shortcuts or effortless), and (b) the other based upon slower or effortful reflective judgement, deliberatively arriving at conclusions. This type of processing is also called 'classical reasoning' (Ziemer and Rothmund, 2024). In Chapters 4 and 6, we will return to the ELM to ask why people believe in enemy images and how they can be countered. One of the first scholars who proposed the *cognitive response approach* was Anthony G. Greenwald (1968). This approach rejects the idea that people are 'spongelike creatures who passively take in information they receive' (Perloff, 2003: 122). Instead, the receiver of a message has an inner monologue, where they counterargue and derogate the messages and even the communicator (Festinger and Maccoby, 1964: 369). Most importantly, people's mental reactions to messages play a critical role in the persuasion process (Perloff, 2003: 122) since 'persuasion occurs if the communicator induces the audience member to generate favorable cognitive responses regarding the communicator or message' (Perloff, 2003: 122). We could also say that the audience members persuade themselves, with the communicator providing the arguments.

The cognitive response approach model has some limitations. Firstly, it assumes that people think carefully about messages (Perloff, 2003: 128). And secondly, this theory does not tell us how to 'devise messages to change attitudes or behavior' (Perloff, 2003: 128–129). Therefore, this approach needs to be complemented with the ELM. As described above, the basic idea of the ELM is to explain when people will, or will not, thoughtfully process and analyse messages (Petty and Cacioppo, 1986). According to the ELM, a lack of *motivation* and *cognitive ability* make people's assessment of messages more superficial (Petty and Briñol, 2012). And depending on the theme of the message, the same individual can in one case lack motivation and cognitive ability and, in other cases, possess both. The important question here is whether enemy images tend to be a case where people have the motivation and cognitive ability to assess the messages. It might be possible to argue that if someone belongs to the target group of an enemy image, e.g. the case of a Jew in Nazi Germany, they will more likely have the motivation and hopefully the cognitive ability to assess the antisemitic rhetoric of that time and context. One prominent example of such heightened sensibility would be Victor Klemperer (1881–1960, see Box 3.1), a German-Jewish scholar who managed to survive during the entire period of Nazi rule from 1933 to 1945. After the war, Klemperer published the seminal work *LTI – Lingua Tertii Imperii* (The Language of the Third Reich, 1947), based on his notebooks and diaries. In *LTI*, Klemperer, a trained philologist who had worked with military censorship during the First World War, noted the small changes in terms, concepts, and use of language that contributed to the consolidation and violent radicalization of totalitarian power. One of the most quoted sentences from the book is: 'Words can be like tiny doses of arsenic: they are swallowed unnoticed, appear to have no effect, and then after a little time the toxic reaction sets in after all' (Klemperer, [1947] 2000: 15–16).

The main audience of antisemitic messages in Germany, on the other hand, tended to be already prejudiced with little knowledge about Jews, and not Jews who were the target of the propaganda. Ergo, their *motivation* and *ability* to make a thorough analysis of the message was probably limited and could easily be exploited by the rhetoric of enemy images.

BOX 3.1 VICTOR KLEMPERER AND *LINGUA TERTII IMPERII*

Victor Klemperer (1881–1960) was born in a formerly German part of Poland in 1881 as the son of a rabbi, but switched his religious affiliation several times during his lifetime. After studies in literature and a career in journalism and writing, he wrote a dissertation in 1913 and was promoted to Associated Professor (German 'Habilitation') in 1914 with work on Montesquieu. After serving in the German army during the First World War, charged with military censorship, he was appointed Professor of Romance Languages at the Technical University of Dresden in Germany. Despite his integration into German culture, he was stripped of his professorship after the Nazi usurpation of 1933 due to discriminatory race laws. Under Nazi rule, he not only managed to survive antisemitic genocidal violence and the destruction of Dresden, but also to keep a diary in which the trained philologist noted the slow change of the German language, facilitating totalitarian rule. The diaries and notebooks were in 1947 used to publish the seminal work *Lingua Tertii Imperii* (*LTI*, or The language of the Third Reich), in which he noted the shift in language related to increasingly totalitarian concepts: 'Making language the servant of its dreadful system, it procures it as its most powerful, most public and most surreptitious means of advertising' (Klemperer, [1947] 2000: 16). In *LTI*, he also directed attention towards how terminology or what today would be called the framing of internal and external enemies changed over the course of 12 years. After the Second World War, he chose to move to Eastern (communist) Germany and became a prominent figure in the cultural and political life of the German Democratic Republic. *LTI* has turned into a standard work of scholarship interested in how linguistic framings can shift under totalitarian conditions and how language contributes to processes of repression, marginalization, and exclusion. For a biography, see Elwert (1980).

Persuasive senders

According to the ELM introduced above, the character of the communicator/ sender *sometimes* plays a role in how the message is elaborated (Perloff, 2003). If the receiver experiences the message as not very relevant to them, with little bearing on their life, they will be less involved and have *less motivation* to assess it carefully. There is thus an increased likelihood of mental shortcuts and peripheral processing. Moreover, if the receiver does not possess the necessary knowledge to comprehend the message, or if they are distracted, their *ability* to process the message is negatively impacted.

Under the effect of these two factors (shortcuts and peripheral processing), the character of the communicator (*who*) is expected to play a bigger role, and *what* is being said a smaller one (Perloff, 2003: 134–136). The question then becomes what characteristics will increase the communicator's persuasiveness and make people accept an enemy image. Two factors appear repeatedly in the literature. The most important of these is *expertise* and other forms of *authority*. Experts appear more credible and authoritative, and 'people have a tendency to look up to authority figures for knowledge and direction' (Jowett and O'Donnell, 2015: 324). And, according to Petty, Cacioppo, and Goldman (1981), the *expertise* of a communicator plays an increasing role if the recipient is less motivated and regards the topic as being of low relevance to them personally (Petty, Cacioppo, and Goldman, 1981: 852). Sometimes a politician does not possess relevant expertise, for instance regarding military threats and enemy intentions. In such cases, they might try to ride on the expertise of others, claiming that experts endorse their policy and 'are backing the politician's proposal with their knowledgeable statements' (Reyes, 2011: 786). Likewise, organizations such as the Red Cross or UN, and religious figures such as the Pope, could play a similar role as they are considered moral or religious authorities.

A second factor is *attractiveness*, often physical. In 1994, Thomas Lee Budesheim and Stephen J. DePaola presented a study investigating the effects of, among other things, the physical appearances of political candidates (Budesheim and DePaola, 1994). As indicated, their study concerns the attractiveness of political candidates, whether good-looking candidates are evaluated more positively. And indeed, they are, at least for an audience that is less knowledgeable and less motivated. To them, physically attractive candidates also appear as having more desirable personality traits and being more successful. It could also impact voter outcomes (Budesheim and DePaola, 1994: 339 and 346–348). However, our focus here is not on voter outcomes in general elections. It is on the persuasiveness of enemy images. Could the physical attractiveness of the source affect the persuasiveness of enemy images? No direct research has been done on this limited question, and in an article from 1979, Shelly Chaiken says that previous research is equivocal regarding 'the effect of communicator physical attractiveness on persuasion' (Chaiken, 1979: 1387). The reason could be that previous research was conducted in a laboratory, and 'the implicit demands of the laboratory may encourage subjects to adopt a highly logical mode of cognitive functioning' (Chaiken, 1979: 1388). In other words, the research participants' thinking did not involve 'simple cues', as the ELM theory suggests. So Chaiken decided to undertake a study in a field setting and found that 'physical attractiveness can significantly enhance communicator persuasiveness' (Chaiken, 1979: 1394).

The link between physical attractiveness and persuasiveness is not only studied by political scientists and other scholars with an interest in political persuasion. It also engages researchers in marketing. In a recent study on consumer-generated feedback and endorsements, Marie Ozanne, Stephanie Q Liu, and Anna S. Mattila summarize several studies indicating that 'unconsciously, people use the "beautiful is good" heuristic to guide their everyday decisions, from making a friend to buying a product' (Ozanne, Liu, and Mattila, 2019: 728). Likewise, 'in advertising, attractive endorsers have a positive influence on customers' brand attitudes and behavioral intentions' (Ozanne, Liu, and Mattila, 2019: 728). The results of their analysis confirm previous research. They studied online reviewers producing customer-generated content on various brands, analysing in particular whether the physical attractiveness of these online reviewers influences customers' brand evaluations. And they found a correlation: 'The study findings demonstrate that customers are positively biased when positive reviews are written by attractive (vs less-attractive) reviewers' (Ozanne, Liu, and Mattila, 2019: 733). Market players know this fact. They avoid having their products endorsed by less attractive individuals in commercials because they could harm the status of the brand (for a more elaborate discussion, see the section on the 'Business sector' below).

Overall, research suggests that the (physical) qualities of the communicator/ sender matter for success in persuasion. This can further be distinguished at three levels, as suggested by Önnerfors (2024):

- 'epistemic trust': the sender manages to establish confidence in their truthfulness.
- 'emotional trust': the sender manages to channel the audience's emotions and create a community.
- 'existential trust': the sender delivers existential explanations of meaning-making.

'Epistemic trust' is defined as 'the willingness to accept new information from another person as trustworthy' (Schröder-Pfeifer et al., 2018: 123–131) – in other words, the sender manages to convince the receiver/audience that their message has a truth value (categories of true and false). For this to happen, the sender either styles themselves as an expert (or refers to experts) or rejects established knowledge as false. Channelling audience emotions involves establishing and reinforcing value judgements (about right and wrong) and creating a community of values/ movement around the message. Emotional trust is created around the messenger as a unifier. Existential explanations serve the purpose of meaning-making on a higher, metaphysical level (for instance explaining the existence of good and evil) and thus answering fundamental why-questions. The sender assumes a position as a quasi-religious herald and leader.

Persuasive messages

In this section, where we discuss persuasive *messages*, we have found it reasonable to put strategies for making messages more persuasive into a few central but overlapping categories. We will start with a discussion of how *emotional messages*, often including fear, can be used as an instrument to make the audience less rational and its assessment of messages more superficial. Then we will discuss the importance of making messages more *credible, consistent,* and *simple*. Lastly, we will discuss how basic human psychological *needs* are considered when producing messages. Our point is that these strategies have two things in common: they aim to increase the likelihood of the receivers applying mental shortcuts and thus decrease their motivation and cognitive ability to critically assess the rhetoric.

The list of factors that enhance persuasiveness discussed below is by no means comprehensive and could be extended. It is simply a shortlist of factors that we believe are relevant to making enemy images persuasive and that are stressed as vital in the academic literature, where they appear frequently. We will discuss the following:

1 Emotional appeal
2 Credibility
3 Consistency
4 Simplicity
5 Human needs.

Emotional appeal

An important way to produce a persuasive message is to exploit the audience's emotions. Fear, disgust, anger, guilt, sadness, envy, and pride are some of the most frequently used emotions (Braddock, 2020: 163–165) and often used in enemy images. Of course, positive emotions can be used in persuasive messages, too.

We already know from Chapter 1 that an enemy image constructs the other as a real, serious, and imminent threat to our vital interests. Fear is invoked rhetorically to mobilize the masses (Wodak, 2015). Moreover (see Chapter 2, Table 2.1), despite our superiority, 'we' are considered vulnerable to the enemy. This means that an enemy image can easily be translated into a fear-mongering message and one that underpins pride and anger: 'we' are superior, and 'they' threaten what rightfully belongs to 'us'. Moreover, since enemy images are often produced in the shadow of a real conflict, we believe that their content combined with an actual conflict could negatively impact both the audience's motivation and its cognitive ability to critically assess messages involving enemy images. This might lead to a more superficial assessment and acceptance of enemy images, and to 'mental shortcuts' such as those explained through the ELM (Perloff, 2003: 132). There is also an increased risk that an audience, particularly during a conflict, would trust authorities more (rallying around the flag) and assess the quality of the arguments to a lesser degree, and that their thinking would involve 'simple cues' (Perloff, 2003: 133–135). Emotional appeal might also refer to rhetorical performance as such. As research in populism posits, there exists a particular 'political style' which entails a Manichean worldview, 'bad manners' (breaking with conventions), and the permanent evocation of crisis, breakdown, and threat (Moffitt, 2016: 42–50). It is easy to adapt such a rhetorical strategy to the expressions of enemy images in which leaders claim to speak on behalf of the people and against those who betray them, evoking existential threats, even if it means being vulgar or indecent. Such a rhetorical scheme can be perceived as being on the side of the people and taking their concerns seriously.

Credible messages

Credible messages will, as a rule, have a greater chance of being persuasive. One factor increasing the credibility of a message is *rationality*, the impression that it is the fruit of extensive reflection and deliberation. The content must appear as having 'been made after a heeded, evaluated and thoughtful procedure' (Reyes, 2011: 786), and not hastily made. You describe the message as having been investigated, involving consultation with experts and academics, and perhaps based on statistics. For instance, prior to the American invasion of Iraq in March 2003, the United States Congress amended a law (Public Law, 2002: 107–243) giving 'Authorization for use of military force against Iraq'. The fact that the invasion was preceded by debates in Congress, leading to a law arguing in detail for the invasion, contributed to the impression that the invasion was indeed based on rational reflection.

A second, related strategy to make a message appear credible is to produce *two-sided messages*. This means the arguments of the opponent are not hidden, but rather presented. You thereby give the impression of being open, of having nothing to hide (Perloff, 2003: 178). And such messages are more influential than one-sided ones provided that the opponent's argument is refuted after having been presented. Another effect of this strategy is not only that your arguments appear more credible, but also that the audience might be made resistant to messages produced by an opponent. The reason is that having been presented with the opponent's arguments, which are then refuted, the audience has been inoculated. If the opponent tries to influence the audience, the latter has already heard the arguments and knows their weaknesses. The inoculation theory (developed further in Chapter 6) was originally developed by William J. McGuire (1961), and his idea was to explain how to make audiences immune to others' attempts to influence them. According to this theory,

> just as people's bodies could be inoculated against disease through exposure to initial mild doses of the disease, people's beliefs could be inoculated against attack by exposing those beliefs to initial mild attacks that were easily refuted.
>
> *(Tormala, 2008: 225)*

A third strategy seeking to build credibility is to make use of *symbols of power*. It is believed that messages from people in power have more impact, and people in power know it. Therefore, in decisive moments, politicians and other actors use symbols of power to rally around. A politician appearing before the national flag in times of crisis uses a symbol of power, claims to represent the nation-state as a whole, and exploits the symbolic power invested in national symbols. The national flag has emotional effects, since when standing 'in front of a huge flag, an emotional association is transferred to the speaker' (Jowett and O'Donnell, 2015: 282). There are more symbols than national flags and crests. If you enter a building belonging to an important transnational corporation, its lobby might very well have 'marble floors; guards at the elevators; tall, live trees and plants; fountains; and a large, imposing reception desk' (Jowett and O'Donnell, 2015: 327). Also 'expensive art on the walls and rare objects of art are additional visual symbols of power' (Jowett and O'Donnell, 2015: 327). And this is nothing new. Emperors have often used various kinds of symbols in portraits to communicate power and invincibility. Ancient empires could have monumental complexes, such as the Acropolis of Athens, the Forbidden City of Imperial China, or the Roman Forum in Rome.

The public, the intended audience, is often cynical and suspects self-interest to lie behind political messaging. A fourth way to increase a message's credibility is to make it appear *altruistic*. According to Reyes, it is important that the senders 'make sure their proposals [do] not appear driven only by personal interests' (Reyes, 2011: 787). But maybe this is not enough. Self-interest is not only personal but could also be national. Noam Chomsky exclaimed, 'It's the oil, stupid!' in a discussion where he alleged that the American invasion of Iraq in 2003 was really motivated by access to Iraq's crude oil (Chomsky, 2012: 87–91). In any case, political leaders must present themselves, their policies, and their motives as serving the voters, a common good (Reyes, 2011: 787), or even universal principles like democracy and freedom.

Although propaganda, including enemy images, blurs the line between fact and fiction, it should avoid 'blatant falsehoods or obviously biased intentions' (Taillard and Giscoppa, 2013: 13) as a fifth strategy to make a message more credible. Instead, senders should try to 'incorporate as much truth as possible in the message' (Taillard and Giscoppa, 2013: 6). And if a sender aims to spread extreme or biased messages, they could start with relatively moderate messages that the receivers will accept. Later, the sender could introduce new messages based on the same narrative, but more extreme. Such habituation makes the receivers 'more susceptible to accepting propaganda messages that are more extreme' (Taillard and Giscoppa, 2013: 13).

A similar argument is that one should try not only to avoid falsehoods but to incorporate *evidence* to substantiate one's claims (Perloff, 2003). This means that the sender of the message should anchor their message outside themselves and refer, for instance, to experts, data, and science in support of their claims. In a discussion about 'Finnish Russophobia', the Finnish professor of communication studies, Heikki Luostarinen, agrees, claiming that 'enemy images are often built around a kernel of real properties, but yarns are then spun around this kernel to dress the enemy in the clothes of Satan' (Luostarinen, 1989: 127). Real and lasting hostilities increase the chance that the enemy image will be understood as true and thereby become more persuasive. In the case of the ongoing war between Russia and Ukraine, for instance, President Putin claimed in an address on 24 February 2022 that Ukraine was run by neo-Nazis (Putin, 24 February 2022). Of course, this is not true, but Putin is also using a kernel of truth since some units, such as the infamous Azov battalion, have right-wing extremists in their ranks and their use of right-wing symbolism is abundant.

To conclude, the six strategies to enhance credibility can be summarized as follows:

- *Rationality*: present your argument as rational.
- *Inoculation*: incorporate arguments of your opponent and refute them.
- *Status*: use symbols of power.
- *Altruism*: present your argument as if it is in the interest of the receivers.
- *Accuracy*: avoid blatant falsehoods.
- *Proofs*: include supporting evidence (a kernel of truth).

Consistent messages

Consistent messages tend to be more persuasive than shifting ones, and academic literature suggests two main reasons. Firstly, persuasion is not usually something that happens instantaneously. On the contrary, 'persuasion takes time' (Perloff, 2003: 8), and for this process to be completed, messages must be consistent over time.

A second argument, based on the tenets of cognitive consistency theory (CCT) and to be discussed in detail in Chapter 4, is that messages have a greater impact when they are consistent with opinions, beliefs, and dispositions already existing in a population. In other words, they are supportive of, rather than discrepant from, the population's commonly held views (Jowett and O'Donnell, 2015: 279–280). People tend to favour messages that are in accordance with existing ideas, neglecting or even rejecting those that fundamentally contradict what is generally believed. The reason is that people prioritize an understanding of the world that is simple, coherent, and confirms established beliefs since it reduces emotional tensions such as cognitive dissonance (Festinger, 1957: 1–31). Therefore, when producing a message, it is important to be aware of and in line with the audience's 'past experiences, its collective memory' (Rutherford, 2004: 6).

There are numerous cases illustrating the use of consistency. One recent example is how the discussion in Sweden following the Russian invasion of Ukraine is in line with centuries of Swedish fear of Russia. The threats that Russia issued after Sweden considered NATO membership in the spring of 2022 (Krasny, 2022) thus rekindled existing and deep-rooted fears. Sue Veres Royal brings up another case. In her article (2011) exploring the narrative after al-Qaeda's terror attacks against the United States and the subsequent 'war on terrorism', she suggests that the propaganda aimed at the American public was successful as it was consistent with established values and views (Royal, 2011: 405). Existing stereotypes about Muslims and Arabs facilitated the acceptance of the enemy image (Royal, 2011: 406).

It is not only people in power who are aware of the importance of cognitive consistency. Mass media also tend to reinforce ideas that are already part of popular wisdom (Petersson, 2006: 27). One reason is purely financial. Media actors know that controversial news stories contradicting established ideas might be rejected by the audience. Controversial news stories might jeopardize market share and, in the end, profit. It is therefore safer to produce news stories that are consistent with what the audience already knows.

Simple messages

Yet another strategy to make the message persuasive is to make it simple. Messages that are simple and repeated are usually more memorable (Taillard and Giscoppa, 2013: 15). According to Taillard and Giscoppa, 'a message will not be memorable if it is complex, confusing, or greatly detailed' (Taillard and Giscoppa, 2013: 14). It is a discouraging fact, but it seems that 'full analyses of the truth lack the novelty of being figuratively clever and, as a result, tend to fail at keeping the audience interested' (Taillard and Giscoppa, 2013: 14). One clear example for this communication strategy is political slogans such as Nigel Farage's 'Breaking Point' catchphrase during the 2016 Brexit campaign (Bergmann, 2021). The United Kingdom Independence Party (UKIP) party leader toured the country with a campaign bus covered with a poster showing a threatening anonymous caravan of immigrants together with the main message of a breaking point that demonstrated how 'the EU has failed us all' and the one-liner 'We must break free of the EU and take back control of our borders'. The image and text communicate a simple yet powerful message of 'us' versus 'them' and place the blame on 'them' (the immigrants and the EU). More examples of powerful visual expressions of enemy images will be discussed in Chapter 7.

Human needs

A last strategy to make a message persuasive is to exploit the audience's needs and desires (Ellul, [1965] 1973: 4). In motivational theories, to be extensively presented in Chapter 4, it is assumed that humans have important needs, and that these needs explain people's behaviour. Since motivational theory is not one single theory, but an assortment of competing theories, different motivational theories identify different types of needs and assess their role differently. The American psychologist Abraham Maslow (1908–1970), for instance, identifies (usually) five hierarchically organized categories of *need*, ranging from *physiological* (Maslow, 1943: 373), *safety* (Maslow, 1943: 376), *love and belonging* (Maslow, 1943: 380), and *(self) esteem* (Maslow, 1943: 381) to *self-actualization* (Maslow, 1943: 382). According to his scheme, people focus on one need at a time, starting with the most basic ones. Ergo, we focus first on food and other physiological needs. When they are met, we move up to other needs in his suggested hierarchy of needs.

The American psychologist Clayton Alderfer (1940–2015) modified Maslow's theory, suggesting that human needs may be grouped under three categories (existence, relatedness, and growth) and not organized on a strictly hierarchical basis (Alderfer, 1969). People can, depending on the situation, focus on one of the needs and move to another, but not in a strict order. A third scholar within motivational research, Douglas C. McClelland (1917–1998), argues that people obtain three types of needs (achievement, affiliation, and power), but to different extents and in different combinations (McClelland and Burnham, 1976; McClelland and Boyatzis, 1982). So each person has a unique combination of needs: for some, achievement needs are prominent; and for others, it could be power.

In this chapter, our take is that human needs can be exploited and used in ways that make messages about the enemy more persuasive. Firstly, we believe that needs relating to our existence and survival are indeed important, and if a message is constructed in such a way that 'they' are convincingly described as a threat to 'our' survival, it will probably be more persuasive or at least receive more attention. As discussed earlier, fear-mongering gives messages more impact and attention, and a threat to our life and security creates fear. If, in addition to that, there is a collective memory of historical and traumatic events where 'they' killed 'us' or starved 'us' to death, a past war or genocide, any reminder of threats to our basic needs will probably have a great impact.

Secondly, and this will also be discussed in the next chapter, the theorists above seem to agree on the importance of being accepted by a group that provides us with love and belonging. And the fear of rejection can be used to raise the persuasiveness of a message. Messages encoded in the slogan 'if you are not with us, you are against us' have a strong impact. They imply that you will be rejected, maybe regarded as one of 'them', if you do not accept 'our' narrative of the conflict and depiction of the enemy. In 1920, before a group of educational workers, Vladimir Lenin, at the time the head of government of Soviet Russia, stated:

> It is with absolute frankness that we speak of this struggle of the proletariat; each man must choose between joining our side or the other side. Any attempt to avoid taking sides in this issue must end in fiasco.
>
> *(Lenin, 1920, 3 November)*

A third common denominator for these theories is the need for a good self-image, and enemy images seem tailor-made to fulfil this kind of need in their audience. As we said in Chapter 2 (see Table 2.1), 'we' are *superior*, and yet vulnerable. This claim to superiority buys into our need for self-esteem and negative attribution towards the out-group. This human need may be one reason why thoughts of white supremacy persist. White supremacism, with roots in pseudosciences such as racial biology and scientific racism, suggests that white people are naturally superior to those of other 'races' (Jenkins, 2024) and thus have the right to dominate them. Racial biology and scientific racism have long since been completely refuted, but white supremacism lives on. A plausible explanation is that this idea buys into lighter-skinned people's need for self-esteem and negative attribution towards the out-group.

Effective propaganda machinery

The last section in this chapter about persuasion concerns the efficiency of the propaganda machinery. A point of departure is that efficient propaganda machinery 'must create a total environment of persuasion, using all available media and leaving no gaps to be filled with opposing views' (Soules, 2015: 8). This, we believe, requires

1 harmony between the enemy images (re)produced in the public sphere and the ones (re)produced in the private sphere;
2 harmony between verbally expressed enemy images and different policies; and
3 consensual elite discourse.

The discussion below will follow these three points to structure our arguments.

Public and private spheres

It is important to know that socialization into norms and attitudes takes place in different spheres of society. Enemy images, for instance, are not only produced and reproduced by elites and not only in the public sphere, but also in everyday situations and by ordinary people in private spheres. Before moving on, it could be of interest to mention that in the 1960s, the German sociologist Jürgen Habermas renewed the discussion about the separation between public and private spheres (Habermas, [1962] 1989). According to Habermas, the public sphere is defined as a common place where beliefs and information can be deliberated freely. The private sphere is usually the home, a place where the individual has some authority, relatively free from governmental institutions. Even if it is possible to see the public sphere as a democratic space where ideas and beliefs are discussed, it can also be a place where so-called discursive elites (see *unanimous elite discourse* below) dominate.

Although elites dominate the public sphere, socialization into the norms desired by the political elite is not a straightforward top-down process. On the contrary, the impact of the private sphere should not be underestimated. According to Taillard and Giscoppa,

> When people receive a message from a trusted acquaintance, such as a friend, family member, or co-worker, regardless of the validity of the message, they are prone to be more receptive to the content of the message because they have a certain degree of trust (or at least respect) for the individual conveying it.
>
> *(Taillard and Giscoppa, 2013: 23)*

An important argument in this section is that when there is *discursive harmony* between the private and public spheres, in other words when similar and/or compatible messages are (re)produced in the private and public spheres, messages produced by political elites are best positioned to have a strong impact. We cannot expect conversations in everyday situations in the private sphere to be the same as political rhetoric in the public. What is important is that the narratives are in harmony and perhaps even mutually reinforcing. In any case, without the private sphere on their side, political leaders would be fighting an uphill struggle and it would be hard to win people over and make them accept enemy images.

If the political elite is aware of popular attitudes and norms (re)produced in the private spheres, it can exploit and build on them. There must therefore be some room for feedback loops (see Figure 3.2), with the receivers of messages also having a chance to react to messages and the political elites at least somewhat sensitive to their reactions (Jowett and O'Donnell, 2015: 330). In this way, the political elite can adjust/fine-tune their messages so that their discourse is in harmony with that in private spheres. As Thierry Balzacq puts it, 'a successful message should identify with the audience's feelings, needs, and interests ... to tune his/her language to the audience's experience' (Balzacq, 2011: 9).

Children's lives are of particular interest. Not only are they particularly impressionable, but they also exist under the influence of the two spheres, the public sphere represented by the educational system and the private sphere by home (Killen, Richardson, and Clark, 2010: 102). In their early life, the parents' and the family's norms and attitudes are of particular importance. Later, in adolescence, parents mean less, and peers' norms and attitudes are more influential (Killen, Richardson, and Clark, 2010: 102 and cf. Killen, Lee-Kim, McGlothlin, and Stangor, 2002). This implies that a wider social context begins to take over (Oppenheimer, 2006: 275).

To make our case, consider the following thought experiment: imagine a German family in the 1930s, at a time when negative remarks about Jews were particularly common. In their depiction of Jews, parents and other adults in the private sphere would probably not use the same vocabulary as elites in the public one, but the narratives could very well be compatible. Imagine adult family members at dinner, discussing Jews, and the young children overhearing the conversation. The prejudice would impact the children, especially if they heard compatible ideas on the radio. In school, they might also hear more, mutually confirming stories. Schoolbooks, children's books, and teaching (representing the public sphere) would give mutually confirming variants of the same antisemitic theme. During their lunch break, kids might be reproducing, in their childish way, attitudes inculcated when a Jewish schoolboy is not allowed to be part of the fun and games. In a way, the strategy in a society like Nazi Germany resembles brainwashing taking place in cults. In 1995, Margaret Thaler Singer published a study on brainwashing in which she outlined a series of simple, yet highly effective measures taken consistently by cults who successfully utilized brainwashing methods. One of her points in a later book was that successful cults 'control the person's social and/or physical environment; especially control the person's time' (Singer, 2003: 65). People involved in cults are isolated and deprived of influence and support from outside. On a much larger scale, this was also done in Nazi Germany, as well as in other totalitarian systems. The Nazi propaganda machinery did not leave anything to chance. More or less all aspects of children's lives were controlled. We have already mentioned the importance of the educational system. But children's leisure activities were also controlled by the Nazi regime, for instance through the Nazi youth organizations *Hitlerjugend* and *Bund Deutscher Mädel*. Even board games children were supposed to play after school could have a Nazi and antisemitic message (see Figure 3.1). This means that 'the propaganda can emanate from parents, age mates, media of various kinds, teachers and other sources of information in society' (Sternberg and Sternberg, 2008: 133). And since the propaganda comes from so many sources, and the hatred against 'them' is repeated with different variations and in terms of multiple stories, they appear to be true. What is stated here could of course also be applied to an analysis of computer and video games in our own time. A host of examples ranging from the invention of the printing press to online memes will be presented in Chapter 7.

To reinforce the point, the arguments presented above in the section 'consistent messages' can here be expressed visually. The model below (Figure 3.2) attempts to capture two important dimensions to achieve the impact of an enemy image in political communities over time. It has two components:

1 discursive consistency over time
2 discursive consensus/harmony across political space (public and private spheres and their interaction).

FIGURE 3.1 Selection of Nazi German board games.

Source: leewrightonflickr under Creative Commons 4.0 licence.

The (horizontal) timescale expresses the ideal that optimizing the impact of a message is facilitated by consistency over time. Variations concerning the content of an enemy image may develop, yet need to be compatible with each other and have a long 'time of decay'. For instance, anti-Jewish propaganda morphed from accusing Jews of the murder of Christ to the blood libel and finally modern forms of cultural, economic, and social antisemitism (for an extensive discussion, see Chapter 7). Another example would be the development from conventional racism (based on 'race') to neo-racism (based on culture).

The (vertical) spatial dimension of the model refers to the discursive consensus between the public and private spheres as reciprocal senders and receivers. We posit that the public sphere is heavily influenced by elite discourse: actors with means to influence what and how it is expressed in public space. However, the success of this elite discourse is determined by its capacity to persuade the private sphere of its significance. For instance, elite discourse might appeal to threats to vital interests (see definitions in previous chapters) or simply voice public opinion. However, success in communicating an enemy image is also relative to the feedback provided from the private sphere, which can in turn be exploited. One explanation for this is approached in system justification theory (SJT, see also Chapters 4 and 5), where Jost (2019: 3) has explained the process of reciprocal endorsement as follows:

> In other words, 'top-down' processes of elite communication (the 'discursive superstructure') necessarily meet up – or interact – with 'bottom-up' psychological needs and interests (the 'motivational substructure'), so that system-justifying messages find their audiences and vice versa.

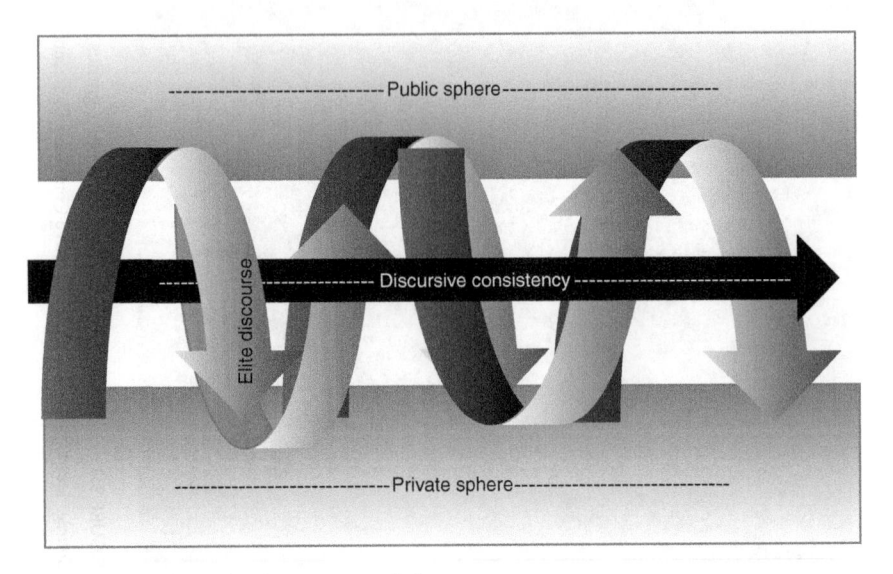

FIGURE 3.2   Discursive harmony model.

Source: Created by the authors.

Propaganda and policies

Enemy images are not only produced by discursive elites in *verbal* messages. It is also important for verbal messages to be followed up with practical policies confirming them. In other words, it is beneficial if there is harmony between what political elites *say* and what they *do*. Let us take a few examples. Israel has built the West Bank barrier separating most Palestinians on the West Bank from Israel. The point is that this barrier, in addition to allegedly reducing the risk of terrorism, also confirms the dominant discourse in Israeli society that people on the other side of the wall are 'our' enemy and potentially dangerous. The barrier is not only a practical instrument for physical safety but also makes a statement about the Palestinians (see Figure 3.3).

FIGURE 3.3 Israeli warning sign.

Source: Flickr/Kyle Taylor under Creative Commons 2.0 licence. No changes have been made to this image.

*https://*flickr.com/photos/95672737@N00/4264579636

The same thing can be said about President Donald Trump's unfinished wall on the border with Mexico or the EU border regime in the Mediterranean and the East.

Practical policies could of course involve more than erecting physical barriers. Visa policies also communicate whom we trust and whom we do not. Between some countries, citizens can travel visa-free or perhaps even without a passport. Citizens from other countries need to undergo a complicated visa process.

At the time of writing this book (2022–2024), the Russian invasion of Ukraine is ongoing. Along with verbal protests, the European Union and the United States implemented numerous policies primarily designed to harm and weaken the Russian economy – and in the long run, Russia's military capacity, too. Some policies were more symbolic, like the boycotts of the Russian national ice hockey and football teams, and of individual athletes. Others were practical, involving donations and arms shipments to the Ukrainian army. In any case, these policies strengthen the credibility of the verbal condemnations of the Russian invasion. They could also be seen as statements reinforcing the enemy image of Russia. The current visa policy in many EU countries, which restricts ordinary Russians' chances of obtaining visas and travelling to European countries, also contributes not only to the image of the Russian regime as an enemy, but also to the idea that Russians at large pose a risk.

Some of these policies and measures were *not* directly ordered by political leaders. Under combined pressure from political leaders and public opinion, leaders of different sports clubs and both national and international sports federations decided to boycott Russian and Belorussian athletes, clubs, and sports federations. We see similar boycotts within the music industry (for instance Eurovision Song Contest) and with consumer products. Companies, too, took action against Russia and Belarus that went beyond the sanctions agreed on by the EU and the United States. Taken as a whole, these policies, in addition to their direct effects on the Russian and Belarusian economies, gave weight to the verbally expressed enemy images, making them more believable and trustworthy. Through them, the enemy images appeared to be more than mere rhetoric.

In the last section of Chapter 2, we constructed two contrasting enemy images, one benign and the other malign (Table 2.3). In the benign one, we posited a clear separation between 'their' leaders and the population, underlining the importance of distinguishing between an aggressive political elite and the people in general. If we return to some of the policies adopted against Russia in 2022–2023, there is a risk that they can contribute to a malign enemy image, where Russians in general become 'our' (arch)enemy. What we mean is that the policies currently being implemented target not only Russia's political elite and the clique around President Putin supporting his aggressive invasion of Ukraine. They also affect people in general just because of who they essentially are (Russians), not because of what they have done. The policies target the purchasing power of Russians; they target Russian athletes, artists, and cultural professionals in general. And if the United States and the European Union are implementing various sanctions that will affect many more people than are responsible for the Russian invasion, there is a risk of such policies confirming a malign enemy image with an unclear separation between 'their' leaders and the general population (Table 2.3).

Unanimous elite discourse

The third component in an efficient propaganda machinery is a unanimous elite discourse. In contemporary propaganda, political leadership uses all available media – press, radio, television, film, the internet, Facebook, Twitter, YouTube and other video-sharing platforms such as TikTok, email, smartphones, videos, cartoons, and so on (Jowett and O'Donnell, 2015: 321). The reason is that the political elite alone cannot persuade its population. It must make use of several other key communicators (Taillard and Giscoppa, 2013: 6), or elites, beyond the government and its agencies (Figure 3.4). In our age of synthetic media (i.e. digitally generated content), that would mean 'influencers' taking to social media to make the case. The Russian war of aggression against Ukraine has in many instances become a

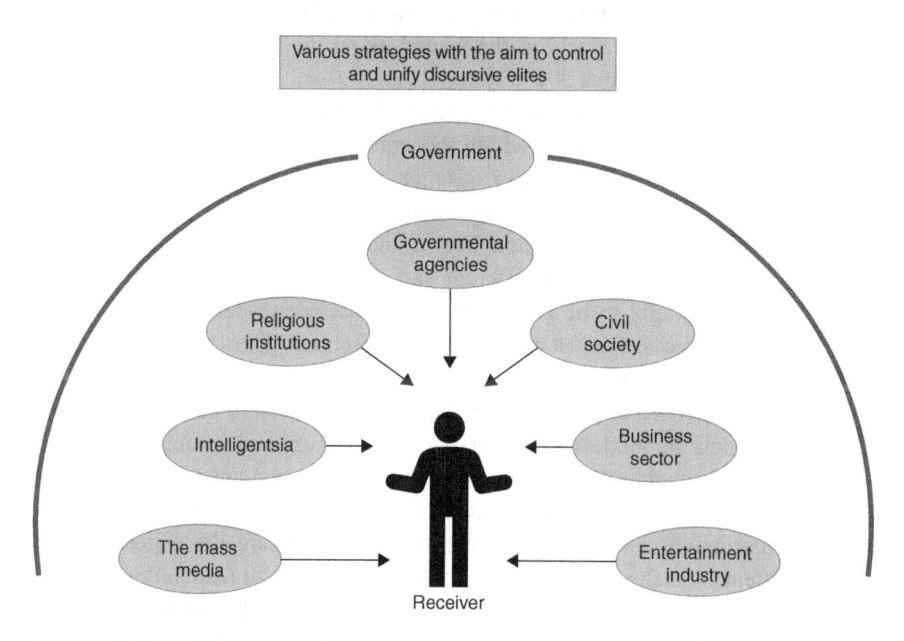

FIGURE 3.4 Elite consensus strategy.

Note: The model expresses the formation of elite consensus through the control and unification of various discursive elites on behalf of a government. The receiver of messages (a member of a political community) is exposed to the discourse of various actors, ranging from highly organized (governmental) to looser expressions (e.g. through entertainment).

Source: Created by the author.

war of influencers on platforms like Instagram, Twitter, and TikTok. For political messages to be convincing, they should be very similar or at least compatible with those produced by governing elites. In other words, 'to influence mass audiences, it requires the cooperation and agency of major communication channels' (Soules, 2015: 6). Together with them, political leaders should develop a unanimous and coordinated elite discourse regarding the enemy.

The concept of 'elite', which we have referred to a couple of times, is not self-evident. Here, an elite refers to a limited group in society that has 'significant control over the means of production of public opinion' (van Dijk, 1993: 45). Such elites usually have access to both material and immaterial resources and means. The material ones include a solid and widely branched infrastructure facilitating access to the audience. Until the introduction of state schools in Sweden, the Church of Sweden (part of the state until 2000) was the organization with probably the best infrastructure for the dissemination of religious and political messages. During the modern era, mass media was introduced, and the (competing) actors controlling them turned into a new discursive elite. Immaterial assets are independent of financial ones but make an elite appear *attractive* and *trustworthy*, thereby giving its discourse an impact through 'knowledge or moral superiority' (Soules, 2015: 12). Immaterial resources are highly important because the influence of a message 'depends just as much on the source as on the content of the message itself' (Taillard and Giscoppa, 2013: 18).

There is not one fixed set of discursive elites. They vary in time and space, from one society to another. Moreover, within the same population, different segments assess communicators differently. For instance, young and old citizens often rely on and trust very different elites. Even among modern societies, the assortment of elites varies. In a democratic and liberal society, having many independent discursive elites, giving voice to different and contrasting interests in society, is vital. The citizens ought to be informed by various independent voices/elites to make informed choices, for instance in general elections. Those growing up in a democratic society have been taught that our mixture of contrasting public voices is collectively supposed to give us the perspectives we need to become informed citizens. Although the mixture of discursive elites varies even among democratic societies, it is reasonable that the government and its public agencies are central to a system aimed at achieving discursive harmony (Figure 3.4). Among the most important discursive instruments in governmental power are the education and military systems. Teachers do not merely tell children how to read and write, and officers do more than show their men how to load a gun. They homogenize cultures within the national border (Hettne, Sörlin, and Østergård, 1998: 165–166) and give large segments of the population a national worldview, defining who 'we' are, whom 'we' can trust, and who the enemy is. In his 1976 essay *The Mesh of Power*, French philosopher Michel Foucault explained how education and the military turned into institutions of disciplining and controlling the members of modern states (Foucault, [1976] 2007: 153–162). By alignment and training of body and mind, the modern state increasingly exercised power over its population.

In addition to these government-run discursive structures, the ideal of a democratic society should have an array of independent opinion-forming actors (Figure 3.4). In many countries, established churches, or similar religious institutions, belong (or perhaps belonged) to one such category of independent actors of civil society. In a democracy, the so-called intelligentsia[1] should not only be independent of the state but also take a critical position on various political issues. Mass media, civil society, and the business sector are other important categories of actor that ideally should be independent of the state, representing a variety of interests and having the capacity to influence public opinion and contribute to public debate. Even the entertainment industry should have such a role (Taillard and Giscoppa, 2013: 6) and similarly be independent of the government. But for efficient propaganda machinery to develop, converging towards consensus in a unified public space, these seemingly independent and disparate entities of elite discourse must adopt messages that either directly reproduce the state's enemy images or produce messages that in other ways confirm them. In totalitarian regimes, diversity is reduced to achieve total convergence in the informational space. Yet, as we will see, these sealed modes of information control are challenged by new technological developments.

Religious institutions

In early modernity, it was important in emerging Protestant states to tie the church close to the government because of its infrastructure and the trust the church enjoyed from the people. As an effect of modernization and secularization, the role of religious institutions has gradually decreased in many parts of the world. Still, churches and comparable religious institutions have played a legitimizing role in wars, confirming enemy images throughout the twentieth century (Barbeau, 2016: 24 and Jenkins, 2014). Writing about the First World War, the prominent American scholar of propaganda Harold Lasswell stated that 'the church of practically every description can be relied upon to bless a popular war, and to see in it an opportunity for the triumph of whatever godly design they choose to further' (Lasswell, 1927: 72). It seems that wars, including current ones, trigger religious rhetoric. In the ongoing Russian attack on Ukraine, for instance, the Russian Orthodox Church is understood as a vital instrument in the Russian propaganda system (Smith, 2022). Still, the church has a problematic Christian pacifist message that must be dealt with. Ironically, Lasswell says that

> In Christian countries precautions must be taken to calm the doubts of those who undertake to give such a book as the Bible an inconvenient interpretation. It is always expedient to circulate the arguments of the preachers and priests who

are willing to explain how you can follow Jesus and kill your enemies. There are always enough theological leaders to undertake the task.

(Lasswell, 1927: 97)

Having a peace-loving creed, the priests have 'to facilitate the transition from the condemnation of wars in general, which is a traditional attitude on the part of the Christian sects, to the praise of a particular war' (Lasswell, 1927: 72). The fact that the church is supposed to teach love of one's neighbour and turning the other cheek could be used as an argument. If even the church realizes that a certain out-group poses an imminent threat, then there should be a real justification for our military violence.

Enemy images produced by a religious elite are usually not identical to secular ones. But if the former are in harmony with those produced by political elites, they can contribute to the justification of war and the creation of enemy images in their unique way. Religious institutions can contribute with religious rhetoric confirming the political rhetoric in at least six ways.

First, religious rhetoric can sanctify warfare and transform a conflict into a *holy war* (Jenkins, 2014: 5–9). This kind of language gives the war a particular meaning. The Russian Orthodox Patriarch Kirill argued along these lines, proclaiming on 6 March 2022 that 'we have entered into a struggle that has not a physical, but a metaphysical significance' (Smith, 2022). *Second*, religious rhetoric can justify the *cause* of war, the so-called jus ad bellum (Barbeau, 2016: 26), claiming that God is on 'our' side and that the nation's cause is also God's will (Jenkins, 2014: 2–5 and 9–11). Maybe we are fighting for our faith and its preservation. Sometimes, as with Christian evangelical theology, eschatology and salvation history are used to justify conflict. In these cases, God has a divine order and plan for the salvation of humanity, but the enemy, usually Islam, together with Satan, tries to divert it (Steiner and Lundberg, 2018: 152). Likewise, during the twentieth century, Protestant churches spread ideas about German 'chosenness', divine purpose, and 'sense of mission' (*Sendungsbewusstsein*) (Moses, 1999: 7–11). In Britain during the First World War, with the Church of England clergy defining 'the sins of Germany, British intervention appeared more and more imperative and morally' (Barbeau, 2016: 38). It was Britain's duty to protect civilization from German militarism and modernism and 'it was Britain's duty to inoculate Germany by force' (Bontrager, 2002: 779). A *third* rhetoric, related to the previous one, contributes to the enemy image by demonizing the enemy. Since the nation is fighting against an enemy that violates God's plan and cause, the enemy is not only a political opponent but potentially God's enemy. This rhetoric turns the enemy into an evil actor representing satanic forces (Jenkins, 2014: 9–11). *Fourth*, if 'our' leaders, in stark contrast to 'theirs', are depicted as fighting alongside God and furthering His cause, the religious elite can easily legitimize 'our' political leaders since they are fighting a divine cause. *Fifth*, religious discourse could also be used to provide fighters with status and sometimes a promise of salvation. In ISIS propaganda, martyrs have been promised a place in Paradise, and in Palestine, martyrs enjoy a high status in some Palestinian circles. Religious discourse could also increase the willingness to sacrifice and describe it as an opportunity for martyrdom (Barbeau, 2016: 26). Sometimes they would 'turn fallen soldiers into heroes' (Bontrager, 2002: 777). A *last* kind of religious rhetoric, which might not contribute to an enemy image, is generally dystopian. In some Christian circles, there is this idea that since mankind has fallen, humanity cannot build peace between nations, at least not before the return of Christ. This theology might not always legitimize a specific war, but it makes wars be comprehensible as something natural and to be expected, portraying the strife for lasting peace as a utopian aspiration (Moses, 1999: 10 and Steiner and Lundberg, 2018: 150).

One could ask *why* religious institutions would support the creation and dissemination of enemy images. In some cases, religious leaders genuinely believe in the cause and confirm enemy images out of conviction. In other cases, they might support the political elite to secure their position in society. For a dominant religious institution like the Church of England in the First World War, it was a way to restore its pre-eminence in the context of secularization (Barbeau, 2016: 27) and a chance to call the flock 'back to the fold' (Barbeau, 2016: 47). The Church of England also had various internal conflicts (Barbeau, 2016: 32), for which the war and its rhetoric presented a potentially unifying function. And lastly, during the First World War, most Church of England clergy 'lacked knowledge of the intricacies of foreign policy, the purpose for the war and the nature of the enemy' (Barbeau, 2016: 34–35). Hence, as Albert Marrin puts it, they became at the same time 'the targets, the creators, and the disseminators of propaganda' (Marrin, 1974: 102).

Intelligentsia

As stated above, the intelligentsia should ideally have an independent voice and a critical position regarding enemy images and thereby provide society with moral and rational guidance. Regrettably, that is not always the case, particularly not before or during a war. Lasswell had already discovered in the First World War that intellectuals are not at all immune to war fever. They become diligent and willing producers and reproducers of enemy images, contributing to a consensual elite discourse. 'German scholarship leaped to the colours in the last War in the famous and unforgettable manifesto, signed by ninety-three of her most illustrious intellectuals' (Lasswell, 1927: 51; see Box 3.2).

BOX 3.2 MANIFESTO OF THE NINETY-THREE

On 4 October 1914, 93 German scientists, composers, artists, writers, and educators signed a manifesto ('To the civilized world') endorsing German participation in the First World War. It was published in all major German newspapers. In the very first line, the manifesto accused Germany's enemies of lying (Meyer-Rewerts and Stöckmann, 2010). The manifesto also justified German war crimes in neutral Belgium and the necessity to resort to military might. It refuted depictions of the German Kaiser as a new Attila and condemned the supposed fact that 'Mongolians and Negroes are agitated to fight against the White race' (more about how this idea emerged, see Chapter 7). The manifesto was seen as a typical example of wartime propaganda and the complacency of intellectuals. Only a few weeks later, more than 3000 German professors signed another declaration with the same aim: to justify German warfare and contest accusations of brutal German 'militarism'.

In the discussion above on persuasive messages, we underlined that credibility is an asset in providing messages, including enemy images, with an enhanced impact. We also stated that messages produced or condoned by authorities depicting policies as rational would have a good chance of being influential. The point is that in an ever-more secularized society, the intelligentsia has become an increasingly important actor in giving messages, including enemy images, credibility. It is therefore in the interests of political elites to control or at least turn the intelligentsia into a useful tool. And it comes as no surprise that the Russian regime tries to control universities and the intelligentsia. In Russia, the Russian Union of Rectors, a major national public organization, issued a statement supporting the invasion of Ukraine by the Russian Federation, leading to a reaction from the European University Association. Maybe Putin has found it harder to control other parts of the intelligentsia. Already before the invasion, some Russian intellectuals called on their country's leadership to de-escalate the hostilities in Ukraine and avoid an 'immoral, irresponsible, and criminal' war (*The Moscow Times*, 2 February 2022).

Media

A third discursive elite is the media. Ideally, the media should also be independent of the state and one of its tasks should be to question indoctrination, enemy images, and war rhetoric. But as we will see, that is often not the case.

Authoritarian states regularly control the media, particularly in times of war. It therefore comes as no surprise that President Putin makes a great effort to control Russian media during the ongoing invasion of Ukraine. Russian media is restricted in what to write and how to portray the invasion, and the president has signed into a law criminalizing reporting that contradicts the government's version of events (Reporters without Borders, 2022).

But in democratic societies, too, there is a risk that the media gets streamlined in times of war to follow the needs and rhetoric of political leaders (Knightley, 1975). In Chapter 7, we will extensively cover how warfare in televised news has developed over the last decades on a spectrum ranging from outright propaganda to independent coverage. The situation during the Vietnam War was probably an exception. In that instance, journalists challenged the official narrative and demonstrated how US forces were committing war crimes. Since then, attempts to control the media image have increased, culminating during the American invasion of Iraq in 2003, when US President George W. Bush decided to invade on the pretext that Iraq possessed weapons of mass destruction. The war was initially not supported by the American public. According to Paul Rutherford, the Pentagon and the newsrooms tried to 'sell the war to a variety of domestic and foreign audiences' (Rutherford, 2004: 4).

> The intervention became a branded war, a co-production of the Pentagon and of newsrooms, processed and cleansed so that it could appeal to the well-established tastes of people who were veteran consumers of popular culture.
>
> *(Rutherford, 2004: 4)*

War rhetoric in the media is not usually orchestrated in this way. And neither the Pentagon nor the White House imposed censorship in the domestic arena; the newsrooms did it voluntarily: 'Very few of the voices called upon to comment during the war were drawn from the ranks of the anti-war movement' (Rutherford, 2004: 189). And the question lingers in the air: why does the media reproduce enemy images?

The first argument is that journalists and broadcasters can also be steeped in dominant narratives, 'subject to received wisdom, patriotic pride and cultural values' (Soules, 2015: 202). Just like the religious elites discussed above, media can be simultaneously the 'targets, the creators, and the disseminators of propaganda' (Marrin, 1974: 102). And if this is the case, the media is inevitably less critical.

A second argument concerns access to sources. During the Vietnam War, journalists had access to diverse sources and produced news stories that fuelled a growing domestic opposition to the unsuccessful warfare. But having analysed the situation closely, the Pentagon took various measures to limit media access to sources in post-Vietnam conflicts. In his analysis of media coverage of the 1991 Persian Gulf War, Philip M. Taylor showed how most American media now depended on the same military-controlled sources. This meant that newspapers, radio channels, and TV channels with completely different styles, ideologies, and target groups referred to the same sources and news material that were uncritically conveyed. Taylor calls it 'monopoly in the guise of pluralism' (Taylor, 1992: 268).

Another way for political elites to discipline the media is the fear of future repercussions. Access to sources within government and other important decision-making bodies is an important resource for the journalistic profession. These contacts are valuable. Journalists who report critically on political decisions risk becoming pariahs and losing their relationship with these inside sources. In Chapter 7, we present Daniel Hallin's theory of journalistic objectivity in war, according to which journalists and media opposing the official narrative are readily pushed out of the accepted mainstream. These dynamics might influence journalists aiming to maintain good relationships with valuable inside sources to neglect critical reporting.

A fourth argument for why the media is uncritical in its war coverage is financial. In times of war, there is a great demand for *fast* reporting. Critical assessments of sources would mean a slower news service. Delays and critical reporting could lead to lost market share, so this dynamic contributes to conformism.

A discussion about the media's role in propaganda machinery and in producing unanimous elite discourse would not be complete without mentioning Edward S. Herman and Noam Chomsky's book *Manufacturing Consent: The Political Economy of the Mass Media*, first published in 1988 (see Box 3.3). In it, Herman and Chomsky developed a propaganda model primarily designed for the United States. Their main point is that in a democratic society, despite formally independent media and a lack of overt coercion, media is also filtered (Herman and Chomsky, 1988: xi) and tends to 'carry out a system-supportive propaganda function' (Herman and Chomsky, 1988: 306), fostering consent for governmental politics. Although the media occasionally criticizes the government and its decision-making, the critique, according to Herman and Chomsky, is of 'limited nature' (1988: 2).

BOX 3.3   EDWARD S. HERMAN AND NOAM CHOMSKY –
MANUFACTURING CONSENT

Noam Chomsky has had various research interests, having first studied linguistics and built a connection to philosophy there. His views on the mind and origins of language were initially questioned by many. After a fellowship at Harvard University and writing his dissertation at Pennsylvania University, he accepted a teaching position at MIT. Some years later, he gained more recognition in linguistics, with some even calling him revolutionary (Tymoczko and Henle, 2000), but many remained sceptical about his ideas. In terms of political work prior to *Manufacturing Consent*, he published the two-volume book *The Political Economy of Human Rights* (1979) concerning the struggles in East Timor, Indonesia. In his earlier essay *The Responsibility of Intellectuals* (1967), he puts the responsibility of educating the masses on intellectuals with power, such as journalists, focusing on the American role in the Vietnam War and how it was not communicated – or even concealed – by the media. His article *What Makes Mainstream Media Mainstream* argues that specific public elites control the way the media presents itself, and that the media has a high influence on ordinary people especially in times of war (Chomsky, 1997). The term Mainstream Media and its abbreviation MSM has gained its own prominence and is today regularly used to denounce the impartiality of the journalistic profession. Edward S. Herman, the co-author of *Manufacturing Consent*, was a business school professor who had published works such as

> *Corporate Control, Corporate Power: A Twentieth Century Fund Study* (1981). What brought them together to write *Manufacturing Consent* was their shared critical view on the connection between the government and the media regarding information control. In 2000 Herman revisited their work and put their model in retrospective (Herman, 2000). Public reaction to *Manufacturing Consent* was mixed. Some scholars saw it as ground-breaking for journalism, sociology, and political science; and in 1996 a movie adaptation was published. Nevertheless, critics object that it describes journalists as being part of a conspiracy. Also, as it was mainly focused on the United States and its media relations, its broader relevance is questioned (Corner, 2003).
>
> Another critique was that the propaganda model presented in *Manufacturing Consent* was too similar to the 'gatekeeper model' of media. Klaehn argues that there is a significant difference here as the propaganda model is structural, focusing on power and social class, whereas the gatekeeper model is concerned with theories of social psychology (Klaehn, 2003). Even after more than 20 years, this model is still controversial.

According to Herman and Chomsky, it is not only the political elite that influences media production. They go further to claim that the media 'serve, and propagandize on behalf of, the powerful societal interests that control and finance them' (Herman and Chomsky, 1988: xi). Their model aims to trace 'the route by which money and power are able to filter out the news fit to print, marginalize dissent and allow the government and dominant private interests to get their messages across to the public' (Herman and Chomsky, 1988: 2). In our discussion on unanimous elite discourse, we focus on the links between political elites and the media. Herman and Chomsky, on the other hand, focus on underlying economic power structures.

This entire section on media and its role in reproducing and aligning to enemy images must be read against the backdrop of homogeneous media ecosystems with clear relationships between media producers and consumers. In an age of social and digital media, these borders are increasingly blurred, a topic we will return to at the end of this chapter.

Civil society

Ideally, self-organized civil society organizations are supposed to work in the interest of citizens, or different segments of citizens, operating outside of the governmental and the for-profit sector. Civil society includes labour unions, non-profit organizations, service agencies, and religious congregations except state churches (as discussed above). When working in the interest of citizens, some of them safeguard their interests in relation to employers, the state, and industry. Specifically, they monitor government policies and hold governments accountable.

In the case of weak states and conflict-ridden societies, they deliver social and other services to the poor and underserved, working for reconciliation. Some organizations defend human rights, work to change social norms, and act as an important source of information (Cooper, 2018: 2).

Civil society organizations play such an important role in society, enjoying a high level of trust, that they might also have the resources to make them an influential elite category. State actors therefore need to influence and even control them, making them contribute to a coordinated enemy image.

In the increasingly dictatorial Russia, it is hard to find a truly independent civil society. In dictatorships, civil society is seen as a nuisance, even an adversary. Through a variety of repressive measures enacted several years ago, the Russian regime began tightening its grip on civil society (Berls, 2021). And now, Russian trade unions, for instance, have to publicly support the invasion and endorse the pro-war rhetoric. And the current situation in Russia is not unique. In Nazi Germany, for example, the term 'Gleichschaltung' referred to the consolidation of institutional power and the total subordination of civil society to the dictatorship's agenda.

If political regimes control civil society too tightly, it ceases to be a genuine civil society and might also lose some of the trust people have in it. Its opinion-forming impact is weakened. In that case, the political elite could try to mask its pressure on civil society organizations, to make messages emanating from such organizations appear as genuine and stemming from an independent source. This masking process is sometimes called 'astroturfing'. Astroturf is a type of fake grass, and astroturfing is making a state-controlled organization appear to be part of an independent grassroots movement (Taillard and Giscoppa, 2013: 24).

Business sector

Another category of actors influencing norms and values in society is the business sector. These for-profit actors are often understood to represent their financial self-interests, and this might reduce their credibility and impact. Therefore, they often unite with think tanks led by skilled people who, like the intelligentsia, provide their arguments with more credibility.

It is reasonable to suppose that the business community, in times of international conflict, will reproduce enemy images for at least two reasons. Firstly, the business community needs to create favourable conditions for its commercial activities. Taking an anti-government position would probably not benefit business, particularly if it concerns vital issues like international conflict. Russia's President Putin has also been fairly successful in this respect, managing to turn the most important representatives of the Russian business sector, sometimes called the oligarchs, into close allies. Many of them got wealthy through corruption and contacts with Putin and owe their wealth to him (Markus, 2022). With a few exceptions (Gilchrist, 2022), they have sided with Putin in the war.

The business sector might also be inclined to reproduce enemy images for other reasons. During a conflict, people representing the enemy probably have low status. 'They' are probably despised. In their research on television commercials, Robert M. Entman and Andrew Rojecki saw a trend that

> Blacks attain less visibility than Whites in ads for luxury products like vacations: in other words, those where advertisers are selling myths and promising fulfilment of especially vague needs.
>
> *(Entman and Rojecki, 2000: 10)*

Sternberg and Sternberg discuss this analysis and conclude that 'certain high-status products like cars or perfume are rarely advertised with Black actors at all' (Sternberg and Sternberg, 2008: 160). What we are trying to say is that in pursuit of making money and avoiding marketing failures, companies launching large marketing campaigns tend to avoid creating controversial ads and commercials. During a violent conflict, it is unlikely that people representing the enemy would be used in commercials as representatives of the company and its products since they would probably not enhance the attractiveness of the products and the company producing them. This does not mean that this elite would explicitly and intentionally produce enemy images in commercials. Still, there is a risk that they confirm them implicitly. A recent event illustrates this. The Danish multinational producer of dairy products, Arla, has for years produced and sold kefir, a fermented milk drink, on the Swedish market. For a long time, the cardboard package was adorned with a stylized image of a typical Russian church with onion-shaped domes. In 2022, production was temporarily stopped because of the Russian invasion of Ukraine, and later, when the product was reintroduced, the cardboard package appeared without the Russian dome (Flores, 2022).

Entertainment industry

We previously argued that successful propaganda states try to control more or less all aspects of children's lives. This is also true for adults. It is therefore no surprise that the entertainment industry, which provides diversion and amusement in adults' leisure time, is also involved in (re)producing enemy images. Political humour has been used as a persuasive instrument since long before entertainment became a part of the modern economy and industrialized means of production. Jesters and jokers were not commonly instruments of those with political power. Often, people in power feared them. In Chapter 7, we will discuss the expression of enemy images in various media over time more closely. The examples provided here relate to the discussion of the entertainment industry as part of controlled elite discourses.

The modern entertainment industry emerged around 1900 with the development of motion pictures. The rapid development of the entertainment industry could be seen as the combined effect first of rising productivity, giving most people more leisure time, and creating a demand for entertainment. And secondly, the technological development within the entertainment industry has been remarkable, from the very first motion pictures, television, videocassette recorders, computer games, and so on. This industry is still growing very fast and makes up a fairly large part of the economy (Bakker, 2003).

The entertainment industry is important not only economically, but also in forming a population's identity, ideology, and values. Different political actors have tried either to use or control it. One could say that what is produced within this industry reflects both financial interests of the producers and political needs (Berny, 2020: 27). During the Second World War and then in the Cold War, the film-making industry in particular was seen as a potential weapon to be used for the benefit of the war effort and as a powerful tool in need of control (Cramer Brownell and Raymond, 2020).

In a few cases, things can go in the other direction, with the film industry producing enemy images that are not in line with the public foreign policy. For instance, both the United States and Sweden were neutral during the Second World War (in the American case, until December 1941). In these two cases, as the states tried to remain neutral, their governments had no interest in producing enemy images that might provoke Germany. But at least some parts of the entertainment industry produced provocative, and politically unwanted, enemy images. In the United States, there was a fear, particularly among American isolationists in the Senate, that the American film industry, allegedly controlled by war-mongering foreigners, was producing enemy images of the Germans that would compromise American neutrality in the Second World War and provoke Germany (Cramer Brownell, 2014: 42). Senator Nye (R-ND) was alarmed, and according to Cramer Brownell,

> by using glamorous actors and the allure of entertainment, Jewish studio executives had 'insidiously' coerced audiences into supporting military involvement in the war abroad.
>
> *(Cramer Brownell, 2014: 42)*

This all changed after the Pearl Harbor Attack. It was then that the film industry was identified as an asset to enhance patriotism and morale. Hollywood was now cooperating with the Office of War Information (OWI) and the Department of the Treasury (Cramer Brownell, 2014: 44). With some speed, the film industry was fully integrated into the war effort (Cramer Brownell, 2014: 54).

> The motion picture emerged as a powerful weapon of war as it helped to mobilize civilians on the home front, taught proper wartime behavior, motivated troops, attacked enemies with 'black propaganda,' and dramatized to others around the world the intense ideological and military struggles that entangled the United States and its allies.
>
> *(Cramer Brownell, 2014: 44)*

During the Second World War, particularly after December 1941, numerous war-related films were produced. Three of the most memorable and important American films contributing to the war effort were *The Great Dictator* (1940), *Waterloo Bridge* (1940), and *Casablanca* (1942). Even the cartoon industry and Donald Duck were 'participating in propaganda intended to inspire patriotism and motivation to defend one's nation against a threat' (Taillard and Giscoppa, 2013: 6). The film *Der Fuehrer's Face* (1943) features a German Donald Duck in a nightmare factory in Nazi Germany where he is working diligently as an arms manufacturer on an assembly line and being increasingly abused to produce more quickly, constantly saluting Hitler, until it is all shown to be a bad dream (Taillard and Giscoppa, 2013: 21).

The cooperation between Hollywood and the Federal government did not stop after the Second World War but continued into the Cold War.

> During the early years of the Cold War in America the language and the views of anticommunism filled the American media, affecting not just the news but Hollywood as well, censoring scenes, actors, and shows that might be labelled 'pink' or 'red'.
>
> *(Rutherford, 2004: 187)*

Also more recently, in the 1980s, there has been a close cooperation between the Pentagon and Hollywood:

> The Pentagon's Film Liaison Unit wanted Hollywood's help with recruitment and personnel retention and to justify America's involvement in conflicts around the globe. The Pentagon provides advisors, locations and weaponry in exchange for positive portrayals of soldiers and their motivations. The 1986 film Top Gun (directed by Tony Scott) was so successful in glorifying military training that recruitment centres were set up in theatre lobbies.
>
> *(Soules, 2015: 134)*

Soules also says that Pentagon threatened to withdraw financial support unless the films 'justify military operations and the actions of soldiers' (Soules, 2015: 134). A few remarks need to be made here. First, the United States is not the only country whose government tries to exercise some level of pressure on the entertainment industry: that is also true of other democracies. And of course this is a core strategy in every totalitarian society, from the Soviet Union, the Soviet Bloc during the Cold War, and Nazi Germany to present-day communist China. On the Soviet side, films like *Mashenka* (1942) and *Two Soldiers* (1943) are worth noting. In Nazi Germany, films within various genres were produced to strengthen morale. Here we find documentaries like *Feldzug in Polen* (The Campaign in Poland, 1940), *Jud Süß* (Süss the Jew, 1940), and historical films like *Das Herz der Königin* (The Heart of a Queen, 1940).

The model described above (Elite consensus strategy, Figure 3.4) portrays the traditional and homogeneous propaganda machinery in *modern* society well. But things change, particularly after the advent of new Information and Communication Technology (ICT) and social media. In the model above, elites, who had access to financial resources, time, and labour, dominated (Bahar, 2020: 36). Now, when all that is required is time, relevant language skills, a computer, a camera, a stable internet connection, and a potentially receptive audience, propaganda, and other messages are disseminated in new ways. Since the production and dissemination of propaganda have changed drastically, the model above needs modification. The production and dissemination of messages, including enemy images, have changed in a few – fundamental – ways. Firstly, the optimist would say this new situation has democratized the production and dissemination of messages. We see new producers, sometimes called influencers, who, without major financial resources, develop an immense impact on media audiences. Secondly, 'propaganda can no longer be viewed as a traditional top-down process alone' (Wanless and Berk, 2020: 86). Back in 1965, long before the advent of social media, Jacques Ellul realized that propaganda could be made by inside groups (i.e. not from the top) and stem from their participants (Ellul, [1965] 1973: 81). Now, with the internet and social media, his ideas have acquired a renewed relevance. And thirdly, 'the traditional and established boundary between producers and consumers of propagandistic content no longer seems to be clearly delineated' (Wanless and Berk, 2020: 85). This means that in practice, the target of propaganda messages is no longer a passive recipient but also a partaker/consumer and creator/producer ('prosumer') in 'hypermedia environments', uniting a dynamic between online and offline presence (Önnerfors, 2021: 178–193). This qualitatively new phenomenon in propaganda studies is sometimes called 'participatory propaganda'(Wanless and Berk, 2020: 86) and implies that the traditional targets of propaganda in comment sections and the like confirm and further horizontally disperse the message in their social media networks. This kind of participation in propaganda 'significantly increases its reach and potential influence' (Wanless and Berk, 2020: 92).

> Participatory propaganda moves beyond a traditional, unidirectional 'one-to-many' form of communication, to a 'one-to-many-to-many more' form where each 'target' of influence (an individual or group which is the object of persuasion) can in theory become the new 'originator' (subject) of content production and distribution, spreading persuasive messaging to others in a 'snowball' effect.
>
> *(Wanless and Berk, 2020: 92)*

When messages are embraced by receivers, there is a chance that their impact will be manifold since receivers will not merely receive the propaganda, but comment on it in a confirmatory way, redesigning and redistributing it. On the other hand, this system also means that political leaders (can) no longer control all parts of the propaganda machinery. If propaganda is not well received, negative comments and ridicule can cause serious backlashes.

Lastly, the character of social media and the internet has turned it into a very important battlefield for military powers with different agendas. Major military powers try both to control social media platforms and exert influence within them (Chen, Chen, and Xia, 2022). Social media can be identified by some national actors as a national security threat (Chen, Chen, and Xia, 2022: 13). Even in a hegemonically controlled media environment such as Russia during the war against Ukraine, the new realities of digital media production and consumption must be considered. Outside the strictly Kremlin-controlled media outlets, war bloggers have challenged the hegemony of the informational space through several social media outlets such as Telegram channels and on the Russian Facebook equivalent, 'VKontakte'. While the older segments of society are shaped by news disseminated through heavily state-controlled propaganda on television and radio, younger generations have resorted to other channels, potentially located outside the discursive hegemony. It is possible that situations like these imply the empowerment of certain segments of media consumers. This occasioned President Putin to meet a wide range of war correspondents from both establishment and non-establishment (social) media in an attempt to regain control (President of Russia, 2023).

Summary

In this chapter, we have discussed the different ways of making enemy images persuasive. A central factor regarding cognition is the motivation and ability to assess messages, as explained by the ELM. Shortcuts in cognition impact the persuasiveness of enemy images. This happens frequently in combination with a biased perception of the senders and an apparent preference for the more attractive ones.

Persuasive messages are directed to appeal to the emotions and needs of the receivers/audiences, using the elements of credibility, consistency, and simplicity to project an enemy image. Their goal is to result in the use of mental shortcuts, which leads to less motivation and cognitive ability to critically assess the rhetoric. As described, propaganda machinery needs an environment of persuasion which includes the media and does not leave room for opposing opinions. Therefore, there must be a sort of harmony between the enemy images that appear in the public and those that appear in the private sphere. Also, the policies need to be consistent with enemy images, just as the elite discourse must be consensual. The supposedly independent institutions in a democracy, such as the 'intelligentsia', the entertainment industry, and the mass media, should be aligned with the dominant narrative – the enemy image – to be part of an efficient propaganda machinery. As mentioned, there have been changes in recent decades involving the emergence of the internet and the rise of social media, which influences communication in society. In the past, the elites with financial and other resources had the most influence. Nowadays the field has opened up for anyone with the relevant skills. This could be seen as democratization. And as communication has opened up and become accessible to almost everyone, propaganda does not exist as a process that only starts at the top anymore. This means that the traditional boundaries between producers and consumers of propagandistic content now seem to be less clear.

Study questions

- 'Words can be like tiny doses of arsenic': reflect on this famous Klemperer quote and see if you can find good examples for the shift of rhetoric enabling enemy images.
- Why do you think human beings prefer to process information quickly and intuitively rather than slowly and reflectively (ELM)?
- Studies suggest that messages such as enemy images are more readily accepted when they are presented by an attractive messenger. Discuss some examples of this.
- Construct an argument rationalizing violence by appealing to emotions and that is simple, credible, consistent, and addresses human needs.

Potential essay or thesis suggestion

Based on the reasoning presented in this chapter, create an analytical framework to help you analyse strategies for making enemy images persuasive. Then select a conflict you are familiar with and the source material for which you can read in the original language. Choose the data you need to carry out your study. Analyse that data and reveal the strategies used to make the enemy image persuasive.

Recommended further reading

Chick, K. (2020) Crossing Enemy Lines in Ken Loach's Ae Fond Kiss/Just a Kiss: Representing Muslims and New Ethnicities in the Shadow of 9/11. In Maillet, J. and Dudouyt, C. (eds.) *Creating the Enemy, Angles, New Perspectives on the Anglophone World* (Volume 10, pp. 1–23). https://doi.org/10.4000/angles.428
In this article, Kristine Chick convincingly argues that Western films have since the very beginning depicted Muslims negatively and inferior. She evaluates the influence of media on the public's perceptions and understanding of Muslims.

Klemperer, V. ([1947] 2000) *The Language of the Third Reich*. London, New York, NY: Continuum.
Victor Klemperer's book is a classic for understanding how the use of words, concepts, and terms frames the perceptions of audiences under totalitarian conditions. It demonstrates how shifts in meaning are constructed to entice and influence audiences, and how deep these manipulations run at the population level.

Lean, N. (2017) *The Islamophobia Industry, How the Right Manufactures Hatred of Muslims*, 2nd ed. London: Pluto Press.

Nathan Lean's book is a must-read book for those who want to understand how different actors, mainly on the right, create enemy images of Muslims. Lean's arguments are in many respects in accordance with those in this chapter when he describes Islamophobia as 'the product of a tight-knit and interconnected confederation of right-wing fear merchants' (Lean, 2017: 14).

Perloff, R. M. (2003) *The Dynamics of Persuasion, Communication and Attitudes in the 21st century*, 2nd ed. Mahwah, NJ: Lawrence Erlbaum Associates Publishers.
In this book, Richard M. Perloff not only offers a good overview of theories explaining persuasion but also provides greater skills in resisting unwanted attempts at influence, giving deeper insight into persuasion as it occurs in twenty-first-century society.

Rutherford, P. (2004) *Weapons of Mass Persuasion, Marketing the War against Iraq.* Toronto: University of Toronto Press.
In this important book, Paul Rutherford analyses the marketing campaign for the war against Iraq, how it was constructed and carried out. He covers speeches, editorial cartoons, media political commentary, and events such as the bombing of Baghdad and the toppling of Saddam Hussein's statue.

Note

1   The term intelligentsia entered the Russian language in the 1860s (Malia, 1960: 441). In this book, it refers to an educated elite which thinks independently and critically (cf. Malia, 1960: 442) and possesses cultural and political influence.

Bibliography

Alderfer, C. P. (1969) An empirical test of a new theory of human needs. *Organizational Behavior & Human Performance* 4(2): 142–175. https://doi.org/10.1016/0030-5073(69)90004-X

Bahar, H. (2020) Social media and disinformation in war propaganda: How Afghan government and the Taliban use Twitter. *Media Asia* 47(1–2): 34–46. https://doi.org/10.1080/01296612.2020.1822634

Bakker, G. (2003) Entertainment industrialized: The emergence of the International Film Industry, 1890—1940. *Enterprise & Society* 4(4): 579–585. www.jstor.org/stable/23700093

Balzacq, T. (2011) A Theory of Securitization, Origins, Core Assumptions, and Variants. In Balzacq, T. (ed.) *Securitization Theory, How Security Problems Emerge and Dissolve* (pp. 1–30). London, New York, NY: Routledge.

Barbeau, A. E. (2016) Christian empire and national crusade: The rhetoric of Anglican Clergy in the First World War. *Anglican and Episcopal History* 85(1): 24–62. www.jstor.org/stable/43973280

Bergmann, E. (2021) The Eurabia conspiracy. In Önnerfors, A. and Krouwel, A. (eds.) *Europe: Continent of Conspiracies. Conspiracy Theories in and about Europe* (pp. 36–53). London: Routledge.

Berls, R. (2021) Civil Society in Russia: Its Role under an Authoritarian Regime, Part I: The Nature of Russian Civil Society. The Nuclear Threat Initiative. www.nti.org/analysis/articles/civil-society-russia-its-role-under-authoritarian-regime-part-i-nature-russian-civil-society/, accessed 8 November 2022.

Berny, M. (2020) The Hollywood Indian Stereotype: The Cinematic Othering and Assimilation of Native Americans at the Turn of the 20th Century. In Maillet, J. and Dudouyt, C. (eds.) *Creating the Enemy, Angles, New Perspectives on the Anglophone World* (Issue 10, pp. 1–25). https://journals.openedition.org/angles/279

Bontrager, S. (2002) The imagined crusade: The Church of England and the mythology of nationalism and Christianity during the great war. *Church History* 71(4): 774–798. www.jstor.org/stable/4146192

Braddock, K. (2020) *Weaponized Words: The Strategic Role of Persuasion in Violent Radicalization and Counter-Radicalization.* Cambridge: Cambridge University Press.

Budesheim, T. and DePaola, S. (1994) Beauty or the beast? The effects of appearance, personality, and issue information of evaluation of political candidates. *Personality and Social Psychology Bulletin* 20(4): 339–348. https://doi.org/10.1177/0146167294204001

Chaiken, S. (1979) Communicator physical attractiveness and persuasion. *Journal of Personality and Social Psychology* 37(8): 1387–1397. https://doi.org/10.1037/0022-3514.37.8.1387

Chen, L., Chen, J. and Xia, C. (2022) Social network behavior and public opinion manipulation. *Journal of Information Security and Applications* 64: 1–15. https://doi.org/10.1016/j.jisa.2021.103060

Chomsky, N. (1997) What makes Mainstream Media Mainstream. *Z Magazine.* https://chomsky.info/199710__/

Chomsky, N. (2012) *Making the Future: Occupations, Interventions, Empire and Resistance.* San Francisco, CA: Open Media Series, City Light Books.

Cooper, R. (2018) What is Civil Society? How is the term used and what is seen to be its role and value (internationally) in 2018? K4D Helpdesk Report. Brighton: Institute of Development Studies. www.gov.uk/research-for-development-outputs/what-is-civil-society-its-role-and-value-in-2018

Corner, J. (2003) The model in question: A response to Klaehn on Herman and Chomsky. *European Journal of Communication* 18(3): 367–375. https://doi.org/10.1177/026732 31030183004

Cramer Brownell, K. (2014) *Showbiz Politics: Hollywood in American Political Life.* Chapel Hill, NC: University of North Carolina Press. www.jstor.org/stable/10.5149/978 1469617923_brownell

Cramer Brownell, K. and Raymond, E. (2020) Hollywood and Politics. In *Oxford Bibliographies; Cinema and Media Studies.* New York, NY: Oxford University Press http://doi.org/10.1093/obo/9780199791286-0195

Ellul, J. ([1965] 1973) *Propaganda: The Formation of Men's Attitudes.* New York, NY: Vintage Books.

Elwert, W. T. (1980) Klemperer, Viktor. In: *Neue Deutsche Biographie* 12 (1980), p. 35. www.deutsche-biographie.de/pnd11856319X.html, accessed 30 June 2023.

Entman, R. and Rojecki, A. (2000) *Black Image in the White Mind Media and Race in America.* Chicago, IL: University of Chicago Press.

Festinger, L. (1957) *A Theory of Cognitive Dissonance.* Stanford, CA: Stanford University Press.

Festinger, L. and Maccoby, N. (1964) On resistance to persuasive communications. *Journal of Abnormal and Social Psychology* 68(4): 359–366. https://doi.org/10.1037/h0049073

Flores, J. (2022, March 21) Hornbach bojkottar sibirisk lärk – Arla slutar sälja Kefir. [Hornbach boycotts Siberian larch – Arla stops selling Kefir] *Dagens Nyheter.* www.dn.se/ekonomi/arla-slutar-salja-kefir-uppfattas-som-opassande/, accessed 8 November 2022.

Foucault, M. ([1976] 2007) The Meshes of Power. In Elden S. and Crampton J. (eds.) *Space, Knowledge and Power: Foucault and Geography* (pp.153–162). London: Routledge. https://doi.org/10.4324/9781315610146

Gilchrist, K. (2022, March 2) War can never be the answer: Russia's wealthy elite speak out against Putin's invasion. CNBC. www.cnbc.com/2022/03/02/russias-oligarch-elite-speak-out-against-putins-invasion-of-ukraine.html, accessed 8 November 2022.

Greenwald, A. (1968) Cognitive Learning, Cognitive Response to Persuasion, and Attitude Change. *Psychological Foundations of Attitudes*. New York, NY: Academic Press Inc.

Habermas, J. (1962] 1989) *The Structural Transformation of the Public Sphere: An Inquiry into a Category of Bourgeois Society*. Cambridge: Polity Press.

Hallahan, K., Holtzhausen, D., van Ruler, B., Verčič, D. and Sriramesh, K. (2007) Defining strategic communication. *International Journal of Strategic Communication* 1(1): 3–35.

Herman, E. (2000) The Propaganda Model: A retrospective. *Journalism Studies* 1(1): 101–112. http://doi.org/10.1080/146167000361195

Herman, E. and Chomsky, N. (1988) *Manufacturing Consent: The Political Economy of the Mass Media*. New York, NY: Pantheon Books.

Hettne, B., Sörlin, S. and Østergård, U. (1998) *Den globala nationalismen, Nationalstatens historia och framtid* [Global Nationalism, the History and Future of the Nation-State]. Stockholm: SNS Förlag.

Jenkins, P. (2014) *The Great and Holy War: How World War I Became a Religious Crusade*. San Francisco, CA: HarperOne.

Jenkins, P. (2024) White supremacy. *Britannica Online*. www.britannica.com/topic/white-supremacy, accessed 11 February 2024.

Jost, J. (2019) A quarter century of system justification theory: Questions, answers, criticisms, and societal applications. *British Journal of Social Psychology* 58(2): 263–314. https://doi.org/10.1111/bjso.12297

Jowett, G. and O'Donnell, V. (2015) *Propaganda and Persuasion*. Los Angeles, CA: SAGE.

Killen, M., Lee-Kim, J., McGlothlin, H. and Stangor, C. (2002) How children and adolescents evaluate gender and racial exclusion. *Monographs of the Society for Research in Child Development* 67(4): vii–vii. https://doi.org/10.1111/1540-5834.00218

Killen, M., Richardson, C. and Kelly, M. (2010) Developmental Perspectives. In Dovidio, J., Hewstone, M., Glick, P. and Esses, V. M. (eds.) *The SAGE Handbook of Prejudice, Stereotyping and Discrimination* (pp. 97–114). SAGE Publications Ltd. https://dx.doi.org/10.4135/9781446200919

Klaehn, J. (2003) Behind the invisible curtain of scholarly criticism: Revisiting the propaganda model. *Journalism Studies* 4(3): 359–369. https://doi.org/10.1080/1461670 0306487

Klemperer, V. (2000) *The Language of the Third Reich*. London, New York, NY: Continuum, 1947.

Knightley, P. (1975) *The First Casualty: The War Correspondent as Hero, Propagandist and Myth Maker from the Crimea to Vietnam*. London: André Deutsch.

Krasny, R. (2022, March 12) *Russian Official Warns Finland, Sweden Against Joining NATO*. Bloomberg. www.bloomberg.com/news/articles/2022-03-12/russian-official-warns-finland-sweden-against-joining-nato, accessed 8 November 2022.

Lasswell, H. (1927) *Propaganda Technique in World War I*. Cambridge, MA: MIT Press.

Lenin, V. (1920, November 3) Speech Delivered at an All-Russia Conference Of Political Education Workers of Gubernia and Uyezd Education Departments. Lenin's Collected

Works (4th ed.) Progress Publishers, Moscow, 1965. 31: 340–361. www.marxists.org/archive/lenin/works/1920/nov/03.htm

Lindberg, S. and Wennman, M. (2023, June 11) Här dumpas H&M-kläderna du "återvinner", Så håller kläderna vi köper på att skapa en miljökatastrof på andra sidan jorden. *Aftonbladet.* www.aftonbladet.se/nyheter/a/O8PAyb/har-dumpas-h-m-kladerna-du-ate rvinner, accessed 12 February 2024.

Luostarinen, H. (1989) Finnish Russophobia: The story of an enemy image. *Journal of Peace Research* 26(2): 123–137. www.jstor.org/stable/423864

Malia, M. (1960) What is the intelligentsia? *Daedalus* 89(3): 441–458. www.jstor.org/sta ble/20026591

Markus, S. (2022, March 4) Meet Russia's oligarchs, a group of men who won't be toppling Putin anytime soon. *The Conversation.* https://theconversation.com/meet-russias-oligar chs-a-group-of-men-who-wont-be-toppling-putin-anytime-soon-178474, accessed 8 November 2022.

Marrin, A. (1974) *The Last Crusade: The Church of England in the First World War.* Durham, NC: Duke University Press.

Maslow, A. (1943) A theory of human motivation. *Psychological Review* 50(4): 370–396. http://doi.org/10.1037/h0054346

McClelland, D. C. and Boyatzis, R. E (1982) Leadership, motive pattern and long-term success in management. *Journal of Applied Psychology* 67(6): 737–743.

McClelland, D. C. and Burnham, D. H. (1976) Power is the great motivator. *Harvard Business Review* (March–April): 100–110.

McGuire, W. (1961) Resistance to persuasion conferred by active and passive prior refutation of same and alternative counterarguments. *Journal of Abnormal Psychology* 63(2): 326–332. https://doi.org/10.1037/h0048344

Meyer-Rewerts, U. G. and Stöckmann, H. (2010) "Das "Manifest der 93": Ausdruck oder Negation der Zivilgesellschaft?. In Klatt, J. and Lorenz, R. (eds.) *Manifeste: Geschichte und Gegenwart des politischen Appells* (pp. 113–1349). Bielefeld: transcript Verlag, 2010. https://doi.org/10.1515/transcript.9783839416792.113

Moffitt, B. (2016) *The Global Rise of Populism. Performance, Political Style and Representation.* Stanford, CA: Stanford University Press. https://doi.org/10.2307/j.ctvqsdsd8

Moses, J. (1999) Justifying war as the will of God: German theology on the eve of the First World War. *Colloquium* 31(1): 3–20.

Önnerfors, A. (2021) Researching Right-Wing Hypermedia Environments: A Case-Study of the German Online Platform einprozent.de. In Asche S., Busher J., Macklin G. and Winter A. (eds.) *Researching the Far Right: Theory, Method and Practice* (pp. 178–194). Routledge Studies in Fascism and the Far Right. London: Routledge. https://doi.org/10.4324/9781315304670

Önnerfors, A. (2024) *Konspirationsteorier – meningsskapande berättelser i historia och nutid.* Lund: Nordic Academic Press.

Oppenheimer, L. (2006) The development of enemy images: A theoretical contribution. *Peace and Conflict: Journal of Peace Psychology* 12(3): 269–292. https://doi.org/10.1207/s15327949pac1203_4

Ozanne, M., Liu, S. and Mattila, A. (2019) Are attractive reviewers more persuasive? Examining the role of physical attractiveness in online reviews. *Journal of Consumer Marketing* 36(6): 728–739. https://doi.org/10.1108/JCM-02-2017-2096

Perloff, R. (2003) *The Dynamics of Persuasion: Communication and Attitudes in the 21st Century* (2nd ed.). Mahwah, NJ: Lawrence Erlbaum Associates, Publishers.

Petersson, B. (2006) *Stereotypes about Strangers, Swedish Media Constructions of Socio-Cultural Risk.* Lanham, MD: University Press of America.

Petty, R. and Briñol, P. (2012) The Elaboration Likelihood Model. In van Lange, P., Kruglanski, A. and Higgins, E. (eds.) *Handbook of theories of social psychology: volume 1* (pp. 224–245). SAGE Publications Ltd. https://dx.doi.org/10.4135/9781446249 215.n12

Petty, R. and Cacioppo, J. (1986) The elaboration likelihood model of persuasion. *Advances in Experimental Social Psychology.* 19: 123–205. https://doi.org/10.1016/S0065-2601(08)60214-2

Petty, R. E., Cacioppo, J. T. and Goldman, R. (1981) Personal involvement as a determinant of argument-based persuasion. *Journal of Personality and Social Psychology* 41(5): 847–855. https://doi.org/10.1037/0022-3514.41.5.847

President of Russia (2023) "Meeting with war correspondents", Website President of Russia, 13 June 2023. http://en.kremlin.ru/events/president/news/71391, accessed 8 November 2022.

Public law 107–243 (2002, October 16) Authorization for Use of Military Force against Iraq, Resolution of 2002. www.govinfo.gov/content/pkg/PLAW-107publ243/pdf/PLAW-107 publ243.pdf

Putin, V. (2022, February 24) Address by the President of the Russian Federation. http://en.kremlin.ru/events/president/news/67843, accessed 8 November 2022.

Reporters without Borders (2022, March 5) War in Ukraine: Putin delivers the final blow to Russia's independent media. https://rsf.org/en/news/war-ukraine-putin-delivers-final-blow-russias-independent-media, accessed 8 November 2022.

Reyes, A. (2011) Strategies of legitimization in political discourse: From words to actions. *Discourse & Society* 22(6): 781–807. https://doi.org/10.1177/0957926511419927

Royal, S. (2011) Fear, rhetoric, and the "Other". *Race/Ethnicity: Multidisciplinary Global Contexts* 4(3): 405–418. https://doi.org/10.2979/racethmulglocon.4.3.405

Rutherford, P. (2004) *Weapons of Mass Persuasion, Marketing the War against Iraq.* Toronto: University of Toronto Press.

Schröder-Pfeifer, P., Talia, A., Volkert, J. and Taubner, S. Developing an assessment of epistemic trust: A research protocol. *Research in Psychotherapy: Psychopathology, Process and Outcome*, 21(3): 123–131. https://doi:10.4081/ripppo.2018.330

Singer, M. (2003) *Cults in Our Midst: The Continuing Fight against Their Hidden Menace* (Rev Upd Su ed.). San Francisco, CA: Jossey-Bass.

Smith, P. (2022, March 8) Russia's Patriarch Kirill defends invasion of Ukraine, stoking Orthodox tensions. *National Catholic Reporter.* www.ncronline.org/news/people/russias-patriarch-kirill-defends-invasion-ukraine-stoking-orthodox-tensions, accessed 8 November 2022.

Soules, M. (2015) *Media, Persuasion and Propaganda.* Edinburgh: Edinburgh University Press.

Steiner, K. and Lundberg, A. (2018) Loving Violent Arabs: A Study of Radicalism Within the Israeli Messianic Movement. In Önnerfors, A. and Steiner, K. (eds.) *Expressions of Radicalization: Global Politics, Processes and Practices* (pp. 147–180). London: Palgrave Macmillan. https://doi.org/10.1007/978-3-319-65566-6_6

Sternberg, R. and Sternberg, K. (2008) *The Nature of Hate.* Cambridge: Cambridge University Press.

Taillard, M. and Giscoppa, H. (2013) *Psychology and Modern Warfare, Idea Management in Conflict and Competition*. New York, NY: Palgrave Macmillan.

Taylor, P. (1992) *War and the Media, Propaganda and Persuasion in the Gulf War*. Manchester: Manchester University Press.

The Moscow Times (2022) Russian intellectuals call on Kremlin to end Ukraine invasion threats. *The Moscow Times*, 2 February. www.themoscowtimes.com/2022/02/02/russian-intellectuals-call-on-kremlin-to-end-ukraine-invasion-threats-a76221, accessed 8 November 2022.

Tormala, Z. (2008) A New Framework for Resistance to Persuasion. The Resistance Appraisals Hypothesis. In Crano, W. and Prislin, R. (eds.) *Attitudes and Attitude Change* (pp. 213–234). New York, NY: Psychology Press. https://doi.org/10.4324/9780203838068

Tymoczko, T. and Henle, J. (2000) *Sweet Reason: A Field Guide to Modern Logic*. New York, NY: Springer-Verlag.

van Dijk, T. (1993) *Elite Discourse and Racism*. Newbury Park, CA: Sage Publications.

Wanless, A. and Berk, M. (2020) The Audience Is the Amplifier: Participatory Propaganda. In Baines, P., O'Shaughnessy, N. and Snow, N. (eds.) *The SAGE Handbook of Propaganda*. (pp. 85–104). Newbury Park, CA: Sage Publications Ltd. https://dx.doi.org/10.4135/9781526477170

Welch, D. (2003) Propaganda. In Nicholas, J. C., Cullbert, D. and Welch, D. (eds.) *Propaganda and Mass Persuasion. A Historical Encyclopaedia, 1500 to the Present*. Santa Barbara, CA: ABC Clio.

Wodak, R. (2015) *The Politics of Fear: What Right-Wing Discourses Mean*. London: Sage.

Ziemer, C. and Rothmund, T. (2024) Psychological Underpinnings of Disinformation Countermeasures: A Systematic Scoping Review. *Journal of Media Psychology* https://doi.org/10.1027/1864-1105/a000407

4

WHY ARE ENEMY IMAGES ACCEPTED?

Individual and structural factors

CHAPTER OBJECTIVES

- To offer an overview of theories that allow readers to understand why enemy images are accepted
- To introduce theories explaining why some individuals more readily accept enemy images than others
- To introduce theories explaining why enemy images seem to spread more rampantly under certain socio-political conditions

Introduction

No one is immune to the impact of enemy images. On the contrary, the acceptance of enemy images is often an effect of normal cognitive and psychological processes. Most people might embrace them given the right circumstances (cf. Allport, 1954). As a rule, people are uncritical of messages describing 'the other' as a threat to 'our' interests. In his book on the First World War, historian Philip Jenkins studied private notes written by soldiers on the battlefields. These indicate that the propaganda had influenced the soldiers:

> Even when they were writing in diaries or journals that were never intended to be read by official eyes, soldiers expressed very standard views about God and country and the virtues and vices of the respective sides. The words of ordinary British soldiers show how many really did believe they were engaged in a war for righteousness's sake, in issues such as the defense of outraged Belgium. German or French soldiers likewise needed little urging to see their war as a

DOI: 10.4324/9781003279570-4

desperate defense of national survival, while the letters of ordinary Russian soldiers regularly asserted their belief in 'Faith, Tsar, and Fatherland,' in that order.

(Jenkins, 2014: 4)

The purpose of this chapter is to give plausible answers to the question of why this is the case, and why people in general, not only soldiers, accept enemy images. We will review and draw from a wealth of literature and approaches within various social science disciplines. We aim to consult relevant literature and come closer to an informed understanding of the acceptance of enemy images. Unlike the previous chapter, which concerned persuasive communicators, messages, and their propaganda machinery – *senders* – this chapter deals with the *recipients* of messages.

Human beings tend to divide fellow humans into those belonging to 'us' and those who do not – 'the other' (see 'othering' Chapter 1). This human tendency is fundamental and has been identified and exploited throughout history. It is already evident in Exodus 34, where Moses (or God) defined how His people, Israel, should live and be different from other nations. Similarly, in ancient Greece, a clear separation was constructed between 'us' and the 'barbarians'. People not only identify with their group but also organize in groups for various tasks. In other words, to belong to and thrive in groups is deeply human.

Since the early nineteenth century, this human tendency has been of academic interest in several disciplines such as sociology, psychology, and social psychology (Cole, 2004: 578). For instance, Gordon Allport underlines in his seminal work *The Nature of Prejudice* (1954) that 'in strict logic, an in-group always implies the existence of some corresponding out-group' (Allport, 1954: 41). Regrettably, it is not just division into 'us' and 'them' that is normal. Being prejudiced against outsiders is also an effect of a normal cognitive process (Allport, 1954: 17).

There is scant research or academic literature specifically on the acceptance of enemy images. But as we know from Chapter 1, enemy images resemble prejudice and stereotypes. Both prejudices and enemy images see the other as inferior in important aspects. Stereotypes and enemy images tend to make strong generalizations, simplified and rigid depictions of the other. What is unique about an enemy image is that it adds *threat*, the sense that the out-group constitutes a threat to 'us' and 'our' vital interests. Research discussing the human tendency to accept prejudices and stereotypes thus provides important input to enhance our understanding of why people accept enemy images.

This chapter is divided into five sections. In the first two, we discuss general human capacities to further our understanding of enemy image acceptance, with the first focusing on human needs and drawing mainly from social psychology and motivational theories, and the second drawing from research on cognition. In the remaining three sections, the variance in the prevalence of enemy images is discussed. We consider how certain societal structures increase the risk of enemy images being accepted (third section), how individuals with certain traits are more likely to accept enemy images (fourth section), and finally whether the need for consolation after violent actions can increase the risk of accepting enemy images (fifth section).

Throughout all these sections, one question will be repeated, almost like a mantra: why do people accept enemy images? The idea is that each section can contribute to the answer, based on its respective theoretical perspective.

Human needs

This section borrows its basic *structure* from the ideas of the American psychologist Abraham Harold Maslow (1908–1970, see Box 4.1). In Chapter 3, we briefly mentioned his theory of the hierarchy of needs, belonging to a large category called motivation theories in which the foundations and drivers of human behaviour are investigated (Cottam et al., 2016: 25). According to Maslow, human needs can be divided into a few categories, from the most basic (physiological) ones to more abstract ones such as self-actualization (see Figure 4.1). Although research has progressed since 1943, when Maslow introduced an early version of this model, and although many aspects of the model have been questioned, it serves the purpose of organizing our discussion in this section, not as its theoretical foundation. This means that we will start the discussion with physiological and safety needs and move up to esteem needs.

A second point of departure in this section is functionalism (Perloff, 2003: 73), also called functional psychology. This school is an outgrowth of Darwinism and focuses on the usefulness of human behaviour, particularly for survival. From

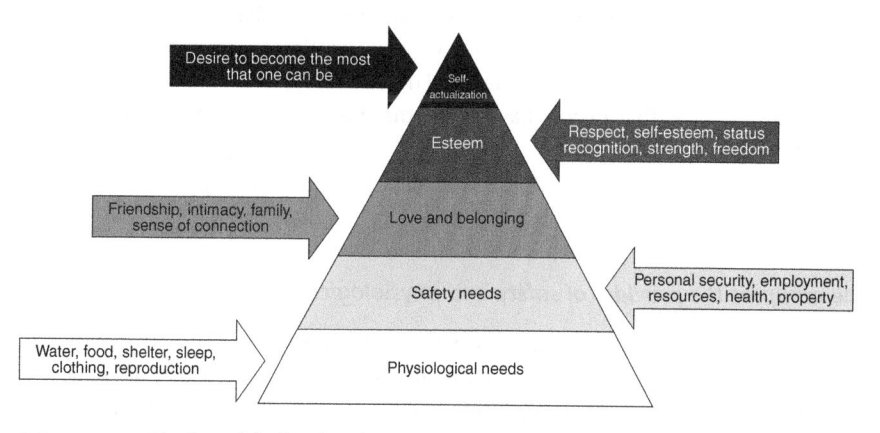

FIGURE 4.1   Abraham Maslow's Hierarchy of Needs.

Source: Adapted by the authors from Maslow (1943).

this point of view, the acceptance of enemy images could be explained due to their function. In Chapters 1 and 2, we discussed their political usefulness for *leaders*, usually political; they legitimize, mobilize, and dehumanize. Here we focus on their usefulness for the *receivers*, and this can explain why people tend to accept them. It seems reasonable to assume that enemy images can have multiple functions for the individual, which can explain why they are accepted (cf. Perloff, 2003: 79).

BOX 4.1   ABRAHAM MASLOW'S HIERARCHY OF NEEDS

Abraham Maslow (1908–1970) was an American psychologist and a psychology professor at Brandeis University, Brooklyn College, the New School for Social Research, and Columbia University. He is the tenth most cited psychologist of the twentieth century (Haggbloom, 2002: 146) and is most famous for creating *Maslow's hierarchy of needs* – the idea, first proposed in 1943, that the needs motivating humans can be organized into a hierarchy ranging from more concrete ones such as food and water to abstract concepts such as self-fulfilment (Maslow, 1943: 370). The five basic categories he proposes are physiological, safety, love, esteem, and self-actualization (see Figure 4.1), and according to this scheme, when a 'lower' need is met, the next one in the hierarchy becomes the focus of attention. Maslow's hierarchy is often portrayed in the shape of a pyramid, with the largest and most fundamental needs at the bottom and the need for self-actualization at the top. Although the ideas behind the hierarchy are Maslow's, the pyramid illustration does not appear anywhere in his original work.

While Maslow presented his needs in a hierarchy, he acknowledged that people do not have to completely satisfy one need for the next need in the hierarchy to emerge. He suggests that, at any given time, most people tend to have each of their needs partially met, and that needs lower on the hierarchy are typically the ones that people have made the most progress towards fulfilling (Maslow, 1943: 388).

The group as the provider of safety and physiological needs

In a physical sense, human beings are vulnerable and easily exposed to external threats such as weather conditions, dangerous animals, or other human adversaries. But humans have an extraordinary intellectual capacity for language, planning, and perspective-taking. Moreover, they have one additional important capacity enhancing their survivability: the capacity to organize in protective groups. And this capacity is indeed important since it is 'the group, not the individual, [that] is the unit of survival' (Frank and Melville, 1988: 199 and cf. Allport, 1954: 46). It is likely that people's physical weakness and vulnerability combined with their intellectual abilities and excellent collaborative and organizational skills make them disposed towards a lifestyle characterized by obligatory interdependence with others (Schaller, Conway, and Peavy, 2010: 84). We have already stated that people belong to numerous different groups and can have different identities. But our starting point here is people's physical weakness and dependence on *safety-providing* groups. Therefore, it is not unreasonable to assume that a group providing physiological and safety needs (see Figure 4.1) will be particularly important to individuals and that they will develop loyalty towards it. It does not automatically follow from this loyalty that enemy images are created. However, it makes sense to explore whether in-group loyalty also can lead to scepticism or even hostility to out-groups that could potentially threaten them and their safety-providing group. The question is therefore whether people's total dependence on their own protective group for their most physiological needs contributes to the acceptance of enemy images. Two arguments will illustrate the plausibility of this assumption.

First, groups usually experience competition for vital resources such as water and food. It is not unreasonable to suppose that negative images are easily created – and eventually also enemy images about groups competing for these resources. This tendency is discussed in greater detail later in this chapter, in the section *Realist group conflict theory and relative deprivation theory*.

Second, the tendency to see out-groups as enemies and to accept enemy images may also have a genetic component. This argument (also prevalent in evolutionary psychology) may seem far-fetched and perhaps even controversial, but it can provide us with a *partial* explanation of our overall question relating to the human tendency to accept enemy images. The American psychologist Mark Schaller and his colleagues have summarized research on the development of prejudice from an evolutionary perspective (Schaller, Conway, and Peavy, 2010). According to them, the development of prejudices can partly be seen as the effect of a 'cultural evolution' in which ideas and beliefs about the 'other' develop and spread and are partly an effect of 'human evolutionary biology' (Schaller, Conway, and Peavy, 2010: 81–82). In the introduction to their discussion of evolutionary biology and the psychology of prejudice, they lay the following meta-theoretical foundation:

Evolutionary inquiry into human psychology assumes that if

a) some specific psychological tendency has some genetic basis, and
b) that psychological tendency, relative to alternative tendencies, promotes reproductive fitness (i.e. the perpetuation of genes into subsequent generations), then
c) that specific psychological tendency (along with its genetic basis) will become increasingly widespread within a population.

(Schaller, Conway, and Peavy, 2010: 83)

A key concept in this reasoning is reproductive fitness. This refers to the ability of an individual to successfully reproduce and pass on their genetic material to the next generation.

At the risk of forming an overly simplified interpretation of this research, one could ask the following questions: all other things being equal, which individuals are more likely to be reproductively fit? Is it individuals who are sceptical of unknown individuals from out-groups and refrain from unnecessary contact with them, or those who are open-minded and have frequent contact with out-groups? The answer is that the first category is likely to have a greater chance of survival, especially in childhood and adolescence. In addition to this, it also seems that people who have 'a desire to form and maintain social bonds [with members of the in-group] would have both survival and reproductive benefits' (Baumeister and Leary, 1995: 499). Through such bonds, the survival of one's offspring increases. Despite a certain amount of biologism (the use of biological explanations for social phenomena) involved in such reasoning, it might be argued that humans have gradually become more sceptical of out-groups and increasingly willing to cooperate within the group.

Before we continue the argument, there may be cause for moderation. Firstly, like Schaller, Conway, and Peavy, we are painting with a broad brush, describing large and complex research in a few words. Secondly, the argument assumes that the psychological tendency to be sceptical of out-groups is not entirely a learned attitude but has a genetic basis established by evolutionary development, which is a controversial claim. Finally, the fact that acceptance of stereotypes and prejudices has some genetic basis should not be understood as implying that people are slaves to or programmed by genetics. On the contrary, they can unlearn conscious prejudice against outsiders through ethically inspired education and socialization (Phelps et al., 2000: 729).

Let us return to the overarching question of this chapter: why do people accept enemy images? Based on the reasoning in this section, there is research suggesting that the combination of people's total dependence on their own protective group for access to scarce and necessary resources (water, shelter, food, protection), combined with natural selection, increasingly enlarges the genetic base of prejudice within a population, making them susceptible to enemy images. Or in other words, the individual's heavy dependence on the group and the genetic base of prejudices could be abused and exploited. Enemy images confirm people's gut feelings that 'they' constitute a threat to 'my' or 'our' safety and most vital needs, and that 'my' group provides safety and physiological safety.

Need for love and belonging

A second important human need is the need for 'love and affection and belongingness' (Maslow, 1943: 380), the need to have place and belongingness in a group and affectionate relations with people in the group (Maslow, 1943: 380). To be accepted by a group is emotionally rewarding for people. This need for belonging has been confirmed by many scholars and is considered a strong motivating factor. It is possible to state that people are not *only* dependent on others for physiological and safety reasons. No, 'we rely on others for support, validation and understanding' (Allen, 2021: 1). It is through the sense of belonging to groups that 'we find much of our meaning, identity, relevance and satisfaction in life' (Allen, 2021: 1). And knowing that one is appreciated, included, and valued 'fosters wellbeing, self-esteem, and confidence' (Buckley, Winkel, and Leary, 2003: 14). Moreover, for these beneficial effects to manifest, people need to stay connected with groups they see as important to them and to maintain bonds with such groups (Baumeister and Leary, 1995: 497). Lastly, if people fail to connect with such groups, they will suffer emotionally and even risk mental and physical illness (Baumeister and Leary, 1995: 511). This idea about the importance of belongingness goes against Sigmund Freud's theories. He regarded sexuality and aggression as major driving psychological forces. The perspective adopted here, by contrast, 'depicts the human being as naturally driven toward establishing and sustaining belongingness' (Baumeister and Leary, 1995: 499) and sees this need as universal regardless of age, gender, class, or culture (Allen, 2021).

What does belonging mean? It is not a quantitative concept, not about having many connections. It is rather a qualitative concept. It is an experience of approval, of fitting in, of being accepted into a group for who one is. If that is the case, people can experience a deep sense of belonging. The ideal sense of belonging assumes that you are approved by a group without adjustments or attempts to try to fit in. You are accepted just as you are (Brown, 2010: 25). Such ideal conditions rarely prevail. People adjust to fit in. One strategy is to imitate (Chartrand and Bargh, 1999) or mimic (Cialdini and Goldstein, 2004: 609) the group. People laugh when others in the group laugh. They follow fashion. They buy things they believe could make them accepted. They try to be helpful and respond affirmatively to requests for help (Cialdini and Goldstein, 2004: 598).

Research indicates that to a great extent groups share prejudice and stereotypes of out-groups (Sechrist and Stangor, 2001: 645). This does not mean that stereotypes of out-groups necessarily are static. They can change, but when they do, they often do so in consensus, i.e. most of 'us' change 'our' attitude towards 'them' (Madon et al., 2001: 1008). An important strategy for obtaining social approval – and this is where enemy image acceptance comes in – is to identify the dominant social norms in a group and adjust to them. By for instance accepting enemy images (or other dominant norms in the group), the individual aspires to 'the social approval of others, to build rewarding relationships with them, and in the process, to enhance their self-esteem' (Cialdini and Goldstein, 2004: 610). This human tendency is probably universal, although some differences across cultures exist (Cialdini and Goldstein, 2004: 610).

A consequence of this emotional dependence on groups and social approval is that people also fear *exclusion* and *rejection*. Exclusion and rejection seem to be even more potent than acceptance (Buckley, Winkel, and Leary, 2003: 26), particularly for children. In fact, 'people who are socially deprived should exhibit a variety of ill effects, such as signs of maladjustment or stress, behavioural or psychological pathology, and possibly health problems' (Baumeister and Leary, 1995: 500). It is hardly surprising, therefore, that solitary confinement and ostracization are considered harsh punishments.

To conclude, research suggests that people need groups for emotional reasons, employing a variety of strategies to ensure inclusion and acceptance in a group and avoid rejection and exclusion. One strategy relevant to a discussion about the acceptance of enemy images is to identify the central norms in a group and adjust to the norms people think the others in the group embrace (Sechrist and Stangor, 2001: 651 and Perloff, 2003: 75). An important kind of norm concerns enemies and threats. Without being aware of it, people might be searching for the answers to the question, 'Whom do we hate, fear, and love in this group?'. The point is that when an enemy image has gained momentum and become the dominant norm in a group, then there is an imminent risk that people will adjust to this norm as a strategy to secure membership of the group (Yzerbyt, 2010: 153–154). And if people question dominant norms in the group, just as August Landmesser did in Figure 4.2, refusing

FIGURE 4.2 August Landmesser's abstention from Nazi salute.

August Landmesser was a worker at the German shipbuilding company Blohm und Voß in Hamburg. In 1936, he refused to perform the Nazi salute in a large public gathering of workers at the shipbuilding company.

Source: Public domain via Wikimedia Commons.

to raise his hand in a Nazi salute, they are jeopardizing group membership and risking rejection. From this it follows that people seem to accept enemy images to secure group membership.

The group as the provider of esteem needs

Another kind of need is for *esteem*. According to Maslow, all people in society (with a few pathological exceptions) have a need or desire for a stable, firmly based, (usually) high evaluation of themselves, for self-respect or self-esteem (Maslow, 1943: 381). Maslow's idea about a *hierarchy* of needs (Figure 4.1) has been questioned, but the human need for self-esteem has been confirmed by many studies, both theoretical and empirical (Yzerbyt, 2010: 151).

People might improve their self-esteem by receiving praise for their accomplishments (Crocker and Knight, 2005: 202), but their self-evaluation is also related to group membership, particularly if individuals 'have internalized their group membership as an aspect of their self-concept' (Tajfel and Turner, 2004: 284). This is sometimes called 'the self-esteem hypothesis' (Hogg and Abrahams, 1990) and explained by the social identity theory (SIT), originally formulated by social psychologists Henri Tajfel and John Turner in the 1970s and 1980s. The purpose of this theory is to increase understanding of how people form and maintain their social identities. According to SIT, belonging to a group with a *high status* – and that is in the eyes not only of its group members but also of outsiders – can help people to feel good about themselves (Tajfel and Turner, 2004: 283), affording them a positive self-image (Oppenheimer, 2006: 271). The self-esteem derived from membership of such high-status groups makes people loyal to them (Deschamps and Devos, 1998: 6).

If people feel good about belonging to high-status groups, does that also imply that denigrating and criticizing another group makes people feel better about their own group and themselves? Some studies do indeed point in that direction. People defend the group that provides them with self-esteem (Jones, 2002: 78), and in their inclination to judge their group favourably compared with other groups, they derogate others. Several studies have shown how stereotyping and prejudice can strengthen or maintain self-esteem in this way (Gilovich et al., 2016: 414). People tend to judge their groups 'more favourably than they do other groups' (Stangor, 2000: 4; cf. Tajfel, Billig, and Bundy, 1971: 172 and Tajfel 1970). This is common and 'is known as in-group favouritism' (Stangor, 2000: 4). People thus defend the group that is providing them with self-esteem (Jones, 2002: 78). One factor that seems to trigger and accentuate the need to derogate an out-group is situations where people's self-esteem is threatened (Fein and Spencer, 1997: 33).

It is clear that people have a strong 'us' versus 'them' mentality and a tendency to defend their own group's status. According to Henri Tajfel and John C. Turner, the tendency to think of one's group better than others can arise even in constructed situations where people are assigned group membership based on arbitrary and seemingly meaningless criteria. This tendency has been extensively documented in experiments and can lead to cognitive biases such as motivated reasoning (Gilovich et al., 2016: 414 and Tajfel and Turner, 2004: 282). Since this tendency can be identified in experiments where groups were created solely for the sake of experimentation, it means that the desire to protect the status of one's own group (and by extension the status of the self) may arise even if 'there is neither a conflict of interests nor previously existing hostility between the "groups"' (Tajfel and Turner, 2004: 282).

Groups can be compared to each other on various dimensions. Countries, for instance, are regularly compared in different ways. For example, both international governmental and non-governmental organizations compare and rate countries in terms of welfare, human development, economic growth, protection of human rights, and in many other ways. The World Values Survey (WVS) measures different levels of survival versus self-expression values and traditional versus secular values among different nations and cultural macro-spheres. In the Olympic Games, people compare countries' sporting successes. Our point is that when people try to defend the status of their group, one way is to choose advantageous comparison points. People highlight the comparisons that tend to make their group appear successful (Turner, 2004: 287). For instance, if Sweden loses an international ice hockey match against Finland, a Swede may choose to downplay the importance of ice hockey and instead point out that Sweden is certainly better than Finland at football. According to Tajfel and Turner (2004), people are creative when it comes to protecting their own group's status. In addition, in order to choose favourable metrics of comparison, people might change

> the values assigned to the attributes of the group, so that comparisons which were previously negative are now perceived as positive. The classic example is 'black is beautiful'.
>
> *(Tajfel and Turner, 2004: 287)*

And lastly, people can also change the out-group with which the in-group is compared. For instance, if Sweden is no longer better than Finland at ice hockey, Swedes would avoid this group as a comparative frame of reference. Such a comparison would no longer improve Swedish self-esteem. In that case, people could choose another out-group with whom the Swedes could be compared favourably – for instance the Danes – since Sweden is still a lot better than Denmark at ice hockey.

Now let us return to this chapter's recurring question: why do people accept enemy images? And can SIT help us to understand this? It makes sense to assume that enemy images and similar ideas (see the discussion about white supremacy in Chapter 3) exploit people's need for self-esteem and thereby their need to belong to a high-status group. In Chapter 2, while constructing the ideal–typical enemy image, it was stated that 'we' (according to the enemy image) are superior to 'them' (see Table 2.1). Such a narrative is attractive to the status-hungry individual and will have a good chance of being accepted. In other words, it is reasonable to believe that people are open to enemy images since they confirm 'our' high status and 'their' inferiority.

Second, enemy images underscore that 'they' pose a threat to 'us' and 'our' vital interests and assets. Fein and Spencer's experiment from 1997, showing that people's need to denigrate an out-group increases when self-esteem is threatened, may be relevant in this context. It seems that the enemy image exploits people's fragile egos and that the content of the enemy image, where the enemy is constructed as a threat to 'us' and 'our' assets, legitimizing political and military actions against them, becomes an attractive narrative.

Autofavouritism

Esteem needs are drivers to seek inclusion in a high-status group combined with a desire to be set apart from that group (Dawson, 2017: 8), enjoying a unique, visible, and glorious position within it. People want not only to be a part of a high-status group, but also to achieve a prominent position within such a group. In other words, as well as viewing their group favourably over an out-group, they wish to see themselves as better members than others in the group (Hinton, 2000: 124). People playing ice hockey do not just want to belong to the winning team. They want to be the celebrated goal scorer.

When it comes to acceptance of enemy images, we would argue that in general they are better at promoting in-group favouritism ('our' group is better than other groups) than autofavouritism (I am better than most in my group). As a rule, enemy images are directed at groups rather than individuals. Still, they might indicate what behaviour and characteristics might give the individual a prominent position within the group or how to become a heroic figure (Cottee and Hayward, 2011: 976). We know that the purpose of enemy images is to mobilize the in-group to take part in violence against the out-group, and that sacrifices for the group are hailed as a virtue. The celebration of terrorists and sometimes children as martyrs is one example of this logic. For soldiers and others who see themselves as key to the protection of the group against external threat, the message of enemy images is therefore attractive. It speaks directly to people's need to be special and even better than most other members of their group since enemy images tell 'us' to make sacrifices for the group, and when 'we' are on the frontline in the defence of 'our' group and all 'we' hold dear, 'we' will be celebrated and rewarded a glorious position.

Ultimate meaning

Let us now return to Maslow's hierarchy of needs for the last time. According to the most widely disseminated version of his model, self-actualization is at the top (see Figure 4.1). However, Maslow produced different versions of his model, and in later writing and reflection, he did not put self-actualization at the top, but rather self-transcendence, resulting in the individual seeking to 'further a cause beyond the self' (Koltko-Rivera, 2006: 303). Here, Maslow underlined that the individual seeks a cause (sometimes called 'ultimate values') and needs to experience communion beyond the boundaries of the self through peak experience (Maslow, 1993: 162–163 and 259–261). When people feel that they are doing something vital for the group, like protecting it from external threats, and thereby doing something beyond themselves, they might experience essential meaning. Being important to the group and its survival gives people a sense of communion beyond the self. 'We' are immersed in the group, and the group survives because of 'us'. One such cause beyond the self could be to sacrifice oneself for the protection of one's group, even to 'kill and die for each other' (Atran, 2010: xi). According to the Finnish professor of information studies, Heikki Luostarinen, war constitutes a situation that

> might increase the social meaning of the individual's life. It gives him a clear objective and enables him to participate in a meaningful collective project. He is involved in something important, together with the rest of the community.
>
> *(Luostarinen, 1989: 126)*

Enemy images tend to describe existential situations where the entire group is under attack. Fighting for 'our' survival, 'we' participate in something essential, with the ego no longer at the centre. And in such a situation, when entire societies are mobilized, people can be led to believe that they are doing something important and meaningful such as a sacrifice for the community. And participating in such endeavours can give people an experience of significance, 'to be someone, to have respect' (Kruglanski, Bélanger, and Gunaratna, 2019: 42), a sense of making 'a mark in the world' (Dawson, 2023: 45).

Exploiting the need for meaning, enemy images can both mobilize a population and make the population embrace the message. An enemy image can potentially construct a message that tells ordinary citizens they are participating in a decisive moment for the group. In the Second World War, the home front (i.e. the participation of ordinary citizens in the war effort) was indeed important. Messages urging civilians to be active in this way were both mobilizing and appealing. Messages exploiting people's need for meaning have indeed the potential to be accepted.

Cognitive limitations

Leaving socio-psychological theories on human needs and motivations aside, a second approach explaining the acceptance of enemy images can be derived from research on cognition. Cognition is usually defined as the mental process by which people acquire knowledge and understand reality through thought, experience, and the senses (Frith, 2008: 2033). Research on cognition can fruitfully complement socio-psychological factors and contribute to explanations of why people accept and/or hold on to enemy images.

Research on cognition is extensive and has a long tradition. In this section we focus on two relevant perspectives contributing to an explanation of enemy image acceptance: (a) reduction of complexity and (b) cognitive consistency. We will summarize and conclude this section with a discussion on (c) confirmation bias.

Reduction of complexity

A starting point in this discussion is that people's five senses produce an abundance of stimuli. In fact, the senses produce many more stimuli than the human brain can manage and process. Simply put, people see and hear far more than their brains can handle. Since the human brain cannot cope with all this, it uses two main strategies to make incoming stimuli manageable: (a) filtering out unnecessary information and (b) reducing their complexity. In this section, we consult some relevant discussions on the human need to reduce complexity.

BOX 4.2 GORDON W. ALLPORT AND *THE NATURE OF PREJUDICE*

The American Gordon W. Allport (1897–1967) was a Harvard professor of social psychology. His research focused on human personality and his main contribution concerned personality psychology and intergroup prejudice (Pettigrew, 2015: 562), with two well-known monographs published in those areas: *Personality: A Psychological Interpretation* (1937) and *The Nature of Prejudice* (1954).

Another influential book, co-authored with Leo Postman, was *The Psychology of Rumor* (1947), in which the authors discuss the nature and dynamics of rumours and their impact on society. One important finding was that rumours tend to spread in situations of ambiguity (Allport and Postman, 1947: 32–35). In the book, the authors also present a few experiments, the most famous being the razor experiment. In this, participants were shown a picture of an argument between a well-dressed Black man and a white man with a razor (see Chapter 1). The participants were asked to pass the story on. White participants tended to distort the scene, depicting the Black man as the aggressor (Allport and Postman, 1947: 71).

A book that is of particular relevance to enemy images is *The Nature of Prejudice*, which discussed people's willingness to accept intergroup prejudice. One important claim Allport makes here is that prejudice is a response to the necessity of mental shortcuts. These exist to facilitate the processing of stimuli with as little effort as possible. In the same book, Allport also suggests that intergroup contact could, under certain conditions, mitigate and counter prejudice (see Chapter 6). *The Nature of Prejudice* remains the most cited work regarding research on prejudice (Dovidio, Glick, and Rudman, 2005: 1).

It is undeniable that Allport's research has been of great importance for later research in social psychology, not least in the field of prejudice. For instance, 25 years after the publication of *The Nature of Prejudice*, Allport's student Thomas Pettigrew stated in a tribute article that the book is 'balanced, ahead of its time, and elegantly written. It has organized the study of prejudice over the past half century' (1999: 415). His research in general, Pettigrew said, was characterized by eclectic balance offering original solutions to central problems (1999: 417–419). A full 25 years after that, John F. Dovidio, Peter Glick, and Laurie A. Rudman published an edited volume commemorating the 50th anniversary of the publication of *The Nature of Prejudice*. In the introduction, they largely echoed what Pettigrew had said 25 years earlier, underlining the profound impact of his research, particularly *The Nature of Prejudice* (Dovidio, Glick, and Rudman, 2005: 14).

One way to reduce complexity is to simplify people's understanding of the world using simple categories, or stereotypes, using them to provide mental shortcuts. This has been known since the 1920s. An early thinker in this field worthy of mention is the American writer and journalist Walter Lippmann (1889–1974) and his classic work *Public Opinion* (1922). In this book, Lippmann discusses democracy and the role of mass media. Of relevance is his idea that the outside world is too complicated for the human brain and that

> We are not equipped to deal with so much subtlety, so much variety, so many permutations and … we have to reconstruct it on a simpler model before we can manage with it.
>
> *(Lippmann, [1922] 2007: 16)*

According to Lippmann, people simplify by using stereotypes. He also claims that people are provided with stereotypes externally and are thereby 'told about the world before we see it' (Lippmann, [1922] 2007: 55), giving actors who 'create and maintain the repertory of stereotypes' a subtle and pervasive influence on how the world is perceived (Lippmann, [1922] 2007: 55).

Another early scholar who claimed that people need stereotypes as shortcuts in cognitive processes was Gordon W. Allport (1897–1967, see Box 4.2). In his seminal book *The Nature of Prejudice* (1954), he describes the use of stereotypes as tools to facilitate cognition. In the 1950s, when this book was published, it was assumed that only a minority were prejudiced. Allport recognized individual differences: some people are more prejudiced than others, but the differences are relatively small (1954: 79). Still, Allport's research was ground-breaking since he realized that not only a minority is prejudiced. He started writing *The Nature of Prejudice* only nine years after the Second World War. In the shadow of the Holocaust and the ongoing racism in for instance the United States and South Africa, there was an urgent need to understand the processes leading up to stereotypes, prejudice, and discrimination. What was new in Allport's research is his claim that prejudice and stereotypes were effects of *normal* processes in the human mind, in which all ordinary people partook. According to him,

> the human mind must think with the aid of categories. ... Once formed, categories are the basis for normal prejudgment. We cannot possibly avoid this process.
>
> *(Allport, 1954: 20)*

What he says is that people *need* categories, or stereotypes, as the basis for their assessment and their processing of incoming stimuli. He even stated that although open-mindedness is considered a virtue, it cannot occur (Allport, 1954: 20). People *need* shortcuts, and they use stereotypes as a tool to facilitate perception (Allport, 1954: 21) since 'we cannot handle each event freshly in its own right' (Allport, 1954: 20). So, stereotypes are useful since they 'allow the individual to simplify and reduce complex information to a manageable size' (Jones, 2002: 9–11). They give people the ability to understand new and unique situations with a minimum of cognitive effort (Gilbert and Hixon, 1991: 509). This also gives humans a capacity for fast detection of dangers, separating a protective 'us' from a threatening 'them', which can be life-saving (Méndez-Bértolo, 2016).

A significant step in research on the reduction of complexity is the concept of 'heuristics', introduced by the American political scientist Herbert Simon in 1955. In his research, he challenged an important assumption of traditional economic theory: rational choice. Rational choice theory assumes that people, motivated by self-interest, make decisions based on rational assessments of costs and benefits and choose alternatives that maximize their wellbeing. Simon, on the other hand, claimed that 'there is a complete lack of evidence that, in actual human choice situations of any complexity, these computations can be, or are in fact, performed' (Simon, 1955: 104). His research drew on psychology that had long criticized the rational man axiom. Simon concluded that decision-makers use heuristics – simplified rules of thumb or 'gut feeling' – as tools to make shortcuts in decision-making and in assessing probability. And surprisingly, this was the same for people scoring high on IQ tests (Stanovich, 2009: x–xi).

In the 1970s, Israeli cognitive psychologists Amos Tversky (1937–1996) and Daniel Kahneman (b. 1934) used the concept of 'cognitive bias' (Tversky and Kahneman, 1974) to challenge traditional rational choice theory. They demonstrated that people are usually not utility maximizers; instead, their decision-making has limited rationality and is based on biased beliefs. In decision-making processes, people

> rely on a limited number of heuristic principles which reduce the complex tasks of assessing probabilities and predicting values to simpler judgmental operations.
>
> *(Tversky and Kahneman, 1974: 1124)*

They concluded that their research participants were influenced in decision-making by a combination of heuristic shortcuts and cognitive biases.

The research on people's need to simplify and reduce complexity in cognitive processes and decision-making continued in the 1980s and the 1990s. In 1984, Susan T. Fiske and Shelley E. Taylor presented the 'cognitive miser approach' in *Social Cognition*. According to Fiske and Taylor (1984: 12), decision-making takes time and energy: 'People are limited in their capacity to process information, so they take shortcuts whenever they can'. The fundamental argument in this approach is that the human brain is a 'cognitive miser' due to its tendency to seek resource-efficient ways to process cognitive data. This idea is not unique but has become generally accepted in psychology (Dunn and Risko, 2019: 1). Moreover, being resource-efficient does not only concern cognitive processes but 'the entire behavior of an individual is at all times motivated by the urge to minimize effort' (Zipf, 1949: 3). We will return to this cognitive energy-saving process when discussing appropriate interventions against enemy images, but already now it is appropriate to mention the elaboration likelihood model (ELM) according to which information is processed in two speeds: (a) quick and intuitive, and (b) slow and reflective.

In his later writing on intelligence tests, Keith E. Stanovich claims that intelligent people too tend to undertake shallow information processing (Stanovich, 2009: 71–72). As a matter of fact, 'most people can carry out fully disjunctive reasoning when they are explicitly told that it is necessary' (Stanovich, 2009: 71). According to Stanovich, 'people make the easiest (incorrect) inference from the information given and do not proceed with the more difficult (but correct) inference that follows from fully disjunctive reasoning' (Stanovich, 2009: 71). It has also been shown that people accept false information faster when it provides quick answers to pressing questions (Vosoughi, Roy, and Ara, 2018).

How does all of this relate to the acceptance of enemy images? Based on the theoretical discussion in this section, it seems that enemy images are uniquely functional since they are a kind of stereotype that facilitates fast, effortless cognition and decision-making. But not only that, enemy images are also a tool for the brain to rapidly separate friends from foes, in-group from the out-group, and thereby identify and avoid danger. So enemy images could be seen as a highly useful tool with two important functions. First, they seem to facilitate fast, effortless cognition, information processing, and decision-making, making them attractive to people's overloaded brains. Second, they might be perceived as life-saving since they help the brain to immediately separate a potentially dangerous stranger from the safe in-group. They help people to rapidly identify and avoid danger. This dual functionality is probably one reason why the human brain accepts them.

Cognitive dissonance

Considered from a cognitive miser approach, enemy images appear to be cognitively useful. Yet another cognitive perspective discussed in the subsequent section, cognitive dissonance theory (CDT), promises to explain a further function. The American social psychologist Leon Festinger (see Box 4.3) and his colleagues open their ground-breaking book *When Prophecy Fails* (1956) with the following words:

> A man with a conviction is a hard man to change. Tell him you disagree and he turns away. Show him facts or figures and he questions your sources. Appeal to logic and he fails to see your point.
>
> *(Festinger, Riecken, and Schachter, 1956: 3)*

Festinger's discussion on cognitive consistency can help us to understand why and how people tend to *hold on to* and *keep* an enemy image despite being confronted with clear contradictory empirical evidence. This section will draw on both Festinger's early (Festinger, 1957; Festinger, Riecken, and Schachter, 1956) and later writings.

A core concept in this theory is *cognitive dissonance*, which refers to the mental or psychological *stress* or *discomfort* that people experience if they simultaneously hold two or more contradictory beliefs, ideas, or values; or when they perform an action that contradicts one of those beliefs, ideals, or values. The antonym is *cognitive consistency*. Thus, cognitive dissonance is what people try to avoid, and cognitive consistency is what they try to achieve (Festinger, 1957: 29–30). A simple example of cognitive dissonance would be when people know that smoking is hazardous but cannot stop smoking. Smoking will, in addition to harming people's physical health, also cause mental stress and discomfort since they know they are doing something harmful to their bodies. Convinced that smoking is dangerous, they are motivated to change, to stop smoking. If they manage to quit smoking, they will reduce the experience of mental stress. In that case, they will resolve the discomfort by accepting medical advice and changing their behaviour. Their beliefs and behaviour will be in harmony.

Not all cognitive dissonance gives people the same level of psychological stress or discomfort. It seems that strong beliefs mean a lot to people, analogous to religious conviction, and if they are challenged by new information, the dissonance will be greater (Allport, 1954: 25–26). To question ideas that people see as the foundation of their life is therefore emotionally very stressful and uncomfortable. Or expressed otherwise, the cognitive miser approach emphasizes the brain's cognitive limitations and people's *need to simplify*. CDT emphasizes their *emotional needs* to be provided with information that confirms and does not contradict their fundamental beliefs.

BOX 4.3 LEON FESTINGER AND COGNITIVE DISSONANCE THEORY

Leon Festinger (1919–1989) was an American social psychologist famous for his cognitive dissonance (1957) and social comparison (1954) theories. During his years at university, he became inspired by social psychologist Kurt Lewin, who was concerned with testing theoretical constructs through innovative field research and experiments (Hatfield et al., 2014). This led Festinger to focus his own research on how people set goals for themselves (Hertzman and Festinger, 1940). Most of it was based on laboratory experiments, but he also used real-life experience, for instance when he and his colleagues infiltrated a cult and published *When Prophecy Fails* (Festinger et al., 1956). In 1957, he published his research on cognitive dissonance, which has been seen as one of the most influential theories in social psychology (Jones, 1985). Combining cognition with motivation was revolutionary at the time. In 1997, Aaronson published a review of Festinger's theory, his main point being how powerful the influence of this theory still is, having made a comeback under new names in social psychology. Festinger's book has been cited over 45,000 times in published research. The theory has been developed since, especially regarding the factors of 'commitment purpose and freedom', the 'consequence of the act purpose' and the 'self-involvement'. It has not only been used in research on human beings but also on non-human primates such as birds and rats (Hatfield et al., 2014).

Stopping smoking is not easy, and giving up one's fundamental beliefs is emotionally burdensome. Therefore, they tend to disregard new evidence or only admit new information that confirms their previous beliefs (Allport, 1954: 23). They can also try to reinterpret new information, to make it consistent with their beliefs. This tendency can be bolstered if the convictions are *deep-rooted* (the foundation of their life) and paired with *commitment* (Festinger, Riecken, and Schachter, 1956: 3–4).

> Suppose an individual believes something with his whole heart; suppose further that he has a commitment to this belief, that he has taken irrevocable actions because of it.
>
> *(Festinger, Riecken, and Schachter, 1956: 3)*

Moreover, there is also a social component. If people are surrounded by others who share their beliefs, as in a sect or the army, it will be easier to keep their convictions despite contradictory evidence (Festinger, Riecken, and Schachter, 1956: 3–4).

Factors such as these seem to make 'the belief resistant to change' even if people are challenged by 'undeniable disconfirmatory evidence' (Festinger, Riecken, and Schachter, 1956: 3–4). And this is what the quote at the beginning of this section referred to. Festinger, Riecken, and Schachter's early study was conducted on an American religious movement led by Mrs Marion Keech, a self-proclaimed prophetess and claimed that 'messages … are sent to her by superior beings from a planet called "Clarion"' (1956: 30). According to her messages, North America would soon be overflooded and only her followers would be rescued. The prophecy failed, which of course caused cognitive dissonance for the members of the sect. Their beliefs were challenged since the flood never came. Yet still a core group remained faithful to the religious group and its 'prophet(ess)'.

This early study is ground-breaking and important, and the theory emanating from it has become a mainstay. And although the study was criticized, particularly its methodology (Dawson, 1999: 61), its main results have been confirmed in later research on other religious cults. Despite the prophecy proving obviously false, movements like Mrs Keech's survive, at least for a time (Dawson, 1999: 62), and loyal members undertake various strategies to explain why the prophecy failed. People generally have an emotional need for cognitive consistency and, therefore, strive for it. A similar case has occurred with the more recent Q-Anon movement. In November 2021 and June 2022, thousands of believers in the conspiracy theory that the United States is ruled by a corrupt 'deep state' rather than by its legally elected leaders gathered in Dallas to await the second coming of John F. Kennedy Jr., his father, and other celebrities (Kornfield, 2021). These promises failed to materialize on both occasions, but people within the movement still stick to the belief that the resurrection of these personalities will occur and restore dignity to the US political system and society.

Although Festinger's theories cannot completely explain the general human tendency to embrace enemy images, they can potentially teach us two things. *First*, cognitive consistency theory can explain what kind of enemy image people usually embrace. It is reasonable to say that they are more willing to embrace enemy images that are in accordance with deeply rooted *previous beliefs*. Such enemy images might generate psychological balance and emotional wellbeing since they confirm what people always 'knew'. To be concrete, antisemitism was not something created from scratch by the Nazi Party in the 1920s and 1930s. On the contrary, it was something cultivated within Christianity for centuries where Jews were blamed, among other things, for the killing of Christ. In Adolf Hitler's propaganda, this was not the primary reason for hatred towards Jews ([1925–26] 1999). In *Mein Kampf*, for instance, the Jews had a different – but still compatible – role from the one taught in church. Nazi propaganda would thus probably generate for most Germans more cognitive consistency, psychological balance, and wellbeing than stress because it was compatible with what they had already been taught. The same could be said about white supremacy. The current alt-right movements are using ideas that not only exploit white people's need for self-esteem but also confirm what white people 'know' and are therefore more easily accepted. In Chapter 7, we will elaborate on how antisemitic ideas survived over five centuries and were expressed in different media.

Second, cognitive consistency theory can also explain why people cling to certain notions as an enemy image despite being confronted with refutations. One explanation is that it is *painful* to abandon old beliefs. Abandoning an enemy image means embracing information that contradicts what they previously believed, leading to cognitive dissonance and inner pain. Another argument is that enemy images are also *deep-rooted* since they concern matters of life and death; and as stated above, deep-rooted convictions are particularly rigid. Moreover, imagine also that a soldier has 'taken irrevocable actions' because of an enemy image, killing or maybe even committing war crimes in its name. In that case, it will be very hard to abandon the idea that justifies his actions (we have a longer discussion about this in Chapter 6, see *Healing of the perpetrators* and *Healing of victims*). And lastly, an enemy image is maintained socially. In wartime, an entire nation or army has probably to some degree accepted, evolved, and reproduced it. This means that, just as Festinger, Riecken, and Schachter (1956) state, people in this situation are surrounded by others who believe in and reproduce the enemy image, making it even harder to let go of this conviction. They would be surrounded by people convinced that 'the others' constitute a threat, and who support 'us' against the other's hostile intentions. Adding to what in Chapter 3 we termed creating discursive consistency over time, these psychological drivers help to explain why such strategies are successful.

Confirmation bias

As it has emerged, human perception is neither objective nor unfiltered. People are not like video or audio devices that mechanically record everything. The human brain has filters selecting stimuli and a biased cognitive process impacts what it sees. In Allport's words, 'Nothing that strikes our eyes or ears conveys its message directly to us. We always *select* and *interpret* our impressions of the surrounding world' (1954: 165, italics in original). In the preceding sections, we introduced two completing approaches to explaining people's filters and biased interpretations. Each perspective contributes to our knowledge about why people accept and maintain enemy images and why such beliefs 'can survive potent logical or empirical challenges' (Ross and Anderson, 1982: 149). Although these two approaches explain this tendency differently, the effect is similar. In the following, we will summarize the discussion on cognition by presenting three types of confirmation bias: information seeking, interpretation of information, and lastly learning and remembering.

Information seeking

When people search for information, they tend to seek out evidence consistent with their existing beliefs and avoid anything that challenges them (Nickerson, 1998: 177–184 and Kunda, 1999: 112–115). There is a risk that when people have made up their minds, they will be 'building a case to justify a conclusion already drawn' (Nickerson, 1998: 175). They likely gather data selectively or give undue weight to data supporting their position while neglecting to gather, or discounting, evidence that would tell against it (Nickerson, 1998: 175). Sometimes they know they are deliberately selecting information to justify their position. But more often it is done unconsciously, and it is this unwitting selectivity that is in focus here (Nickerson, 1998: 175).

This selectivity does not only occur in uneducated people. On the contrary, Toby Dodge in his research on President George W. Bush's advisers found that

> individuals defend the internal consistency of their belief system by discrediting information that does not make sense within its boundaries. Ironically, this process of 'cognitive consistency' is likely to be much more rigid in expert policy-makers.
>
> *(Dodge, 2012: 467)*

As the German historian Ragnhild Fiebig-von Hase argues, this cognitive rigidity spills over into decision-making processes through the reproduction of system-inherent enemy images and the inability to challenge established cognitive schemas of enemy perception and evaluation (1997: 9–10). In other words, there is a risk that stakeholders are limited by an inbuilt perceptual path dependency with which the enemy is imagined.

If people were confronted with unequivocal information that contradicted their flawed beliefs, maybe it would influence and correct them. But in real life, they are not surrounded by unequivocal data. This is especially evident in a crisis or conflict situation, where it is not uncommon to be faced with conflicting information. Some information will probably confirm their enemy images. Were people encountering only data contradicting their enemy images, it would be harder to search and find information confirming their beliefs. That was probably the case right after the end of the Cold War. But again, since people usually have access to information supporting their ingrained enemy images, research indicates that they will favour such information.

Lastly, people's propensity to seek affirmative information is reinforced by the invisible algorithms used in various search engines and social media. There is a risk that these systems will serve the information that people wish to receive (Haider and Sundin, 2022: 4–10).

Interpretation of information

Imagine that people are confronted with undeniable information contradicting their fundamental beliefs. Imagine that their enemy is suddenly acting morally and peacefully, even consistently so. In such a case, people cannot turn a blind eye to reality but will still try to avoid concluding that their enemy has indeed changed and now is peaceful. To confirm their deeply rooted beliefs, they will probably *interpret* the challenging data in a way that supports their existing beliefs, including their enemy images.

At the beginning of Chapter 1, an enemy image was presented as a kind of stereotype and cognitive schema used by social perceivers to 'process information about others' (Dovidio et al., 2010: 7). Such schemas 'filter and organize ... information' (Fiebig-von Hase, 1997: 8). The problem is that enemy images/ stereotypes/cognitive schemas are rigid by definition. Not only do they make people misunderstand a situation, as discussed in Chapter 1, but they also *perpetuate* people's beliefs. Therefore, in addition to influencing perception, attention, memory, interpretation, and expectations (see Chapter 1), enemy images also have self-reinforcing effects. And in a conflict situation, information is often unreliable and ambiguous, expanding the scope for interpretation. When people receive such information, they tend to 'assume the worst about the enemy' (Silverstein and Flamenbaum, 1989: 53).

In Chapter 1, we also presented Table 1.2, explaining good and bad behaviour. We pointed out that once an enemy image has been accepted, people develop malevolent thinking, assuming the worst in a logic of bad faith. People expect their enemy to deceive them and tend to see their good behaviour as an effect of situational factors ('they' perform good behaviour because 'they' must) and bad behaviour as an effect of dispositional factors ('they' perform aggressive behaviour because that is who 'they' are). The logic presented in that table not only impacts 'our' perception of the enemy and causes people to make bad decisions. It also makes people perpetuate their enemy images and could be called an 'ultimate attribution error' (Pettigrew, 1979: 464). No matter that the enemy is behaving peacefully, once people embrace an enemy image, there is an imminent risk that they interpret behaviour contradicting it to fit their enemy image (Pettigrew, 1979: 469). The logic would be 'the enemy is undoubtedly behaving more peacefully, but that is by no means a change of heart, it is by force of circumstances'.

And again, it seems that intelligence is of little avail in this case. Biased interpretation of information occurs among all kinds of people and 'is particularly unrelated to intelligence' (Stanovich, West, and Toplak, 2013: 263).

Learning and remembering

Confirmation bias not only impacts information seeking and interpretation of information. This kind of bias also impacts what people *learn* and *remember*. They tend to remember the enemy's hostile actions and accusations against them more easily than good behaviour and exculpations (Silverstein and Flamenbaum, 1989: 53).

As early as 1943, Jerome M. Levine and Gardner Murphy conducted a study analysing how much confirmation bias affected learning and remembering of controversial material. That year, the United States was allied with the Soviet Union against Nazi Germany, but anti-Soviet and anti-Communist values persisted in American society. In this test, two small homogenous groups of students were selected, with only five in each (Levine and Murphy, 1943: 509). One group was pro-Communist, the other anti-Communist. Both felt strongly about their beliefs. The two groups were supposed to study two texts, one 'excitedly anti-communist, the other more moderately pro-communist' (Levine and Murphy, 1943: 509). The participants met with the researcher in private, not in a group. They were told to read the first short text twice, after which they and the researcher talked about unrelated things for 15 minutes. Then they were told:

'Reproduce as accurately as possible the paragraph which was presented to you. Make an effort to have your reproduction as accurate and as nearly identical with the original paragraph as you possibly can. Be sure to have your reproduction not only accurate but as complete as the original paragraph.' The procedure was then repeated with the second text. This represented the learning period. Thereafter, at weekly intervals for four weeks, the memory of the two selected texts was tested. This the researchers called the 'forgetting period'.

(Levine and Murphy, 1943: 510)

The researchers found that the participants with pro-Communist attitudes learned more of the moderately pro-Communist text and forgot less of it. The anti-Communist participants, on the other hand, learned more and forgot less of the 'excitedly anti-communist' text (Levine and Murphy, 1943: 510–514). A similar effect was tested by Allport and Postman (see Box 4.2 and Chapter 1), who showed an image to participants about an alleged razor attack in a subway car, testing racial prejudices.

Our point is that once people have embraced an enemy image, there is a risk that it functions as a schema, making them remember negative facts about the enemy more easily and reject facts showing the enemy's behaviour and intentions in a good light. Thus, the way human memory works might perpetuate people's enemy images.

Societal structures

In the preceding sections, we consulted scholars and theories in cognition and social psychology to comprehend the more general reasons why humans frequently and willingly accept and/or hold on to enemy images. But we know that the prevalence of enemy images varies in time and space. At certain times and in certain geographical areas, they dominate and acquire a more prominent position in society. In this section, we will discuss a few theories that help us understand why enemy images have an increased impact under certain conditions, starting with socio-economic ones. Specifically, the section will elaborate on (a) realist group conflict theory (RGCT) and relative deprivation theory (RDT), and (b) relative gratification theory (RGT).

Realist group conflict theory and relative deprivation theory

When groups experience external competition for limited resources or perceive that they have been deprived of something essential other groups have, it is reasonable to assume an elevated risk of enemy image acceptance.

One theory that emphasizes how unfortunate structures propel intergroup conflict is the RGCT (Campbell, 1965). This theory demonstrates that when resources are limited and groups compete for them in a zero-sum game, feelings of resentment, prejudice, and discrimination are a likely result (Khan and Samarina, 2007: 726) – and so, it seems fair to infer, is the acceptance of enemy images. We have stated before that groups are important to people because they are essential providers of various needs. That means they might develop hostile attitudes towards each other even when not competing for limited resources (Tajfel, Billig, and Bundy, 1971: 151 and Tajfel and Turner, 2004: 281). What the realistic group conflict theory underlines is that the presence of a 'real conflict of group interests causes intergroup conflict' (Campbell, 1965: 287), particularly if it concerns scarce resources (Tajfel and Turner, 2004: 276).

This idea has been questioned and developed. It seems that objectively presented conflicts of interest are not enough to develop feelings of resentment, prejudice, and discrimination. It is important that a group also *perceives* a situation as conflictual for an awareness of competition for resources to exist (Sherif, 1966). In a 1989 study on Israeli citizens' attitudes to the ultra-Orthodox Jewish minority in Israel, Naomi Struch and Shalom H. Schwartz analysed the role of conflict perception, finding that

> perceived conflict promotes dehumanizing the out-group, so its members do not deserve the humane treatment enjoined even by universal norms.
> *(Struch and Schwartz, 1989: 371)*

The sad effect is that when people perceive a zero-sum conflict between groups, it also affects how *individuals* in opposing groups perceive each other. Members of the opposing group tend to lose their individuality, and 'the individuals who are members of the opposite groups will behave toward each other as a function of their respective group memberships' (Tajfel and Turner, 2004: 277).

BOX 4.4   MUZAFER SHERIF AND THE ROBBERS CAVE EXPERIMENT

Muzafer Sherif (1906–1988) was a Turkish-born American social psychologist who grew up in a well-to-do family in the final years of the Ottoman Empire and experienced the rise of the Turkish Republic. Those years were characterized by the collapse of empires, war, nationalism, and the Armenian genocide. In Izmir, Sherif witnessed the war between Turkey and Greece. He was not only a renowned social psychologist but also a political activist, both an academic and an activist for peace and cooperation.

Sherif conducted his first academic studies in Turkey, transferring to the United States in 1926 for his MA and PhD studies at Harvard, though he completed his PhD thesis at Columbia University (Kayaoğlu, Batur, and Aslıtürk, 2014: 831). One of the teachers who influenced him was Gordon Allport. After completing his PhD, Sherif returned to Turkey and, being anti-Nazi and anti-fascist, became politically involved. After the Second World War, his politically controversial status in Turkey prompted a return to the United States.

His political and academic interests were in symbiosis and led him to research competition and conflicts. He fought individualistic and reductionist explanations of human behaviour, underlining the importance of the social structure for the human mind.

Sherif has been primarily remembered by posterity, and especially students, for the 1954 Robbers Cave experiment (see below for details). Conducted together with his wife Carolyn Wood Sherif, this demonstrated the dynamics of realist group conflict. He found that social structural factors such as competition for scarce resources undermine relations between groups.

The social psychologist Muzafer Sherif (see Box 4.4) and his associates pioneered empirical research in this area, testing the realistic group conflict theory (Tajfel and Turner, 2004: 276). In 1954, they conducted a study on 11-year-old boys. The experiment took place at a secluded summer camp, Robbers Cave State Park in Oklahoma, and aimed to investigate the effects of intergroup conflicts. When selecting the boys, the idea was that they would be relatively similar to each other so that 'the groups would be composed as similarly as possible' (Sherif et al., [1961] 1988: 58): if conflicts arose, they could not be attributed to any factor other than resource availability.

The 22 subjects who were finally selected were relatively homogeneous… All were from established Protestant families. All were well adjusted both in school and at home, according to observations and school and home interviews. According to school records, all the subjects were doing average or above school work.

(Sherif et al., [1961] 1988: 57)

Researchers, who doubled as counsellors at this summer camp, divided the participants into two different groups, each assigned cabins far from the other. During the first stage, the groups were not aware of the existence of the other group. The boys developed an attachment to their respective groups during the first week of the camp through doing various activities together. They chose names for their respective groups, *The Eagles* and *The Rattlers*, which they put onto shirts and flags (Sherif, 1966: 80). In this 'in-group formation' phase, members of the groups got to know each other, social norms developed, and leadership and structure emerged.

Then the second phase started, in which the groups encountered each other and a group conflict began. The researchers organized a four-day competition between the groups, with prizes promised to the winners. Prejudice became apparent between the two groups. This was initially only expressed verbally, through teasing or name-calling, but as the competition progressed, it began to be expressed more directly, with one group burning the other's flag or ransacking their cabin. The groups became too aggressive with each other to control, and the researchers had to separate them physically (Sherif et al., [1961] 1988: 110).

The researchers then gave all boys a two-day cooling-off period and asked them to list the characteristics of the two groups. The boys tended to characterize their group highly favourably and the other group very negatively. The researchers then tried to reduce prejudice between the groups and found that simply increasing their contact with each other made matters worse. One factor seemed to help. They made the two groups work together to reach superordinate – or common – goals (Sherif, 1966: 128–130). Thus, in this conflict resolution phase, it was shown that superordinate goals reduce conflict far more effectively than did communication or contact.

The 1954 experiment and a precursor abandoned in 1953 have come under recent scrutiny, with a particular interest in the manipulation and provocation of the underage participants by the scientists, and possible confirmation bias by Sherif. Still, the RGCT is today a well-established theory with robust research support from both laboratory and field studies (Khan and Samarina, 2007: 725).

Another relevant theory, introduced by Samuel A. Stouffer and his colleagues in a study on American soldiers during the Second World War (Stouffer et al., 1949), is the relative deprivation theory (RDT). Relative deprivation is a social psychological concept, describing 'a subjective state that shapes emotions, cognitions, and behavior' (Pettigrew et al., 2008: 386). Relative deprivation could be both individual and collective, but our focus is on group relative deprivation (GRD). People who experience relative deprivation are often of lower socioeconomic status (Pettigrew et al., 2008: 395). A major assumption in the theory is that

> a person's or group's satisfaction is not related to their objective circumstances but, rather, to their condition relative to other persons or groups. This implies, for example, that objectively disadvantaged people may feel less deprived than objectively advantaged people because of the chosen target for their social comparisons.
>
> *(Dambrun et al., 2006: 1032)*

The point is that the feeling of relative deprivation is not based on *objective facts* (for instance 'our' objective wealth) but is a perception 'that a group that one identifies highly with is deprived relative to an outgroup' (Yzerbyt, 2010: 151), that 'we' are poorer than others, that 'we' have less than 'we' feel entitled to (Mummendey et al., 1999: 229). In other words, GRD focuses on the perceived relative distribution of vital assets between groups and 'challenges conventional wisdom about the importance of absolute deprivation' (Pettigrew et al., 2008: 386). According to social psychological research on GRD, it is a predictor of prejudice (Pettigrew et al., 2008: 386, 390, and 395) and is 'fueled by perceptions that members of one group are losing ground to members of another group in matters of voice or material well-being' (Anderson and Christie, 2001: 179). The point is that perceptions of GRD, particularly if they are intensifying, 'have a powerful influence on the development of intergroup enmity' (Anderson and Christie, 2001: 179 and cf. Gatto, Guimond, and Dambrun, 2018: 2), and groups experiencing GRD are more likely to express hostility towards the more privileged group (Grant and Brown, 1995). Dambrun et al. conclude that 'relative deprivation has consistently been identified as being a strong and robust predictor of intergroup attitudes' in different countries and cultures (2006: 1032).

To summarize, social structures can create conditions favourable for the growth and acceptance of enemy images. In situations where people experience a shortage (sometimes relative) of important resources and groups compete for them in a zero-sum game, it is reasonable to believe that the prevalence of enemy images increases. An image of the 'other' as a threat to 'our' vital interests will be increasingly credible and believable, and this can be exploited by political leaders.

Relative gratification theory

In the previous section, it was stated that there is probably a relationship between GRD and the acceptance of enemy images. Counterintuitively, research indicates that well-off people *also* tend to accept prejudice (and we assume therefore enemy images). The concept of *relative gratification* is the antonym of relative deprivation and refers to people who perceive that they are better off than others. Its effect is less studied than the effects of relative deprivation (Dambrun et al., 2006: 1033), with the first experimental tests conducted by the French social psychologists Serge Guimond and Michaël Dambrun in 2002.

As stated, it would intuitively be reasonable to suppose that if GRD leads to intergroup hostility and a propensity to accept enemy images, relative gratification should lead to the opposite, to tolerance and benevolence. This assumption can however be challenged. Guimond and Dambrun found in their 2002 experiment that research participants experiencing relative gratification actually 'expressed in a consistent and reliable manner more negative attitudes toward outgroups' than those in the control group (Guimond and Dambrun, 2002: 904). Dambrun et al. call this seeming contradiction 'the V-curve hypothesis' (2006). In other words, *both* relative deprivation and relative gratification increased the level of prejudice towards relevant out-groups (2006: 1033 and 1040). The reason could be that 'when people perceive economic relative gratification, they are motivated to maintain their advantaged position by derogating groups that are perceived as potential competitors' (Dambrun et al., 2006: 1034).

The idea that economically and socially advantaged individuals or groups 'stigmatize those of lower status to justify their advantages' (Crocker, Major, and Steele, 1998: 509) has not only been proposed in RGT. It also recurs in social dominance theory (SDT), to be discussed later in this chapter, which holds that dominant groups create 'hierarchy-enhancing legitimizing myths' (Pratto et al., 1994: 741 and cf. Sidanius and Pratto, 1999: 45 and 84), something that can inform dominant narratives in a society, and which we will return to in Chapter 6.

Let us recap. In this section, we sought to gain an increased understanding of the societal structures that tend to escalate the acceptance of enemy images. It seems that large social divides could be a fertile ground for enemy images since they give economically and socially advantaged people incentives to seek arguments to justify and maintain their advantaged position, and this can be done in part by derogating or stigmatizing those of lower status.

Individual traits

The previous section discussed socio-economic conditions that increase the risk of proliferation and acceptance of enemy images. In this section, the focus is instead directed towards theories analysing whether and how individuals' characters and traits impact the acceptance of enemy images. In this context, we will discuss the importance of low self-esteem, authoritarian personalities, and social dominance orientation (SDO).

Low self-esteem

The discussion above suggests that belonging to a high-status group can help people feel good about themselves and give them a positive self-image. Therefore, people tend to favour their group and derogate other groups, potentially also accepting enemy images about them. This seems to be a universal tendency. However, we now want to explore whether this tendency is more pronounced, on an individual level, in those with *low self-esteem*.

The idea that people with low self-esteem are likely to derogate out-groups is not unique. On the contrary, several theories 'predict an association between low self-esteem … and out-group derogation' (Golec de Zavala et al., 2020: 742). This is in line with the SIT briefly mentioned in a previous section and starting from which social psychologists Michael A. Hogg and Dominic Abrams formulated two hypotheses (sometimes called the 'self-esteem hypotheses'), the second of them reading:

> Depressed or threatened self-esteem promotes intergroup discrimination because of a need for self-esteem. Self-esteem is an independent variable, a motivating force for specific forms of intergroup behaviour.
>
> *(Hogg and Abrams, 1990: 33)*

It is confirmed that out-group derogation is a way to boost group members' self-esteem (see discussion above, Rubin and Hewstone, 1998). However, it has been more difficult to see a correlation when the variables change, as in Hogg and Abrams' hypothesis. Researchers who have examined the results and data from several studies (i.e. a meta-analysis) have not been able to establish a clear relationship between low self-esteem (independent variable) and out-group derogation (dependent variable) (Martiny and Rubin, 2016).

In a recent article, psychologist Agnieszka Golec de Zavala presented together with colleagues a series of ambitious studies in which she retested Hogg and Abrams' hypothesis. By checking for intervening variables and considering *collective narcissism* as an intermediate variable, she was able to establish clear support for the hypothesis. She defined collective narcissism 'as a belief that the in-group is exceptional and entitled to privileged treatment, but it is not sufficiently recognized by others' (Golec de Zavala et al., 2020: 742) – in other words, it is an 'unrealistic belief about the unparalleled greatness of an ingroup' (Golec de Zavala et al., 2009: 1074). She and her co-authors claim that people with low self-esteem 'may demand privileged treatment and recognition of their in-group to compensate for their personal shortcomings' (2020: 743). And what is worse, 'demanding special treatment for the in-group, they do not shy away from derogating out-groups' (Golec de Zavala et al., 2020: 743). And again, by thoroughly testing the hypothesis in seven studies, she confirmed that 'low self-esteem conduces to out-group derogation. However, this effect was indirect, mediated by collective narcissism' (Golec de Zavala et al., 2020: 761). If she and her co-authors are correct, it seems more than probable that individuals with low self-esteem are more susceptible to enemy images than others.

The authoritarian personality

The authoritarian personality (briefly mentioned in Chapter 1) describes someone who prefers a society with a strong leader who can maintain order, and who is willing to obey them (perhaps completely). Are people with an authoritarian personality more susceptible to enemy images? Although very little research has been conducted on this specific question, we will consult the authoritarian personality theory (APT) to see if it can contribute to our understanding of enemy image acceptance.

Research on the authoritarian personality has a long tradition and gained fresh momentum after the Second World War (Cottam et al., 2016: 28). At the time, there was a need to understand why so many Germans had embraced Nazism and participated in Nazi war crimes and human rights violations. Together with Else Frenkel-Brunswik, Daniel J. Levinson, and R. Nevitt Sanford from the University of California at Berkley, Theodor Adorno formed a research group focusing on the 'the authoritarian personality'. In their research, they saw the need to identify and measure factors they believed contribute to antisemitic and fascist traits. They tried to establish whether certain people had pathological personalities, making them susceptible to anti-democratic propaganda, and even fascism. Their research appeared in an extensive volume published in 1950. Although it was a collective effort, for consistency we will refer to these perspectives as Adorno's research.

BOX 4.5   THEODOR ADORNO'S RESEARCH ON THE AUTHORITARIAN PERSONALITY

Theodor Adorno was a German philosopher (1903–1969) who also worked in fields such as sociology, psychology, and musicology. He taught at the Goethe University Frankfurt in Germany but had to flee to England in 1934 after the Nazis came to power. There, he continued teaching at the University of Oxford. After three years he moved to the United States to work at Princeton University. In 1949 he returned to Frankfurt and rebuilt the Institute for Social Research with his colleague Max Horkheimer. They also participated in bringing the *Frankfurt School of Critical Theory* back to life. This greatly influenced the German intellectual turn after the war. His research on the authoritarian personality has influenced research into prejudices.

Adorno's major topic was the tendency of civilization to destroy itself, leading to fascism. Together with Horkheimer, he published the widely known book *Dialektik der Aufklärung* (Dialectic of Enlightenment, 1947).

His work on the authoritarian personality was a response to the Nazi regime in Germany. It attempted to identify the characteristics of people who favour playing a role in a social system with a strong authority figure. The authoritarian individual could be the strong ruler themselves or their unconditional follower.

This type of person often tends to have negative feelings towards minority groups. Through a questionnaire-study, Adorno et al. generated a scale to define fascist personality traits, called the F-scale (1950: 222–280). Its main purpose was to find the basic structure of an authoritarian personality and to be able to predict fascist or anti-democratic ideological potential.

Noelle M. Nelson (2020) points out that the sample size during Adorno's study was limited. Additionally, she states that the selection of the participants was biased from the beginning as Adorno chose them through formal organizations.

The research conducted by Adorno et al. (and to some extent Altemeyer's study – see below) has received a lot of criticism, mostly because of its methodology. Their research was for some time influential – but harmful to the field, according to its critics. Martin (2001) in particular sees it as politicized psychology rather than political psychology. He states that Adorno et al.'s method consists of two deficient processes. First, he criticizes Adorno's mixing of nominalist research methods, in which empirical results were supposed to characterize respondents, with realistic character interpretations. There he came to the result that certain people simply were authoritarian and others were not. Martin also observed that Adorno had not spent much time on the psychodynamics of liberals, concluding that Adorno's study on the authoritarian personality was therefore biased and interpretative (Martin, 2001).

F-Scale variables (Adorno et al., 1950: 228)

a   *Conventionalism*
    Rigid adherence to conventional, middle-class values
b   *Authoritarian submission*
    Submissive, uncritical attitude towards idealized moral authorities of the in-group
c   *Authoritarian aggression*
    Tendency to be on the lookout for, and to condemn, reject, and punish people who violate conventional values
d   *Anti-intraception*
    Opposition to the subjective, the imaginative, the tender-minded
e   *Superstition and stereotypy*
    Belief in mystical determinants of the individual's fate; disposition to think in rigid categories
f   *Power and 'toughness'*
    Preoccupation with the dominance–submission, strong–weak, leader–follower dimension; identification with power figures; over-emphasis on the

> conventionalized attributes of the ego; exaggerated assertion of strength and toughness
> g *Destructiveness and cynicism*
>   Generalized hostility, vilification of the human
> h *Projectivity*
>   Disposition to believe that wild and dangerous things go on in the world; projection outwards of unconscious emotional impulses
> i *Sex*
>   Exaggerated concern with sexual 'goings-on'

Founded on some of Sigmund Freud's psychoanalytic arguments, Adorno's study regards the personality as stable over a person's lifetime, as 'an organization of needs', and most importantly as 'a determinant of ideological preferences' (Adorno et al., 1950: 5), making it an important topic to analyse right after the Holocaust and Nazism. According to Adorno,

> one of the major findings of the present study [is] that individuals who show extreme susceptibility to fascist propaganda have a great deal in common. (They exhibit numerous characteristics that go together to form a 'syndrome' although typical variations within this major pattern can be distinguished).
> *(Adorno et al., 1950: 1, second parenthesis in original)*

Adorno and his co-authors summarized the characteristics that make people susceptible to fascism in a list of variables (presented in Box 4.5), but two common traits of the authoritarian personality are a 'rigid adherence to conventional, middle-class values' and 'submissive, uncritical attitude toward idealized moral authorities of the ingroup' (Adorno et al., 1950: 228). Based upon this list of variables, Adorno formulated the so-called F-scale, where F stands for fascism, intended to measure the authoritarian personality (Adorno et al., 1950: 222–280) and more specifically to 'construct an instrument that would yield an estimate of fascist receptivity at the personality level' (Adorno et al., 1950: 279).

Another theme in this research project concerned factors contributing to an authoritarian personality. According to Adorno, this personality was the product of an authoritarian upbringing with demanding, controlling parents who also used severe disciplinary techniques (Adorno et al., 1950: 340, 519, 529, and 544).

Although Adorno and his co-authors never spoke of enemy images per se, it is not unreasonable to assume that researchers would corroborate that people with authoritarian traits consistent with the findings of Adorno's team are likely to recognize their thoughts in an enemy image and embrace the core arguments of an ideal–typical enemy image.

The research by Adorno et al. was just the beginning of research into the authoritarian personality and attitudes. In the 1980s, it was renewed by

American psychologist Robert Altemeyer (b. 1940) in his pathbreaking book *The Authoritarian Specter* (1996), where he abandons Adorno's psychoanalytical foundations. Unlike Adorno, Altemeyer does not see right-wing authoritarianism as an essential personality trait, but rather as something learned (Altemeyer, 1996: 78). Yet he borrows three of Adorno's personality traits, stating in his introduction that 'right-wing authoritarianism' is 'the covariation of three attitudinal clusters in a person':

Authoritarian submission – a high degree of submission to the authorities who are perceived to be established and legitimate in the society in which one lives.

Authoritarian aggression – a general aggressiveness, directed against various persons, that is perceived to be sanctioned by established authorities.

Conventionalism – a high degree of adherence to the social conventions that are perceived to be endorsed by society and its established authorities.

(Altemeyer, 1996: 6)

Later in the same book, Altemeyer discusses how right-wing authoritarians think and make decisions. He claims that people with these tendencies have, in contrast to others,

not spent much time examining evidence, thinking critically, reaching independent conclusions, and seeing whether their conclusions mesh with the other things they believe. Instead, they have largely accepted what they were told by the authorities in their lives, … which … leaves them underpracticed in thinking for themselves.

(Altemeyer, 1996: 93)

Another trait that seems to characterize right-wing authoritarians is that they

stand about ten steps closer to the panic button than the rest of the population. They see the world as a more dangerous place than most others do, with civilization on the verge of collapse and the world of Mad Max looming just beyond.

(Altemeyer, 1996: 100; c.f. Son Hing and Zanna, 2010: 167)

However, this does not mean that right-wing authoritarians believe everything they hear. On the contrary, 'they carry quite a list of "false teachings" and rejected ideologies in their heads'. But they lack the capacity to identify 'falsehoods on their own because they are not as prepared to think critically' (Altemeyer, 1996: 95). Their profile also makes them 'particularly vulnerable to an insincere communicator who tells them what they want to hear' (Altemeyer, 1996: 109).

Previously, in Chapter 1 and earlier in this chapter, we discussed the concept of 'attribution error': people tending to believe that their enemy's good behaviour is an effect of situational factors ('they' perform good behaviour because 'they' must) and bad behaviour an effect of dispositional factors ('they' perform aggressive behaviour because that is who 'they' are). Altemeyer found that attribution error is far more common among right-wing authoritarians, particularly when they agreed with the message (Altemeyer, 1996: 109).

Lastly, Altemeyer never discusses enemy image acceptance, but he does make a case that comes close. Conducting his research during the Cold War, he draws the following conclusion about the most war-prone individuals in the two superpowers:

> Who formed the front ranks of the Cold War warriors, on both sides? Which Russians tended to believe their country had a right to intervene in their neighbors' affairs that the United States did not have? Which Americans tended to think they were building nuclear weapons only because of the Russian threat? Which Russians thought their leaders truly wanted peace and freedom around the world while the American leaders did not? Which Americans believed their government invaded other countries because it cared about the people living there? Which Russians believed the United States would launch a surprise nuclear attack if it could get away with it? You will not be surprised by the answer, in all cases: largely the right-wing authoritarians.
>
> *(Altemeyer, 1996: 127)*

Now the question must be asked: is the authoritarian personality more susceptible to enemy images? Considering the quote above, the answer is almost a given and would resonate well with Altemeyer. Enemy images are usually communicated by people in a position of authority and make use of established beliefs in the group. They talk about threats to 'our' most central assets. All of this adds up to the fact that enemy images are most likely compatible with the cognitive processes of right-wing authoritarians. Ergo, such personalities would most likely accept them.

A recent review article on contemporary research into authoritarianism by Schnelle, Handjar, and Boehnke (2021) provides a valuable overview of later developments within this field. As we have seen in the research by Adorno's team and by Altemeyer, the authoritarian personality was perceived as something stable, either formed in early childhood or even genetic. In the more recent research that Schnelle, Handjar, and Boehnke present, a different view emerges of how the authoritarian personality arises: the emergence of authoritarian traits is seen as something dynamic and determined by the current environment and situational and contextual influences alike (Schnelle, Handjar, and Boehnke, 2021). It seems that life-long socialization combined with fear-laden situations in which the individual experiences different forms of threat are stimuli that have a bearing on the development of authoritarian traits.

Social dominance orientation

SDT was originally formulated by the psychologists Jim Sidanius and Felicia Pratto in the 1990s and ties together several established social science theories (Sidanius and Pratto, 1999: 31). According to this theory, all societies are composed of stable group-based hierarchies (Sidanius and Pratto, 1999: 31), and individuals who belong to a powerful group can dominate others even if they lack individual characteristics such as charisma and intelligence (Rios Morrison and Ybarra, 2007: 894). SDT describes societies as usually having three kinds of hierarchy, based on *gender* (men have higher status than women), *age* (the middle-aged have higher status than young and old), and an arbitrary category that differs from one society to another (Sidanius and Pratto, 1999: 35–40). An important point in this theory is that people with a SDO seem to embrace and accept these hierarchies and favour an unequal, hierarchical, dominance-oriented relationship among groups. High scorers simply want their in-group to dominate out-groups (Pratto et al., 1994: 741). And, as Altemeyer says, people with a high SDO believe that

> equality should not be a central value of our society or a goal toward which we should strive. It is a mistake to intervene in the law of the jungle. To social dominators, 'equality' is a sucker-word in which only fools believe.
>
> *(Altemeyer, 2004: 425)*

And lastly, social dominators enjoy power and would not hesitate to hurt someone who blocks their plans. In other words, they act with relatively little moral restraint (Altemeyer, 2004: 425).

In this theory, Sidanius and Pratto also present an SDO *scale* that differentiates people who prefer social group relations to be equal or hierarchical, and by the extent to which they want their in-group to dominate an out-group (Sidanius and Pratto, 1999: 67). In their SDO scale, they aim to identify how much the research participants agree with or reject values such as 'increased social equality', 'increased economic equality', and 'equality' in general (see the full list below). The scale below was published in 1999 and is one of several slightly different versions. Here Sidanius and Pratto ask research participants to agree or disagree with 14 statements, and the researchers can assess their score and SDO based on their replies.

1. Some groups of people are simply not the equals of others.
2. Some people are just more worthy than others.
3. This country would be better off if we cared less about how equal all people were.
4. Some people are just more deserving than others.
5. It is not a problem if some people have more of a chance in life than others.

6. Some people are just inferior to others.
7. To get ahead in life, it is sometimes necessary to step on others.
8. Increased economic equality.
9. Increased social equality.
10. Equality.
11. If people were treated more equally we would have fewer problems in this country.
12. In an ideal world, all nations would be equal.
13. We should try to treat one another as equals as much as possible. (All humans should be treated equally.)
14. It is important that we treat other countries as equals.

(Sidanius and Pratto, 1999: 66)

Societies marked by injustice and great social differences are often affected by conflict. Those who benefit from the established order and dominate in such societies have an interest in maintaining it and undermining the legitimacy of those working for change. This group is most likely to produce myths justifying inequalities between the groups (Sidanius and Pratto, 1999: 45, 84) as an instrument to 'minimize group conflict by creating consensus on ideologies that promote the superiority of one group over others' (Pratto et al., 1994: 741). In other words, groups benefitting from the societal hierarchy create an ideology that legitimizes existing differences between groups. Most commonly, in SDT, ideology aims to passivate, to legitimize discrimination and stabilize oppression. Pratto et al. call these hierarchy-legitimizing myths (Pratto et al., 1994: 741). But this theory also claims that social dominators can produce an ideology legitimizing war if the social structure is jeopardized.

According to Altemeyer (2004) and Sidanius and Pratto (1999), people with an SDO have a few things in common with authoritarian personality types. For instance, both are 'expected to be relatively racist, sexist, homophobic, ethnocentric, and politically conservative, and to show little empathy for lower-status others' (Sidanius and Pratto, 1999: 74). Both are most likely prejudiced and keen on law and order. Both probably dislike various minorities and people who deviate from the norm in some way. They also have similar attitudes to market-oriented economic policies (Altemeyer, 2004: 426). But there are also some differences. Social dominators want to dominate. The authoritarians probably accept being dominated and submit. The SDOs have little or no religious background, while authoritarians have received a religious upbringing and probably still attend church services (Altemeyer, 2004: 426). SDOs could be seen as amoral and without ideology, while the authoritarians are dogmatic. Lastly, although both are prejudiced, it seems that this attitude has different causes. According to Altemeyer, 'social dominators' prejudice seems to spring from personal drives to dominate. Authoritarians' prejudice ... appears to arise largely from fear and self-righteousness' (Altemeyer, 2004: 426).

What can we learn from social domination theory? Can it inform us about the acceptance of enemy images? It is important to note that social domination theory was not created to discuss enemy image acceptance but for other purposes. We believe, however, that it is still possible to draw some tentative conclusions.

To social domination theory, social dominators are susceptible to various ideologies that legitimize their position in a hierarchy and such ideologies correlate with SDO (Pratto et al., 1994: 742). Moreover, SDO does not exist in isolation. It seems that 'SDO serves as an orientation in shaping new attitudes' (Pratto et al., 1994: 742). So, people with an SDO are probably also susceptible to ethnic prejudice, racism (like white supremacy), cultural elitism, sexism, political-economic conservatism (and thus against generous welfare programmes), militarism, punitive policies, and to chauvinist nationalism (Pratto et al., 1994: 742–743 and 754 and Sidanius and Pratto, 1999: 83–93). And in their study conducted during the Gulf War 1990–1991, Pratto and his co-authors found that social dominators were associated with pro-war sentiment (Pratto et al., 1994: 753). Since SDO has shaped political attitudes in this way, particularly the tendency to militarism and national chauvinism, high scorers most probably have attitudes to out-groups and violence that are compatible with an enemy image, and social dominators would likely embrace important elements of the ideal–typical enemy image presented in Chapter 2. The idea that 'we' are superior to 'them' and that violent responses to perceived threats are legitimate is probably not alien to them.

The need for consolation

In the previous two sections, we have explained how socio-economic conditions and individuals' characters and traits affect their acceptance of enemy images. In this last section, a situational factor will be explored: our susceptibility to enemy images after committing violent actions.

It makes intuitive sense to assume that humans *first* hear, read, watch, and then intellectually accept and internalize an enemy image *before* acting violently, that enemy images programme us to commit acts of violence. However, as elaborated in Chapter 1, people tend to commit violent acts for other reasons, too. Being under the pressure of authority and peers, as well as physically distant from a victim, can facilitate participation in violence and even the committing of war crimes. It appears worthwhile to explore if enemy images could have a comforting function *after* horrendous violent acts have been committed. When conscience strikes after such acts, people seek consolation to justify what they did. And enemy images can serve as comfort after the actor aggresses against the victim since enemy images justify their aggressive behaviour (Worchel and Andreoli, 1978: 550).

In Chapter 1, various consequences of enemy images were discussed. Using ideas from Albert Bandura's moral disengagement theory (2016), as well as from Michael Taillard and Holly Giscoppa (2013), we discussed the emotional *effects* of enemy images, how they can justify participating in violence because most people feel a certain amount of guilt after committing violent actions (Bandura, 2016: 29), and seeking relief from guilt is a typical strategy of psychological comfort (Taillard and Giscoppa, 2013: 108). Under peaceful circumstances, people try to behave by their standards of right and wrong and refrain from violating collective norms (Osofsky, Bandura, and Zimbardo, 2005: 371). And they punish themselves when they do not, self-sanctioning for behaviour they think violates their norms (Bandura, 2016: 1). When people follow their moral compass, on the other hand, they experience satisfaction and a sense of self-worth (Bandura, 2016: 1). That is one important reason why people usually act morally. In war, on the other hand, people sometimes must do things that violate their moral standards.

> When soldiers are sent into battle with questionable justification or in the context of national discord over the morality of the cause, they pay a heavy social and psychological price. They are viewed by many as having fought for an illegitimate rather than a noble cause. Some return haunted by their combat experiences and guilt ridden over moral breaches that led to some of their military actions.
>
> *(Bandura, 2016: 49–50)*

And in such situations, people's self-respect suffers, as does their sense of self-worth. They might begin to loathe themselves, and self-loathing is harmful and devastating for emotional wellbeing. In his research and writing, Bandura explains how people retain their self-respect after misconduct (Bandura, 2016). In Chapter 1, we discussed in detail how enemy images can legitimize war crimes and how enemy images can help perpetrators of violence disengage morally. For instance, enemy images can help people sanctify immoral violent behaviour by claiming it was informed by a moral *purpose*. Enemy images can also help to *displace responsibility* for the violence onto the victim, seen as an enemy who has been violent at an earlier stage of the conflict and brought it on themselves. And enemy images can also help people to dehumanize the victims of our violence. With the help of enemy imagery, they can tell themselves that they did not kill humans.

Our point is that enemy images are likely to be in demand even *after* people have carried out acts of violence. When their conscience torments them because of what they have done, people should confess their actions. But no, instead they search for a narrative that frees them from guilt. Therefore, when their soul is distressed by guilt, people are at their most susceptible to enemy images. Accepting such images becomes a strategy for emotional recovery.

Summary

What is most striking in the description of the theories and reasoning above is how functional enemy images are. All the theories appear to indicate that enemy images are accepted because they fulfil important functions for both the individual and the group.

Hardly any research or literature exists directly addressing the question, 'Why do we accept enemy images?'. But informed by various approaches explaining individual and structural factors, we have explored the human tendency to accept enemy images.

Firstly, starting with motivation theory, it appears to be a reasonable claim that enemy images are compatible with people's need for their group, and with their predisposition to fear outsiders. It also feeds their need for belonging, meaning, and status.

Secondly, research on cognition explains that enemy images are useful since they are a form of stereotype, facilitating simple, swift, and fast processing of stimuli. And once people embrace an enemy image, they tend to avoid or explain away information that questions it. In other words, they tend to avoid cognitive dissonance. Internalized enemy images become self-perpetuating.

Thirdly, social structures also matter. Realistic group conflict theory and relative deprivation theory explain why it is likely that social structures where people experience a (relative) shortage of important resources boost the prevalence of enemy images. The same could also be said of people experiencing that they are better off than others since they might embrace prejudice, with enemy images perhaps justifying their advantaged position.

Fourthly, we also consulted research focusing on the individual level, discussing factors such as low self-esteem, the authoritarian personality, and SDO. Literature on this analytical level should be read with some degree of caution. But there is evidence that people with low self-esteem are inclined to out-group derogation, and since enemy images have an element of out-group derogation, it is reasonable to assume that there may be a correlation between low self-confidence and acceptance of enemy images. Likewise, since people with an authoritarian personality tend to see the world as dangerous, and since they tend to embrace aggressive authoritarian messages, it is likely that they would be more disposed to accept enemy images. It is also reasonable to assume that people with an SDO, and its concomitant tendency to believe in hierarchy and dominance, would also recognize themselves in and accept the enemy image's thoughts about 'our' superiority.

Lastly, moral disengagement theory might explain why people are particularly susceptible to enemy images after they have carried out morally questionable acts of violence. In this situation, people will search for narratives like those offered by enemy images to justify their actions and liberate them from guilt. Their tendency to see the enemy as subhuman and as a threat to their legitimate assets functions as a narrative of innocence. In such a situation, it is tempting to accept the enemy image.

Study questions

- Revisit Gordon Allport and Leo Postman's subway experiment (1947) and the image used. Do you think this kind of image still is relevant today? Try to design an image that would represent the psychological processes involved in the visualization of prejudices today.

- Leon Festinger's theory on cognitive dissonance can help us to understand why and how people tend to *hold on to* and *keep* an enemy image. Can you come up with an example of 'cognitive dissonance' and how it impacts the perception of adversaries?
- Revisit Muzafer Sherif's famous 'Robbers Cave' experiment. Have you been exposed to similar dynamics in groups you belonged to? If so, how did this dynamic affect you, your group, and your relationship to the out-group?

Potential essay or thesis suggestion

In SDT, Jim Sidanius and Felicia Pratto presented an SDO scale differentiating people who prefer social group relations to be equal or hierarchical. Design and carry out a study based on the SDO scale. Reflect on the following:

- How would you design a study based on SDO?
- How would you gather data?
- What research ethics problems would the study have?

Recommended further reading

Cottam, M., Dietz-Uhler, B., Mastors, E., and Preston, T. (2004) *Introduction to Political Psychology*. Mahwah, NJ: Lawrence Erlbaum Associates Publishers.
Published in several editions, this is a comprehensive and easy-to-read textbook that deals with the psychological origins of political behaviour. What makes it particularly relevant for students with an interest in enemy images is that it touches on issues such as cognition, the political psychology of media, race, genocide, nationalism, and terrorism. It also discusses conflict resolution and reconciliation.

Gilovich, T., Keltner, D., Chen, S. and Nisbett, R. E. (2018) *Social Psychology* (5th ed.). New York, NY: WW Norton & Company.
This is a much appreciated and widely used textbook on social psychology that has been published in several editions. Since many of the arguments in this chapter are taken from social psychology, it might be a good idea to read an accessible textbook in the area. This one is relevant.

Sidanius, J. and Pratto, F. (1999) *Social Dominance: An Intergroup Theory of Social Hierarchy and Oppression*. Cambridge: Cambridge University Press.
In this classic book, Jim Sidanius and Felicia Pratto present SDT. The authors are social psychologists who seek answers to questions concerning the causes of oppression and discrimination against people from other groups, and why this oppression is so hard to eliminate.

Bibliography

Adorno, T. W., Frenkel-Brunswik, E., Levinson, D. J. and Sanford, R. N. (1950) *The Authoritarian Personality*. New York, NY: Harper and Row.

Allen, K.-A. (2021) *The Psychology of Belonging*. Abingdon, Oxon: Routledge.

Allport, G. W. (1937) *Personality: A Psychological Interpretation*. New York, NY: Holt, Rinehart & Winston.

Allport, G. W. (1954) *The Nature of Prejudice*. New York, NY: Basic Books.

Allport, G. W. and Postman, L. (1947) *The Psychology of Rumor*. New York, NY: Henry Holt and Company.

Altemeyer, B. (1996) *The Authoritarian Specter*. Cambridge, MA: Harvard University Press.

Altemeyer, B. (2004) Highly dominating, highly authoritarian personalities. *The Journal of Social Psychology* 144(4): 421–447. https://doi.org/10.3200/SOCP.144.4.421-448

Anderson, A. and Christie, D. J. (2001) Some contributions of psychology to policies promoting cultures of peace. *Peace and Conflict: Journal of Peace Psychology* 7(2): 173–185. https://doi.org/10.1207/S15327949PAC0702_07

Atran, S. (2010) *Talking to the Enemy: Violent Extremism, Sacred Values, and What It Means to Be Human*. London: Allen Lane.

Bandura, A. (2016) *Moral Disengagement, How People Do Harm and Live with Them-Selves*. New York, NY: Worth Publishers.

Baumeister, R. and Leary, M. (1995) The need to belong: Desire for interpersonal attachments as a fundamental human motivation. *Psychology Bulletin* 117(3): 497–529. https://doi.org/10.1037/0033-2909.117.3.497

Brown, B. (2010) *The Gifts of Imperfection: Let Go of Who You Think You're Supposed to Be and Embrace Who You Are*. Center City, MN: Hazelden.

Buckley, K., Winkel, R. and Leary, M. (2003) Reactions to acceptance and rejection: Effects of level and sequence of relational evaluation. *Journal of Experimental Social Psychology* 40(1): 14–28. https://doi.org/10.1016/S0022-1031(03)00064-7

Campbell, D. T. (1965) Ethnocentric and Other Altruistic Motives. In Levine D. (ed.) *Nebraska Symposium on Motivation* (pp. 283–311). Lincoln, NE: University of Nebraska Press.

Chartrand, T. L. and Bargh, J. A. (1999) The chameleon effect: The perception–behavior link and social interaction. *Journal of Personality and Social Psychology* 76(6): 893–910. https://doi.org/10.1037/0022-3514.76.6.893

Cialdini, R. B. and Goldstein, N. J. (2004) Social influence: Compliance and conformity. *Annual Review of Psychology* 55: 591–621. https://doi.org/10.1146/annurev.psych.55.090902.142015

Cole, A. (2004) What Hegel's master/slave dialectic really means. *Journal of Medieval and Early Modern Studies* 34(3): 577–610.

Cottam, M., Dietz-Uhler, B., Mastors, E. and Preston, T. (2016) *Introduction to Political Psychology* (3rd ed.). Mahwah, NJ: Lawrence Erlbaum Associates Publishers.

Cottee, S. and Hayward, K. (2011) Terrorist (E)motives: The existential attractions of terrorism. *Studies in Conflict and Terrorism* 34(12): 963–986. https://doi.org/10.1080/1057610X.2011.621116

Crocker, J. and Knight, K. M. (2005) Contingencies of self-worth. *Current Directions in Psychological Science* 14(4): 200–203. https://doi.org/10.1111/j.0963-7214.2005.00364.x

Crocker, J., Major, B. and Steele, C. (1998) Social Stigma. In Gilbert, D., Fiske, S. and Lindzey G. (eds.) *Handbook of Social Psychology* (4th ed., pp. 504–553). Boston, MA: McGraw-Hill.

Dambrun, M., Taylor, D. M., McDonald, D. A., Crush, J. and Méot, A. (2006) The relative deprivation–gratification continuum and the attitudes of South Africans toward immigrants: A test of the V-curve hypothesis. *Journal of Personality and Social Psychology* 91(6): 1032–1044. https://doi.org/10.1037/0022-3514.91.6.1032

Dawson, L. (1999) When prophecy fails and faith persists: A theoretical overview. *Nova Religion: The Journal of Alternative and Emergent Religions* 3(1): 60–82. https://doi.org/10.1525/nr.1999.3.1.60

Dawson, L. (2017) *Sketch of a Social Ecology Model for Explaining Homegrown Terrorist Radicalisation*. The Hague, NL: International Centre for Counter-Terrorism.

Dawson, L. (2023) The Social Ecology Model of 'homegrown' Jihadist Radicalization. In Awan, A. N. and Lewis, J. R. (eds.) *Radicalisation: A Global and Comparative Perspective* (pp. 33–56). London: Hurst & Company.

Deschamps, J. and Devos, T. (1998) Regarding the Relationship between Social Identity and Personal Identity. In Worchel, S., Morales, J., Páez, D. and Deschamps, J. (eds.) *Social Identity: International Perspectives* (pp. 1–12). London: Sage Publications, Inc. https://doi.org/10.4135/9781446279205.n1

Dodge, T. (2012) Enemy images, coercive socio-engineering and civil war in Iraq. *International Peacekeeping* 19(4): 461–477. http://doi.org/10.1080/13533312.2012.709756

Dovidio, J. F., Glick, P. and Rudman, L. A. (2005) Introduction: Reflection on the Nature of Prejudice: Fifty Years after Allport. In *On the Nature of Prejudice: Fifty Years after Allport*. Malden, MA: Blackwell Publishing.

Dovidio, J. F., Hewstone, M., Glick, P. and Esses, V. M. (2010) Prejudice, Stereotyping and Discrimination: Theoretical and Empirical Overview. In *The Sage Handbook of Prejudice, Stereotyping and Discrimination* (pp. 3–28) London: SAGE Publications.

Dunn, T. L. and Risko, E. F. (2019) Understanding the cognitive miser: Cue-utilization in effort-based decision making. *Acta Psychologica* 198: 1–10. https://doi.org/10.1016/j.actpsy.2019.102863

Fein, S. and Spencer, S. J. (1997) Prejudice as self-image maintenance: Affirming the self through derogating others. *Journal of Personality and Social Psychology* 73(1): 31–44.

Festinger, L. (1957) *A Theory of Cognitive Dissonance*. Stanford, CA: Stanford University Press.

Festinger, L., Riecken, H. and Schachter, S. (1956) *When Prophecy Fails*. Minneapolis, MN: University of Minnesota Press.

Fiebig-von Hase, R. (1997) Introduction. In Fiebig-von Hase, R. and Lemkuhl, U. (eds.) *Enemy Images in American History* (pp. 1–40). Providence, RI; Oxford, NY: Berghahn.

Fiske, S. and Taylor, S. (1984) *Social Cognition*. New York, NY: Random House.

Frank, J. and Melville, A. (1988) The Image of the Enemy and the Process of Change. In Gromyko, A. and Hellman, M. (eds.) *Breakthrough: Emerging New Thinking* (pp. 198–207). New York, NY: Walker.

Frith, C. D. (2008) Social cognition. *Philosophical Transactions: Biological Sciences* 363(1499): 2033–2039. www.jstor.org/stable/20208607

Gatto, J., Guimond, S. and Dambrun, M. (2018) Relative gratification and outgroup prejudice: Further tests on a new dimension of comparison. *The Open Psychology Journal* 11: 1–14. http://dx.doi.org/10.2174/1874350101811010001

Gilbert, D. T. and Hixon, J. G. (1991) The trouble of thinking: Activation and application of stereotypic beliefs. *Journal of Personality and Psychology* 60(4): 509–517.

Gilovich, T., Keltner, D., Chen, S. and Nisbett, R. E. (2016) *Social Psychology* (4th ed.). New York, NY: WW Norton & Company.

Golec de Zavala, A., Cichocka, A., Eidelson, R. and Jayawickreme, N. (2009) Collective narcissism and its social consequences. *Journal of Personality and Social Psychology* 97(6): 1074–1096. http://dx.doi.org/10.1037/a0016904

Golec de Zavala, A., Federico, C. M., Sedikides, C., Guerra, R., Lantos, D., Mroziński, B., Cypryańska, M. and Baran, T. (2020) Low self-esteem predicts out-group derogation via collective narcissism, but this relationship is obscured by in-group satisfaction. *Journal of Personality and Social Psychology: Personality Processes and Individual Differences* 119(3): 741–764. http://dx.doi.org/10.1037/pspp0000260

Grant, P. R. and Brown, R. (1995) From ethnocentrism to collective protest: Responses to relative deprivation and threats to social identity. *Social Psychology Quarterly* 58(3): 195–211. https://doi.org/10.2307/2787042

Guimond, S. and Dambrun, M. (2002) When prosperity breeds intergroup hostility: The effects of relative deprivation and relative gratification on prejudice. *Personality and Social Psychology Bulletin* 28(7): 900–912.

Haggbloom, S. J. (2002) The 100 most eminent psychologists of the 20th century. *Review of General Psychology* 6(2): 139–152. https://doi.org/10.1037/1089-2680.6.2.139

Haider, J. and Sundin, O. (2022) *Paradoxes of Media and Information Literacy: The Crisis of Information*. London: Routledge.

Hatfield E., Carpenter, M., Thornton, P. and Rapson, R. (2014) In Oxford Biographies, *Leon Festinger*. http://doi.org/10.1093/OBO/9780199828340-0157

Hertzman, M. and Festinger, L. (1940) Shifts in explicit goals in a level of aspiration experiment. *Journal of Experimental Psychology* 27(4): 439–452. https://doi.org/10.1037/h0055195

Hinton, P. (2000) *Stereotypes, Cognition and Culture*. New York, NY: Psychology Press.

Hitler, A. ([1925–26] 1999) *Mein Kampf*. New York, NY: A Mariner Book, Houghton Mifflin Company.

Hogg, M. and Abrams, D. (1990) Social Motivation, Self-Esteem and Social Identity. In Abrams, D. and Hogg, M. (eds.) *Social Identity Theory: Constructive and Critical Advances* (pp. 28–47). New York, NY: Harvester Wheatsheaf.

Horkheimer, M. and Adorno, T. (1947) *Dialektik der Aufklärung* [Dialectic of Enlightenment]. Amsterdam: Querido-Verlag.

Jenkins, P. (2014) *The Great and Holy War: How World War I Changed Religion Forever*. Oxford: Lion Books.

Jones, E. E. (1985) Major Developments in Social Psychology during the Past Five Decades. In Lindzey G. and Aronson E. (eds.) *Handbook of Social Psychology* (pp. 47–107). New York, NY: Random House.

Jones, M. (2002) *Social Psychology of Prejudice*. Upper Saddle River, NJ: Prentice Hall.

Kayaoğlu, A., Batur, S. and Aslıtürk, E. (2014) The unknown Muzafer Sherif. *The Psychologist* 27(11): 830–833.

Khan, S. and Samarina, V. (2007) Realistic Group Conflict Theory. In Baumeister, R. and Vohs, K. (eds.) *Encyclopaedia of Social Psychology* (pp.725–726). Thousand Oaks, CA: SAGE Publications.

Koltko-Rivera, M. (2006) Rediscovering the later version of Maslow's hierarchy of needs: Self transcendence and opportunities for theory, research, and unification. *Review of General Psychology* 10(4): 302–317. https://doi.org/10.1037/1089-2680.10.4.302

Kornfield, M. (2021) Why hundreds of QAnon supporters showed up in Dallas, expecting JFK Jr.'s return. *Washington Post*. 2 November 2021. www.washingtonpost.com/nation/2021/11/02/qanon-jfk-jr-dallas/, accessed 8 November 2022.

Kruglanski, A. W., Bélanger, J. J., and Gunaratna, R. (2019) *The Three Pillars of Radicalization: Needs, Narratives and Networks*. New York, NY: Oxford University Press. https://doi-org.proxy.mau.se/10.1093/oso/9780190851125.001.0001

Kunda, Z. (1999) *Social Cognition: Making Sense of People*. Cambridge, MA: The MIT Press.

Levine, J. M. and Murphy, G. (1943) The learning and forgetting of controversial material. *The Journal of Abnormal and Social Psychology* 38(4): 507–517. https://doi.org/10.1037/h0062586

Lippmann, W. ([1922] 2007) *Public Opinion*. Wilmington, NC: NuVision Publications, 1922.

Luostarinen, H. (1989) Finnish Russophobia: The story of an enemy image. *Journal of Peace Research* 26(2): 123–137. www.jstor.org/stable/423864

Madon, S., Guyll, M., Aboufadel, K., Montiel, E., Smith, A., Palumbo, P. and Jussim, L. (2001) Ethnic and national stereotypes: The Princeton trilogy revisited and revised. *Personality and Social Psychology Bulletin* 27(8): 996–1010. https://doi.org/10.1177/0146167201278007

Martin, J. L. (2001) "The Authoritarian Personality," 50 years later: What lessons are there for political psychology? *Political Psychology* 22(1): 1–26. www.jstor.org/stable/3791902

Martiny, S. E. and Rubin, M. (2016) Towards a Clearer Understanding of Social Identity Theory's Self-Esteem Hypothesis. In S. McKeown, R. Haji and N. Ferguson (eds.) *Understanding Peace and Conflict through Social Identity Theory: Contemporary Global Perspectives* (pp. 19–32). New York, NY: Springer. http://dx.doi.org/10.1007/978-3-319-29869-6_2

Maslow, A. (1943) A theory of human motivation. *Psychological Review* 50(4): 370–396. http://doi.org/10.1037/h0054346

Maslow, A. (1993) *The Farther Reaches of Human Nature*. New York, NY: Arkana.

Méndez-Bértolo, C., Moratti, S., Toledano, R., Lopez-Sosa, F., Martínez-Alvarez, R., Mah, Y., Vuilleumier, P., Gil-Nagel, A. and Strange, B. (2016) A fast pathway for fear in human amygdala. *Nature Neuroscience* 19(8), 1041–1049. https://doi.org/10.1038/nn.4324

Mummendey, A., Kessler, T., Klink, A. and Mielke R. (1999) Strategies to cope with negative social identity: Predictions by social identity theory and relative deprivation theory. *Journal of Personality and Social Psychology* 76(2): 229–245. https://doi.org/10.1037/0022-3514.76.2.229

Nelson, E. (2020) *Levinas, Adorno, and the Ethics of the Material Other*. New York, NY: State University of New York Press.

Nickerson, R. S. (1998) Confirmation bias: A ubiquitous phenomenon in many guises. *Review of General Psychology* 2(2): 175–220. https://doi.org/10.1037/1089-2680.2.2.175

Oppenheimer, L. (2006) The development of enemy images: A theoretical contribution. *Peace and Conflict: Journal of Peace Psychology* 12(3): 269–292. https://doi.org/10.1207/s15327949pac1203_4

Osofsky, M., Bandura, A. and Zimbardo, P. (2005) The role of moral disengagement in the execution process. *Law and Human Behavior* 29(4): 371–393. https://doi.org/10.1007/s10979-005-4930-1

Perloff, R. (2003) *The Dynamics of Persuasion, Communication and Attitudes in the 21st Century* (2nd ed.). Mahwah, NJ: Lawrence Erlbaum Associates, Publishers.

Pettigrew, T. F. (1979) The ultimate attribution error: Extending allport's cognitive analysis of prejudice. *Personality and Social Psychology Bulletin* 5(4): 461–476. https://doi.org/10.1177/014616727900500407

Pettigrew, T. F. (2015) Allport, Gordon W (1897–1967). In *International Encyclopedia of the Social & Behavioral Sciences* (2nd ed., pp. 562–565). Amsterdam: Elsevier. https://doi.org/10.1016/B978-0-08-097086-8.61001-2

Pettigrew, T. F., Christ, O., Wagner, U., Meertens, R. W., van Dick, R. and Zick, A. (2008) Relative deprivation and intergroup prejudice. *Journal of Social Issues* 64(2): 385–401. https://doi.org/10.1111/j.1540-4560.2008.00567.x

Phelps, E., O'Connor, K. J., Cunningham, W. A. and Funayama, S. (2000) Performance on indirect measures of race evaluation predicts amygdala activation. *Journal of Cognitive Neuroscience* 12(5): 729–738. https://doi.org/10.1162/089892900562552

Pratto, F., Sidanius, J., Stallworth, L. M. and Malle, B. F. (1994) Social dominance orientation: A personality variable predicting social and political attitudes. *Journal of Personality and Social Psychology* 67(4): 741–763. https://doi.org/10.1037/0022-3514.67.4.741

Rios Morrison, K. and Ybarra O. (2007) Social Dominance Orientation. In Baumeister, R. and Vohs, K. (eds.) *Encyclopedia of Social Psychology* (pp. 894–895). SAGE Publications, Inc. https://dx.doi.org/10.4135/9781412956253

Ross, L. and Anderson, C. (1982) Shortcomings in the Attribution Process: On the Origins and Maintenance of Erroneous Social Assessments. In Kahneman, D., Slovic, P. and Tversky, A. *Judgment under Uncertainty: Heuristics and Biases.* Cambridge: Cambridge University Press.

Rubin, M. and Hewstone, M. (1998) Social identity theory's self-esteem hypothesis: A review and some suggestions for clarification. *Personality and Social Psychology Review* 2: 40–62. http://dx.doi.org/10.1207/s15327957pspr0201_3

Schaller, M, Conway III, L. G. and Peavy, K. M. (2010) Evolutionary Processes. In *The Sage Handbook of Prejudice, Stereotyping and Discrimination* (pp. 81–96). London: SAGE Publications. https://doi.org/10.4135/9781446200919

Schnelle C., Baier, D., Handjar, A. and Boehnke, K. (2021) Authoritarianism beyond disposition: A literature review of research on contextual antecedents. *Frontiers in Psychology* (Volume 12, pp. 1–10). http://doi.org/10.3389/fpsyg.2021.676093

Sechrist, G. and Stangor, C. (2001) Perceived consensus influences intergroup behavior and stereotype accessibility. *Journal of Personality and Social Psychology* 80(4): 645–654.

Sherif, M. (1966) *Group Conflict and Co-operation: Their Social Psychology.* London: Routledge & Kegan Paul Ltd.

Sherif, M., Harvey, O. J., White, B. J., Hood, W. R. and Sherif, C. W. ([1961] 1988) *Intergroup Conflict and Cooperation.* Middletown, CT: Wesleyan University Press.

Sidanius, J. and Pratto, F. (1999) *Social Dominance: An Intergroup Theory of Social Hierarchy and Oppression.* Cambridge: Cambridge University Press. https://doi.org/10.1017/CBO9780113917504

Silverstein, B. and Flamenbaum, C. (1989) Biases in the perception and cognition of the actions of enemies. *Journal of Social Issues* 45(2): 51–72. https://doi.org/10.1111/j.1540-4560.1989.tb01542.x

Simon, H. A. (1955) A behavioral model of rational choice. *The Quarterly Journal of Economics* 69(1): 99–118. https://doi.org/10.2307/1884852

Son Hing, L. S. and Zanna, M. P. (2010) Individual Differences. In *The Sage Handbook of Prejudice, Stereotyping and Discrimination* (pp. 163–178). London: The SAGE Publications Ltd. https://doi.org/10.4135/9781446200919

Stangor, C. (2000) *Stereotypes and Prejudice.* Philadelphia, PA: Psychology Press.

Stanovich, K. E. (2009) *What Intelligence Tests Miss: The Psychology of Rational Thought.* New Haven, CT: Yale University Press.

Stanovich, K. E., West, R. and Toplak, M. (2013) Myside bias, rational thinking, and intelligence. *Current Directions in Psychological Science* 22(4): 259–264. https://doi.org/10.1177/0963721413480174

Stouffer, S. A., Suchman, E. A., DeVinney, L. C., Star, S.A. and Williams, R. M. Jr. (1949) *The American Soldier: Adjustment during Army Life* (Vol. 1). Princeton, NJ: Princeton University Press.

Struch, N. and Schwartz, S. (1989) Intergroup aggression: Its predictors and distinctness from in-group bias. *Journal of Personality and Social Psychology* 56(3): 364–373. https://doi.org/10.1037/0022-3514.56.3.364

Taillard, M. and Giscoppa, H. (2013) *Psychology and Modern Warfare: Idea Management in Conflict and Competition.* New York, NY: Palgrave Macmillan US.

Tajfel, H. (1970) Experiments in intergroup discrimination. *Scientific American* 223(5): 96–103. www.jstor.org/stable/24927662

Tajfel, H., Billig, M. G., Bundy, R. P. and Flament, C. (1971) Social categorization and intergroup behaviour. *European Journal of Social Psychology* 1(2): 149–178. https://doi.org/10.1002/ejsp.2420010202

Tajfel, H. and Turner J. C. (2004) The Social Identity Theory of Intergroup Behavior. In Jost, J. and Sidanius, J. (eds.) *Political Psychology: Key Readings* (pp. 276–293). London: Routledge. https://doi.org/10.4324/9780203505984

Tversky, A. and Kahneman, D. (1974) Judgment under uncertainty: Heuristics and biases. *Science* 185(4157): 1124–1131. www.jstor.org/stable/1738360

Vosoughi, S., Roy, D. and Ara, S. (2018) The spread of true and false news online. *Science* 359(6380): 1146–1151. https://doi.org/10.1126/science.aap9559

Worchel, S. and Andreoli, V. (1978) Facilitation of social interaction through deindividuation of the target. *Journal of Personality and Social Psychology* 35(5): 549–556. https://doi.org/10.1037/0022-3514.36.5.549

Yzerbyt, V. (2010) Motivational Processes. In *The SAGE Handbook of Prejudice, Stereotyping and Discrimination.* London: SAGE Publications.

Zipf, G. K. (1949) *Human Behavior and the Principle of Least Effort: An Introduction to Human Ecology.* Cambridge, MA: Addison-Wesley Press.

5
WHO IS TARGETED BY ENEMY IMAGES?

Socio-psychological and cognitive drivers

CHAPTER OBJECTIVE

- To introduce theories and models furthering the readers' understanding of why some (out-)groups become targets of enemy images

---

Introduction

We know from previous discussions that people tend to divide humanity into 'us' and 'them', in-groups and out-groups. However, not all out-groups are considered enemies. The overarching question we aim to answer in this chapter is *why* certain out-groups become targets, often repeatedly, of enemy images. What factors and conditions seem to cause some out-groups to be perceived that way?

In most cases, enemy images emerge in conflicts and wars. In this vein, it is unsurprising that many Ukrainians should create an enemy image of President Putin and Russia. However, in this chapter, we are concerned with groups that have been identified as enemies time after time without any apparent reason. We consult various relevant approaches to the subject, drawing specifically from the literature that discusses *scapegoating, system justification theory* (SJT), *illusory correlation, crossed categorization* and *double out-group theory*, and lastly *stereotype content model* (SCM).

Scapegoating

Scapegoating, placing blame on other individuals or groups, is an age-old strategy to deflect responsibility and to explain why 'bad things happen to good people', as Seneca the Younger discussed two millennia ago in his essay *De Providentia.*

DOI: 10.4324/9781003279570-5

The American social psychologist Peter Glick, a leading expert in the field, defines scapegoating as an extreme form of prejudice and as a process 'in which an out-group is unfairly blamed for having intentionally caused an in-group's misfortune' (Glick, 2005: 244).

That people tend to create scapegoats is well known, but the reasons for scapegoating are debated in scholarship: and in different periods, scapegoating has been explained and theorized in different ways. An important early tradition in the field is based on Sigmund Freud's psychoanalytic theory. According to Glick, Sigmund Freud claimed that

> people are born with drives, primarily for sex and aggression, that society (with parents as its primary agents) attempts to control ... People who are unable to deal with inner conflict adaptively (i.e., those with weak, infantile personalities), according to the psychoanalytic approach, are likely to project their psychologically unacceptable impulses (e.g., desire to aggress) onto others, who serve as projective screens. Thus, the individual's own moral shortcomings are transformed into the perceived flaws of others, who become targets of what would otherwise be self-directed aggression.
>
> *(Glick, 2008: 125–126)*

According to this view, people are thus grappling with *internal* conflicts. Two types of internal conflicts concern sexuality and aggression. Society regulates such drives heavily, and the child is told to inhibit them and is punished when acting inappropriately on them. Inevitably, this makes frustration build up, which needs to be vented. Since people do not want to be recognized for these impulses, they are instead attributed to the scapegoat (Glick, 2002: 118). This tradition also envisages that 'devalued minority groups make a convenient projective screen because they are not in a position to fight back and it is socially acceptable to view and treat them in a hostile manner' (Glick, 2008: 126).

In research after the Second World War, Freudian perspectives lost some of their prominence in scapegoating research. Instead, *external* conditions – for instance frustration – were emphasized. In other words, post-Freudian frustration–aggression theory underlines *external* causes. According to this classic frustration–aggression theory, when people experience difficult life conditions that frustrate universal psychological needs like being 'able to influence important events in one's life', this can give rise to 'psychological processes in individuals and whole groups of people, and social processes in groups, that are destructive' (Staub, 2008: 248).

In recent years, based on the frustration–aggression theory, Peter Glick has further developed scapegoating theory and formulated *the ideological model* (Glick, 2002 and 2005). This model emphasizes that although scapegoating is 'irrational (in the sense that demonstrably false beliefs are held about the scapegoat) and maladaptive (because violence against the scapegoat fails to remove the frustrations that instigated it)', and can ultimately lead to horrific actions, it is usually the result of normal cognitive and motivational processes 'by which people try to explain and to solve shared misfortunes' (Glick, 2008: 115 and 124). According to the ideological model, scapegoating is also a collective process that can lead members of a group to have the same understanding and explanation of something negative that happened to them, thereby collectively blaming an innocent group (Glick, 2008: 124). In the end, an idea can develop where negative treatment and violence are seen as necessary solutions to group misfortunes (Glick, 2008: 124). An important point in Glick's ideological model of scapegoating is that this experience of frustration must be *collective* (not individual) and lead to shared worldviews.

> Such negative events demand explanation because they threaten people's wellbeing, motivating them both to diagnose the causes of the events and, guided by their perceptions of causality, to seek solutions.
>
> *(Glick, 2008: 127)*

Particularly useful in Glick's ideological model is the way it describes and explains how collective frustrations develop into scapegoating where an out-group is unfairly blamed for having caused an in-group's misfortune. His model holds that the lack of resources individuals or groups are exposed to always needs to be understood in relation to something, whether it is the *real* absence of resources or merely a *perceived* one.

Glick highlights three main reasons why scapegoating 'without being the result of fundamentally irrational processes' can go horribly wrong (2008: 127). The first is that misfortunes are usually the consequence of complex processes, and 'information about the causes [are] so limited that people are ill equipped to explain them' (Glick, 2008: 127–128). When the causes of pandemics, wars, and poverty are difficult to comprehend, and when even researchers cannot see unambiguous reasons for them, there is room for fanciful explanations. Here, then, is an opportunity to interpret events so that blame is placed on 'them' since political, social, and economic frustrations 'motivate people to seek plausible explanations at a collective level' (Glick, 2002: 114). The second reason reconnects to our discussion about human needs. Narratives about scapegoats promise the fulfilment of various human needs: if 'we' eliminate the scapegoat, 'our' problems will be solved. According to the American historian Peter Fritzsche (1998), most Germans were more attracted by the Nazis' promises about a better tomorrow than their antisemitic messages. And in difficult times, people have an increased need for security, self- and group esteem; they are open to messages confirming 'our' high status and 'their' inferiority. According to Glick, people are more open to explanations that blame another group for failures, poverty, and misfortunes. These are 'more attractive than blaming one's own group, which would threaten collective self-esteem' (Glick, 2008: 128 and cf. Glick, 2002: 114), and the need for positive self-esteem and for belonging to high-status groups is heightened during difficult life conditions (Glick, 2008: 141). A third explanation that Glick puts forward reconnects to our argument in Chapter 4 about people's emotional need for cognitive consistency and their greater willingness to embrace messages that accord with deeply rooted *previous beliefs*. In a society and cultural context where people believed not only that witches existed but also that they could cause harm, blaming witches for the plague made sense (Glick, 2005: 253).

According to Glick, 'people's explanations for events are guided by established cultural ideologies, fostering shared social realities that can entrench false beliefs, such as stereotypes that increase the likelihood of blaming a specific group for having caused widespread misfortunes' (Glick, 2008: 128). He elaborates:

> The ideological model of scapegoating suggests that it is the specific content of these well-established stereotypes that determines which groups are at risk of being scapegoated when shared misfortunes strike.
>
> *(Glick, 2008: 129)*

Moreover, scapegoat movements attract followers by 'offering simpler, culturally plausible explanations and solutions for shared negative events' (Glick, 2005: 253).

Beyond established stereotypes, Glick mentions one additional factor that increases the risk of being scapegoated: groups that are viewed as 'having the opportunity to cause harm' (Glick, 2008: 141). Historically, it was usually groups living in close proximity to 'us' who allegedly competed with 'us' for resources and were thus seen as having both the opportunity and the interest in harming 'us'. So it is not unusual for neighbours or out-groups in 'our' midst to become the target of scapegoating (Glick, 2008: 123). The Jews in the Third Reich, for example, who lived together with other Germans and were believed to have control over a large sector of the economy, were blamed for economic problems. In Chapter 1, we discussed the danger of philosemitism and how supposedly philosemitic beliefs can easily evolve into antisemitism. If a philosemite believes that Jews have special qualities (intelligence, industriousness), this can be seen as a benign stereotype in good times but can easily turn into antisemitism during periods of economic hardship. It is not only Jews that have been scapegoated in this way: similar things happened, and for similar reasons, to the Armenians in Turkey and the Tutsi in Rwanda (Glick, 2005: 254).

However, Glick asks himself why negative circumstances are not blamed on structural factors or impersonal or natural forces (Glick, 2008: 128), advancing the idea that if the cause of the misfortune is attributed to natural forces or structure, then people cannot influence them. It is more psychologically attractive to see a *group and collective of people* as a cause because in that case 'there are actions that could remedy the problem' (Glick, 2008: 129).

Along with these factors behind scapegoating as an effective mechanism to project blame, 'aggrieved entitlement' is yet another driver (Kimmel, 2013: 21).

Aggrieved entitlement rests upon a feeling of having been stripped of rights to something – or as Fiona McDonald puts it:

> a perception that the benefits and/or status you believe yourself entitled to have been wrongfully taken away from you by unforeseen forces. This perception can lead to feelings of humiliation and, in turn, violence.
>
> *(McDonald, 2022)*

Those who are identified as culprits behind this loss of status/influence are thus easily targeted as enemies.

In conclusion, let us return to the overarching question of this chapter: why are some groups more likely to be selected as targets of an enemy image? Although Peter Glick's theory concerns scapegoating and not enemy images per se, we think that it is also helpful for our question, particularly the third factor in his model. Simply put, it seems to be the case that once a prejudice against a particular group has been established, even if it was way back in history, there is an increased risk that this group will become the repeated target of an enemy image. And one reason for this may be that the human brain is a 'cognitive miser' due to its tendency to seek resource-efficient ways to process cognitive data. For reasons of efficiency, humans choose narratives that they recognize. Thus, it is easier for the brain to accept an enemy image that is in line with previously held beliefs than to question them. Moreover, groups that are perceived as having the capacity to harm 'us', like those in 'our' midst who are perceived as influential, are particularly vulnerable to enmification.

System justification theory

Another theory that could potentially help us explain why certain groups are selected to become targets of enemy images is the SJT. SJT was first formulated in 1994, in a joint article by social psychologist John T. Jost and psychologist Mahzarin R. Banaji. Just like relative deprivation theory and relative gratification theory as discussed in Chapter 4, SJT theorizes the role of status in societies, with unequal distribution of resources between groups. Jost and Banaji confirm that people accept stereotypes, and thus enemy images, which serve *ego-justification* functions (I am better than you) and *group justification* functions ('we' are better than 'you') (Jost and Banaji, 1994: 2 and 6. See also the discussion on human esteem needs in Chapter 4). But Jost and Banaji build on these 'to propose a third category of justification' which they term *system justification* (1994: 2). They define system justification as 'the psychological process by which existing social arrangements are preserved in spite of the obvious psychological and material harm they entail for disadvantaged individuals and groups' (Jost and Banaji, 1994: 10). According to Jost, many intellectuals over the years have observed people's apparent tendency to willingly, 'even enthusiastically', submit to and accept oppressive and humiliating social and political systems 'inflicted by the powerful' (Jost, 2020: 2). SJT explains this tendency as 'a social psychological propensity to defend and bolster the status quo, that is, to see it as good, fair, legitimate, and desirable' (Jost and Liviatan, 2007: 966).

This process has a few important *consequences*. Firstly, 'people will ascribe to themselves and others [with] traits which are consonant with their social position' (Jost and Banaji, 1994: 11). Concretely, it means that when people occupy a dominant position in society, they ascribe flattering stereotypes to themselves and derogatory ones to less successful groups (Yzerbyt, 2010: 151 and cf. Kay et al., 2007). Consequently, the powerful are given characteristics that explain or justify their success (Jost and Banaji, 1994: 13), e.g. being industrious, clever, and hard-working. Likewise, the powerless and poor are stereotyped (and self-stereotyped) in such a way that their plight is well-deserved and similarly justified (Jost and Banaji, 1994: 13). They are thus often stereotyped as lazy and indolent (Esses, Jackson, and Bennett-AbuAyyash, 2010: 229). This can also lead to favoured groups experiencing increased self-esteem while disadvantaged groups undergo a lowering of self-esteem (Jost and Liviatan, 2007: 967).

A second consequence is that people's *social position is given an explanation and legitimized*. The rich and powerful hold their social position rightfully due to their hard work, intelligence, and industriousness. The poor and powerless, on the other hand, have only themselves to blame. They are stereotyped (and self-stereotyped) in such a way that their plight is well-deserved and similarly justified (Jost and Banaji, 1994: 13). A third consequence is that the *socioeconomic* system is also *perceived as legitimate*. People are stereotyped in such a way that 'the existing social order, with its attendant degree of inequality, is seen as legitimate and even natural' (Jost and Liviatan, 2007: 967). Moreover, the poor accept negative stereotypes of themselves 'rather than question the order or legitimacy of the system' which made them poor and powerless (Jost and Banaji, 1994: 11).

The question that then arises is *why* people preserve and justify social arrangements that are harmful to disadvantaged individuals and groups. We can understand why people who benefit from a social arrangement support it.

> For members of advantaged groups – system justification is consistent with ego and group justification motives to maintain or enhance personal and collective self-esteem, respectively. For members of advantaged groups, therefore, it appears that system justification is positively associated with self-esteem, ingroup favouritism, and psychological well-being.
>
> *(Jost, 2018: 14)*

But this cannot be said for members of disadvantaged groups. In their case, system justification *conflicts* with ego and group justification motives (Jost, 2018: 14). Disadvantaged individuals and groups do not support the overarching social system more than the advantaged. Still, 'what is remarkable to me is that disadvantaged groups – such as members of the working class – subscribe to the legitimacy of the status quo as much as they do' (Jost, 2018: 12). This fact is confirmed by the American historian and political scientist, Howard Zinn:

> rebellion is only an occasional reaction to suffering in human history; we have infinitely more instances of forbearance to exploitation, and submission to authority, than we have examples of revolt.
>
> *(Zinn, [1968] 2002: 16-17)*

One kind of explanation that is often referred to is based on the idea that people tend to see the world as a just place where people get what they deserve. The American social psychologist Melvin J. Lerner develops these ideas in his book *The Belief in a Just World: A Fundamental Delusion* (1980). A basic idea is that we have strong motives to believe in a just and fair world where people get what they deserve. Imagine that there is a good person 'out there' who suffers undeservedly, say a good and peaceful person dying in a car accident. According to Lerner, 'under certain circumstances, people who become aware of that person's fate will construe events, including the personal attributes of the victim, so that the victim appears to "deserve" his suffering' (1980: 12). People who know the deceased might be asking themselves if they were driving too fast, not wearing a seat belt, had bad tyres, and so on.

Lerner suggests three possible reasons why people construct events in this way. One may be the *culture* we live in, where 'suffering often results from the violation of laws of man and nature' (Lerner, 1980:13). Thus, we have been culturally influenced to believe that evil actions have consequences. When a person experiences difficulties in life, people look for evil actions in the past, i.e. the reasons behind the difficulties. People seek causality. A second reason is 'the way our minds work'. Again, people seek causality, and 'we are inclined to believe that goodness, happiness, beauty, virtue, and success are connected causally, just as are misery, ugliness, sin, inferiority, and suffering' (Lerner, 1980: 14). Finally, the belief in a just world is functional. 'People want to and have to believe they live in a just world so that they can go about their daily lives with a sense of trust, hope, and confidence in their future' (Lerner, 1980: 14). The opposite would be intolerable. And this makes most people want to 'perceive existing authorities and institutions as largely benevolent and legitimate' (Jost and Liviatan, 2007: 966). These conditions also make members of disadvantaged groups believe that 'the existing social system is legitimate and justified' (Jost, 2018: 3).

A consequence is that the existing social order, with its attendant degree of inequality, is seen as *legitimate* and even *natural*. People feel safer in the status quo than in times of radical change. Therefore, most disapprove of protests and radical change. 'There is probably a sense of security in the prevailing existing social, economic, and political arrangements, even if they are suboptimal for parts of the population, and they are preferred to alternatives to the status quo' (Jost and Liviatan, 2007: 966), even if those would be an improvement.

Let us now return to the most important question: can SJT help us to understand why some groups are targeted by enemy images? Again, we must emphasize that the theory was not formulated with this question in mind. With that said, we dare to formulate some tentative thoughts. We believe that two conditions highlighted by this theory are of relevance. *First*, the powerless and people of low socioeconomic status are stereotyped in a negative way that justifies their social position in society (Jones, 2002: 11). In other words, they are stigmatized from the outset. *Second*, there is a belief in the legitimacy of the existing socioeconomic system, with such systems possibly even being regarded as natural. Imagine people with low socioeconomic status questioning the existing system like the African National Congress (ANC) did in 1980s South Africa. Since most people prioritize order and stability, particularly those who benefit from that order and stability, ANC (representing a low-status group) and the radical changes they proposed could well have been regarded as undesirable. As radical reformers, they might have been construed as a threat to the foundations of society – potentially as an enemy. Our point is that low-status groups and individuals who demand far-reaching social change would probably be in the line of fire for enemy images.

Illusory correlation

In our quest to increase our understanding of why certain out-groups become targets, often repeatedly, of enemy images, it is important to discuss the concept of *illusory correlation,* originally formulated by American psychologist Loren J. Chapman in 1967. Illusory correlation describes a phenomenon where people tend to perceive a relationship between variables, for instance between *people* and *behaviour*, or more specifically an illusory correlation between minorities and unwanted behaviour – for instance immigration and crime. We believe Chapman's reasoning and the research conducted in its wake can advance our understanding of why certain groups become targets of enemy images. A starting point in this reasoning is that people tend to focus on what diverges from our expectations of 'normalcy' (relative to what is perceived and constructed as the measuring point or the mainstream).

> Research on cognitive processes suggests that we tend to focus on distinctive stimuli in our environment. We notice the unusual, the atypical ... We notice anyone who is distinctive within a social context such as a man within a room full of women.
>
> *(Jones, 2002: 88)*

Imagine that you are a teacher in nursing education and your class has many female students but only one male. Unknowingly, you will probably pay more attention to the male student. And imagine that your single male student fails a practical test on intramuscular injection techniques. In this case, there is an increased risk that you will see relationships between the minority group (the male student in this context) and his failure (cf. Jones, 2002: 89). Maybe you would think that men are not suited to be nurses, since it is a female occupation, and that they lack relevant female qualities to cope with duties associated with nursing. And this tendency to focus on what diverges from our expectations – 'distinctive stimuli' – and to infer a false correlation can contribute to the development of stereotypes and prejudice (Jones, 2002: 88).

An early study that focused on how illusory correlation affects social perception and the way we make judgments about other people was conducted by David L. Hamilton and Robert K. Gifford in 1976. In this study, they started from Chapman's findings and developed hypothetical reasoning to be analysed in an experiment:

> Given this framework, the implication of Chapman's (1967) finding is that, even if the distribution of desirable and undesirable behavior is the same for both blacks and whites, the pairing of 'blackness' with 'undesirable behavior' would lead the typical white observer to infer that those two events co-occur more frequently than they actually do.
>
> *(Hamilton and Gifford, 1976: 394)*

The results of their study confirm the hypothesis and show an illusory correlation, with an 'overattribution of undesirable behaviors to the smaller group' (Hamilton and Gifford, 1976: 397 and 399–400):

> While unusual or infrequent events are themselves distinctive, the co-occurrence of two distinctive events presumably would be particularly noticeable, differentially drawing the observer's attention to the fact that these events co-occurred.
>
> *(Hamilton and Gifford, 1976: 405)*

In other words, most people act within the confines of preconceived norms. Suppose that most people where you live belong to the majority population. If an ethnic minority person in your neighbourhood acts against the norms and thereby does something undesirable, then this will attract attention. Similarly, there is a risk that people overinterpret and believe that these events co-occur more frequently than they actually do. Moreover, we believe that if the unwanted behaviour is violent and threatening, the coincidence might contribute to the development of enemy images. In this case, there is an increased risk that people will see a connection/correlation between group affiliation and threatening behaviour.

Hamilton and Gifford's (1976) study shows that the phenomenon of illusory correlation is an effect of normal cognition, indicating that normal cognitive processes could contribute to the formation of stereotypes – and, as we imagine, perhaps also to enemy images. But Hamilton and Gifford do not deny the importance of 'socially learned or culturally transmitted bases of stereotypes' (1976: 405). In fact, they suggest that learning and illusory correlation are mutually reinforcing. Moreover, it is also possible that some stereotypes originally had a purely cognitive basis but are subsequently transmitted to others and become acquired (Hamilton and Gifford, 1976: 406).

We have so far described *how* the phenomenon of illusory correlation appears and what its consequences might be. However, we have not discussed *why* human cognitive processes function in this way. There is no room in this section for extensive discussion of the causes of illusory correlation, and it probably is a multicausal phenomenon. Still, one important reason may well be that the human being is a *cognitive miser* (see Chapter 4).

In conclusion, let us return to the overarching question of this chapter: why are some groups more likely to be selected to become targets of an enemy image? The phenomenon of illusory correlation may not give us the complete answer, but the mere fact that a group is a minority in a social context makes it more vulnerable. The group, its members, and their behaviour will receive more attention. And should group members act in an undesirable or even threatening way, there is a risk that this negative behaviour will be linked to the group. Outside observers would thus see a correlation between the two, an illusory correlation. Such unwanted actions could be seen as typical of the group and thus a prejudice (and in some cases an enemy image) has come to life.

Crossed categorization and double out-group theory

In the following section, we will introduce and discuss the social psychology models, crossed categorization, and double out-group. As previously stated, categorization is a main feature of human cognition. We have a tendency to divide people into different categories, to separate 'us' from 'them'. Categorization frequently relies on simple visual features such as race, gender, and age in order to save cognitive resources (Nicolas, de la Fuente, and Fiske, 2017: 621). People also tend to see the world with an in-group bias and evaluate 'our' own group more positively than out-groups. This also happens when 'our' group is a so-called trivial one (see Chapter 4). In the previous chapter, we also mentioned how the ability to separate a protective 'us' from a threatening 'them' can be life-saving. The downside is that the human tendency to think in terms of 'us' and 'them' ultimately might lead to intergroup bias and even enemy images.

Our reasoning in the previous chapter was based on 'single demographic categorization, or distinctions between two groups' (Nicolas, de la Fuente, and Fiske, 2017: 621), 'us' versus 'them', or 'us' versus the enemy. In the real world, people belong to more than one group simultaneously and interact with others who simultaneously belong to more than one group. For instance, people can belong to two groups along the same categorical space (being both Black and white) or different spaces (e.g. race and gender) (Nicolas, de la Fuente, and Fiske, 2017: 622). And 'current categorization research has begun to focus on targets who can be categorized into multiple social groups' (Nicolas, de la Fuente, and Fiske, 2017: 622). Several social psychological studies have examined the effects of crossed categorizations on group bias (Mullen, Migdal, and Hewstone, 2001: 722).

> In these studies, crossed categorization typically refers to the crossing of two independent dichotomous dimensions, resulting in four groups: The double-ingroup, the double-outgroup, and two mixed groups. The double-ingroup (or, ingroup-ingroup) refers to people who share ingroup membership on both dimensions. The double-outgroup (or, outgroup-outgroup) refers to people who are in the outgroup on both dimensions. The two mixed groups (ingroup-outgroup and the complementary outgroup-ingroup) refer to people who share ingroup membership on one dimension but retain outgroup membership on the other dimension.
>
> *(Mullen, Migdal, and Hewstone, 2001: 722)*

In a clearly racially divided context with a substantial lack of gender equality, an example of what the authors propose could be as follows: for a white man, a Black woman belongs to a double out-group; another white man would be perceived as belonging to a double in-group; and a white woman would belong to a mixed group for the white man. The fact that people usually belong to more than one group can both reduce and increase the risk of being targeted by enemy images. According to the so-called additive model, people might judge individuals or groups belonging to double out-groups rather than mixed groups more negatively (Nicolas, de la Fuente, Fiske, 2017: 623; Echebarria Echabe and Fernández Guede, 2006: 83 and Mullen, Migdal, and Hewstone, 2001: 732).

Following this logic, there is a risk that a white Christian would judge a Black Muslim (double out-group) more negatively than they would a Black Christian. But on the other hand, an African American woman might recognize experiences and to some extent identify with a white American woman. This can reduce the risk of enemy images being created. But in this context, our main message is that if an individual or a collective is seen as a double out-group, there is an elevated risk of their encountering negative prejudice and a greater risk of enemy images developing.

In a 2006 study, Agustin Echebarria Echabe and Emilia Fernández Guede develop these thoughts further, claiming that categorization influences social perception, that we judge out-groups differently from people belonging to 'us' – and double out-groups even more so. However, not all group belonging has the same effect. There seems to be a hierarchy: belonging to a different class had a greater effect than belonging to another ethnicity (2006: 93).

We conclude that there is reason to suspect that double out-groups are more likely to be selected as targets of enemy images than single out-groups. This conclusion also resonates with what we proposed in Chapter 1: that one way to create enemy images and make them accepted and believable in society is to depict 'them' as completely different from 'us', so 'we' have nothing in common with 'them'. These mechanisms make it easier to neglect feelings of empathy. Therefore, enemy images exaggerate differences between 'us' and 'them'. And the actor who communicates an enemy image can more easily claim that 'we' have nothing in common with 'them' if 'they' are perceived as a double out-group.

Stereotype content model

To advance our understanding of why some out-groups might become targets of enemy images, we will now consult the SCM. Just like the previous model, SCM is based on the idea that people tend not only to divide individuals and collectives into 'us' and 'them', but also to describe 'us' as a little better than 'them'. In the SCM, this idea is developed and nuanced, 'suggesting that out-groups can be liked (even if not respected) or respected (even if not liked)' (Cuddy et al., 2009: 2). Usually when thinking about attitudes to out-groups, prejudices and stereotypes are seen as unidimensional, 'falling along a single general goodness–badness dimension' (Cuddy et al., 2009: 3) where 'we' are better than 'them'. What SCM discovers is that 'stereotypes are neither univalent nor unidimensional' (Cuddy et al., 2009: 3), and that the *types* of stereotypes 'we' attribute to out-groups are developed, discussed, and explained. The SCM was created by social psychologist Susan Fiske and her colleagues Amy Cuddy, Peter Glick, and Jun Xu in two articles at the turn of the millennium. One of them (2002) opens with the following statement:

> Not all stereotypes are alike. Some stereotyped groups are disrespected as incapable and useless (e.g., elderly people), whereas others are respected for excessive, threatening competence (e.g., Asians). Some stereotyped groups are liked as sweet and harmless (e.g., housewives), whereas others are disliked as cold and inhuman (e.g., rich people). Surely, such differences matter.
>
> *(Fiske, Cuddy, Glick, and Xu, 2002: 878)*

This means that not all stereotypes or prejudices about out-groups have negative content. What is new and unique in this model is that it proposes that stereotypes are captured by two dimensions – warmth versus competence (see Table 5.1) – and that these two dimensions can predict stereotype content (Fiske, Cuddy, Glick, and Xu, 2002: 878).

This model has the same starting point as the discussion in Chapter 4 regarding the group as a provider of safety. There, we underlined that humans are vulnerable and survive only as members of organized groups. And since 'we' are vulnerable,

TABLE 5.1 Four types of out-group

		Competence	
		Low	*High*
Warmth	High	**Paternalistic prejudice** Low status, not competitive Pity, sympathy (e.g. elderly people, disabled people, housewives)	**Admiration** High status, not competitive Pride, admiration (e.g. in-group, close allies)
	Low	**Contemptuous prejudice** Low status, competitive Contempt, disgust, anger, resentment (e.g. welfare recipients, poor people)	**Envious prejudice** High status, competitive Envy, jealousy (e.g. Asians, Jews, rich people, feminists)

Source: Adapted from Fiske, Cuddy, Glick, and Xu (2002: 881).

'we' are suspicious of strangers. Therefore, according to the SCM, 'we' initially assess out-groups or strangers regarding their intent: do 'they' want to harm or help 'us'? This reaction is powerful and seen as deriving from evolution. To survive, 'we' need to be instantaneously able to distinguish between those who have the intention to harm 'us' and those who might help 'us'. Knowing another's intent for good or ill matters to our survival, making this competence relevant from an evolutionary perspective (Cuddy, Fiske, and Glick, 2008: 89). According to the SCM, this need to protect oneself against 'them' is seen as two-dimensional:

> Evolutionary pressures are reflected in social perception: on encountering others, people must determine, first, the intentions of the other person or group and, second, their ability to act on those intentions.
>
> *(Fiske, Cuddy, and Glick, 2007: 77)*

In other words, 'people ask two questions: Do they intend to harm me; and are they capable of harming me?' (Cuddy et al., 2009: 3). Moreover, these two dimensions seem to be 'universal dimensions of human social cognition, both at the individual level and at the group level' (Fiske, Cuddy, and Glick, 2007: 77). These two dimensions, *warmth* and *competence*, were known to be important in intergroup relations long before Fiske et al. created this model. What is new is that they combined them into one cohesive model.

As said, the dimension called *warmth* concerns the *intentions* of the out-group and their expected behaviour (Fiske, Cuddy, and Glick, 2007: 80). Can 'we' expect 'them' to compete with 'us' for resources or perhaps even constitute a threat? In that case, the warmth in intergroup relationships is categorized as *low*. If 'we' cannot predict any threat or competition from 'them', 'they' are potential partners, and 'we' might categorize 'them' as *high* in warmth. Maybe 'we' even like 'them'.

The dimension called *competence* concerns 'their' *status* and hierarchical position and *capacity* to 'act upon their intentions' (Yzerbyt, 2010: 153). Groups and individuals who score high on this dimension are respected (Cuddy et al., 2009: 3). Combining the two dimensions could say something about how people perceive an out-group socially.

Let us consider Table 5.1 and its four categories again. Two of them could be labelled *unambiguous*. They receive either positive evaluations on both dimensions or double negatives. The category to the bottom left of the table is evaluated as neither warm nor competent. This is a category 'we' neither respect nor like. In this case, there is a risk that 'we' harbour *contemptuous prejudice* towards them. 'We' regard them with disgust, anger, and resentment. This group may consist of welfare recipients and poor people. Although 'they' do not constitute any direct threat because of their incompetence, 'we' might see them as a liability in society. The category in the upper right corner of the table is diametrically different since people evaluate it as both warm and competent. Since 'we' trust this category, 'we' do not fear the competence of its individuals and groups. On the contrary, 'we' *admire* them, and 'we' regard 'them' as allies or potential allies. Perhaps this is how Europeans viewed Americans right after the Second World War.

The two remaining categories are those that the SCM defines as ambivalent since they comprise a positive evaluation on one dimension and a negative one on the other (Cuddy, Fiske, and Glick, 2008: 68). The upper left category consists of collectives and individuals whom 'we' consider to be high on warmth but low in competence. 'We' tend to like people in this category since 'we' do not expect any harmful behaviour from 'them'. But because 'we' consider 'them' to have low competence, 'we' tend to develop *paternalistic prejudice* against 'them'. There is a risk that 'we' pity them. In this category, one might find the elderly, the disabled, and housewives.

In the second ambivalent category, the shaded part of the table in the bottom right, we find a group that 'we' regard as cold and competent. There is a risk that 'we' harbour *envious prejudice* against groups and individuals within this category, and that 'we' perceive 'them' as sly. Instead of admiring 'their' capacity and resources, 'we' envy and sometimes fear 'them' since 'they' not only have a high status but 'we' see 'them' as competing with 'us'. This group may consist of Asians, Jews, rich people, or feminists.

In the same vein as the SCM, Chip Berlet (2009: 10 and 26) analysed typical target groups in conspiracy theories and distinguished for the US context between (a) corrupt elites and (b) undeserving outsiders or 'elite parasites' and 'lazy, sinful, and subversive parasites'. These two groups correspond roughly to the two bottom categories of the SCM. Berlet moreover proposes that those who engage in conspiratorial meaning-making frequently see themselves as squeezed in between these two groups and therefore direct what we would call enemy images in two directions: upward and downward. The targets of downward scapegoating and repression are for instance Black people, immigrants, welfare mothers, and people of colour in general, who are portrayed as lazy. Moral judgements are directed against 'sinful' or 'subversive' groups such as abortionists, homosexuals, feminists, social and economic justice activists, or militant labour activists. But the feeling of being conspired against is also an impression of being squeezed and abused from above. Anger is therefore also directed upward to the elites who are identified as secretive groups, malign insiders, international bankers, shady freemasons, Jews, globalists, liberal secular humanists, and government bureaucrats. In this binary scheme, loss and decline are orchestrated from above, and wealth and resources can be sucked out from below, resulting in deprivation from two directions for those exposed to this cabal. In the minds of those who feel exposed to these threats from above and below, enemy groups can also form malign coalitions and coordinate their actions. During the refugee crisis in 2016, a wealthy businessman, George Soros, could be styled as orchestrating mass migration to Europe.

These dynamics can be illustrated by two examples, the first related to the antisemitic blood libel and the other to the Islamophobic idea of the 'Great Replacement'. From these examples, a few general conclusions about the construction of enemy images can be derived. Let us start with blood libel. Not long after the invention of the printing press, at the end of the fifteenth century, a story about the supposedly ritual murder of a Christian boy, Simon of Trent, was turned into a book (Caumanns and Önnerfors, 2020: 441–456). With images on the left and text on the right, the book claimed that the boy was killed so his blood could be used to bake Jewish bread, *matzah*, for Passover. But Simon's alleged fate was also turned into a play and a sculpture group in a Catholic church converted into a place of pilgrimage. The blood libel myth has survived throughout history into Nazi propaganda and contemporary neo-Nazi activism. It was referred to in a manifesto by a San Diego synagogue shooter in 2019, turned into bad art by an Italian artist during the pandemic, and now retold in a new version: that elites are abducting children to extract the mysterious substance adrenochrome to help make them immortal. The story shows that across time and media, the idea of Jews as conspiring against and killing Christians to collect their blood has survived as a powerful trope that has motivated extremist violence and genocide.

The second example is the 'Great Replacement'. About 20 years ago, several writers started to spread the idea of Eurabia, an alleged plot between liberal European elites and dangerous Muslim outsiders with the aim of overthrowing European nation-states. Norwegian terrorist Behring Breivik was inspired by Eurabia literature. These theories were subsequently condensed into 'The Great Replacement', which went even further and claimed that the end goal is a total replacement of the original populations of Europe with Muslim foreigners from the Middle East and North Africa. The origins of this conspiracy theory are the writings of the French author Renaud Camus (Önnerfors, 2021: 76–96). It was widely referred to in the French 2022 presidential elections but figured more prominently as the motivation for the Christchurch, NZ, terrorist attack in 2019 and proved extremely influential in European and American right-wing populism, where it is also sometimes called 'white genocide', expressing in other words the fear that the white race is exposed to wilful extinction. Europe is portrayed as the naïve frog, transporting the Muslim scorpion to its own shores, where hordes of 'rapefugees' are just waiting to grab power with violence, especially directed against women and girls. A future is invoked in which European culture is slowly erased and fades out until nothing remains.

These two examples illustrate how enemy images of Jews and Muslims are similar yet different. Firstly, they conflate religion and race/ethnicity – all Israelis and Jews are assumed to belong to a perverted and dangerous religious cult which threatens European children. Likewise, with Muslims, all people from MENA countries must automatically be of Islamic faith and preprogrammed to perpetrate crimes and commit sexual violence, threatening European women. When it comes to Jews, who historically were allowed to trade in precious metals and lend money at interest despite exclusion from other professions, there is a strong idea about their alleged superiority. Today many people believe in the trope of 'powerful Jewish bankers', of greedy Jewish businessmen and media owners, which also was expressed in the 'Protocols of the Elder of Zion', a forgery alleging a Jewish plot for world domination. Jews are thus perceived as a privileged and powerful yet corrupt elite out-group. Despite their status as a religious and racial minority, they are superior to – and will manipulate and enslave – 'us'. Muslims are on the contrary perceived as an underprivileged, underdog out-group. Their sole purpose is to invade and overrun Europe and Western civilization by brutal force. They are also a minority out-group, yet inferior to 'us', despicable *Untermenschen* and underserving outsiders. Both groups pose threats against children and women, through barbarian blood rituals or rape. The killing and manipulation of children are a threat to 'our' future. Muslim over-fertility is portrayed as a biopolitical weapon in the 'war of the wombs'.

In both cases, the plot is a mixture of internal and external enemies. The enemies inside are colluding with forces outside our societies to bring them down. It is possible to scapegoat both groups with negative events such as the plague, decline, crises, pandemics, and war. Throughout history, both groups have also been dehumanized and portrayed as demons with genuinely evil and satanic intentions. In the European psyche, the meaning of Europe as a geopolitical entity as much as a cultural construction has been created in this tension between internal dissolution and external extermination (Önnerfors and Krouwel, 2021: 9–11). This means that Europe, lacking any consistent or clear self-definition either geographically or culturally, has imagined itself as being as strong as its weakest parts and as weak as its perceived outside and existential threats, ranging from non-Roman barbarians to Huns, from Muslims, the 'Yellow Peril', Muslims again and now to non-European autocratic and illiberal Russian imperialists paired with resurgent Chinese power bent on total domination. And at the same time, inside Europe, subversive elements have supposedly threatened its internal cohesion. Most of them are minorities belonging to imagined or real external enemies or powerful elites and destructive and decadent groups who could be portrayed as a threat and by whom the chaos of internal dissolution has been released through a string of orchestrated revolutions, crises, and manipulation strategies. Enemy images against these target groups have come as an expression of virulent self-doubt and existential fears. The imagined threats relate to the combined fears of demographic extinction, profound political transformation, economic deprivation, religious annihilation, and cultural erasure of European identity (Gualda, 2021: 54–75).

What can we learn, then, from the SCM and related models? How can it help us understand why some groups are more likely to be depicted as enemies? We conclude that groups and individuals who fall within an ambivalent category, and who are simultaneously categorized as 'low' along the warmth dimension and 'high' on the competence dimension (the shaded part of Table 5.1), can appear as a real threat. Not only are 'they' malevolent, but 'they' also have the competence and resources to harm and threaten 'us'. Since Jews in Nazi propaganda were often considered to combine these characteristics, this may explain why during the Third Reich, 'many Germans viewed the Jews as a hyperpotent enemy that had to be destroyed' (Fiske et al., 2002: 899). But does that square with our ideal–typical enemy image constructed in Chapter 2 since we said the enemy is inferior to 'us'? We think so. One could say that the enemy image must satisfy two needs. To be accepted, it must satisfy 'our' esteem needs, 'our' need to appear a little better than 'them'. But the enemy has one clear competence: it can threaten and harm 'us'. And this competence adds to a seemingly realistic assessment.

Summary

Let us return to the question informing this chapter: why do some out-groups become targets, often repeatedly, of enemy images? Firstly, illusory correlation and SJT can be helpful when it comes to explaining why this is the case for inner or proximate out-groups. According to illusory correlation, the mere fact that a group is a minority gains its members and their behaviour more attention than the majority, particularly its unwanted behaviour. As the name of the theory indicates, people tend to see a correlation between minorities and their unwanted behaviour, although the correlation usually is illusory. That is how prejudices can come to life. And we believe that if the unwanted behaviour is violent, violence and threats become correlated to the group and are seen as defining it. We therefore believe there is reason to assume that the mere fact of a group constituting a minority means there is an increased risk that it will become a target of an enemy image.

Another kind of minority group living among 'us' that can easily become subject to critical scrutiny is, according to SJT, people of low socioeconomic status. The majority, at least the wealthy and influential, tend to stereotype the poor in a negative way so that their subordinate position in society is justified. For example, people tend to describe poor people as lazy. The rich, on the other hand, are often described as industrious and rational. A second idea in the same theory is that people tend to believe in the legitimacy of the existing socioeconomic system, even if it is oppressive. People generally, including the poor, support the status quo more than radical change. With these premises as a starting point, it is reasonable to claim that people of low socioeconomic status demanding radical social, economic, or political changes will become targets of enemy images and perhaps be portrayed as a threat to the foundations of society.

The presence of a threat is a core characteristic of an enemy image. The other is depicted as an imminent, real, and possibly growing threat to our most vital interests. We believe that out-groups that can easily and credibly be described as genuine threats will likely become targets of enemy images. Theories on scapegoating and stereotype content suggest certain conditions that make it possible to convincingly describe an out-group as a major threat. If a group is perceived as *influential*, living *close* to 'us', and believed to have *malevolent intentions*, it can more easily be depicted as a credible threat. An enemy image of such a group could perhaps be perceived as reasonable and convincing. Groups perceived in this way could therefore become an easy target of enemy images.

Another condition that can make an out-group a likely target for enemy images is if it is perceived as a double out-group. The starting point in this reasoning is that dehumanization is both an objective of an enemy image – it is much easier to harm a dehumanized enemy than a humanized one – and also a facilitator: if an out-group is perceived from the outset as completely different from 'us', perhaps even dehumanized, it is easier to portray it as an enemy. On the other hand, it is harder to portray an out-group with whom we have good and close ties as an enemy, as we learned from the intergroup contact theory. If the other is a double out-group, there is a risk that people perceive it as more deviant than other groups, perhaps believing that 'we' have nothing in common with 'them'. There is thus a risk that such a group may become the target of an enemy image.

Finally, a fact that has been highlighted several times is the human need for cognitive consistency, our tendency to prioritize empirical evidence that reinforces already established beliefs and avoids those that challenge them (Chapter 4). The reasoning above about scapegoating also highlighted this fact. The need for cognitive consistency affects human acceptance of enemy images, too. Groups that have historically been subjected to verbal attacks and described as dangerous, violent, unreliable, and so on will constitute a vulnerable group when these descriptions are accepted, and can thus become a target for new verbal attacks such as enemy images.

Study questions

- Based on what you now know about factors and conditions explaining how and why some groups are more likely to be selected as targets of enemy images, which groups do you think risk being perceived as enemies in your context today?
- In 1993, the Tutsis in Rwanda were designated enemies of the Hutus. What factors do you think led to this? What theories and arguments in this and previous chapters have helped you understand developments in Rwanda?
- Based on the theories and arguments presented in this chapter, how would you explain why African Americans, non-white European immigrants, and indigenous populations have become the target of enemy image constructions?

Potential essay or thesis suggestion

Based on the theories and models presented in this chapter, create an analytical framework to help you can analyse why some (out-)groups become targets of enemy images. Choose a case you are familiar with where a group has been identified as an enemy and subjected to senseless violence, and whose source material you can read in the original language. Choose the data you need to carry out your study. Analyse the data and reveal the properties that are attributed to this group.

Recommended further reading

Campbell, C. (2011) *Scapegoat: A History of Blaming Other People*. London: Duckworth Overlook.
In this easy-to-read book, Charlie Campbell analyses the human habit of blaming others, discussing several historical cases starting from the Black Death and the blaming of Jews. His study also provides a chapter explaining the psychology of scapegoating.

Glick, P. (2005) Choice of Scapegoats. In Dovidio, J. F., Glick, P. and Rudman, L. A. (eds.) *On the nature of prejudice, Fifty years after Allport.* (pp. 244–261). Malden, MA: Blackwell Publishing.
Peter Glick is an authority on scapegoating but has not written a monograph on the subject. We therefore recommend reading the book chapter 'Choice of Scapegoats' and his other texts (see Bibliography below). In addition, we would also like to refer to his website, which presents his research work and where relevant lectures are linked: https://faculty.lawrence.edu/glickp/

Jones, M. (2002) *Social Psychology of Prejudice*. Upper Saddle River, NJ: Prentice Hall.
This is an accessible and systematic textbook written by Melinda Jones, discussing different forms of prejudice and various theories explaining them. Jones also describes the psychological processes maintaining prejudice, how marginalized groups and individuals cope with it, and how it can be reduced.

Bibliography

Berlet, C. (2009) *Toxic to Democracy: Conspiracy Theories, Demonization & Scapegoating.* Somerville, MA: Political Research Associates.

Campbell, C. (2011) *Scapegoat: A History of Blaming Other People.* London: Duckworth Overlook.

Caumanns, U. and Önnerfors, A. (2020) Conspiracy Theories and Visual Culture. In Butter, M. and Knight, P. (eds.) *Routledge Handbook of Conspiracy Theories* (pp. 441–456). London: Routledge.

Chapman, L. J. (1967) Illusory correlation in observational report. *Journal of Verbal Learning and Verbal Behavior* 6(1): 151–155.

Cuddy, A. J., Fiske, S. T. and Glick, P. (2008) Warmth and competence as universal dimensions of social perception: The stereotype content model and the BIAS map. In Zanna, M. P. (eds.) *Advances in Experimental Social Psychology* (Volume 40, pp. 61–149). Elsevier Academic Press. DOI: 10.1016/S0065-2601(07)00002-0

Cuddy, A. J. C., Fiske, S. T., Kwan, V. S. Y., Glick, P., Demoulin, S., Leyens, J.-P., Bond, M. H., Croizet, J.-C., Ellemers, N., Sleebos, E., Htun, T. T., Kim, H.-J., Maio, G., Perry, J., Petkova, K., Todorov, V., Rodríguez-Bailón, R., Morales, E., Moya, M., Palacios, M., Smith, V., Perez, R., Vala, J. and Ziegler, R. (2009) Stereotype content model across cultures: Towards universal similarities and some differences. *British Journal of Social Psychology* 48(1): 1–33. https://doi-org.proxy.mau.se/10.1348/014466608X314935

Echebarria Echabe, A. and Fernández Guede, E. (2006) Crossed-categorization and stereotypes: Class and ethnicity. *RIPS/IRSP* 19(2): 81–101. www.cairn-int.info/article-E_RIPSO_192_0081--crossed-categorization-and-stereotypes.htm, accessed 10 October 2023.

Esses, V. M., Jackson, L. M. and Bennett-AbuAyyash, C. (2010) Intergroup Competition. In Dovidio, J. (ed.) *The SAGE Handbook of Prejudice, Stereotyping and Discrimination.* (pp. 225–240). London: SAGE.

Fiske, S. T., Cuddy, A. J. C. and Glick, P. (2007) Universal dimensions of social cognition: Warmth and competence. *TRENDS in Cognitive Sciences* 11(2): 77–83. https://doi.org/10.1016/j.tics.2006.11.005

Fiske, S. T., Cuddy, A. J. C., Glick, P. and Xu, J. (2002) A model of (often mixed) stereotype content: Competence and warmth respectively follow from perceived status and competition. *Journal of Personality and Social Psychology* 82(6): 878–902. https://doi.org/10.1037/0022-3514.82.6.878

Fritzsche, P. (1998) *Germans into Nazis.* Cambridge, MA: Harvard University Press.

Glick, P. (2002) Sacrificial Lambs Dressed in Wolves' Clothing: Envious Prejudice, Ideology, and the Scapegoating of Jews. In Newman, L. S. and Erber, R. (eds.) *Understanding Genocide: The Social Psychological Holocaust* (pp. 113–142). New York, NY: Oxford University Press.

Glick, P. (2005) Choice of Scapegoats. In Dovidio, J. F., Glick, P. and Rudman, L. A. (eds.) *On the Nature of Prejudice, Fifty Years after Allport* (pp. 244–261). Malden, MA: Blackwell.

Glick, P. (2008) When Neighbors Blame Neighbors: Scapegoating and the Breakdown of Ethnic Relations. In Esses, V. M. and Vernon, R. A. (eds.) *Explaining the Breakdown of Ethnic Relations: Why Neighbors Kill* (pp. 123–146). Malden, MA: Blackwell Publishing.

Gualda, E. (2021) Metaphors of Invasion: Imagining Europe as Endangered by Islamisation. In Önnerfors, A. and Krouwel, A. (eds.) *Europe: Continent of Conspiracies. Conspiracy Theories in and about Europe* (pp. 54–75). London: Routledge.

Hamilton, D. L. and Gifford, D. K. (1976) Illusory correlation in interpersonal perception: A cognitive basis of stereotypic judgments. *Journal of Experimental Social Psychology* 12(4): 392–407. https://doi.org/10.1016/S0022-1031(76)80006-6

Jones, M. (2002) *Social Psychology of Prejudice.* Upper Saddle River, NJ: Prentice Hall.

Jost, J. T. (2018) A quarter century of system justification theory: Questions, answers, criticisms, and societal applications. *British Journal of Social Psychology* 58(2): 263–314. https://DOI:10.1111/bjso.12297

Jost, J. T. (2020) *A Theory of System Justification.* Cambridge, MA: Harvard University Press.

Jost, J. T. and Banaji, M. R. (1994) The role of stereotyping in system-justification and the production of false consciousness. *British Journal of Social Psychology* 33(1): 1–27. https://doi.org/10.1111/j.2044-8309.1994.tb01008.x

Jost, J. T. and Liviatan, J. (2007) System Justification. In Baumeister, R. and Vohs, K. (eds.) *Encyclopedia of Social Psychology* (pp. 894–895). SAGE Publications, Inc. https://dx.doi.org/10.4135/9781412956253.n573

Kay, A. C., Jost, J. T., Mandisodza, A. N., Sherman, J. V., Petrocelli, J. V. and Johnson, A. L. (2007) Panglossian Ideology in the service of system justification: How complementary stereotypes help us to rationalize inequality. *Advances in Experimental Social Psychology* 39: 305–358. https://doi.org/10.1016/S0065-2601(06)39006-5

Kimmel, M. (2013) *Angry White Men, American Masculinity at the End of an Era.* New York, NY: Bold Type Books.

Lerner, M. J. (1980) *The Belief in a Just World: A Fundamental Delusion.* New York, NY: Springer Science+Business Media.

McDonald, F. (2022) The 'freedom convoy' protesters are a textbook case of 'aggrieved entitlement'. *The Conversation*, 16 June 2022. https://theconversation.com/the-freedom-convoy-protesters-are-a-textbook-case-of-aggrieved-entitlement-176791, accessed 10 October 2023.

Mullen, B., Migdal, M. J. and Hewstone, M. (2001) Crossed categorization versus simple categorization and intergroup evaluations: A meta-analysis. *European Journal of Social Psychology* 31, 721–736. https://doi.org/10.1002/ejsp.60

Nicolas, G., de la Fuente, M. and Fiske, S. T. (2017) Mind the overlap in multiple categorization: A review of crossed categorization, intersectionality, and multiracial perception. *Group Processes & Intergroup Relations* 20(5): 621–631. https://doi.org/10.1177/136843021770886

Önnerfors, A. (2021) Der Grosse Austausch: Conspiratorial Frames of Terrorist Violence in Germany. In Önnerfors, A. and Krouwel, A. (eds.) *A Continent of Conspiracies? Conspiracy Theories in and on Europe* (pp. 76–96) London: Routledge.

Önnerfors, A. and Krouwel, A. (2021) Between Internal Enemies and External Threats: How Conspiracy Theories Have Shaped Europe – An Introduction. In Önnerfors, A. and Krouwel, A. (eds.) *Europe: Continent of Conspiracies. Conspiracy Theories in and about Europe* (pp. 1–21). London: Routledge.

Staub, E. (2008) The Origins of Genocide and Mass Killing, Prevention, Reconciliation, and Their Application to Rwanda. In Esses, V. M. and Vernon, R. A. (eds.) *Explaining the Breakdown of Ethnic Relations: Why Neighbors Kill* (pp. 245–268). Malden, MA: Blackwell Publishing.

Yzerbyt, V. Y. (2010) Motivational Processes. In *The SAGE Handbook of Prejudice, Stereotyping and Discrimination.* London: SAGE Publisher.

Zinn, H. ([1968] 2002) *Disobedience and Democracy: Nine Fallacies on Law and Order.* Cambridge: South End Press.

6

HOW TO COUNTERACT ENEMY IMAGES

Interventions and measures

CHAPTER OBJECTIVES

- To offer an overview of interventions and measures counteracting enemy images
- To describe the challenges when countering enemy images
- To offer relevant examples of organizations and projects aimed at countering enemy images

Introduction

Since enemy images have the potential to desensitize and mobilize their target audiences and to legitimize war, it is hugely important to address if and how they can be counteracted. In this chapter, we will suggest some interventions and measures, making it mainly normative.

For countermeasures to be effective, any interventions need to acknowledge the challenges faced. First, political leaders have both the interest and resources to spread malign enemy images (Chapter 3). Political leaders planning to go to war are aware of the potential of enemy images (Chapters 1 and 2) and have vast resources at their disposal to marginalize dissenting voices and form a powerful, unanimous elite discourse (Chapter 3). Second, as well as being useful to political leaders, enemy images are persuasive due to their cognitive and psychological functions (Chapter 4). This is why they are so often accepted and why recommending appropriate and effective interventions against them is not an easy task.

To systematize our reasoning and increase clarity, we have chosen to categorize the countermeasures into four levels of analysis we call *sender, receiver, message,*

DOI: 10.4324/9781003279570-6

and *social structure* (Figure 6.1). We combine these four levels with a horizontal temporal dimension that we divide into three phases: *preventive measures* that can be undertaken before indoctrination by enemy images begins; measures during ongoing indoctrination; and *curative measures* that can be taken after enemy image indoctrination. In total, we have identified eight relevant strategies. This number, of course, is not set in stone but is how we understand and organize existing research and literature in the area. Our model is to some extent inspired by the Hungarian social psychologist and political scientist Péter Krekó's discussion about countering conspiracy theories (Krekó, 2020).

At the *sender level*, we have identified two important strategies. The first concerns the *diversification of elite discourse* to avoid a unanimous discourse about the enemy, where all (or almost all) important elites in a society spread similar or at least compatible enemy images (see Chapter 3). Secondly, at this analytical level, we also find *regulation* of the freedom of expression, i.e. how to limit the supply of enemy images. There is usually no political interest in restricting access to enemy imagery during conflict, but there sometimes is before – and after – conflict occurs.

At the *receiver level*, we first find a strategy we call *media and information literacy (MIL)*. This is where 'immunization' can take place, interventions aiming at developing critical thinking and preventing individuals or groups from accepting (malign) enemy images (Krekó, 2020: 247). This type of measure can take place before a conflict or the spread of enemy images, and also in later phases. Media literacy training needs to be a continuous process since, like milk, it is perishable, and the abilities one develops in a pre-war situation are often forgotten when a conflict arises. On the same level of analysis, we also find *healing processes* taking place after exposure to enemy images.

On the third analytical level, we discuss *messages*, and how the dispersion of counter-narratives could potentially neutralize enemy images. Here we consult the literature on peace journalism but also briefly return to the reasoning about benign enemy images in Chapter 2. The spread of counter-narratives can in principle take place both before and after a conflict and at the same time as enemy images spread.

On the fourth and final level, we discuss *structural changes* – political, social, and economic – that potentially make both *individuals* and *communities* more resilient to enemy images or their dissemination. In focus here is Gordon Allport's famous *intergroup contact theory* (ICT), but also *social and political reforms*. Intergroup contacts and reforms overlap in Figure 6.1 because different types of reform are also a component of Allport's theory.

The discussion of the different counteracting measures will include a description of each one and what it aims to achieve, presenting the associated challenges and historical cases where it has been used, and where relevant discussing the ethical and democratic dilemmas involved.

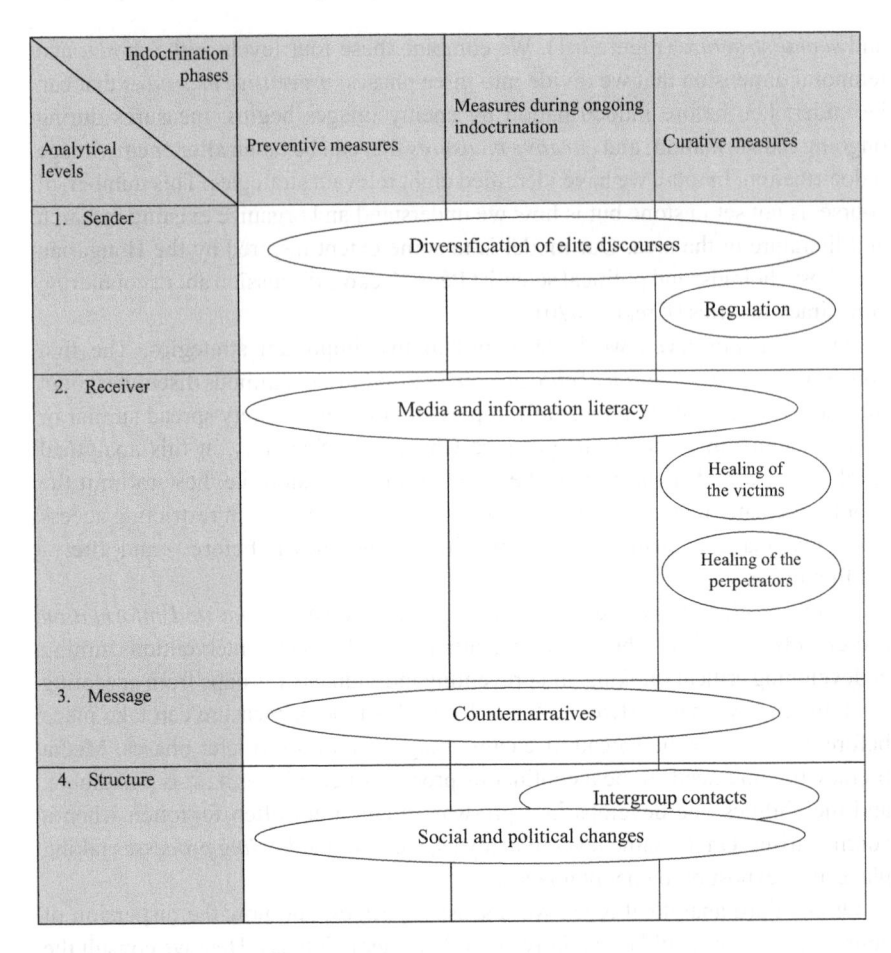

FIGURE 6.1 Counteracting measures.

Source: Created by the authors.

The sender level

As stated in the introduction, the purpose of the discussion at the sender level is to describe how we can break up a hegemonic enemy image producing elite discourses and to discuss how we can limit their supply and the harm they do.

Diversification of elite discourses

The greatest desire of political leaders is to create a situation in which supposedly independent actors 'voluntarily' side with them in the event of an armed conflict. As established in Chapter 3, political leaders know that they alone cannot persuade their population of the necessity or legitimacy of war. It is thus of great importance for them to create a situation where more or less all key communicators in society loyally develop a unanimous and coordinated elite discourse regarding the enemy. This situation is difficult for the receivers/citizens. After all, citizens in a democracy must be given *different* arguments based on which they can form their own opinions. Thus, a first and highly relevant counteracting measure at the sender level is to create a *diversification* of dominant elite discourses. Discourses creating enemy images of the 'other' should not go unchallenged because of their effects. We would even argue that it is a moral obligation for non-state discursive elites to free themselves as far as possible from the rhetoric of the state in cases where it spreads enemy images. Many of the discursive elites (Figure 3.4) have important societal roles. For example, it is often said that democratic societies have a free press, not only to disseminate information but also to act as an independent scrutinizer of power and ensure transparency. Likewise, the role of the intelligentsia is to think independently and critically; parts of civil society should monitor human rights; the church and other religious institutions should preach love for fellow human beings, and so on. Our normative point is that discursive elites that the state tries to turn into obedient tools have a moral duty to detach themselves and produce counter-narratives questioning enemy images.

It is easy to preach this moral stance, especially for those of us who are not in a situation of war or living in an authoritarian society. And we must understand the methods by which the state can discipline discursive elites, and which can be turned against them in case of dissent. The price of questioning enemy images, especially those sanctioned by the state, can be high. In this context, it is worth re-reading the section *Unanimous elite discourse* again in Chapter 3 and reflecting on the price that dissent can have for different elites. In Chapter 7, we also present Hallin's 'sphere of deviance' theory, illustrating how different zones of consensus, legitimate controversy, and deviance are shaped in journalism (particularly in wartime). Strong pressure for consensus diminishes the leeway for dissenting voices to be publicized. Let us also return to *Need for love and belonging* in Chapter 4. In that section, we described how important the group is to people for 'support, validation and understanding' (Allen, 2021: 1), outlining how they therefore seek group acceptance and try to avoid rejection. An important strategy for obtaining social approval is to identify the dominant social norms in a group and then adjust to them. In the event of a conflict, enemy images are one such social norm. In other words, if discursive elites question a state-sanctioned enemy image during an ongoing conflict, they can expect to be rejected, considered traitors, and subjected to hate campaigns. These groups might experience what most fear: exclusion and rejection.

During war, there have been important organizations or sometimes individuals who have questioned war propaganda and enemy images. One example is the creation of *Die bekennende Kirche* (the Confessing Church) in Germany in 1933. The background is the emergence, a few years earlier during the Weimar Republic, of a Protestant racist and antisemitic movement that attempted to 'Aryanize' the

German Church. During the Third Reich, a German Nazi Protestant church called *Die Deutsche Evangelische Kirche* (The German Evangelical Church) was created on these foundations. As a reaction, a countermovement, *Die Bekennende Kirche* (The Confessing Church), was formed. Famous representatives of this church were Karl Barth (1886–1968), Dietrich Bonhoeffer (1906–1945), and Martin Niemöller (1892–1984). Bonhoeffer was executed after it was revealed that he had participated in a conspiracy against Hitler, and Niemöller spent several years in a Nazi concentration camp. Although the movement failed to influence political developments in Nazi Germany, the fate of these leaders shows the price that dissenters may have to pay.

In the United States during the Vietnam War, dissenting actors were more successful. First, the United States is a democracy, so dissenting voices, albeit marginalized, were not executed. Second, as we wrote in Chapter 3, the media were able to work independently during this war and successfully promoted reporting that did not confirm the official American picture. A famous example of reporting that influenced American public opinion was a photo taken by Huỳnh Công Út, known professionally as Nick Ut (b. 1951, he subsequently won the Pulitzer Prize for Breaking News Photography in 1973). His photo depicts Vietnamese children running away from an American napalm bombing attack (see Figure 6.2).

In addition to the media, other key American communicators also played a major role during the Vietnam War. These include the linguist Noam Chomsky (mentioned in Chapter 3), the folk singer and social activist Pete Seeger (1919–2014), and the Baptist pastor and activist Martin Luther King (1929–1968).

FIGURE 6.2 'The terror of war'.

Source: Nick Ut, first published by Associated Press in 1972 without a copyright notice.

Regulations

In his text on countering conspiracy theories, Péter Krekó discusses strategies to target sources of misinformation 'in order to reduce the chance that the target audience will encounter the undesirable piece of information' (Krekó, 2020: 248). Since it is the state that has the power to limit the supply of enemy images, the state would probably not limit the spread of enemy images during or right before a war. We therefore imagine a post-conflict situation (see Figure 6.1) where the state could have an interest in building peace, but where enemy images might linger and be reproduced by non-state actors.

After the Second World War and at the start of the Cold War, there was a political will in Western Europe, especially among the members of the recently founded European Coal and Steel Union, to heal the wounds of the world wars and create a peaceful new Europe. But, of course, the attitudes of war lingered among the population and some discursive elites. There was thus a risk that enemy images would be reproduced against the wishes of the state.

In a way, the tables were now turned. With the European states no longer at war and pursuing a peacebuilding agenda, there was a risk of actors who reproduced enemy images feeling they were out in the political cold. And further, there was now a possible political motivation to undermine the position of those actors. Krekó discusses not only the discursive elites that we dealt with in Chapter 3, but also the responsibility and role of social media platforms with the removal of social media accounts (Krekó, 2020: 248). If the state wants to regulate the supply of enemy images today, in the era of the internet and social media platforms, it must regulate both traditional discursive elites (Figure 3.4) and the plethora of actors using the internet and social media to create and disseminate enemy images. A famous example of a key communicator being silenced after violence was the radio channel (RTLM) in Rwanda (see Chapter 7). After the genocide in 1994, in addition to the legal aftermath, RTLM was shut down and Rwanda implemented a media reform to prevent a repeat of what had occurred (Staub and Pearlman, 2006: 236).

Regulation, censorship, or other measures to limit the production and dissemination of enemy images are not without controversy. In open and democratic societies, this kind of intervention can be perceived as problematic, even undemocratic, not least in terms of societal deliberation and freedom of expression.

The receiver level

On this analytical level, we focus on the receivers of enemy images, first discussing research and programmes dealing with MIL as a way of boosting resilience to enemy images before going on to consider the *healing of victims* and *perpetrators*. The common aim of the three sections in this level is a reduction in the demand for enemy images and similar rhetoric.

Media and information literacy

In modern society, when enemy images are spread, mass media and social media are often engaged. One strategy for countering enemy images requires receivers to develop an ability to access and search for sound information, analyse and evaluate media content, and develop an understanding of how such information is circulated in complex digital information environments. The underlying normative expectation with increased MIL is that citizens (receivers) are enabled and empowered to make informed decisions in democratic societies, such as during elections, and to arrive at well-balanced judgements about the accuracy of claims made in public space. This includes the ability to develop and apply source criticism, an understanding of how information is gathered and communicated through various media formats (such as developing digital skills), how knowledge is formed in society, as well as an understanding of rhetorical strategies of persuasion. MIL is thus focused on skills that protect receivers from the negative effects of media, particularly new technological developments in which images, film, music, and text are combined in order to increase their impact (Potter, 2019: 3).

As media technology changes, so does MIL. UNESCO (2023) is a leading actor in promoting MIL across educational systems with the goal of enabling 'people's ability to think critically and click wisely' and a host of related aims such as participation in peacebuilding, equality, and sustainable development. Such a view of MIL requires a relatively stable knowledge environment with clear rules of quality control and an ideal that neutral knowledge (with a commitment to truth values) does in fact exist. Yet, as information studies researchers Jutta Haider and Olof Sundin (2022) argue, the laudable aims of MIL are compromised by several paradoxes. Contemporary societies are undergoing a crisis of information involving fragmentation and individualization driven by emotional engagement with (digital) media content. It is no longer clear what constitutes a shared societal knowledge basis in a context of growing 'algorithmic culture' shaped by privately owned platforms, individual choices, and partisan preferences. Establishing 'trust in public knowledge [...] requires collectively shared and societally accepted methods for producing, challenging, and vetting knowledge', but that is undercut by fragmentation (Haider and Sundin, 2022: 6). This makes the contemporary information environment particularly vulnerable to manipulation and divisive messages such as enemy images. These need to be countered online, but the mechanisms of algorithmic amplification mean that instead they risk being pushed to the core of societal deliberation since controversial messages attract interaction both pro and con. The amalgamation of media producers and consumers into a 'prosumer' (see Chapter 3) further obscures the extent to which the social reality supposedly communicated in media is real or imagined since a high amount of likes and shares, for instance, is frequently seen as a proof of its salience. As discussed at the end of Chapter 3, today it requires significantly fewer financial resources for a citizen to become a producer of media content. It is no longer reserved for a small elite with large financial resources to produce and spread media content. Currently, therefore, MIL is not just about the competence to be a critical consumer but should also be about being a responsible prosumer of content.

Altogether, these processes undermine societal trust and, significantly for our topic, limit the possibilities to develop sound counterstrategies to toxic enemy images. However, according to Haider and Sundin (2022), trust is the basis of both societal and cognitive order since it is a prerequisite for a shared worldview. MIL has been identified as a tool for restoring trust in information (and its truthfulness) and has been taken up in different curricula and strategies for combatting and countering disinformation, most importantly among audiences. It therefore seems to be an unproblematic intervention to bolster citizens' information skills and critical thinking and thus 'inoculate' them against messages relying on cognitive shortcuts, emotional appeals, and rhetorical manipulation. Yet Haider and Sundin also identify a problem with placing the responsibility for informed (and rational) decisions on the individual. Can we rely on citizens (or rather 'consumers of information') being truly enabled to autonomously analyse the overwhelming flows of information in the digital age? It requires considerable technical competence to be able to verify, for instance, if media content represents reality, is manipulated, or is completely faked. In war propaganda and for the sake of disseminating enemy images, this problem is even increased.

Moreover, if information consumers are trained to always be critical towards and question information, its meaning and interpretation, there might be a risk that none of it is trusted, which also would entail information that contradicts enemy images. The voices of experts or peacebuilders, for example, risk being rejected by such criticism. This brings us back to the issue of information trust, if and how audience trust can be established, in particular when the purpose is to actively deconstruct messages like enemy images. In this vein, the goal of MIL training is first to help audiences process news stories and other media content critically (Scharrer, 2002: 354) by learning how such messages often 'serve to rationalize existing social norms and expectations' (Ramasubramanian, 2007: 252). One could interpret such an approach as using MIL to inoculate against the persuasive power of enemy images as outlined in Chapter 3 and exemplified extensively in Chapter 7.

An important measure could therefore be to train audiences to identify, deconstruct, and resist the appeal of enemy images and develop resilience against them. We will talk more about the level of messages later and instead remind the reader here of what we said about *persuasive* communicators in Chapter 3. Due to cognitive shortcuts and peripheral processing in audiences, the person communicating the message can sometimes develop trustworthiness by playing on expertise and authority. As a counterstrategy, it is therefore important to train audiences in understanding what constitutes legitimate expertise and authority. During the pandemic, it was for instance possible to see that actors wrongly claimed and mimicked both expertise and authority to push false narratives. They invented positions and organizations that were not recognized internationally – for instance, a completely arbitrary so-called tribunal with the aim of sentencing political leaders for their interventions against COVID-19 (Önnerfors, 2024). A further factor connected to persuasiveness was identified in Chapter 3 as the *attractiveness* of the messenger. In the case of enemy images, it is difficult to speculate how a sceptical attitude towards these factors (in line with MIL) can be developed since enemy images are as a rule expressed by legitimate official authorities in leading powerful positions. This means that a critical attitude towards expertise and authority is to a certain extent inevitably formed in opposition to the dominant societal discourse.

Likewise, it is also of great importance that the receivers of messages understand the propagandists' strategies. In *Public and private spheres* (Chapter 3), we explained that a message has the potential to be accepted when there is *discursive harmony* between the private and public spheres, when the top-down elite discourse is in accordance with established ideas among the receivers. We also wrote that discursive consistency is important – i.e. the enemy images produced are consistent over time. Finally, strategies controlling and unifying discursive elites, convergence towards absolute consensus in one shared public space, are a feature of totalitarian/ authoritarian information regimes. What we want to say, then, is that it is important for the receivers of messages to understand this three-pronged approach in order to become increasingly media literate.

Healing of victims

This section deals with individuals and groups who have been subjected to extreme violence in war or genocide. It is inspired by texts written by one of the most prominent experts in the field, the American psychologist Ervin Staub (see Box 6.1), by his and colleagues' reconciliation work in field settings.

According to Staub, groups or individuals who have experienced violence against them or other forms of intense victimization are deeply affected in many ways (Staub, 2008: 253), often greatly traumatized (Staub and Perlman, 2006: 215). Even individuals who have not been subjected to violence themselves but belong to a targeted group are affected (Staub, 1998: 231). Just being a member of a victimized group and knowing that mere membership makes you a potential target of violence has an impact on individuals, who can develop different symptoms of trauma. They can suffer from survivor guilt or experience devaluation of themselves and their group, insecurity, and vulnerability. They might perceive the world and other groups (particularly the perpetrating group) as hostile and dangerous (Staub, 1998: 231 and 2008: 253).

BOX 6.1 ERVIN STAUB

Ervin Staub (b. 1938) is a Hungarian-born American professor of psychology, and emeritus at the University of Massachusetts Amherst. Surviving the Holocaust as a child, thanks in part to an active bystander, has probably influenced his choice of research field and its applications (Staub, 2019: 60).

Staub is well-known for his studies both in influences that lead to caring, helpful, altruistic behaviour and in the social processes that lead to mass violence, mass killing, and genocide. Over a long career, he has published several books and peer-reviewed articles on these themes.

In addition to his academic work, Professor Staub has worked on various projects in field settings such as programmes to train police officers in different parts of the United States to avoid unnecessary violence and to improve Dutch–Muslim relations in Amsterdam. One goal was to turn police officers into 'active bystanders who attempt to prevent or stop unnecessary harmful or violent behavior by fellow officers' (Staub, 2019: 61).

Starting in 1999, five years after the Rwanda genocide, Staub conducted workshops and training there for the staff of community organizations, national leaders, people in the media, and others. He did so in collaboration with clinical psychologist Dr Laurie Anne Pearlman and US and Rwandan assistants. In 2004, he also founded the *Psychology of Peace and Violence Program* at the University of Massachusetts Amherst, which trains doctoral students in social psychological theory to translate their work into policy and practical applications.

According to Staub and Perlman, violence between groups can resume after a peace treaty (Staub and Perlman, 2006: 214), and if power relations are reversed, the victim group can become a perpetrator (Staub, 1998 and 2008). Ergo, violence begets violence. One example is Rwanda. The violence perpetrated by Hutus in 1994 against Tutsis was not the first wave of violent repression in Rwanda. Under German and Belgian colonial rulers, Tutsis were favoured over Hutus. Until 1959, Hutus were severely repressed and exploited. When the power relations changed in the Hutus' favour, the old victims became the new perpetrators (Staub, 2008: 247).

The point is, it is reasonable to assume that members of a victimized group who see themselves as vulnerable and the world and other groups as dangerous have a higher propensity to accept enemy images, especially those depicting the group that subjected them to violence and suffering. That makes both individual and collective healing of trauma caused by war and violence a potentially important strategy to reduce the attractiveness of enemy images after conflict, or as we wrote in the preamble to this section, a way to reduce the demand for them.

How, then, should such healing be approached? The purpose of this section is not to elaborate on this issue in detail, but it is still relevant to mention a few important conditions and measures that facilitate healing and reconciliation. As indicated above, we will refer to the writings of Ervin Staub and his colleagues and their experiences in field settings, compiling a few central and reoccurring ideas in their writing.

The first prerequisite for reconciliation and healing concerns political structures. This includes institutions upholding physical security, democratic structures, and a fair and efficient legal system. Since the victims of war or genocide have terrible experiences of physical violence, they are sensitive to physical insecurity, and physical security is thus required for healing to begin, preferably with efficient and fair institutions maintaining it (Staub and Pearlman, 2006: 216). Moreover, although this is difficult to achieve in a post-conflict situation, stable democratic institutions and a democratic constitution can also contribute to the start of a healing process (Staub and Pearlman, 2006: 216). But democracy can be a double-edged sword. At worst, democracy could be the rule of a threatening majority over a vulnerable minority. Therefore, a constitution that safeguards the rights of minorities, as well as strong and honest democratic institutions to uphold them, is crucial for the healing process. A third vital political structure is a functioning legal system that can administer justice and sentence the perpetrators of violence to fair penalties and sometimes also restorative justice (Staub, 2008: 261). But in addition to sentencing perpetrators, a functioning legal system can establish what has been done to the victims, itself a form of acknowledgement of their suffering (Staub, 2008: 260; 1998: 233) that can help them feel innocent (1998: 233) and promote healing. After war or genocide, the number of criminal investigations and perpetrators can be very large. This was the case in Rwanda. And in addition to that, the judiciary was severely strained post-genocide since a significant proportion of Rwanda's lawyers had been murdered, fled the country, or were themselves accused of perpetration (Staub, 2014: 505). The UN therefore assisted Rwanda in 1994 by creating the *International Court in Rwanda* to try high-ranking government and army officials. To cope with the handling of the tens of thousands of cases in local society, a traditional legal system, often called the *gacaca courts,* was introduced.

> In the gacaca process, the populace elected 250,000 people from the general population in October 2001. These people would serve as judges, in panels of 19, in about 9000 locations around Rwanda.
>
> *(Staub and Perlman, 2006: 227)*

And in addition to that, community members were legally required to attend the trials (Staub, 2014: 507). Because the process was transparent and because so many attended the trials or were part of the courts, the anticipated effect was that the population would accept the verdicts (Staub and Perlman, 2006: 229).

In these trials, the suspects were held accountable to the inhabitants of the villages where the crimes had been committed, and there was a stated intention that the process would promote reconciliation and healing for the victims. Legal certainty, on the other hand, was considered low, as the defendants had to pursue their own defence and the judges had limited legal training. Still, it cannot be stressed enough how important it is for the victims and their healing that the killings and crimes are investigated and that those who are guilty are convicted. Alongside the courts, the Rwandan *Truth and Reconciliation Commission* also played an important role, 'communicating to the victims that the world considers what was done to them as wrong, immoral, and unacceptable by the community of nations' (Staub, 1998: 233).

Another prerequisite for reconciliation and healing concerns social justice and having basic economic and social needs met. Much of the work for reconciliation in Rwanda was led from the central political level. For example, soon after the genocide, Rwanda's new government established a *National Unity and Reconciliation Commission* (NURC), which held public meetings in different parts of the country with various categories of people who were allowed to express what they needed to reconcile. In Rwanda, there had been unjust social arrangements for a long time. In one period 'there was strong Tutsi dominance in wealth and power, especially under Belgian rule, followed by strong Hutu dominance' (Staub, 2008: 257). And things worsened during the genocide. Many Tutsis had lost everything; many women had lost their husbands and needed resources to support their families and provide education for their children (Staub, 2014: 506). According to Staub, counteracting poverty, equal distribution of resources, and work against discrimination are necessary for the healing process (Staub, 2006: 879). His ideas resemble what we wrote in *Realist group conflict theory and relative deprivation theory* (Chapter 4). In other words, equal distribution of resources could be a way to reduce the attractiveness of enemy images.

In addition to these prerequisites, Staub emphasizes the importance of a new rhetoric or ideology that is inclusive, counteracts stereotypes and prejudices, and creates a shared collective memory (Staub, 2008: 263). This new constructive rhetoric should be expressed on all levels in society and by a diverse allocation of senders (see the discussion about senders above and the message below). Firstly, it is important that a 'we' is created that includes all ethnic groups – in Rwanda's case, Tutsis, Hutus, and Twa. These groups should also be described as important assets for the nation. In some conflicts, the regime has grandiose plans for a bright future for the group. The only obstacle to this bright future manifesting here and now is 'they', who must therefore be annihilated (Staub, 2008: 251). Here the enemy is not described as a threat to 'our' current assets, but the enemy robs 'us' of a bright and glorious future. One example is the Khmer Rouge in Cambodia, who advocated a society of total social equality. But allegedly there were groups in society – the former ruling class, intellectuals, and others – who stood in the way of this wonderful society and had to be eliminated (Staub, 2008: 250). This kind of rhetoric is devastating and must be replaced by a vision where a new and inclusive 'we' is created, including the former enemy. Staub also discusses the importance of rhetoric that does not stereotype the out-group but sees the good examples among 'them' (Staub, 2008: 250). This recalls what we wrote in Chapter 2 about benign enemy images and the humanization of the enemy.

The wounds of the killing-time could also be healed by meeting with others within the victim group. A large part of Ervin Staub's discussions underlines the importance of one's own group for healing from the trauma of past victimization, and the importance of person-to-person healing. Still, this must be done with caution and should not be rushed.

> Healing requires mourning. Mourning requires remembering. While some people may need distance, initially, from the horrible events they have experienced, over time it is important that they engage with what has happened to them. Healing is facilitated by others' acknowledgment of the group's suffering, as well as by finding hope for a better future.
>
> *(Staub, 2008: 253)*

Staub thus seems to mean that reconciliation work should not be rushed; temporal distance from the events may be required. In the case of Rwanda, the number of people involved was enormous. About 700,000 Tutsis, or about 75% of the ethnic group, were murdered, and so were 50,000 moderate Hutus. In addition, many were subjected to torture and psychological violence, with countless women raped and mutilated (Staub, 2006: 869). This means that the number of people affected, both victimized survivors and perpetrators, amounts to several millions. Professional counselling is not feasible. There are simply not enough professional counsellors to deal with all traumatized people (Staub and Pearlman, 2006: 216). Ordinary fellow human beings must play a central role. And when ordinary fellow human beings listen to each other and confirm each other's stories, a healing process can take place (Staub, 2008: 253).

> People can help each other heal by becoming witness to each other's experiences, especially their painful experiences during the genocide, with empathy and caring.
>
> *(Staub, 2008: 253)*

In Staub's and his co-workers' fieldwork in Rwanda, a large group of people, called facilitators, were trained to lead the conversations.

> These people were professional helpers with various backgrounds and positions. Some were trained trauma counselors, others public educators for the national unity and reconciliation commission, still others front-line staff in local NGOs; a few were staff of religious organizations.
>
> *(Staub and Pearlman, 2006: 217)*

In these conversations, it is important to listen to and acknowledge the participants' stories of abuse and violence, and to convey hope for a better future. Similarly, learning about other genocides and similar suffering and examining their psychological and social roots 'can help people see their common humanity with others' (Staub and Pearlman, 2006: 219) and facilitate healing. In the case of Rwanda, Staub and Perlman tell us that when victims learned that similar genocides had occurred on other occasions, they felt they were not outside history – 'they seemed moved and rehumanized by the understanding that what had happened in their society is a human, albeit horrific, process' (Staub and Pearlman, 2006: 221). According to Staub and Perlman, one woman said, 'If this has happened to other people, then it doesn't mean that God abandoned the people of Rwanda' (Staub and Pearlman, 2006: 221). Some research indicates that 'encouraging people to talk about their painful experiences, or exposure, can overcome the avoidance that maintains trauma symptoms' (Staub and Pearlman, 2006: 219), but opinions are divided on this.

In addition to this interpersonal process, public commemoration and memorialization also have great significance. In Israel, Holocaust Remembrance Day on the 27th of Nisan (a spring month in the Hebrew calendar) is an important date in memory of all those who were murdered. In Armenia, a genocide museum opened (Staub, 1998: 234). However, these public rites must not stop at the memories of the unbearable but also highlight the hope for a future, preferably one that includes the perpetrators.

In addition to the in-group healing process discussed above, intergroup contacts can also be valuable. There is a well-established theory and research tradition based on Gordon Allport's research on intergroup contacts and this will be discussed in detail below (see the section on ICT). Here a brief discussion on Staub's use of intergroup contacts will suffice. It must be emphasized that not all intergroup contact contributes to healing. Staub underlines that for people with traumatizing experiences, ill-considered encounters and superficial intergroup contacts even increase problems (Staub, 2008: 263). However, well-conducted meetings, sometimes in smaller groups (Staub, 1998: 232) characterized by deep engagement by group members, help to diminish feelings of devaluation and are likely to be helpful (Staub, 2008: 263–264). One additional factor is if members of the perpetrating group acknowledge the victims' suffering (Staub, 1998: 232). In Rwanda, Staub and his colleagues worked with both Hutus and Tutsis. Of course, members of the perpetrating Hutu group, even if they participated actively in the workshops in general,

> did not tell the 'stories' of their experiences during the genocide. Still, we believe that hearing the painful stories of Tutsis – stories that mainly focused on what happened to the victims, hardly mentioning perpetrators – could promote empathy in Hutus and contribute to reconciliation.
>
> *(Staub and Pearlman, 2006: 221)*

Let us summarize this section. A starting point in the discussion was that people who are traumatized by organized violence have a higher propensity to accept enemy images because they see themselves as vulnerable and the world and other groups as dangerous, especially the perpetrator group. Thus, healing from the trauma could be one important strategy to reduce the attractiveness of enemy images after conflict, or as we wrote in the preamble to this section, a way to reduce the demand for them.

Healing from trauma is something individual, and some people probably never get rid of the pain from their memories. However, it seems that some conditions facilitate at least partial healing. When a group has lived through situations of lawlessness and powerlessness in which they were subjected to violence, physical security maintained by fair authorities is vital. For the same reason, a political system that safeguards the rights of minorities is of great importance. Another theme is justice and a recognition of the victim group's suffering. This can to some extent be achieved through conversations with others in the participants' own group who listen to and acknowledge their stories of abuse and violence. Similarly, a fair and functioning legal system that administers justice is vital, since the crimes and suffering are thereby publicly recognized. In the same way, museums, the media, and finally even the perpetrators can acknowledge the crimes committed. Moreover, the survivors of war and genocide are not only fighting their inner demons but may also be economically destitute. Social and restorative justice can therefore also contribute to the sense of justice and, by extension, healing. Finally, healing can also be facilitated by the spread of a new ideology in which an inclusive 'we' is created to embrace both victims and perpetrators.

Healing of the perpetrators

War, genocide, and large-scale violence create terrible psychological damage also for the perpetrators and bystanders in the perpetrator group (Staub, 2006: 872; Staub and Perlman, 2006: 215). The psychological damage is particularly severe when the victims of their violence are innocent (Staub, 2008: 255).

In Chapters 1 and 4, referring to Albert Bandura (2016), Michael J. Osofsky, Albert Bandura, and Philip G. Zimbardo (2005), and Michael Taillard and Holly Giscoppa (2013), we stated that people might be particularly willing to accept enemy images *after* committing horrendous violent acts. The reason is that people who engage in intense violence against others tend to be psychologically injured by their own actions and need to find ways to live with themselves. Bandura's entire book from 2016 discusses 'moral disengagement', how people 'can behave inhumanely and still retain their self-respect and feel good about themselves' (Bandura, 2016: 1). He describes eight mechanisms for absolving oneself of moral responsibility. Please go back to Chapter 1, where these were discussed in detail, and compare them with our discussion below. Staub underlines that when the perpetrators are ashamed of their actions, they try to protect themselves from shame and guilt (Staub, 2010: 473). Here we will select and discuss just a few of the perpetrators' strategies.

Two strategies relate to the perpetrators' actions. One is the displacement of responsibility for their actions, where they claim that they were only obeying orders (Bandura, 2016: 3), and comfort themselves by saying that someone else is responsible for their violence and killing. In a second one, they tend to minimize the harm their actions have caused (Staub, 2006: 872; Bandura, 2016: 3 and 34). In this case, as a protective measure, they do not (want to) realize the full consequences of their actions.

Three other strategies concern the relationship to, or judgements and attitudes about the victimized group. Firstly, violence and killing affect perpetrators' and bystanders' relationships with the victims. Staub returns to keeping a distance from the victims as a protective mechanism. Suffering from guilt, empathic distress, and shame, perpetrators and bystanders find it difficult to be close to the victims and to other members of the victimized group and therefore distance themselves from them (Staub, 2006: 872; Staub and Pearlman, 2006: 216). The second common strategy Bandura calls attribution of blame (2016: 3). The idea is simple: blaming the victim by claiming that 'our' behaviour was a response to 'their' actions (Staub, 2008: 255). Allegedly, 'they' threatened 'us' and 'our' legitimate assets, and 'our' acts were pure self-defence. A variation on this theme is to say that 'they' stood in the way of 'our' glorious future. In this case, the perpetrators see their own violence

> as a way of dealing with a group that stood in the way of important, legitimate goals, possibly embodied in a 'higher' ideological vision like communism, Nazism, or nationalism.
>
> *(Staub, 1998: 233)*

By holding on to their ideology and to the notion that 'they' constitute a threat to 'our' assets and goals, 'perpetrators can resist accepting that their actions were immoral and inhumane' (Staub, 2008: 255). A third strategy implies that the perpetrators, during ongoing acts of violence and afterwards, 'justify their actions by seeing the other in a more and more negative light' (Staub, 2010: 166), even dehumanizing them. The longer the violence goes on and the more severe it is, the worse and more vulgar the notions of the victims become (Staub, 2010: 167). In some cases, perpetrators can be seen to 'feel guilty, to apologize, and to attempt to make amends for their actions' (Staub, 2010: 167), but it is more likely that they hold on to their justifying enemy images (Staub, 2010: 167).

Although it is primarily the actual perpetrators who need to protect themselves from the emotional consequences of their actions, bystanders in the perpetrator group who did not participate in the genocide or war also need to protect themselves emotionally, according to Staub and Pearlman, and are likely to act to some extent as described above (Staub and Pearlman, 2010: 216).

Our first point with this list of coping strategies is that the last two strategies – the attribution of blame and the negative depiction of the out-group – are compatible with the ideal-type malign enemy image (see Table 2.3). The enemy image gives perpetrators what they need: a narrative justifying their actions. According to the enemy image, 'they' allegedly threaten 'us' and 'our' most vital assets, and therefore 'our' violence was necessary and legitimate. And moreover, 'their' essence is completely different from 'ours'; 'they' are inferior, perhaps even dehumanized. In Chapter 1, we discussed in detail the consequences of this kind of rhetoric, including emotional ones. In that context, we emphasized that enemy images dull people and that natural feelings of empathy are suppressed. The enemy images prepare people to carry out gruesome acts of violence and also serve as a coping strategy after carrying out acts of violence. And our second point is that, since enemy images probably give guilt-ridden perpetrators the kind of justification they need, it is likely that enemy images are in particular demand by perpetrators after their violent actions since they might protect them against realizing the true nature of their acts. Enemy images are thus likely to be attractive to a tormented soul.

Normatively, one important duty of the peace researcher and peace worker is to formulate and implement strategies that will make enemy images less attractive to perpetrators and thereby reduce the likelihood of them holding on to, or accepting, enemy images. Ervin Staub has devoted much of his academic work to understanding the origins of mass murder and genocide as well as proposing healing and reconciliation strategies. His writing is therefore broader than our question, which merely concerns the attractiveness of enemy images. In the following paragraphs, we will formulate only a few thoughts, inspired by Staub, that are relevant to our more limited question: how can we make enemy images less attractive for perpetrators and reduce their demand for them?

The first step is to make the perpetrators comprehend the consequences and the morally reprehensible nature of their actions. This is not easy because they will resort to the protection and coping mechanisms mentioned above, to protect themselves against guilt and shame. We believe that a major information campaign – perhaps even a propaganda campaign – is required to penetrate the thinking of perpetrators. In Chapter 3, we discussed what kind of senders and messages appear persuasive to an audience and how one can construct a persuasive system of indoctrination. In that chapter, this know-how was deployed in the service of enemy images. But that chapter's lessons can also be used to counter the coping strategies of perpetrators. It was said, among other things, that it is a great advantage if influential actors – we called them discursive elites – communicated the same or compatible discourses. It is therefore vital that different discursive elites in post-conflict societies communicate true messages about what really happened and challenge the perpetrators' imaginations about and justifications for genocide.

In this context, courts can also play a significant role. In the Rwandan case, UN-founded courts that judged high-ranking leaders as well as local ones judging people in the community were important. This was discussed in the previous section. In addition to holding the suspects accountable for their actions, the courts' moral communication was central. They publicly communicated that the killing was wrong, immoral, and unacceptable. In Germany right after the Second World War, the Nuremberg trials had a similar function. In the course of these trials,

> the history and actions of Germany during the Hitler era were laid bare in great detail, using to a large extent materials created by the Nazis and the German bureaucracy (Staub, 1998: 233). [Without this documentary exposition] it is likely that the Germans, once again, would have felt like victims.
>
> *(Staub, 1998: 233)*

A communicating role could also be given to *truth and reconciliation commissions* after conflicts. Such commissions are official bodies tasked with revealing past offences. They are given authoritative status, and through their work, leading figures at least are confronted with their actions.

Further important discursive elites are for instance the mass media, the educational system, and museums. In the previous section, we described how public commemoration and memorialization were important for the victims' healing process. Among other things, we mentioned the Armenian Genocide Museum. This type of public commemoration can also be important in confronting perpetrators and informing bystanders in the perpetrating group. In Germany, there are several monuments not only to honour the victims but also to remind succeeding generations of the perpetrator group of what happened during the Holocaust. With a similar purpose, many of the Nazi concentration camps and death camps are today museums.

Another discursive elite is the mass media. Documentaries and news programmes can contribute to the creation of a new public discourse where abuse and genocide are accurately described and condemned. In Rwanda some time after the 1994 genocide, RTLM was shut down and programmes with peace-making content were broadcast instead. Among others, Staub and his team created educational radio programmes that were widely distributed (Staub, 2019: 62).

Another important actor in this context is the education system, and it can play many key roles in reconciliation (King, 2014). Here, we will confine our discussion to how it can disseminate accurate information after a conflict, for example about mass murder, genocide, and the killing of civilians during war. But this is not an easy task. Integrating teaching about the crimes of one's own group into the general curriculum is delicate. For instance, German policymakers did not include the Holocaust in the school syllabus until nearly 20 years after the end of the Second World War (King, 2014: 153). But concealing a painful history did not only happen in Germany. It is common in many post-war contexts (King, 2014: 153). In any case, the education system must appropriately disseminate information about its own nation's history of violence and trauma, and it is essential to consider children's age and psychological maturity when introducing themes of war, mass murder, and genocide.

Another type of teaching involves the re-education of perpetrators. In Rwanda, perpetrators had to go through re-education under the auspices of the NURC before being released into the community. Similar programmes have also been implemented after other conflicts. However, there is a risk that this type of action could 'lead to compliance, but not necessarily to a transformation' (Staub, 2014: 507), meaning that perpetrators act and say what they think is expected from them, without any real change. But in some cases, they accept their responsibility and renounce malign images of the other. In an article, Ervin Staub describes an event that made a great impression on the then only 17-year-old author Günter Grass:

> The great German author who has written much about the culpability of Germans, was profoundly affected when as a young man the American troops marched him, together with other local Germans, through one of the concentrations (sic) camps.
>
> *(Staub, 1998: 233)*

In addition to mustering important actors in society with the aim of forming a unanimous elite discourse, letting perpetrators face survivors of their violence can be effective. This is a form of intergroup contact mentioned in the previous section. This strategy too is fraught with challenges. Not infrequently, perpetrators want to distance themselves from their victims as a coping strategy (Staub and Pearlman, 2006: 216). But if contacts are still possible, these meetings must be organized with great care. This type of meeting should probably take place later in the process because if a victim is put in a situation where they encounter perpetrators who neither acknowledge their actions nor realize the extent of their consequences, the meeting can be offensive and harmful for the victim. The meeting should therefore take place on the victims' terms. However, well-conducted meetings in which the perpetrators begin to understand the magnitude of their actions can lead to healing for the victims, increase empathy in the perpetrators, and contribute to reconciliation (Staub and Pearlman, 2006: 221).

Sometimes it is not possible to influence perpetrators through information or intergroup contacts. In that case, another strategy could be useful: to publicly dissuade people from discriminating behaviour or from prejudiced utterances. This is a kind of learning-by-doing. This way of shaping behaviours can help in 'developing values, beliefs and action tendencies consistent with the social norms that guide action', even if these norms are imposed by the government (Staub, 2014: 507). In other words, if people are forced to act in a non-discriminatory way, their behaviour could, in the long run, impact their values and beliefs, i.e. learning-by-doing. A version of this strategy is to allow people in post-conflict situations to work towards common goals. According to Staub and Pearlman, 'working together for shared goals, which are superordinate to people's and their groups' separate and at times conflicting goals, can promote this deep engagement' (Staub and Pearlman, 2001: 224). This strategy will be developed and discussed further on, in the section on ICT.

Finally, we want to discuss confession and forgiveness as strategies to make enemy images less attractive to perpetrators. We already know that the attribution of blame and the negative depiction of the out-group are two important coping strategies to protect against guilt and shame. And we described above how the entire society should muster all discursive elites to spread accurate information about wars, mass killing, and genocide so that perpetrators cannot surround themselves with a 'protective shell' of delusions (Staub and Pearlman, 2001: 209); likewise, they should be confronted through intergroup contacts with victims and encouraged to face the consequences of their actions (Staub and Pearlman, 2001: 209). Another strategy to get perpetrators to abandon their enemy images is confession and asking for forgiveness. We saw in the previous section that a local legal system called *gacaca* was established in post-genocide Rwanda, which both convicted the guilty and publicly spelt out and condemned the perpetrators' actions. But since the local courts sought also to promote reconciliation, they aimed not only at uncovering the truth but also 'focused on confession and apology' and asking the victims for forgiveness (Hewstone et al., 2008: 75).

When extreme violence has been committed, it may seem unacceptable to even suggest that victims should be put in a situation where the perpetrators are expected to ask for forgiveness which the victims are supposed to grant. It can be difficult to forgive even passive bystanders or completely innocent members of the perpetrator group. In the case of Rwanda, the violence was immense: not only its quantitative scale, 750,000 killed, but also its nature. In many cases, machetes were used, requiring close contact between perpetrator and victim. And in addition to that, people were killed by neighbours and even relatives, such as a Tutsi married into a Hutu family (Staub and Pearlman, 2001: 211). Against this background, it can be difficult to forgive. And the expectations of the victims to forgive can leave them feeling diminished. Moreover, 'forgiving' perpetrators in this situation may be more like a 'capitulation to a powerful other than real forgiveness' (Staub and Pearlman, 2001: 208). Nevertheless, Staub and Pearlman emphasize that 'forgiving is necessary and desirable' (Staub and Pearlman, 2001: 207) and believe that 'it paves the way for reconciliation and furthers healing, thereby making a better future possible' (Staub and Pearlman, 2001: 207). If Staub is right, forgiving is also relevant to our question.

Let us summarize: it has been emphasized that perpetrators are ashamed of their actions and try to protect themselves from shame and guilt, sometimes by embracing enemy images as a way to justify their actions and conceal the true nature of their acts. In the healing process suggested by Staub, the encounter with victims, taking clear individual responsibility for one's actions and the process of confession and forgiveness could mean that feelings of guilt and shame are reduced. If this is the case, the need for enemy images as a remedy might also be reduced.

The message level

In this section, we discuss how to produce and spread counter-narratives that could potentially counteract enemy images. Specifically, we will first discuss strategies that increase the persuasiveness of counter-narratives, and then the actual content of the counter-narrative.

In Chapter 3 we discussed political leaders' persuasion strategies to make an audience accept enemy images. In addition to persuasive *messages*, we discussed the importance of convincing *communicators* and effective *propaganda machinery*. In a successful counteraction of enemy images, the persuasion strategy presented in Chapter 3 must be countered at every point, but in this section we will discuss the message only. In the same chapter, we developed further factors that make messages about enemy images more convincing. We discussed their *emotional appeal, credibility, consistency, simplicity*, and how they should cater to *human needs*. These factors can also be used in the service of peace and will be discussed briefly.

If messages are to appeal to *emotions*, they must not be based on fear of the other as enemy images are. Instead, they could be based on a hope for a better and brighter future where the 'other' is included and seen as a partner. This was done, for example, in Rwanda after the genocide. It might be possible to enhance the *credibility* of messages by referring to reason, rationality, and symbols of status. In Chapter 3 we highlighted the importance of the messages being *consistent* with established beliefs. It has been said on various occasions (Chapters 3 and 4) that people more easily absorb messages that are compatible with established beliefs. A problem arises here, as countering enemy images in many cases means breaking with an existing and firmly established notion of 'them' as a threat. That means a message counteracting enemy images would not be consistent with what people probably already believe. In this case, it is important to find values and beliefs, probably from a time before a conflict or pre-indoctrination, that can be exploited in the service of peace. Perhaps one can refer to established religious ideas or highlight historical periods of peace prior to the conflict that the audience is familiar with. Peace might thereby, in the eyes of the audience, be understood as morally acceptable and possible.

Peace processes are often complicated. Healing physical and emotional wounds after a war is a lengthy and sometimes painful process. In addition, there are political, economic, and legal issues to be resolved. But messages counteracting enemy images should, whenever possible, avoid going into these details because *simple* messages are more memorable (Taillard and Giscoppa, 2013: 15). Finally, Chapter 3 stated that successful communication must consider people's needs. We also touched on this in the section on the *Healing of the victims* and the *Healing of the perpetrators*. When counteracting enemy images, a future should be presented where human needs, both physiological and psychological, are met.

Let us now turn to the *content* of the counter-narrative, the information that contradicts enemy images. In this section, we take the ideal–typical (malign) enemy image as a background and starting point. After all, it is against this narrative that we want to present alternatives. In Chapter 2, we presented the ideal–typical enemy image as consisting of five elements: (a) separating 'us' from 'them', (b) describing 'them' as inferior to 'us', and yet (c) capable of threatening and harming 'us', especially 'our' core assets. Likewise, enemy images aimed to (d) legitimize 'our' actions to neutralize the threats, and (e) mobilise 'us' to take part in those actions. A large part of the same chapter was devoted to these five elements, describing them in detail and providing illustrations. In the latter part of the chapter, we created two compacted and contrasting enemy images, one we termed malign and the other benign (see Table 2.3). The point is that in Chapter 2, we had already formulated not only an enemy image, but also a counter-narrative. The benign enemy image is a form of counter-narrative. It describes 'us' and 'them' and the threat 'they' pose in a way that does not legitimize violent action. It emphasizes the other's humanity and likeness to 'us' and 'their' ability to improve: 'they' can change and do not have to be 'our' eternal enemies. It thus points to a future where peace is possible. So please read Chapter 2 again, especially the discussion about the benign enemy image. Here you will find some elements of rhetoric that could be included in a counter-narrative.

In writing this book, we are of course not the only ones to have worked with counter-narratives. Another example is *peace journalism*, which emerged as a new field within peace and conflict studies in the mid-1990s (Lynch and McGoldrick, 2007: 248). Peace journalism is a normative theory which claims that journalism should strive (among other things) to reject conflict-generating messages (e.g. enemy images) depicting relationships with 'them' as a zero-sum game and replace them with a win–win orientation. Likewise, it should strive for the humanization of all sides, focusing on suffering overall, and on peacemakers among 'them' (Lynch and McGoldrick, 2007: 251).

It must be underlined that messages countering enemy images are not only a task for established media outlets. On the contrary, such messages should be dispersed everywhere in the public sphere exercising influence over people. However, producing messages that challenge cognitive consistency (see Chapter 4) is a complex task. Over the last decade, the potential of counter-narratives has been explored in research, with mixed results. Nevertheless, important lessons on countering the message of enemy images can be derived from the literature.

Carthy et al. (2020) carried out a scoping study of available research where the effect of interventions could be measured. The authors found that 'counter-narrative interventions which target a specific, dominant narrative can have an effect'. Overall risk factors were better reduced by 'using counter-stereotypical exemplars, alternative narratives and inoculation techniques (eliciting [mental] resistance through the production of counter-arguments)'. Interestingly, 'persuasion did not have a significant effect'. In sum, 'the most pronounced effects were for secondary outcomes' such as 'realistic threat perceptions towards an adversarial group, in-group favouritism and out-group hostility'. The effectiveness of interventions on primary outcomes (intent to act violently) was inconclusive. In other words, 'the concept of using a communication strategy to directly counter a dominant narrative' needs further elaboration (Carthy et al., 2020: 3).

Since counter-narratives 'should address the underlying logic of a dominant narrative', it is important to understand that stories

- are recollections of events which happen in sequence
- contain characters (protagonists and antagonists) that can cause change
- have an identifiable beginning, middle, and end
- present a sequence that is interpreted as a specific order of (key) events.

As social constructions of the world, narratives are embedded in processes of identity formation and serve to provide meaning and explanation, constituting 'among the most effective forms of persuasion, and attitude change' (Carthy et al., 2020: 5).

Narratives frequently have generic features and can be sorted into different types. For a (national) collective, the narrative of historical origin and state formation is for instance a vital piece of identification. It is easy to imagine that a narrator can manipulate such origin stories, saturated with accounts of grievances and abuses, to such a degree that old enmities are mobilized and revived among the target audience of an in-group, in particular in a context of emerging and escalating conflicts. We only need to study the manifold reinterpretations of history that have played out in the information war of strategic narrative dominance between Ukraine and Russia. Another typical form is doomsday or 'end times' narratives, which focus instead on the imminent threat of fall, decline, and ruin of the in-group if the adversary is not terminally confronted. These stories are frequently sorted in the dramaturgical sequence of the golden age – decline (loss of golden age), looming collapse, hope of restoration (to the former golden age) – and are an integrated part of political strategic communication, as immortalized by a slogan such as 'Make America Great Again' (Önnerfors, 2022: 60–79). In this story, it is easy to point out that both domestic and foreign antagonists who have contributed to the downfall are plotting the final collapse and need to be neutralized/eliminated in order for former/lost glory to be restored (by means of violence).

If a dominant narrative (communicating enemy images) is thus identified, the question is whether it is possible to challenge it 'by deconstructing, discrediting, and "demystifying" it'. The aim of counter-narrative strategies must be to present individuals exposed to the dominant narrative with alternative social constructions, for instance by challenging inaccurate historical narratives. Counter-narratives should 'address the underlying logic of a dominant narrative' and its constitutive meaning-making elements by unpicking it, challenging its main themes and delegitimizing the violent means with which the goals of confrontation with the out-group are imbued. The counter-narrative is thus an 'intervention that challenges the rationalization(s) of violence purported in a dominant narrative, which will, in turn, reconstruct the story' (Carthy et al., 2020: 5–6).

In practice, the intervention has been tested in many genres, in video or text format or even as video games. Appealing to cognitive factors of perception, counter-narratives have presented logical arguments with the aim of refuting or debunking the dominant narrative. However, these have proved to be rather ineffective in changing pre-existing baseline attitudes since 'metacognitive experiences [...] are part and parcel of the reasoning process' (Schwarz et al., 2007: 128). This is also an important lesson from measures directed against mis- and disinformation. Factual corrections are not likely to dislodge emotional or existential positions. Counter-argumentation might descend into a contest over the truthfulness of information (and thus the trustworthiness of the messenger) rather than challenging or changing the storyline and its rationalization of violence. Instead, the construction of emotionally evocative counter-narratives focusing on emotions rather than evidence has been proposed (see Box 6.2). Such approaches are geared towards the identification of the in-group with the targeted out-group through various narrative strategies such as personalization, humanization, and normalization. Another variety is alternative accounts of events, presenting the story from a different perspective (as in our example of Swedish state formation above). According to the Elaboration Likelihood Model (ELM), humans process information through two channels: one quick and intuitive (superficial and prone to cognitive shortcuts or effortless), and the other based on slower reflective judgement or an effortful, deliberative arrival at conclusions. This type of processing is also called 'classical reasoning' (Ziemer and Rothmund, 2024). Research has shown that exposing participants to contradictory information about another social group activates the second form of processing information, resulting in lower hostility (Carthy et al., 2020: 6). Finally, another form of counter-narrative is achieved through so-called inoculation, following the same rationale as viral inoculation with self-created counter-arguments analogous to antibodies. The idea is to expose individuals to weakened arguments which then can protect them against stronger arguments of the same nature. This method seems effective at reducing susceptibility to persuasion.

BOX 6.2 EXAMPLES OF COUNTER-NARRATIVE STRATEGIES

- *counter-stereotypical exemplars* (e.g. based on countering stereotypes, needs for reconciliation, priming theory, cognitive and intergroup contact theories)
- *persuasion* (e.g. based on exposing individuals to contradictory evidence about the adversary)

- *inoculation* (presenting weaker arguments to foster resilience against stronger arguments)
- *alternative accounts* (e.g. changing the directionality of the narrative or its impact upon social identity)

Some insights related to the effectiveness of counter-narratives challenging dominant narratives of enemy images can also be derived from research into mis- and disinformation with some overlaps to MIL as discussed above. Why do people endorse false information and how can it be countered? The 'information deficit model' holds that if people misunderstand or lack access to facts, 'a thorough and accessible explanation of facts should overcome the impact of misinformation'. However, this model 'ignores the cognitive, social and affective drivers of attitude formation and truth judgements'. Even after people have received a correction of false information and accept it as true, misinformation can continue influencing their perceptions, a phenomenon called 'continued influence effect' or CIE (Ecker et al., 2022: 13 and 15, see Box 6.3).

Since enemy images distort and exaggerate information about the enemy, target audiences might deny or reject information that challenges their baseline belief systems about the 'other', which can be driven by fears, issues of social identity, or motivated reasoning instead. Therefore, in order to develop appropriate measures to overcome resistance to corrections, it is important to consider both cognitive factors and social context. Enemy images overlap with disinformation insofar as the latter is defined as a wilful intention to harm and deceive.

BOX 6.3 MODEL OF DRIVERS OF FALSE BELIEFS

False beliefs are endorsed by *cognitive drivers* such as

- intuitive thinking (lack of analytical thinking)
- cognitive failures (neglect of sources or knowledge) and
- illusory truth (familiarity and cohesion)

and socio-affective drivers such as

- source cues (elite, attractive in-group senders/messengers)
- emotion (emotive engagement more effective than persuasion) and
- worldview (personal views, partisanship).
  (based on Ecker et al., 2022: 15)

One important lesson that can be learned from the CIE in relation to counter-narratives is the long-term memory-based retention of false information. Countering the false content of enemy images is no quick fix. On the level of socio-affective drivers, the trustworthiness of information is evaluated against source credibility, which in turn is not primarily based on rational factors or truthfulness. Instead, other factors weigh in, such as partisanship, group identity, or various forms of cognitive bias. This also has to be taken into account when designing countermeasures. If the (counter-)messenger has no or low credibility among a target audience, the counter-narrative will most likely not be effective, even when based on expertise since 'people tend to trust sources that are perceived to share their values and worldviews' (Ecker et al., 2022: 17). Acceptance of counter-narratives is thus related to sociocultural identity.

In the most comprehensive study of interventions against disinformation published to date, Ziemer and Rothmund (2024) extensively cover the psychological drivers of susceptibility and focus on a process of knowledge generation called 'motivated reasoning'. Knowledge is processed to fit personal or social identity. Ziemer and Rothmund provide an overview of the most common five types of intervention addressed in research:

1 *Boosting* through (a) knowledge and (b) media literacy (meta-skills subdivided into information, news, digital and science literacy)
2 *Inoculation* through (a) warnings (that content might be false), (b) classic inoculation (being able to counter a small dose of false information builds up resistance), and (c) strategic inoculation (for instance through gamification)
3 *Identity management* through (a) self-affirmation and (b) perspective-taking
4 *Nudging* through promoting (a) accuracy, (b) credibility, (c) lateral reading, and (d) social norms
5 *Fact-checking* through (a) flagging (through experts or peers), (b) social invalidation, and (c) expert correction (through simple rebuttal, narrative correction, consensus correction, and debunking)

When designing counter-narratives against dominant enemy images, all these types of intervention can be explored. Taken together, countering the message level of enemy images requires insights into both cognitive and socio-affective dimensions of why certain (false or manipulated) information is believed among a target group/audience.

The structure level

On the structure level of analysis, we discuss how we can create social, economic, and political structures that disadvantage the acceptance and spread of enemy images and make individuals and communities more resilient to them. We return to Gordon Allport's writings about prejudice. Allport's ICT discusses not only the reasons why people accept prejudice, but also the benefits of intergroup contact as a tool to counteract enemy images. And lastly, we consider the conditions and reforms required for intergroup contact to be successful.

Presentation of intergroup contact theory

The idea that intergroup contacts between people counteract prejudice and hatred is old and consonant with intuitive thinking. A starting point in this theory is that 'most people refuse to behave cruelly toward humanized others' (Bandura, 2016: 90), and under favourable circumstances, intergroup contacts between groups can contribute to humanization of the other. Furthermore, there are numerous examples of how peace-oriented political leaders have tried *after* conflicts and war to facilitate and encourage people from antagonistic groups to meet. One example of such initiatives is sister (or twin) cities across Europe promoting cultural and commercial exchange. Attempts to influence malleable youngsters are quite common. There are several NGOs working to get children to meet each other across conflict boundaries. There are also schools with children from groups that are or have been in conflict. One example is the Hand in Hand schools in Israel, which we present more about below. Another example in local society is race-integration bussing of school children in the United States primarily in the 1950s and 1960s. At the EU level, too, work has been done in this direction. Since 1987, for instance, the EU has implemented the Erasmus programme to promote the mobility of students across Europe. Since then, millions of students have studied in another member state. The Erasmus+ Programme guide mentions neither intergroup contact nor the reduction of enemy images as an objective, but does reference among other things 'social cohesion' and 'strengthening European identity' as a goal (2023). Similarly, the prestigious Fulbright Program promotes the exchange of American students and scholars with those of other nations. In addition to furthering academic development and improving intercultural relations, it aims to promote peace. At Senator J. William Fulbright's funeral in 1995, President Clinton stated that

> The Fulbright Scholarship Program is a perfect example of Fulbright's faith – different kinds of people learning side by side, building what he called 'a capacity for empathy, a distaste for killing other men, and an inclination for peace.'
>
> *(Fulbright, toward a better world)*

Although this contact hypothesis is mostly associated with social psychology and Gordon Allport, enlightenment philosophers such as John Locke and Immanuel Kant were already putting forward similar ideas in the eighteenth century. In his work *Perpetual Peace* (1795), which developed ideas on cosmopolitan law, Kant stated that human beings enjoy an unalienable right to live on any spot across the surface of the earth. He called this right 'hospitality', which underpins a right of free movement, mutual solidarity, and a sort of world citizenship (Kleingeld, 2011: 75–76).

And in the twentieth century, as research in international relations (IR) took off, enlightenment ideas developed further within the liberal IR tradition. One example is the Australian academic writer and diplomat John Burton, who used sociological reasoning to suggest that tight transnational relations between people from different states could help develop new forms of human society. According to the line of thought set out in his book *World Society* (1972), which could be seen as both a description of empirical development and as a normative ideal (1972: 50), Burton suggests a cobweb model of transnational relationships. In this model, individuals have frequent contacts and ties with out-groups beyond their own nation-state, belonging to many different groups and having many different identities (see the left part of Figure 6.3). We believe that this means they are likely to have different interests and loyalties, many of them transnational: religious groups, business groups, labour groups, extended family, and so on. Potentially, the cobweb model points to a world driven more by mutually beneficial cooperation than by antagonistic conflict.

The opposite is to depict states as rock-solid billiard balls (Burton, 1972: 28) (see the right part of Figure 6.3). In this case, the various communities of interest mentioned above are confined to the state. People have very limited experience of the world beyond the borders of the state and should certainly not belong to any communities that can create loyalties beyond the state. Instead, individuals develop nationally marked loyalties and life horizons. Such a model is conservative and in line with realism within the study of IR.

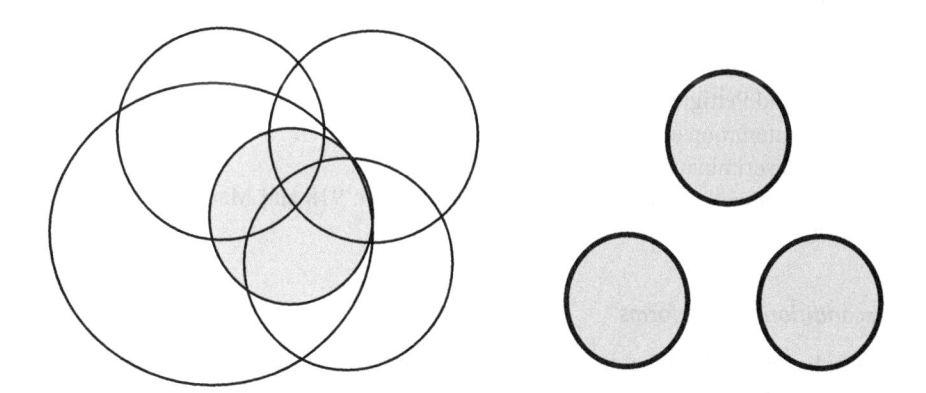

FIGURE 6.3 The cobweb model and the billiard ball model.
Source: Created by the authors.

Probably many of Burton's ideas have materialized in our postmodern age. More and more states are opening not only to transnational trade, but also to transnational interpersonal contacts and relations. And in addition to that, transnational interpersonal communication is increasingly fast, cheap, and safe. The point in our context is that it is likely easier for prejudices and enemy images about out-groups beyond one's own nation-state to take hold in populations living in closed billiard ball-like states, whereas living in a shrinking world with open states and having numerous transnational identities and loyalties would potentially contribute to the humanization of outsiders. But this does not always work. Ties between Russia and Ukraine, for example, have long been tight, intermarriages common. Russians and Ukrainians have friends, colleagues, and relatives on the other side of the border. On 24 February 2022, President Zelensky tried to use this fact by giving a speech in Russian to the Russian people. As we know, he failed to convince the Russian people. President Putin's propaganda was far more successful.

As emphasized above, one researcher who highlighted the benefits of intergroup contacts early on was the American social psychologist Gordon Allport, featured in Chapter 4 (see Box 4.2). In his book *The Nature of Prejudice* (1954), he not only discussed the development of prejudice but also developed and systematized existing research into the 'intergroup contact theory'. As already stated, the idea that intergroup contacts could counteract prejudice and hostility is an old one, and by the 1930s, research had been conducted in this area (Dovidio, Gaertner, and Kawakami, 2003: 6–8), especially in the United States. Allport systematized existing research and suggested that intergroup contact can be a successful way to improve intergroup relations (Allport, 1954: 261). It was already known in the 1940s that 'mere giving of objective general information' (Williams, 1947: 64–65) is not enough to counteract prejudice and hostility. However, under beneficial preconditions, intergroup contact can

1 reduce prejudice – though more strongly affective than cognitive prejudice (Tropp and Pettigrew, 2005),
2 reduce intergroup anxiety (Stephan and Stephan, 2007),
3 reduce discrimination, and
4 increase empathy (Malhotra and Liyanage, 2005: 918 and Mania et al., 2010: 87–90).

Preconditions and reforms

It must be emphasized that intergroup contact is only successful under appropriate conditions. Not all intergroup contacts produce desired effects. In some cases, when the parties in an intergroup contact experience threat, negative images of the other can be reinforced (see the sections *Healing of the perpetrators* and *Healing of the victims* above). Moreover, intergroup contact should not be an opportunity to trade insults, argue, use physical violence, or discriminate against each other. Research has demonstrated that when poorly organized, interracial workplaces and housing can aggravate interracial relations (Pettigrew, 1998: 68). So 'when such deleterious factors cannot be eliminated, it may be best to limit contact until they can be neutralized' (Mania et al., 2010: 91–93). For beneficial effects, the situation must be supportive. Allport suggested four conditions that must be met for intergroup contact to be effective:

1 equal status,
2 common goals,
3 intergroup cooperation (interdependence), and
4 institutional support – law, custom, or local atmosphere (Allport, 1954: 281).

In conflict situations, these conditions are usually not available; indeed, the opposite conditions might prevail. This means that intergroup contacts need to be accompanied by radical reforms to build a more just society. What Allport means by the first condition is that when people meet, they must *have, expect,* and *experience* equal status (Pettigrew, 1998: 66) in the situation where they meet. And in addition to that, the state must treat all citizens equally when providing social services. In his discussion about Rwanda, Ervin Staub mentions the importance of equal status to schools (Staub, 2008: 250). However, this is easier said than done. It might be possible to create such situations in psychological experiments or controlled contexts, but it is harder in real-life post-conflict situations.

Around the world, there are organizations working for peace through intergroup contacts, and they have taken note of the importance of equal status. One of them is the previously mentioned Hand in Hand schools in Israel. This network of 'integrated, bilingual, and multicultural schools and communities' works explicitly for 'inclusion and equality between Arabs and Jews' (Hand in Hand, Annual Report 2021–22: 3). Their strategy is to give the language and culture of both groups demonstrably the same space in every way. They employ as many Arab as Jewish teachers; management functions are also shared; and so on. A complicating factor is that the relationship does not just have to be equal on an objective level. Individuals who meet must also *experience* equality. And if the relationship outside school between two groups has been characterized by inequality or perhaps even by oppression for a long time, there is a risk that the oppressed party will interpret the social interaction as unequal. They are acutely aware of 'their group's devalued status and that they are likely to be seen and evaluated in terms of their devalued group membership. Consequently, they live with a constant threat of becoming targets of 'prejudice and discrimination' (Tropp, 2006: 174). This means that members of disadvantaged groups construe intergroup interactions in different ways than do members of advantaged groups. Specifically, they are less likely to be convinced that they have equal status in the interaction and are more likely to anticipate prejudice and discrimination against them from members of the dominant group.

(Tausch and Hewstone, 2010: 550)

Sadly, outside a controlled context like the school mentioned above, relations in conflict and war are often characterized by power hierarchies, oppression, and inequality. The occupier has almost unlimited power over the civilian population in, for example, Palestine (see Figure 6.4). The relationship between white and Black South Africans during Apartheid was marked by inequality. So, if individuals from antagonistic groups meet under unequal conditions, it will not lead to any improvement in behaviour or attitudes.

The second condition that could make intergroup contacts successful is the experience of *common goals*, with both groups in a post-conflict situation feeling that they are working on a common task or a common superordinate goal (Pettigrew, 1998: 66–67). This condition was mentioned above in the discussion

FIGURE 6.4   Palestinian children encountering Israeli soldiers at a checkpoint.

Source: Flickr/Friends123. The creator of this photo has released it into the worldwide public domain via a Creative Commons 1.0 license.

about Rwanda (see *Healing of the perpetrators* and *Healing of the victims*). Likewise, in Chapter 4 we discussed the Robbers Cave Experiment conducted by Muzafer Sherif, and how two very similar groups of white American middle-class boys developed a prejudice against each other when they had to compete for limited resources. According to Sherif, when people from two groups meet and experience a zero-sum situation in which both groups desire goals that can be attained by one only at the expense of the other, hostility and prejudice are likely to develop (Sherif, 1966: 81–84). Thus, prejudice between groups flourish in zero-sum games, when the groups experience that access to resources is severely limited and other groups are perceived as competitors. The encouraging thing is that people can change when they 'decide that cooperation yields vastly greater benefits to both than antagonism' (Frank and Melville, 1988: 203). So if groups experience a need to cooperate and see that they can gain from cooperation, the picture of the out-group and its members could change (Yzerbyt, 2010: 148). Later in Sherif's experiment, the researchers changed the circumstances so that the two groups would not experience a zero-sum situation but worked instead towards common goals, and prejudice between them diminished (Sherif, 1966: 128–130).

This mechanism could be used at both the grassroots and the political level. One case representing the grassroots level is the Divan Orchestra in Israel, founded in 1999 by Argentinian-Israeli conductor Daniel Barenboim and the Palestinian-American academic Edward Said. The purpose is to have workshops for young musicians to promote coexistence and intercultural dialogue (Divan Orchestra, Founders). Let us return to Figure 6.3 for a moment and the idea of a cobweb-like identity. Applying that model to this case, we can imagine a young Palestinian or Israeli girl or boy who loves playing classical music having more than one identity: they are of course Jews or Palestinians, but in addition to that they are musicians devoted to music. They might experience people on the other side who love classical music just as they do. So, although they are Jews or Palestinians, they have a common identity as musicians. On the orchestra's webpage, Edward Said is quoted as saying

> Humanism is the only – I would go so far as saying the final – resistance we have against the inhuman practices and injustices that disfigure human history. Separation between peoples is not a solution for any of the problems that divide peoples. And certainly ignorance of the other provides no help whatever. Cooperation and coexistence of the kind that music lived as we have lived, performed, shared and loved it together, might be.
>
> *(Divan Orchestra, Founders)*

On a political level, one could imagine states working towards common goals despite a history of conflict. Currently, many countries are experiencing the consequences of global warming and other forms of environmental threats. And solving these environmental problems is indeed a common goal. In the *Healing of the perpetrators* section above, we referred to Staub and Pearlman's work in Rwanda. According to them, the work for reconciliation and against enemy images was based on this logic: after the genocide, the Hutus and the Tutsis started to work together for shared goals (Staub and Pearlman, 2001: 224).

The third condition to be met for intergroup contact to be effective is closely related to the previous one. Here it is emphasized not only that 'we' and 'they' have common goals, but also that 'we' cannot reach 'our' desired goals without help from the other group since 'they' have certain necessary competencies that 'we' do not (and vice versa) (Pettigrew, 1998: 67). By pooling resources, both groups can reach goals that they could not alone. If political leaders discussed water scarcity in the Middle East in such a way that other states were not portrayed as competing for the limited access to water but as necessary and competent partners in solving this common problem, then attitudes could potentially change. Ergo, the effect of working towards a common goal is amplified if the other is not seen as a competitor in a struggle for limited resources but rather as a necessary partner, with our common goal attainable only if the two groups work together by pooling resources.

The last condition that Allport mentions for successful intergroup contacts is the support and sanction of authorities, law, or custom. For intergroup contact to have a lasting effect, some authority on both sides must acknowledge and support the interaction between the groups. In conflict zones and situations where prejudice dominates, grassroots organizations sometimes step in and offer various projects where people meet. There are numerous examples in addition to the Divan Orchestra and the Hand in Hand schools mentioned above. Regrettably, if authorities – and important elites – do not support intergroup contact, the grassroots-level intergroup contact will not have a lasting effect. The experiences that the children may have had in the orchestra or at school are likely to be nullified by the conditions outside. Thus a final conclusion in this section must be that 'Without changing policies that sustain conflict and inequality, bottom-up approaches to peace … are of rather limited effectiveness' (Mania et al., 2010: 89–90).

New developments in intergroup contact theory

One of Gordon Allport's great achievements was that he not only formulated a theory but also became a prominent figure in a large and still-growing field of research. And his basic results have stood the test of time in the more recent research that has been done. Over the past 20-plus years, Thomas F. Pettigrew and Linda R. Tropp have conducted a few meta-studies on intergroup contacts (Pettigrew and Tropp, 2000 and 2006), involving systematic reviews of qualitative and quantitative data from studies within the field to develop a single conclusion.

In a meta-study from 2000 based on 203 individual studies, they found that in 94% of them, 'face-to-face interaction between members of distinguishable groups' reduced prejudice (Pettigrew and Tropp, 2000: 109).

In recent years, research on indirect contact has also been conducted (Dovidio, Eller, and Hewstone, 2011). One type of indirect contact is the extended contact hypothesis, described by Wright, Aaron, McLaughlin-Volpe, and Ropp (1997), which suggests that knowing a member of one's own group has a close relationship with a member of an out-group can lead to more positive attitudes towards that out-group (Wright et al., 1997). This hypothesis has been empirically supported by later studies (Vezzali et al., 2014 and Zhou et al., 2019).

Another form of indirect contact is the kind of contact we can develop over the internet and social media. Earlier in this chapter, we pointed out that the internet and social media can spread and amplify enemy images. But research shows that different forms of e-contact, if perceived positively, can reduce religious prejudice, notably against sexual minorities. In 2012, Ronny Edry created an online movement for peace in the Middle East. It all started with him posting a Facebook image of himself and his daughter declaring, 'Iranians, we will never bomb your country'. This simple statement spread and 'within forty-eight hours, Iranians heeded the Israeli call – on Facebook. Majid, a thirty-four-year-old landscape architect from Iran, launched an Iran-Loves-Israel campaign that reciprocated the message' (Peace Factory, 2024). Thereafter, thousands of people posted a photo of their faces and a short message of peace.

Above, we have discussed Allport's four preconditions for successful contact. Researchers have since built on his ideas and added further factors and processes that enhance the chances for positive intergroup contact. One additional factor is friendship potential (Pettigrew, 1998: 80) – and so on until it almost resembles a laundry list.

Problems

Although most people agree that intergroup contact under the right circumstances is a good way to reduce prejudice, the model also has disadvantages. Some problems are academic and relate to the experiments where the intergroup contact hypothesis is tested. Others are practical and relate to projects where intergroup contacts are used as an in-the-field peacebuilding strategy. In experiments where research participants are aware that intergroup contacts are expected, some people – probably those with the most ingrained negative attitudes towards the out-group – will avoid participating (Pettigrew, 1998: 69). The participants will thus not be representative, and a biased selection has taken place. The same can happen with in-the-field peace projects where intergroup contacts are planned. Those who are the most prejudiced will not participate. This is obvious to us who have participated in various conferences where people from different camps meet. You recognize the faces. It is the same (open-minded, unprejudiced, willing) people who show up. The already 'saved' flock is there. The hardliners or bigots within the different camps are not. Likewise, the kind of parents that send their kids off to school programmes like Hand in Hand to befriend their 'enemies' are usually open-minded. The most prejudiced would avoid this kind of intergroup contact for themselves and for their children. In Chapter 4, we explained that people tend to avoid information that contradicts their existing beliefs. They do not want to be challenged; they want cognitive consistency. There is also a risk that this tendency will affect contacts; people avoid encounters where their positions are questioned.

A second disappointing tendency is that the insights people gain in one context do not affect behaviour in other contexts. Studies published in the 1950s and 1960s showed initially encouraging results, demonstrating that racially integrated workplaces and neighbourhoods led to fewer prejudices or discriminatory actions (Pettigrew, 1998: 67). Regrettably, it seems that the lessons learned in one context do not affect attitudes in new ones (Pettigrew, 1998: 73). In other words, there is a risk that the attitudes and non-discriminatory behaviour that people might display in integrated neighbourhoods, schools, or workplaces do not necessarily carry over to new situations. In more concrete terms, imagine an Israeli Jewish girl or boy attends the Hand in Hand school and has Arab friends and teachers: can we be sure that the attitudes and lessons learned there will inform behaviours and attitudes a few years later when they join the Israeli army and are influenced by new friends, new loyalties, and new authorities?

Thirdly, it is hard to change implicit forms of prejudice, as some people may harbour ideas they are not aware of, making them resistant to challenge. Sternberg and Sternberg write that

> The implicit form of prejudice is more difficult to combat because people experiencing it typically do not identify as prejudiced and therefore may not be willing to engage in actions to reduce prejudice.
>
> *(Sternberg and Sternberg, 2008: 200)*

Summary

Countering enemy images effectively is a difficult task. As we wrote in Chapter 4, people tend to accept enemy images because they accord with human cognitive and socio-psychological drivers of susceptibility. In addition, enemy images are politically useful, at least during a conflict, and strong interests ('military logic') do not want to see them counteracted and questioned. But the situation is far from hopeless. All over the world, we have seen how enemy images have been successfully countered. In some cases, they have even disappeared. This section summarizes our findings. The model presented at the outset (Figure 6.1) systematized useful and relevant counteraction strategies addressed in the literature.

These countermeasures should not be seen as competing alternatives, but rather as a toolbox of complementary tools for different contexts.

A first reflection is how important the state is for peacebuilding in modern society. A strong state with fair and efficient institutions is necessary to maintain physical security. Failed states have never been a recipe for success. And the state is also essential when it comes to enemy images, both for creating and countering them. In peace and conflict studies, it has often been seen as the cause of war and organized violence, and rightly so. And the modern state has the strongest instruments to disseminate enemy images and form a unanimous elite discourse confirming them. But strong state involvement is highly desirable, maybe even required, in all the strategies for counteraction (see Figure 6.1) to be successful. The state is needed for (a) breaking up hegemonic elite-driven enemy images, (b) reducing the demand for enemy images among the receivers, (c) producing and spreading counter-narratives neutralizing enemy images, and (d) allowing for intergroup contacts and carrying out needed reforms.

A second reflection is that the political will to counter enemy images may be (but is not necessarily) greater after a conflict than before. This is tragic. So much would have been gained if enemy images had been countered before an armed conflict erupted. But as long as a conflict is building up or ongoing, there is little political interest in countering enemy images.

A third reflection is that work against enemy images must be both comprehensive and persistent. The human tendency towards cognitive consistency and the psychological function of enemy images have been repeatedly emphasized in our discussions, primarily in Chapters 4 and 6. This means that once an enemy image has been accepted by large parts of a population and become part of its imagination, it is difficult to counteract. The work against enemy images must therefore be comprehensive and mobilize many actors in society. For example, the counter-narratives that are disseminated must dominate the public sphere. Most, preferably all, discursive elites should participate in the dissemination of narratives countering enemy images. And for the same reason, the work of countering enemy images must be done persistently and tirelessly, perhaps for generations to come.

A fourth and final reflection from this chapter is that while the participation of the state and elites in countering enemy effectively images is important and necessary, we must also highlight the role of all other actors. This includes the role of NGOs and the private sphere. NGOs can play a large and important role in reconciliation in local society, for the healing of victims and perpetrators, and for successful intergroup contacts. Likewise, the private sphere of families or local communities plays a significant part. In Chapter 3, we discussed the importance of harmony between enemy images in the public sphere and those in the private sphere for them to gain acceptance. We also emphasized how important the family is for children's socialization. What we want to say in this context is that the role of the private sphere is just as important when it comes to counteracting enemy images. First, it is vital that children are socialized into values promoting inclusion and critical attitudes towards prejudice and enemy images. Likewise, it is important that the private sphere – the family, informal associations, and circles of friends, for instance – becomes a place where messages of peace from the public sphere are accepted. This kind of interaction between actors in the public sphere and ordinary people in the private sphere facilitates and boosts the counteraction of enemy images. The fact that the private sphere and NGOs play such a large role in counteracting enemy images means there is an opportunity for all of us to work in various ways against enemy images by participating in local society organizations and helping to build resilient communities.

Study questions

- Choose a war or similar conflict you are familiar with where key communicators refused to (re)produce enemy images. How did they counteract the enemy images? What price did they have to pay for doing so?
- What would a counteraction strategy of enemy images between Russians and Ukrainians look like (2023) amid the current war? Is it even desirable to work against Ukrainian enemy images of Russia during the war, or are enemy images needed to keep up Ukrainian morale and unite the nation?
- Find out more about the 'Yellow Peril' enemy image (see Chapter 7). Think about how an effective counter-narrative could be constructed in this case, and write it down. What would be needed for a counter-narrative to develop an impact in this situation?
- What would a strategy to counteract enemy images between Israeli Jews and Palestinians look like after the escalation of events since 7 October 2023? Is it possible to counteract enemy images in this situation? Can such peace work do more harm than good?

Potential essay or thesis suggestions

Prepare an analytical framework and research plan based on the discussion of ICT above. Select an organization you are familiar with that brings people from conflicting groups together and whose source material you can read in the original language. Choose the data you need to carry out your study. Analyse the data and the organization's work.

Recommended further reading

Lynch, J. and McGoldrick, A. (2005). *Peace Journalism*. Stroud: Hawthorn.
In this accessible and authoritative book, Jake Lynch and Annabel McGoldrick explain how traditional journalism and media coverage fuel violence and entrench conflicts. The authors attempt to contrast war journalism with peace journalism, showing how the reporting of war, violence, and terror can be made more accurate and constructive.

Staub, E. (2010) *Overcoming Evil: Genocide, Violent Conflict, and Terrorism*. Oxford: Oxford University Press.
In this comprehensive book, Ervin Staub summarizes and describes a large part of his academic and humanitarian work. He sets out the central principles of the origins of violence between groups, and of prevention and reconciliation.

Stephan, W. G. and Stephan, C. W. (2001) *Improving Intergroup Relations*. Thousand Oaks, CA: SAGE Publications.
In this book, Walter G. Stephan and Cookie White Stephan examine various programmes that aim to improve intergroup relations, providing evaluation models and help for practitioners who need help evaluating their programmes. This is a practical guidebook for anyone interested in reducing prejudice and improving intergroup relations.

Williams, T. (2020) Meeting the Enemy, British-German Encounters in the Occupied Rhineland after the First World War. In Maillet, J. and Dudouyt, C. (eds.) *Creating the Enemy, Angles, New Perspectives on the Anglophone World* (Volume 10, pp. 1–19). https://doi.org/10.4000/angles.488
In this chapter, historian Tom Willian analyses several British eyewitness accounts of the post–First World War period in the Rhineland. After the war, the British army occupied the Rhineland until 1930. When British soldiers and civilians entered the area, they were often surprised to discover that Germans they encountered had little in common with the enemy image promulgated by British propaganda during the war. But at the same time, their observations were influenced by the propaganda they had been served.

Bibliography

Allen, K.-A. (2021) *The Psychology of Belonging*. Abingdon, Oxon: Routledge.

Allport, G. W. (1954) *The Nature of Prejudice*. New York, NY: Basic Books.

Bandura, A. (2016) *Moral Disengagement, How People Do Harm and Live with Themselves*. New York, NY: Worth Publishers.

Burton, J. (1972) *World Society*. Cambridge: Cambridge University Press. https://doi.org/10.1017/CBO9780511521669

Carthy, S. L., Doody, C. B., Cox, K., O'Hora, D. and Sarma, K. M. (2020) Counter-narratives for the prevention of violent radicalisation: A systematic review of targeted interventions. *Campbell Systematic Reviews* 16(3): 1–37. https://doi.org/10.1002/cl2.1106

Divan Orchestra (no date) Divan Orchestra. https://west-eastern-divan.org/founders, accessed 11 April 2023.

Dovidio, J. F., Eller, A. and Hewstone, M. (2011) Improving intergroup relations through direct, extended and other forms of indirect contact. *Group Processes & Intergroup Relations* 14(2): 147–160. https://doi.org/10.1177/1368430210390555

Dovidio, J. F., Gaertner, S. L. and Kawakami, K. (2003) Intergroup contact: The past, present, and the future. *Group Processes & Intergroup Relations* 6(1): 5–21. https://doi.org/10.1177/1368430203006001009

Ecker, U. K. H., Lewandowsky, S. and Cook, J. (2022) The psychological drivers of misinformation belief and its resistance to correction. *Nature Revues Psychology* 1: 13–29. https://doi.org/10.1038/s44159-021-00006-y

Erasmus+ (2023) 'Programme Guide', European Commission, 28 November 2023. https://erasmus-plus.ec.europa.eu/sites/default/files/2023-11/2024-Erasmus%2BProgramme-Guide_EN.pdf, accessed 21 February 2024.

Fulbright (no date) *Toward a Better World*. www.fulbright.se/about/, accessed 1 March 2024.

Frank, J. D. and Melville, A. Y. (1988) The Image of the Enemy and the Process of Change. In Gromyko, A. and Hellman, M. (eds.) *Breakthrough Emerging New Thinking* (pp. 199–207). New York, NY: Walker and Company.

Haider, J. and Sundin, O. (2022) *Paradoxes of Media and Information Literacy: The Crisis of Information*. Milton Park, Abingdon, Oxon: Routledge.

Hand in Hand (2022) *Annual Report: Building Shared Society through Integrated Schools and Communities 2021–22*. Jerusalem: Hand in Hand. www.handinhandk12.org/about/annual-report/2021-22-annual-report/, accessed 16 October 2023.

Hewstone, M., Tausch, N., Voci, A., Kenworthy, J., Hughes, J. and Cairns, E. (2008) Why Neighbors Kill: Prior Intergroup Contact and Killing of Ethnic Outgroup Neighbors. In Esses, V. M. and Vernon R. A. (eds.) *Explaining the Breakdown of Ethnic Relations: Why Neighbors Kill* (pp. 61–91). Malden, MA: Blackwell Publishing.

Kant, I. (2003) *To Perpetual Peace: A Philosophical Sketch*. Reprint. Indianapolis, IN: Hacket Publishing, 1795.

King, E. (2014) *From Classrooms to Conflict in Rwanda*. New York, NY: Cambridge University Press.

Kleingeld, P. (2011) Kant's cosmopolitan law: World citizenship for a global order. *Kantian Review* 2: 72–90. https://doi.org/10.1017/S1369415400000200

Krekó, P. (2020) Countering Conspiracy Theories and Misinformation. In Butter, M. and Knight, P. (eds.) *Routledge Handbook of Conspiracy Theories* (pp. 242–255). Abingdon, Oxon: Routledge.

Lynch, J. and McGoldrick, A. (2007) Peace Journalism. In Webel, C. and Galtung, J. (eds.) *Handbook of Peace and Conflict Studies* (pp. 248–264). London: Routledge.

Malhotra, D. and Liyanage, S. (2005) Long-term effects of peace workshops in protracted conflicts. *Journal of Conflict Resolution*, 49(6): 908–924.

Mania, E. W., Gaertner, S. L., Riek, B. M., Dovidio, J. F., Lamoreaux, M. J., and Direso, S. A. (2010) Intergroup Contact: Implications for Peace Education. In G. Salomon & E. Cairns (eds.) *Handbook on Peace Education* (pp. 87–102). New York, NY: Psychology Press.

Önnerfors, A. (2022) Folkhemmet: 'The People's Home' as an Expression of Retrotopian Longing of Sweden before the Arrival of Mass Migration. In Harbison, S., Einhorn, E. and Huss, M. (eds.) *Migration and Multiculturalism in Scandinavia* (pp. 60–79) Madison, WI: University of Wisconsin Press.

Önnerfors, A. (2024) *Konspirationsteorier – meningsskapande berättelser i historia och nutid.* Lund: Nordic Academic Press.

Osofsky, M., Bandura, A. and Zimbardo, P. (2005) The role of moral disengagement in the execution process. *Law and Human Behavior* 29(4): 371–393. https://doi.org/10.1007/s10979-005-4930-1

Peace Factory (2024) 'Israel Loves Iran'.https://thepeacefactory.org/israel-loves-iran/?doing_wp_cron=1708519379.9206678867340087890625, accessed 21 February 2024.

Pettigrew, T. F. (1998) Intergroup contact theory. *Annual Review of Psychology*, 49: 65–89. https://doi.org/10.1146/annurev.psych.49.1.65.

Pettigrew, T. F. and Tropp, L. R. (2000) Does Intergroup Contact Reduce Prejudice? Recent Meta-Analytic Findings. In Oskamp, S. (ed.) *Reducing Prejudice and Discrimination* (pp. 93–114) New York, NY: Psychology Press.

Pettigrew, T. F. and Tropp, L. R. (2006) A meta-analytic test of intergroup contact theory. *Journal of Personality and Social Psychology* 90(5): 751–783. https://doi.org/10.1037/0022-3514.90.5.751

Potter, W. J. (2019) *Seven Skills of Media Literacy*. Thousand Oaks, CA: SAGE.

Ramasubramanian, S. (2007) Media-based strategies to reduce racial stereotypes activated by news stories. *Journalism and Mass Communication Quarterly* 84(2): 249–264. https://doi.org/10.1177/107769900708400204

Scharrer, E. (2002) Making a case for media literacy in the curriculum: Outcomes and assessment. *Journal of Adolescent & Adult Literacy* 46(4): 354–358.

Schwarz, N., Sanna, L. J., Skurnik, I. and Yoon, C. (2007) Metacognitive experiences and the intricacies of setting people straight: Implications for debiasing and public information campaigns. *Advances in Experimental Social Psychology* 39: 127–161. https://doi.org/10.1016/S0065-2601(06)39003-X

Sherif, M. (1966) *Group Conflict and Co-Operation. Their Social Psychology.* London: Routledge & Kegan Paul Ltd.

Staub, E. (1998) Breaking the Cycle of Genocidal Violence: Healing and Reconciliation. In. Harvey, J. H (ed.) *Perspectives on Loss: A Sourcebook* (pp. 231–238) Philadelphia, PA: Brunner/Mazel.

Staub, E. (2006) Reconciliation after genocide, mass killing, or intractable conflict: Understanding the roots of violence, psychological recovery, and steps toward a general theory. *Political Psychology* 27(6): 867–894. www.jstor.org/stable/20447006

Staub, E. (2008) The Origins of Genocide and Mass Killing, Prevention, Reconciliation, and Their Application to Rwanda. In Esses, V.M. and Vernon, R.A (eds.) *Explaining the Breakdown of Ethnic Relations: Why Neighbors Kill* (pp. 245–268). Malden, MA: Blackwell Publishing.

Staub, E. (2010) *Overcoming Evil: Genocide, Violent Conflict, and Terrorism.* New York, NY: Oxford University Press.

Staub, E. (2014) The challenging road to reconciliation in Rwanda: Societal processes, interventions and their evaluation. *Journal of Social and Political Psychology* 2(1): 505–517. https://doi.org/10.5964/jspp.v2i1.294

Staub, E. (2019) Promoting healing and reconciliation in Rwanda, and generating active bystandership by police to stop unnecessary harm by fellow officers. *Perspectives on Psychological Science* 14(1): 60–64. https://doi.org/10.1177/174569161880938

Staub, E. and Pearlman, L. A. (2001) Healing, Reconciliation, and Forgiving after Genocide and Other Collective Violence. In Helmick, R. G. and Petersen, R. L. (eds.) *Forgiveness and Reconciliation: Religion, Public Policy, & Conflict Transformation* (pp. 205–227) Radnor, PA: Templeton Foundation Press.

Staub, E. and Pearlman, L. A. (2006) Advancing Healing and Reconciliation. In Barbanel, L. and Sternberg R. J. (eds.) *Psychological Interventions in Times of Crisis* (pp. 213–243) New York, NY: Springer Publishing Company.

Stephan, W. G. and Stephan, C. W. (2001) *Improving Intergroup Relations.* Thousand Oaks, CA: SAGE Publications.

Stephan, W. P. and Stephan, C. W. (2007) Intergroup Anxiety. In Baumeister, R. F and Vohs, K. (eds.) *Encyclopedia of Social Psychology* (pp. 492–493). Los Angeles, CA: SAGE. https://doi.org/10.1111/j.1540-4560.1985.tb01134.x

Sternberg, R. J. and Sternberg, K. (2008) *The Nature of Hate.* Cambridge: Cambridge UP.

Taillard, M. and Giscoppa, H. (2013) *Psychology and Modern Warfare, Idea Management in Conflict and Competition.* New York, NY: Palgrave Macmillan.

Tausch, N. and Hewstone, M. (2010) Intergroup Contact. In *The SAGE Handbook of Prejudice, Stereotyping and Discrimination* (pp. 544–560). London: SAGE Publishing.

Tropp, L. R. (2006) Stigma and Intergroup Contact among Members of Minority and Majority Status Groups. In Levin, S. and van Laar, C. (eds.) *Stigma and Group Inequality: Social Psychological Perspectives* (pp. 171–191) .Mahwah, NJ: Erlbaum.

Tropp, L. R. and Pettigrew, T. F. (2005) Differential relationships between intergroup contact and affective and cognitive dimensions of prejudice. *Personality and Social Psychology Bulletin* 31(8): 1145–1158. https://doi.org/10.1177/0146167205274854

UNESCO (2023). Media and information literacy. www.unesco.org/en/media-information-literacy, accessed 13 June 2023.

Vezzali, L., Hewstone, M., Capozza, D., Giovannini, D. and Wölfer, R. (2014) Improving intergroup relations with extended and vicarious forms of indirect contact. *European Review of Social Psychology* 25(1): 314–389. http://dx.doi.org/10.1080/10463283.2014.982948

Williams, R. M., Jr. (1947) *The Reduction of Intergroup Tensions: A Survey of Research on Problems of Ethnic, Racial, and Religious Group Relations*. New York, NY: Social Science Research Council.

Williams, T. (2020) Meeting the Enemy, British-German Encounters in the Occupied Rhineland after the First World War. In Maillet, J. and Dudouyt, C. (eds.) *Creating the Enemy, Angles, New Perspectives on the Anglophone World* (Volume 10, pp. 1–19). https://doi.org/10.4000/angles.488

Wright, S. C., Aron, A., McLaughlin-Volpe, T. and Ropp, S. A. (1997) The extended contact effect: Knowledge of cross-group friendships and prejudice. *Journal of Personality and Social Psychology* 73(1): 73–90. https://doi.org/10.1037/0022-3514.73.1.73

Yzerbyt, V. Y. (2010) Motivational Processes. In Dovidio, J. F., Hewstone, M., Glick, P. and Esses, V. M. (eds.) *The SAGE Handbook of Prejudice, Stereotyping and Discrimination* (pp. 146–162) London: SAGE Publishers. https://doi.org/10.4135/9781446200919

Zhou, S., Page-Gould, E., Aron, A., Moyer, A. and Hewstone, M. (2019) The extended contact hypothesis: A meta-analysis on 20 years of research. *Personality and Social Psychology Review* 23(2): 132–160. https://doi.org/10.1177/1088868318762647

Ziemer, C. and Rothmund, T. (2024). Psychological underpinnings of disinformation countermeasures: A systematic scoping review. *Journal of Medical Psychology* 0 (ahead of print): 1–13. https://doi.org/10.1027/1864-1105/a000407

7

EXPRESSIONS OF ENEMY IMAGES

Media and manipulation

CHAPTER OBJECTIVES

- To offer insights into how the development of media impacts the formation of enemy images
- To provide an overview of successive media revolutions and their significance for the expression of enemy images
- To problematize media-specific frames in the construction of enemy images and their role in contributing to the mobilization and desensitization of audiences
- To discuss the accountability of media producers for dehumanizing content

---

Introduction

Pre-Socratic Greek philosopher Heraclitus is frequently quoted as stating that 'war is the father of all things'. Whereas technical innovation in human societies is linked to the needs of warfare or exploited for bellicose purposes, the role of media in communicating enemy images has been less studied than in the development of weaponry. But from pamphlets printed by the field press of the Thirty Years' War (1618–1648) to airdropped propaganda leaflets in the Second World War and elaborate digital information influence operations in our age, the so-called cognitive domain of warfare cannot be neglected. Enemy images are expressed and communicated through different forms of media – news, social media, arts, literature, or film – and are sometimes theorized as 'cultural violence' (Galtung, 1990). This chapter aims to widen the horizon and provide an important outlook on how enemy images are conveyed to a wide range of target audiences through

DOI: 10.4324/9781003279570-7

different forms of expression, i.e. manifestations of enemy images in media. It will discuss classic examples of how the texts and images of literature, film, online memes, etc. communicate representations of the enemy, presenting tools for decoding such content. The communication of enemy images is closely linked to various forms of their medialization (how they are turned into various forms of media). From oral forms of transmission (rumours, sermons, speeches) to print media (pamphlets, newspapers, books) or multi-media outlets (audio-visual news, documentaries, or fictional feature films and new digitally born or synthetic media and their platforms), the rhetoric of enemy images has been expressed over time (Aupers, Craciun, and Önnerfors, 2020: 387–390). Four successive media revolutions have taken place over the last five centuries that have shaped how enemy images have been conveyed:

1 *Analogue media* (fifteenth to eighteenth century)
  This first period (the so-called Gutenberg galaxy according to McLuhan, 1964) is characterized by the invention of the printing press and moveable type, new modes of paper production, and a general increase in literacy. The printing of books, daily newspapers, and journals facilitated the generation of an international readership/audience. Governments discovered the printing press as a tool of propaganda but also of heavy regulation. Official censorship was introduced across the globe. Printed war propaganda was invented during the Thirty Years' War (1618–1648), and European armies were equipped with field press as a tool of warfare, not least during the Napoleonic wars at the beginning of the nineteenth century.

2 *Electronic mass media* (nineteenth and twentieth centuries)
  The second period saw the rise of electronically communicated information, facilitated by inventions such as the telegraph in conjunction with steam-driven railways and vessels disseminating news and the establishment of news agencies. This laid the foundations for the development of radio, TV, cable, and satellite TV, forging the 'global village', an instant international newsroom.

3 *Digital and social media* (twentieth and twenty-first centuries)
  With the advent of the internet, digital information processing rapidly transformed the modes of media production and dissemination, most profoundly during the 1990s with search engines, digital outlets, email, and the first steps towards social media in which information was shared directly between consumers.

4 *Synthetic media* (twenty-first century)
  The early twenty-first century accelerated the development of social media from list servers and email lists to digital platforms, peaking with Facebook, Twitter, Instagram, and others. The development of smartphones created a formidable explosion of user-generated content (UGC) in conjunction with the rapid expansion of high-speed internet. Literally, everyone with access to a smartphone could now take pictures, write texts, record movies and sound,

and instantly share this digital content with others. Yet what first was perceived as a democratization of information and its dissemination was also prone to manipulation and processes of polarization, not least driven by 'algorithmic culture' (a term explained in Chapter 6). At the time of writing, we have entered a period characterized by artificial intelligence (AI)-augmented/generated media. Images, sound, and text are now either manipulated by AI or entirely generated by it, trained by (autonomous) machine learning, and using access to big data across platforms.

While all these revolutions entailed a democratization of the diffusion of knowledge (Doorn et al., 2021: 34), they also were open to the manipulation of collective enemy perceptions, not least by people in power.

Before we turn to examples illustrating these developments, some reflections need to be made about the production, mediation, and reception of media content related to enemy images from the perspective of media studies. In a conventional understanding of communication, there is a unidirectional relationship between the sender, medium, and receiver by which the message is communicated. However, this relationship is exposed to a multitude of variations and feedback loops (see Chapter 2).

Producers of media content are bound by how the message can be communicated and by how is received by its audiences. But is the construction of enemy images always related to the technical means of their dissemination? Did elaborate and symbolically coded images of enemies emerge because copper engravings were invented in the seventeenth century as effective illustrations which could be printed and disseminated easily? And was it likewise the emergence of multicoloured printed political posters during the twentieth century which generated new images and representations? Was the rhetoric of enemy images steeped in how and what could be said on the radio? Questions like these are open for discussion and must remain an ambiguity that cannot be resolved in this chapter.

Yet as we will see, there is clearly an interrelationship between the medium and the way a message can be expressed. Innovations in media technology also add to the way the enemy can be fashioned, from flat to multidimensional, silent to vocal, and monochrome to multicoloured. And the materiality of media, from paper and printing ink to digital electric impulses, bytes, and pixels, together with their modes of diffusion, always constitutes a framework defining the limits of expression and dissemination. Enemy images are specific forms of message (media content) with a particular rhetorical purpose (mobilization and desensitization of an in-group) in a context of supply and demand (susceptibility and target mechanisms) as described in previous chapters. The examples discussed below cover most of these dimensions, and we can see how the production, mediation, and reception of enemy images interact – with potentially catastrophic consequences for their targets.

The 'Yellow Peril' – imagining an antagonistic Other

Enemy images can start as images in the narrower sense and develop violent consequences. The example discussed in this part of the chapter illustrates the formation of discursive consistency as explained in Chapter 3. It also demonstrates how enemy images can morph over time and be adapted to different contexts.

In 1895, the German imperial printing office in Leipzig published a poster measuring 52 × 69.5 cm, designed by no less a personage than the ruling emperor, Kaiser Wilhelm II (1859–1941), and executed by the historical painter Hermann Knackfuß (Deutsches Historisches Museum, 2022, see Figure 7.1). It shows the archangel Michael with his burning sword in front of eight female personifications of the European nations, all dressed in armour and placed on a cliff (suggestive of contemporary representations of Valkyries in, e.g., Wagner's opera of the same title). France, Germany, Russia, Austria, Britannia, Italy, and other nations are united under a radiant cross in the sky. The two ravens of the Norse god Odin, Hugin and Munin, are placed above a potential representation of Scandinavia. What

FIGURE 7.1 The 'Yellow Peril', *Harper's Weekly*, 1898.

Source: Peoples of Europe, guard your dearest goods (1895) Lithograph by: Hermann Knackfuß. Republished in 1898 in *Harpers Weekly*. Accessed via wikimedia commons.

the archangel points at from his elevated position is a violently burning central European river landscape (probably the Rhine, charged with strong meaning in collective identity). The flames of the scorched villages and fields reach up to the sky, where a dark cloud has formed, carrying a flying dragon with thunderbolts and, on top of the dragon, a sitting Buddha. Wilhelm II also handwrote a motto on the print: 'Völker Europas wehret eure heligsten Güter!' (literally 'People of Europe, defend your most sacred assets!', translated to English as 'Nations of Europe! Join in the defence of your faith and your home!' and to French as 'Nations Européennes! Défendez vos biens sacrés!'). Still untouched, and on the side of the united defenders, lies a landscape with buildings forming a line from the ruling German dynasty's Hohenzollern Castle to the 'national' cathedral of Cologne, the cathedral of Berlin, and what appear to be Orthodox churches on the riverbank.

The German newspaper *Illustrirte Zeitung* wrote at the time of the poster's publication that 'the enemy is not only to be understood as the bellicose adversary of and the – to us – alien race of Asians, but all devastating hatred against the shared morals and the shared property of the educated world'. In other words, the image of the enemy divides the world into two separate spheres. The European nations are existentially threatened by the 'fire-breathing dragon' and its destructive consuming flames (*Illustrirte Zeitung*, 1895). Divided into separate nations, but united by a common (Christian) faith and civilization (with references to Norse mythology), they can defend themselves against the looming violent and vicious attack by an external and common enemy of another faith ('Buddhism' as a *pars pro toto*, the part representing everything 'Asian') and race. The image appeared in the context of European colonial expansion into Asia and several setbacks in attempts to divide the East Asian nations like the African continent. With Japan and China fast growing into regional great powers, not least through the domestic adaptation of Western engineering and warfare, Europe imagined itself threatened by the so-called 'Yellow Peril'. This anxiety of external extermination fuelled a steady stream of caricatures and drawings in which the existential clash of civilizations was turned into a strongly stereotyped visual programme (MIT, 2022).

But in the case of Wilhelm II's design, the image also turned into war rhetoric and thence into action. Speaking to his troops five years later on the occasion of an expedition to China to brutally crush the Boxer Uprising (1899–1901), the German ruler stated among other things: 'When you meet the enemy, defeat him! Do not give any pardons! Take no prisoners! Whoever falls into your hands is at your mercy'. Wilhelm also likened the German expedition to the brutal wars of the Huns against the Chinese that were still current in memory, 'so that in a 1000 years no Chinaman will dare to look strangely at a German'. He also sent copies of his 1895 image to be displayed on German warships, sometimes with the additional motto 'No pardon' (Klein, 2013: 160–172).

And indeed, with what has since been called the Kaiser's 'Hun speech', Wilhelm II legitimized the horrendous crimes against humanity committed by the punitive German expedition corps, foreshadowing the 1904–1908 genocide in

German South-West Africa (today Namibia) and the horrors of the First World War. There is also little doubt that contemporary media and politicians were aware of the potentially brutalizing effects of the Kaiser's words. His speech was officially suppressed, a full version only disseminated in a minor newspaper under governmental control. Politicians in the German parliament accused the Kaiser of having incited German troops to brutality during the Chinese campaign. Later, during the First World War, the term 'Hun' was applied to describe German barbarity.

Although it would be worth delving deeper into the manifold expressions of enemy images (and their reversal in often humorous or ironic caricatures) at the zenith of the imagined 'Yellow Peril', the episode with Wilhelm II's design, its execution, dissemination, and active application have some overarching features that this chapter aims to capture. It is not just about the image content and context but also its mode of production and circulation. Wilhelm II was himself an avid amateur artist but left the finalization of his sketch to a popular historical painter, who submitted his artwork to the imperial printing press, where it was reproduced for wide circulation as a poster (and thus, public display). *Illustrirte Zeitung* (which had a print run of tens of thousands) presented its readers with a preprint. An international audience was targeted with the French and English translations of Wilhelm II's words. The American journal *Harper's Weekly* picked up Knackfuß's image in 1898 with the caption 'The Yellow Peril', and a dramatically colourized version with a Russian caption 'Гроза с Востока [Groza s Vostoka]' (The Threat from the East) was disseminated in 1904 as a postcard (May, 2016: 1–5). The 'Hun speech' was widely reported in the press and in the early 2000s, a preserved audio recording of it was even digitally restored.

It is thus fruitful to view the expressions of enemy images connected to their modes of technical (re)production and dissemination. The evolution of media and their content go hand in hand and 'the medium is the message', according to Canadian communication scholar Marshall McLuhan (1964). This implies that mobilization of and desensitization to enemy images are linked to the modes of their expression.

But when did it all start? Images *of* enemies appeared early: on Greek pottery, Marcus Aurelius' column in Rome (displaying 'barbarian' tribes), or the Bayeux tapestry (and of course much earlier in a non-European global context). But an enemy image is more than an illustration of the existential antagonist; it communicates rather a visual programme with distinct features and aims. Such a programme entails what was previously defined (in Chapter 1) as constructing the collective Other as an existential threat against 'our' most vital interests with the aim of mobilizing and desensitizing the in-group to legitimize a response, often violent, against the out-group.

When we apply this definition to unpacking Wilhelm II's image above, it corresponds exactly. The Asian 'other' is constructed as an existential and (anonymous) threat, scorching and pillaging European villages (or as is said in the *Illustrirte Zeitung*, 'landscapes blessed by culture') like a rolling firestorm. Wilhelm II even explicitly mentions 'the most sacred goods' of the European people that are to be secured. Warned by the archangel Michael of the imminent danger, their representatives (in line with conventions in art history portrayed as protective mothers of the nations) are mobilized to defend themselves against this danger.

It is, however, not only the enemy from outside who threaten the assets of the European nations but also the enemies within. Sending the image to the Russian tsar, Wilhelm II noted that the 'united resistance of all European powers [...] also is needed against our shared inner enemies: anarchy, republicanism, nihilism' (May, 2016: 3). Thus, geopolitical unity is invoked when faced with the threat of internal dissolution and external extermination (Önnerfors and Krouwel, 2021: 9–11). Armour-clad and bearing swords and lances, there is no doubt that a collective response on the part of the European nations will be violent. Moreover, references to Christian and Asian religions provide the imagery with an existential ideological meta-frame. The enemy is not only a physical but a metaphysical threat to European civilization.

Knackfuß's image was re-used even after the German defeat in the First World War. Fearing the threat of Communism, the *Osthilfe*, an association supporting voluntary fighters against Bolshevist uprisings in Eastern Europe, replaced the image of Buddha with a fanged skull. More grotesque posters of the same organization showed dehumanized representations of the eastern threat, monsters and skulls with stereotypical 'Asiatic' traits and the motto 'Die Heimat ist in Gefahr!' (The heartland is in danger!, IWM 2022). A satirical image from the German journal *Der Kladderadatsch* in 1934 showed Europe as a woman waking up with red bedbugs with the title 'Vermin: People of Europe, Defend Your Sacred Treasures!' (Cornell University, 2015). The 'Yellow Peril' motif was later recycled in American Second World War propaganda. A film titled *Know Your Enemy: Japan* (1945) was shot, drawing heavily on racial stereotypes of the Japanese totalitarian militaristic government. The slogan 'Slap a Jap', together with racialized depictions of the enemy, was widely disseminated through cartoons, posters, or matchboxes.

But it was the First World War which developed into the first medialized war with a wide dissemination of enemy images. As Jo Fox, a specialist in twentieth-century propaganda explains (and in line with what we previously stated), there were tensions in how the enemy was depicted:

> on the one hand you don't want to minimise the power of the enemy because ultimately you want to prove that you are beating a formidable foe. But equally you don't want to demonise the enemy to the extent that you induce terror in your fighting and producing peoples.

> *(British Library, 2014)*

So these images had to strike a balance between portraying a manageable threat and simultaneously reducing potential fear of enemy superiority (see the definition of an enemy image in Chapter 1 and the discussion on mobilization in Chapter 2). Sometimes subtle codes were used to denote barbarity versus civilization. Postcards displayed Germans killing their rescue dogs for dinner, for example, while others showed Allied soldiers being kind to animals. If we fast forward to our times, a similar logic is expressed today in the Twitter handle @FDF_Ukraine, the 'Feline Defence Force' which since the start of the war has posted more than 1400 Tweets showing cats (and other pets) together with Ukrainian soldiers and civilians. Returning to the First World War, Fox explains that the Germans in turn portrayed the British Empire as a beast devouring the European nations. One book with the title *Das englische Raubtier* (The English Predator) shows an octopus resting on a pile of coins, wrapping its tentacles around the globe (von Hoensbroech, 1919), a visual representation popular within conspiracy theories. The octopus entangling the globe also appeared on the front page of the 1931 German publication *Crisis*, illustrating the burdens of the Versailles treaty building up sentiments of indignation among the German population. During the Second World War, the octopus squeezing the globe was re-used in portraying Churchill as a ruthless Jewish exploiter.

Jo Fox demonstrates further that gender played an important role in propaganda. Bellicose women as national personifications (such as in Knackfuß's image) were disseminated on wartime postcards. Women were also idealized as something to fight for and return to, as symbols of hope, reward, and future national reproduction. But they also represented national loss and sorrow. One postcard in the British Library collections ('The German honour has become a shame') shows a German woman crucified on the iron cross against the backdrop of a destroyed city. When after the war, parts of Germany were occupied by French forces, the alleged mass rape of German women by African soldiers was expressed in heavily racist terms, for instance on a medal designed by Karl Xaver Goetz (1875–1950), perhaps one of the most unexpected medializations of enemy images. Dated in 1920, the medal shows a German woman with her hands tied behind an enormous phallus wearing a French military helmet. Under the motto 'Die schwarze Schande' (for a picture, see 'The black shame', Wikimedia, 2018), we find a symbolic representation of Freemasonry, a radiant all-seeing eye in a triangle (a popular symbol of the 'Illuminati conspiracy' to this day), denoting the alleged Jewish–Masonic plot against Germany. The front of the medal displays a heavily racialized representation of a Black French soldier, highlighting his racial inferiority and barbarity together with the motto of the French Republic of liberty, equality, and fraternity.

However, the history of visual representations of enemy images did not start in the modern era. Before we move on to a more historical panorama across different forms of media, it is worth summing up what the examples can tell us about the interrelationship between enemy images and their medial expression:

1 real or imagined conflicts lead to various (stereotypical) representations of enemies (foes) and their opponents (friends)
2 the media of enemy images are closely related to the context of their origin
3 the medialization of enemy images is to a varying degree coupled with the technical means (media) of their dissemination
4 medial representations of enemy images serve their inbuilt rhetorical purpose

First, real or imagined conflicts lead to the ideation (formation of ideas about) of enemy representations and simultaneously of those who oppose them. This is achieved through a binary scheme where motives like threat (defence, fear), strength, and power (resilience) are portrayed, frequently in a stereotypical manner and using strong symbolism. These stereotypes are related to strategies of visual and rhetorical anonymization, dehumanization, and brutalization of the enemy as opposed to the personalization and humanization of friends and allies and their existential interests, whose violence is described as noble, 'gallant', and justified. It can be expressed in detail: there is for instance a tremendous difference between the 'sword of justice' and the dagger, associated with betrayal, treachery, and assassination. Opposing worldviews and ideologies are condensed into symbols or symbolic references. The portrayal of gender plays another pivotal role – as with, for instance, the female representation of both national strengths but also victimhood. It is also important to notice that once established, enemy images are difficult to eradicate as mental constructs. They 'stick' easily (see Chapter 6) and have the potential to morph over time both in terms of content and the media disseminating them. From evoking European unity against the 'Yellow Peril', the enemy image expressed in Knackfuß's lithography could for instance be reappropriated and recycled after the First World War in another context.

Second, the media of enemy images are closely linked to their originators and the context of origin. In the case of the 'Yellow Peril', designed by the German Kaiser, the image is constructed top-down and disseminated through (semi-)official media outlets. In line with what was stated in Chapter 3, the elite construction of enemy images is aimed at alignment over time in the target audience for discursive consistency.

Third, as in the case presented above, the medialization of enemy images is connected to the technical variety in its dissemination – as image and text, as a (moveable) poster, an article, a performed speech, a recorded speech, a postcard, and so on.

Fourth and possibly most important, the rhetorical purpose of the enemy image as a medial construct is to desensitize and mobilize the target audience to such a degree that organized violence appears as a rational and legitimate response to the perceived threat posed by the enemy. This purpose is evident proactively but can also be employed as an exculpatory reaction to the violence that has already been perpetrated.

Paper trails of persecution – from woodcuts to online memes

When studying the expressions of enemy images, another important insight is that their content can remain relatively stable over time while adapting to the evolution of media. In this section, we follow how antisemitic myths were expressed in different types of media over five centuries, from the invention of the printing press to digital formats.

Perhaps one of the earliest examples of the effective communication of enemy images is the antisemitic blood libel. In 2020, historian Magda Teter published *Blood Libel: on the trail of an anti-Semitic Myth*. The book (and a companion website 'The Blood Libel Trail') explores how accusations that Jews ritually killed Christian children and used their blood emerged in European mediaeval society. Whereas blood libel stories were initially communicated in monastic chronicles, sermons, and local lore, the development of the printing press expanded the audience drastically and amplified the spread of false information and hateful images 'providing a lasting template for hate' (Teter, 2020: 5). Thus, it is possible to follow a 'paper trail' of toxic enemy images from early modernity until today, where the antisemitic imagery of the blood libel was expressed again in connection with the COVID-19 pandemic.

Within the iconography of antisemitic codes, legends surrounding 'ritual murder' occupy a particular position since several narrative strings are united: (a) an allegedly perverted religious cult, (b) a seemingly unambiguous relationship between perpetrator and victim, and (c) strongly charged visual metaphors of the body and of blood (Caumanns and Önnerfors, 2021: 12). Building on the alleged blame for the crucifixion of Jesus, the idea of Jewish ritual murder was incorporated into the Western imagination during the Middle Ages and has been expressed in iconographic programmes as much as performative manifestations ever since. Conspiratorial narratives, such as those involving William of Norwich (1132–1144) or Simon of Trent (1472–1475), were transposed into the modern antisemitism of the nineteenth and twentieth centuries, to the internet, and at times into Islamophobic varieties.

Whereas more attention has been paid in general to the rhetorical strategies of enemy images, the example of ritual murder helps to explain how imagery itself has been vital to the transmission and dissemination of demonizing tropes. Conspiracy theories have, for example, been communicated with several iconographic markers such as 'the dagger', 'the octopus', or 'the string-puller' (Caumanns and Önnerfors, 2020: 442–456). When it comes to the legend of ritual murder, the slaughter knife, a cup for the collection of blood, and instruments of torture such as pincers or prickers were frequently employed to enforce the dramatic and emblematic opposition between innocent victims and inhuman perpetrators. Of particular influence was one of the first printed accounts, the 'History of Simon of Trent', an incunable (early print) printed as early as 1475 with woodcuts in Trent (imagery available on Magda Teter's website thebloodlibletrail. org and see Figure 7.2). The case revolves around a three-year-old Christian boy

FIGURE 7.2 Jews abducting the Christian child Simon.

Source: Woodcut illustration in Albert Kunne's *Hystorie von Simon zu Trient (1475)* as seen in the *Bayrische Staatsbibliothek.*

Simon, who disappeared around Easter of 1475 in Trent (South Tyrol). When his dead body was found three days later, suspicion was immediately directed against the city's Jewish congregation. Under torture, some of its members confessed to the crime and were executed. These 'confessions' were now printed in the History in 12 chapters, accompanied by graphic woodcuts, where the juxtaposition of text on the right and image on the left page reinforces the dramatic nature of the narrative. The book as a media-technical development enables and enhances this complementarity of visual expression and textual explanation, ensuring their rapid dissemination. In other words, the arrangement of books as volumes with successive sheets bound in verso (left page) and recto (right page), as compared to the scroll (a paper roll, also replicated in the digital age as 'scrolling' up and down), opens up other ways of illustration than for instance a framed image, photograph or radio programme.

The first seven chapters describe the horrendous crime in detail: Jews plot the kidnapping of a Christian child; Simon is kidnapped; he is circumcized; his body is tortured; and his blood is collected to bake matzah (Jewish Passover flatbread). Finally, the corpse is hidden but discovered, and the boy is subsequently adored as a martyr on the altar of the Christian church. The last three woodcuts illustrate the torture and execution of the Jewish 'perpetrators'. Even without reading skills, a multi-phased narrative string was thus established:

- a conspiratorial plot to commit ritual murder among the community of perpetrators (enemies) hidden from society
- abduction and brutish murder of an (innocent) child from the community of victims (friends)
- attempts to conceal the body, then the uncovering of the crime by the community of victims (in the presence of the community of perpetrators)
- religious adoration of the victim, in stark contrast to the brutal execution of the perpetrators.

Magda Teter divides the narrative structure into three elements: (a) martyrdom (the ritual murder of the child), (b) victimhood (the dead body as a token of the act of murder), and (c) glorification (the beatification of the victim through his ascent to heaven). For our understanding of how dominant narratives of enemy images work (cf. Chapter 6), it is important to decode such structures.

Once the legend of blood libel was established as an allegedly factual account, it was reproduced for instance in the influential *Schedel'sche Weltchronik* (1493, arguably the first printed encyclopaedia) and two centuries later in Gottfried's *Historische Chronica* (1674). But the storyline was also adapted to other media. During the seventeenth-century Counter-Reformation, the Order of Jesuits wrote an interactive theatre play dedicated to Simon and another very similar alleged victim of Jewish ritual murder, Andreas Oxner. The didactic and rhetorical function of this educational play cannot be underestimated – it was an effective communication device to mobilize religious devotion through an active performance of enemy images on stage in which different forms of medial expressions converged. The inclusion of the spectators, who were encouraged to actively express both disaffection (with the perpetrators/enemies) and sympathy (with the innocent victim/friend) increased the emotional and psychological effect of the narrative. It was also during the Counter-Reformation that the 'Sacred Congregation for the Propagation of the Faith' was established by the Vatican in 1622, officially to support missionary work.

Whereas enlightenment, secularization, and greater tolerance possibly diminished the legend of blood libel over the next centuries, it was alive as late as 1840 in the Ottoman Empire. During the so-called Damascus Affair, Jews were accused by Christians and Muslims of having carried out ritual murder. The narrative was thus transposed into more distinctly political contexts, but the range of victims was also extended from Christian boys to girls and (young) women, thus adding explicit elements of sexual violence and perversion (for instance in the Hungarian Tiszaeszlár affair during the 1880s).

With the advent of new media, antisemitic content was disseminated widely in the form of sensational postcards. The blood libel was also incorporated in the Nazi propaganda journal *Der Stürmer*, which published two thematic issues in 1934 and 1939, respectively. These motifs also informed Nazi movies, shot to discredit, and dehumanize Jews: *Die Rothschilds* (1940), *Jud Suess* (1940), and *Der ewige Jude* (1940) likening the Jews to rats spreading diseases and finishing with purported footage of ritual murder (Welch, 2014). The accusations of child murder and consumption of (Christian) blood have been integral to antisemitic imagery and reproduced not only in Western but also in Middle Eastern media. An inverted Islamophobic myth, that of Muslims consuming Christian blood, was part of Swedish folklore in the nineteenth and twentieth centuries. Dozens of accounts were gathered by folklorists and are accounted for in newspapers where Swedish freemasons were accused of acting as intermediaries of a murky pact between the state and Ottoman rulers, paying back credits that had been given to the Swedish crown in the eighteenth century (Astapova et al., 2021: 18). The story was very similar: Swedish children were said to be abducted and killed by the masons, their bodies (or blood) sent in barrels to Istanbul. It is a typical feature of enemy images to weaponize the alleged abuse of children (as vulnerable victims) as a shorthand for evil. In the US-born conspiracy theories of the Q-Anon movement, the Democrats were accused of running a paedophile ring. Kidnapping and abduction of Muslim children in Sweden by the social services turned in 2022 into a powerful narrative of foreign influence operations. Recycling previous tropes in Russian propaganda, a network of social media activists targeted Sweden (Astapova et al., 2021: 75–82; SR, 2022; Ranstorp and Ahlerup, 2023). The episode demonstrates the increasing trend towards disinformation campaigns as a new type of hybrid warfare targeting the so-called cognitive domain, which we will return to at the end of this chapter.

In the internet age, the blood libel myth has been transferred into the world of digital culture wars. In 2020, Italian artist Gasparro published a neo-classical altarpiece giving new life to the 'martyrdom of Simon of Trent through Jewish ritual murder' (Caumanns and Önnerfors, 2021: 17). Supported by ultra-Catholic circles, the altarpiece was widely disseminated on Facebook before it was taken down and the platform accused of 'censorship', providing the artist with a chance to style himself as a victim of persecution. This was also the case for those opponents of pandemic policies who pinned a yellow Jewish star on their clothes with the caption 'not vaccinated', suggesting they were victims of a totalitarian regime of extermination. Gasparro's Jews take obvious delight in the torture of Simon. Moreover, they seem to stab the baby child with syringes, opening the door towards violent vaccine resistance (also frequently charged with antisemitic tropes) that radicalized a considerable number of people globally during the anti-corona protests between 2020 and 2022. During Passover in 2021, the terrorist organization Nordic Resistance Movement erected a rack outside the synagogue of Norrköping in Sweden with baby dolls smeared in red and a note suggesting that the traditional matzah was prepared with human blood. The purpose of this 'protest' was mainly to get attention and dissemination on social media, a new strategy of so-called hypermedia engagement, blurring the lines between offline performance and online diffusion (Önnerfors, 2020: 178–193).

With its long history of ideas alluding to persisting cultural and religious stereotypes, its dramatic narrative structure, drastic visual language, and performative potential, the blood libel myth is an effective and productive code of conspiratorial antisemitic narratives, trans-mediated by text and images. Due to its juxtaposition of innocent 'victims' (frequently children or women) and perverted Jewish 'perpetrators', the myth can effectively be adapted to the monochrome and binary formula of world explanation that unites enemy images and conspiracy theories alike. In simple terms, the narrative of the enemy image is effective because it builds up a clear black-and-white worldview which explains fundamental antagonisms.

But we can also see how the 'paper trail' of persecution cuts through five centuries of media development, from the very early age of the printing press to digital media and its intricate online–offline dynamics. This explains its longevity and how mythical representations of enemies, both internal and external, can be recycled, reproduced, adapted to crises, and expressed in various forms of media over time.

The 'broadcasting of hatred'

With the invention of the radio, a new and effective tool of communication across space emerged. This section discusses the implications of this development from early twentieth-century propaganda to the genocide in Rwanda. That technical evolution and new modes of disseminating propaganda are intrinsically linked can be illustrated by the German *Volksempfänger 301* (The People's Receiver), a low-budget radio set commissioned by Nazi Reich Minister of Propaganda Joseph Goebbels. Opening a radio exhibition in Berlin, Goebbels claimed that later generations would have to acknowledge that in influencing the spiritual development of the masses, radio broadcasts were like the introduction of the printing press during the Reformation. Almost everyone in Germany could afford this new radio and it would emerge around the country 'as electrification made rapid progress' as a powerful means of mass communication (Meier, 2018). By 1941, it is estimated that around 65% of German households owned a *Volksempfänger*, and it was used to drum enemy images into the population. The development was of course also embraced by the other warring countries, not least by the BBC. A novelty in warfare was the international outreach of 'enemy broadcasts' (*Feindsender* in German) trying to influence perceptions of the conflict on either side and representing the start of proper information influence operations (psychological warfare and black propaganda directed at antagonist audiences). *Nachtsender 1212* was for instance a covert American operation broadcasting programmes in German to give the impression of authenticity. A German poster from 1944 read:

> You are a traitor: if you listen to enemy broadcast stations; if you believe in the slogans of the enemy; if you disseminate the messages of the enemy; if you follow instructions from the side of the enemy; if you make agreements with the enemy [...]
>
> *(Der Spiegel, 2013)*

As communication scholar and journalist Keith Somerville, author of *Radio Propaganda and the Broadcasting of Hatred* (2012) states:

> The use of the electronic media, radio in particular, to promote causes, propagate ideologies, define or develop discourses of identity and also of 'otherness', ridicule, demonize, dehumanize and incite hatred and even violent action was a product of the technological advances of the 20th century.
>
> *(2012: 1)*

Beyond the mere propagation of a discourse of fear and hatred, radio broadcasts (as auditory media types: speech and various types of sound) can encompass a call to actual violence or other collective actions based on media framing and representation. What Somerville defines as 'hate propaganda' (and in consequence 'hate radio') has many similarities with how we have identified enemy images in this book. It is

> aimed by governments, movements and parties at their own populations to develop and maintain support for a regime or a set of policies, elicit active support or at the very least acquiescence in the face of a set of policies or actions

by that regime and, in the extreme cases [...] promote hatred and incite violence towards the objects of that hatred.

(Somerville, 2012: 2)

Somerville argues that the emergence of radio from 1911–1945 created a 'mass audience for propaganda and incitement' (Somerville, 2012: 33). Radio broadcasts were used to disseminate hate propaganda in the United States in the early 1920s and later during the Spanish Civil War. In Italy, Germany, and the USSR in the 1930s, radio turned into a tool for ideological education and indoctrination. A methodological challenge to studying radio broadcasts is access to the material. It is far from standard practice for radio broadcasts to be recorded and preserved for the future. Whereas major speeches by statesmen (such as the one delivered by Kaiser Wilhelm II) might have been recorded and are thus potentially available for analysis by posterity, everyday radio broadcasts – particularly by smaller local radio stations – are lost in the ether. Nazi radio was monitored, though, with transcripts published by the BBC. Interestingly, the potential abuse of radio for propaganda purposes was identified as early as 1936 in the 'International Convention Concerning the Use of Broadcasting in the Cause of Peace' launched by the League of Nations (Baade, 2019: 1365–1369; Potter, 2023: 1–22). Conversely, international wireless broadcasting was identified during the interwar period as a contributor to universal peacebuilding. This international convention constitutes to this day one of the few legal frameworks in international law for assessing the legal consequences of propaganda and disinformation.

Even though by then it had already been overrun by cable and satellite television, the power of radio media (and the spoken word) in the transmission of enemy images was once again demonstrated in 1994 during the Rwandan genocide. As Somerville notes, radio broadcasts were not monitored or transcribed consistently (2012: 152). The most comprehensive collection is available at the Montreal Institute for Genocide and Human Rights Studies (MIGS) and a host of other materials at the Genocide Archive Rwanda at the University of Texas, Austin as well as the Genocide Archive Rwanda (in Kigali). At the media trials of the UN International Criminal Tribunal for Rwanda (ICTR), documentation was made available. We will return to this trial in the final part of the chapter and quote extensively from the court proceedings since they allow us direct insights into the tribunal's reasoning.

However, as mentioned in Chapters 2 and 6, radio broadcasts played a pivotal role in inciting ordinary citizens to take part in the massacres of Tutsi and moderate Hutu neighbours. 'The genocide was carried out with haste but with evident organization and with the media, especially vernacular radio, playing a prominent role' (Somerville, 2012: 153). Two radio stations played a pivotal role in disseminating hate propaganda: public broadcaster Radio Rwanda and Radio Télévision des Milles Collines (RTLM). Radio Rwanda was the official government-owned radio station. RTLM was formed as a private channel in response to previous attempts to reduce hateful content. The channel gained popularity as a snappier alternative to the public broadcaster, playing popular music and encouraging interaction with its listeners, resonating well with unemployed youth and militia members. Between 1993 and 1994, the channel was used by Hutu leaders to advance an extremist Hutu message and anti-Tutsi disinformation. Fear of a Tutsi genocide was spread, and specific Tutsi targets were identified, accelerating the process of genocide (MIGS, 2022). Somerville states that in the months before the genocide, RTLM 'consistently set an agenda of suspicion and hatred of the Tutsi' (2012: 186). Radio Rwanda began to advance a similar message on behalf of the national government, issuing directives on how and where to kill Tutsis. Those who took part in the killings were congratulated (MIGS, 2022). Before and after the genocide, there were many pleas to jam the broadcasts of both stations, yet they continued to incite killings of Tutsis and moderate Hutus until the victories of the Rwandan Patriotic Front (MIGS, 2022). As scholarship and the war crimes tribunal respectively agree, a clear causal connection between radio broadcasts and actual genocidal violence remains difficult to establish. However,

> it is impossible to disentangle the complex web of radio propaganda, exhortations at public meetings and the effects of a strongly ordered and controlled society under the hegemony of first a government and then a Hutu supremacist movement that had the manpower, means and will to enforce its word.
>
> *(Somerville, 2012: 201)*

This aligns with what we described in Chapter 3 as a discursive consistency and consensus between the public and the private.

Enemy images in feature films

Another example of the technical evolution of medial expressions is feature films as a new mode of narration. In this section, we discuss how movies have shaped perceptions of enemies over the course of a century.

The portrayal of defining moments in national histories across the globe frequently revolves around conflicts and war – and consequently around antagonists, both external enemies and enemies within. This confronted the film industry from its inception around 1900 with the task of constructing moving images of the enemy and – when not reduced to mere extras, as the French troops were in the recent Oscar-winning Netflix adaptation of *All Quiet on the Western Front* (2022) – with representing its threatening traits. As we argued in Chapter 3, the formation of elite consensus and discursive consistency in the construction of enemy images also entails the entertainment industry. It is therefore unsurprising that various state-sponsored national film projects should also communicate such ambitions and direct their interest towards both external and internal enemies. It seems that the First World War provided the opportunity to explore moving images as a means of visual propaganda. In Britain, Lancelot Speed (1860–1931), a romantic painter in many ways similar to Knackfuß, was commissioned to produce a cartoon titled *Bully Boy* (1914), ridiculing the German Kaiser waging war in the light of obvious atrocities (BFI, 2022; Welch, 2014). Four years later, Speed produced a cartoon titled *The British Effort*, portraying mobilization across the British Empire and from all walks of life as an honourable sacrifice. The cartoon also shows women contributing to the war industry, creating a war effort on a civilizational par with the Egyptian pyramids. Also, the colonial war theatre is portrayed vividly (British Pathé, 2022).

Any selection of feature films in this section is arbitrary and can be expanded almost infinitely, not least if also considering non-European examples. Nevertheless, the intention is not to be exhaustive but rather just to point out how the medium of moving images allowed for new portrayals of enemies. The ground zero of toxic enemy images on screen is arguably *The Birth of a Nation* (1915), a silent epic film about the defining national conflict of the US Civil War (1861–1865, see Figure 7.3). Although the movie is about a domestic war, it has plenty to offer when analysing how conflict parties, and the dichotomy between villainy and innocence, are portrayed. First, Black men are characterized as intellectually inferior, brutish, and sexually predatory, constantly menacing white women. Black voting rights, part of the peace deal of the reconstruction era, are also repudiated, echoing into the 'stop-the-steal' conspiracy theories of our age. By contrast, the members of the Ku Klux Klan (KKK) are represented as heroes, defending true American values and women as well as safeguarding racial supremacy. The Klan imagined itself as a Christian knighthood placed above the law with the right to exercise indiscriminate capital punishment. Instead of highlighting the injustice of slavery and the structural exclusion of Black people from American society, *The Birth of a Nation* cemented and justified its fundamental division, foreshadowing future conflict lines right into the contemporary 'Black Lives Matter' movement and domestic white supremacy terrorism. The movie is also said to have directly inspired the formation of the second generation of the Klan. In the interwar period, the fraternal order took its violent extremism to new levels, combining white supremacy with conspiracy theories accusing Catholic immigrants to the United States of being enemies undermining American nativist identity (Kendall, 2011: 123–143). This idea of a knighthood defending Christian and Western values against the immigrant and racial 'other' to avert the purported 'white genocide' also informed terrorist Behring Breivik in Oslo and Utøya in 2011 (Önnerfors, 2017: 159–175).

The Birth of a Nation developed an advanced musical score to be played together with its screening. Most notably, German composer Richard Wagner's 'Ride of the Valkyries' was used as a leitmotif for the white rescue ride of the KKK and later also featured prominently in the Vietnam War movie *Apocalypse Now* (1979) during a napalm strike carried out by airborne cavalry. As the editors of the book *The Enemy in Contemporary Film* (2018) state, enemy images serve to 'reassert or redefine a

FIGURE 7.3   Movie poster for *The Birth of a Nation*.

Source: Universal History Archive/Shutterstock.

national identity in the present', triggering a dialogue between different forms of historical perception (past and present) into which issues such as race, ethnicity, and gender are interwoven. Providing a comparative approach, the authors aim to describe 'representative filmic strategies underlying the (de)(re)constructions of the "enemy image" in transnational contexts'. Filmic representations are connected to various national politics of historical memory, where the internal viewpoint is created in relation to the external as a shaping force. The image of the external enemy is needed in the construction of the image of the internal self in a dichotomy of 'us' versus 'them' (Sokołowska-Paryż and Löschnigg, 2018: 1–2 and 4). The same applies to the internal enemy, through which domestic conflicts can paradoxically be externalized. This happens when the enemy within is scapegoated as acting on behalf of foreign interests, as a representation of manipulation and deception in ever-shifting allegiances. The collaborator can never be trusted, even when guilt and lack of loyalty to the in-group are only constructed by mere association, such as being Japanese in the United States during the Second World War.

The trend in contemporary film is, however, ambivalent. On the one hand, new global conflicts such as the war in Ukraine might trigger a reactivation and weaponization of long-standing enemy images. There is a risk that portraying historical events and conflicts might increase nationalism. Even if the ambition is to alleviate past antagonisms, they could potentially be reignited. The coverage of (c)old conflicts might even create new tensions. On the other hand, there are endeavours to 'de-enimize' the past with the aim of promoting transnational/ethnic reconciliation on the basis of an understanding of the motivations of the "enemy" and an acknowledgement of the humanity [and alterity] of the "Other" ', particularly when wartime enemies have become post-war allies. Such an idealistic view tends to tone down past antagonisms, for instance by downplaying or problematizing the concept of the enemy. This resonates well with what in Chapter 2 we theorized as 'malign' and 'benign' enemy images (Sokołowska-Paryż and Löschnigg, 2018: 3, 5, and 10–11). In this vein, a movie like 'Joyeux Noël' (2005), about the Christmas truce on the western front during the First World War, can be interpreted as a manifestation of the contemporary Germano-French alliance and European unity, a hypothetical indication that it was possible and legitimate to overcome exclusionary and destructive constructions of enemies against all odds.

Highlighting the close nexus between film and national cultural memory, it is significant to grasp that the construction of the enemy figure is exposed to transnational and transtemporal paradigms. Some enemy images create sense over long time periods and receive their meaning through sharp stereotypical reasoning. One can, for instance, take the characterization of Nazis in the character Hans Landa (played by Christopher Waltz) in *Inglourious Basterds* (2009) as a shorthand for the enemy evil stereotype. Moreover, a string of atrocities from Nanjing to Auschwitz and Hiroshima (and soon perhaps also Bucha, Ukraine) have reached global audiences and serve as a 'shared archive of experience' in the construction of enemy images (Sokołowska-Paryż and Löschnigg, 2018: 4). The real and imagined threat of terrorist attacks and warfare in Afghanistan and the MENA region has in multiple Western filmic representations since 9/11 or earlier turned 'The Muslim' immigrant 'other' into a strong Islamophobic representation of the unassimilable enemy within (parallel to previous antisemitic codes in both open and more subtle propaganda). Visual codes such as headscarves, mosques, calls to prayer, and religious dress are also employed in political advertising and memes.

In *The Alamo* (1960), autocratic Mexican enemies rebelling against Texas republicans defending a besieged fort are portrayed as faceless, mean, and brutal attackers, turning them into symbolic representations of the enemy as such, and echoing into subsequent treatments in film. The movie was shot against the backdrop of the Cold War and the recent victory over Nazi Germany. It could thus evoke a stereotypical fight between freedom and tyranny, motivating and reproducing a clear distinction between friend and foe. The epic war movie *Zulu* (1964) – also about a siege – was recently identified by a British governmental anti-radicalization programme as promoting white supremacism, which sparked a veritable culture war about the feature film (Bradshaw, 2023). *Zulu* tells the story of a side battle in the colonial Zululand campaign of 1879, in which outnumbered British soldiers defend their camp courageously and victoriously against the superior strength of a tribal army. But the movie, which supposedly aims at a fair portrayal of the warring parties, can also be read as a statement of civilized white Britishness opposing savage Black brutishness. Almost 60 years after its release, *Zulu* has surprisingly created a huge fanbase on social media: its official Facebook page has 30,000 followers, its TikTok account more than 72,000, and its YouTube channel has more than 81,000 subscribers. 'The Zulu Store' sells movie merchandise from coffee mugs to mouse mats and phone cases and mostly T-shirts, one of them with the slogan 'Pro Zulu Anti Woke'. The store claims to have reached out to more than 100 million people worldwide. On social media, the roughly 2-hour movie is cut up into small reels adapted to dissemination, frequently with texts added, turning them into memes. The reels focus on the scenes where white British soldiers kill Black Zulu warriors. Also, the merchandise is much about fixing bayonets to be pushed into Black bodies. Perhaps it is impossible to disentangle romanticized colonial violence from its contemporary usages – or as Peter Bradshaw (2023) put it: ' "Zulu" shows cinema's power to rewrite history [...] by turning an armed invasion into a plucky underdog story'. By focusing on the heroic defence of an insignificant army outpost, 'the movie is arguably part of the cover-up mythology that began almost immediately: the seizing on and inflation of a relatively unimportant event'. Aggressive attackers are turned into noble defenders.

In a globalized world, it is thus even more important to develop sensitivities to both similarities and differences depending on such socio-cultural contexts and agendas related to enemy images in film. There is always a risk that retrospective filmic treatment of enemies guided by extreme nationalism and pride might evoke sentiments of a heroic and glorious past shaped by military victories and strife. The Finnish war epic *The Unknown Soldier* (2017), for instance, does little to change the perception of its Soviet antagonists or to provide more context for Finnish collaboration with the Nazi war machine. *American Sniper* (2015) tells the story of the most lethal of all US snipers in history without reflecting much upon his 200 or so victims, whereas *Battle for Haditha* (2007) paints a very different picture of the same conflict, the Iraq War. As the trailer for the latter movie states, 'there are many ways to see the same story' (IMDb, 2022). In German post-unification cinema and arts in general, there has been a trend to problematize previously clear-cut enemy images by also portraying German victimhood during the end of the Second World War. *Die Flucht* (March of Millions), a two-part film produced by public broadcaster ARD in 2007, sparked controversy with its portrayal of the sufferings of German refugees. It showed them escaping the invasion of the Red Army and in doing so reverted to conventional schemes of victims and perpetrators. One year later, *Anonyma: eine Frau in Berlin* (Anonyma: A Woman in Berlin) came out, a movie exposing 'hitherto suppressed national shame (mass rape of German women by Red Army soldiers)'. Whereas such movies contribute to a reframing of actual events in which Germany's victimhood is emphasized, they also contribute to highlighting 'gender-oriented violence in wartime' (Sokołowska-Paryż and Löschnigg, 2018: 1–2 and 8). Other movies portray the 'forbidden' crossing of boundaries between enemy and ally – for instance women's relations with enemy soldiers.

But as Sokołowska-Paryż and Löschnigg argue, the overarching question to be addressed is 'to what extent filmic representations of the enemy are interpretations of actual threat menacing today's world', or rather 'to what degree they may be considered ideological evocations of fear for the (geo)political needs of the "here and now" of a nation's self-interest' (2018: 5). In analysing enemy images in film, this seems to be a productive formula: is an actual threat being portrayed or is it rather a perceived construct of fear serving internal purposes of meaning-making?

Warfare in televised news – videos on social media

Simultaneously with the development of feature films, moving images were also used to document news events. Unsurprisingly, war and conflict were portrayed together with heavily framed representations of friends and foes. The supposedly documentary capture of conflicts is open to a wide range of manipulation, from the newsreels of the early twentieth century to clips on contemporary social media.

In 2005, documentary filmmaker Mark Daniels released the movie *Enemy Image*, an attempt to examine 'how television news in the US has covered the war from Vietnam to the present day' (IMDb, 2022; Films for Action, 2022). Despite its title, the documentary is not an investigation of enemy images as such but rather portrays how news coverage of wars in the United States has been involved in has changed from the Vietnam War to the early 2000s, something we briefly touched upon in Chapter 3. Whereas journalists during the Vietnam War were allowed access to the battlefield and to civilians experiencing its consequences, the development moved in the direction of ever-closer control over the media image communicated, from ready-made news packages to embedding journalists with regular troops. As the movie's narrator states, 'when great nations go to war it's a big story, and when America goes to war, American television goes to war'. Although the first invasion of Iraq ('Operation Desert Storm' in 1990–1991) only lasted 800 hours, it generated 20,000 hours of video to narrate with. This was due to an almost non-stop 24/7 news coverage. But did this coverage contribute to a better understanding of the conflict?

Since the rise of the periodical press in the early modern period, warfare, and news about the movements of armies, big battles, and conquests have been in the consciousness of news audiences worldwide. It is therefore not surprising that the new medium of the film was both a continuation of such reports and a new way of portraying conflicts through the visual immersion of audiences in real-world events. Perhaps one of the first documentary movies of war was the *Battle of the Somme*, shown to millions of Britons during the First World War (British Library, 2014). From the 1930s up to the 1960s, newsreels provided cinema and later TV audiences with carefully redacted content, in line with official propaganda. (Live) music within the framework of the conventions of classical composition, text, and voiceovers were used to dramatize the message. Their troops and victories were glorified, and enemies were only portrayed as powerless victims as in the genre conventions of the centuries-old military art tradition. First war photography, then televised news about warfare added a sense of realism and immediacy to this conventional formula through the (often abused) truth claims of photography. Media scholars talk about the so-called indexicality of images (Gunning, 2004), the degree to which an image requires external explanation. What was created initially was merely a new way of visually representing friends and enemies, acts of 'bravery' and 'barbarism' and rationalizations of 'collateral damage' civilians (belonging to the collective of enemies) were exposed to.

The soundtrack of news media and how it developed to accompany reporting on wars and conflicts requires a short digression. According to Martin Knust (2021: n p), media and communication scholars have for a long time 'ignored this communicative layer in journalism', even though non-diegetic music (heard only by audiences) has been used in news communication for over a century. Knust also makes the point that such music is different from feature film music since it is linked to 'political opinion shaping and the articulation of political programs and thus more to propaganda' (2021: n p). Whereas Knust does not explicitly treat the audible representation of enemy images in news communication, some important conclusions of his merit further attention. While music in journalism disappeared during the 1950s and 1960s, marking a distancing from abuses in totalitarian systems, it slowly reappeared over the following decades and is today almost intrinsically connected to the genres of news journalism and documentaries. Without being able to generalize, Knust (2021) highlights the recent emergence of sci-fi and horror film music in such contexts, which perhaps offers some clues. In 2018, the Trump administration released a movie ahead of what was the first state visit of a US president to North Korea. It pitched this meeting of geopolitical adversaries as a moment of destiny with fundamentally diverging outcomes: confrontation or cooperation; fate in the hands of two world leaders. The video communicates a binary message, which is also reflected in the musical score, moving between expectation and melancholy, for instance displaying 'formulae of disorder' as opposed to more harmonic tunes. This binary design 'corresponds to the technique of propaganda films and newsreels that were produced during the Second World War' with only two alternatives – defeat or victory. Knust quotes a study of the German propaganda movie *Feldzug in Polen* (Campaign in Poland, 1939), which styled the brutal attack on a neighbouring country as self-defence. Consequently, the German city of Danzig is illustrated with 'serene string music', whereas the Polish threat is expressed as 'dissonant brass fanfares', with the colour black spreading across a map of central Europe. In the repertoire of contemporary digital video production, databases known as music libraries have been created and sorted into categories of mood or other parameters outside of music (think of music for relaxation or study). It is important to add that images are also made available on databases for stock photos. These are also sorted according to 'typical' representations and there are huge risks of inbuilt biases and stereotyping, prone to amplification at a time when synthetic media content is to an increasing extent created by AI.

No systematic research on enemy representations on such platforms has been carried out, but the soundtrack for the enemy has unsettling musical elements involving military timpani, snare drums, martial trumpets, hunting horns, dramatic beats, pulsating string music, or tense sci-fi-type alienating sounds marking the audible distance from what is native and familiar. This, in combination with the speaker's voice, creates a melodramatic effect where the spoken word (verbal information) and music reinforce each other, today mostly through dark male voiceovers creating credibility. In another example, Knust investigates a political campaign movie from a domestic US context, the aim of which is 'to denigrate and vilify the political opponent' and in which the music style 'displays the typical split horror film soundtrack with its low threatening blows and biting high frequencies, leaving the warm middle register void' (Knust, 2021: n p). Together, the campaign movie operates with 'stimuli overload which is a common practice in political agitation. The condensed presentation of information does not give the listener/ viewer time to reflect but creates emotions of shock and alarm…' (Knust, 2021: n p). A third example shows how a Canadian TV production drastically othered Trump and his supporters. The framing effect of sound design contributed to vilification and demonization. What we can learn from these examples is 'that music may pave the way for irrationality and fanaticism in politics' – or even worse, as during the Nazi rule, intoxicate the masses and replace 'rational thinking with emotion in politics' since 'music has both an emotionalizing and fictionalizing effect' (Knust, 2021: n p).

In 1963, the first news coverage of networked television was released by Columbia Broadcasting System (CBS). It coincided with the Vietnam War, conveying direct and unfiltered reporting to the living rooms of the United States and elsewhere. Daniels' documentary (2005) profits from interviews with journalists who had direct access to the war theatre. It is thus possible to get a better understanding of how media (and its ethos) shapes the image of a conflict and consequently the conflicting parties. Is the journalist a reliable witness or even a conscience? In Vietnam, American journalists decided to report against the conventions and to portray the victims of warfare in all their naked exposure to violence. An iconic example was the reporting of the 1965 'Cam Ne incident', a clear breach of the rules of warfare in its creation of unnecessary suffering. When CBS aired the report, no fewer than 30 million Americans watched, and the US president consequently attempted to influence the news corporation to change the news story. Yet, as Daniels' documentary asks rhetorically, 'if American television never showed the face of the enemy, could the war be understood?'. Instead, French news reporters documented the war from the Vietnamese perspective and CBS joined in, narrating a more balanced account of the consequences of American warfare. It was denounced as communist propaganda. The narrative about the war was lost before the war itself and tensions rose across the country and the world: 'The image of war had become an anti-war image', as Daniels' voiceover declares. In this context, it is worth considering the iconic report by LIFE magazine on the My Lai massacre of 1968, which contributed to the growing international opposition to US warfare in Vietnam.

In the early 1980s, it was claimed that this change in media reporting even affected the outcome of the war; a scapegoat was identified on which to pin the blame for the defeat, an inner enemy which – as after the First World War in Germany – was accused of backstabbing the home front with its nefarious daggers. Consequently, independent TV journalists were locked out from subsequent campaigns, but the new Pentagon strategy backfired. During the 1983 invasion of Grenada, official footage was contradicted by uncensored reporting from a French journalist, putting the independence of US media heavily into question. Instead, a new system was introduced, where 'pools' of journalists worldwide were selected to report from the frontlines, yet under heavy control by the US Army public affairs. Yet again, what was reported through filters, for instance during the first attack on Iraq during the Gulf War 1990–1991, was contradicted by footage available from the bombing of Baghdad from the side of independent journalists. Examples like this illustrate how war reporting by conflicting parties is actively concerned with creating enemy images. In general, direct reporting from the frontlines and both sides of the conflict was rare and television studios turned into representations of situation rooms, which gave a central role to presenters/anchormen to decide what story to tell. Accounts of enemy casualties were however filtered out, which seems to point to a rhetorical discrepancy between the enemy image as such and the representation of its lethal consequences. New ways of tracking attacks with real-time footage created the impression of surgically clean warfare using 'smart bombs' without any major side effects or displaying any casualties. But both sides tried to create false impressions of reality, with 'Baghdad Bob' ('Comical Ali'), the information minister under Saddam Hussein, known for his increasingly delusional reports on Iraqi success despite the visible opposite. To preserve a sanitized impression of warfare, the US side continued to hide footage of 'collateral damage', intervening in major broadcasters' decisions. In his analysis of the media coverage of the 1991 Persian Gulf War, Philip M. Taylor showed how most of the American media depended on the same military-controlled sources. This implied that newspapers, radio, and TV channels with completely different styles, ideologies, and target groups referred to the same sources and news material, which were uncritically conveyed. Taylor calls it 'monopoly in the guise of pluralism' (Taylor, 1992: 268).

The next step in this development was the introduction of embedded journalists – reporters integrated directly into military units and reporting from their perspective, turning into something akin to battlefield sports commentators. But as journalist Jon Alpert states in Daniels' documentary, this was a one-sided exercise, and 'there wasn't anyone embedded with an Iraqi family', leading to a big void in reporting from the perspective of those affected by American warfare (Alpert, 2005). Media companies such as the relatively new Al Jazeera (established in 1996) were trying to counteract this considerable bias. However, the failure to report the war accurately likely contributed to fuelling anti-Western sentiment within the affected populations as well as creating momentum for spectacular revelations and leaks, such as the Iraq War Logs in 2010. Mark Daniels' documentary demonstrates how news media contribute to framing the coverage of war and how this coverage is perceived in the domestic context depending on biases among different audiences.

Following up on Knust and his work on the soundtrack of war, James Deaville has written about how music has shaped public opinion since 9/11 and 'a whole sonic realm works with the images to produce their impact' (Deaville, 2006). Again, there is little theorizing on how this affects the portrayal of enemies, but it is evident that news coverage sophisticatedly prepared for setting war to music and signal military might and security to its audiences combined with the insight that fears also had to be represented. Music and imagery interplayed 'to enhance the message of a justified conflict that we can win' but also to employ audio strategies to sanitize the darkest realities of war (Deaville, 2006).

In *When the press fails* (Bennett, Lawrence, and Livingston, 2007), the authors demonstrate how political forces have prevented news media from fulfilling their role of holding power to account as they fall in with the official 'line' or narrative of events. Daniel Hallin suggested back in 1986 that journalistic objectivity during the Vietnam War could be divided into three spheres: (a) *consensus* (where journalists express implicit agreement with official politics), (b) *legitimate controversy* (where issues can be questioned and debated in a spirit of plurality), and (c) *deviance* (where radical views are excluded, ostracized, or ridiculed) (Hallin, 1986). Hallin's spheres assume the existence of a relatively homogenous media environment in which it is possible to identify a singular public opinion and media audience. However, in more fractured media landscapes where there are multiple producers and audiences (as expressed through contemporary alternative media), this clear-cut distinction is less applicable since audiences will direct their attention to self-affirming biases and news sources confirming previously held opinions. When it comes to enmity perception, and given the diversity of media audiences in contemporary societies, it is thus fully perceivable that some expressions that are considered deviant in one type of media–audience relationship are considered consensus in another – in the same media ecosystem and at the same time. This might lead to a larger variety of enemy images – from benign to malign – than in more controlled media environments.

Moving into an age of synthetic media that might even amplify the diversification of audiences, other trends are also discernible that affect the portrayal and perception of enemies and thus enemy images. At the end of Daniels' documentary, it is described how American soldiers were trained for their mission in Iraq with virtual simulations, replacing reality with a prefabricated video game setting. And during the 2010s, it could be observed how the dynamics of IRL-war coverage have increasingly been twisted towards online dissemination. Knust (2021: n p) describes how 'the visual design of news began to resemble that of computer games' and how 'during the second Iraq War even the audio design of US-American news started to imitate that of a computer game', contributing to a fictionalization or even gamification (at the time dubbed 'Nintendoization') of political communication.

Swedish media researcher Michael Krona has spent considerable effort analysing the media world of the terrorist group ISIS. Aesthetically crafted and carefully edited movies of beheadings and other spectacular executions reached a global audience after the 2014 rise to the power of ISIS. The enemy is needed more as an extra since the script has already allocated pre-defined roles. According to Krona and Pennington (2019: 1), this 'clearly illustrated a deliberate strategy of mediation by ISIS – a strategy that aimed to gain global attention through the theatrical beheading of [westerners] and to simultaneously convey the message of the organization as a global phenomenon itself'. The aim of 'terrorism as theatre' is to maximize outreach in a new media ecology where violence and dynamics of viral dissemination intersect. ISIS created its very own media industry that produced and communicated stories designed to reach out to a broad global audience both intentionally and unintentionally targeted by propaganda. This was achieved by coming 'as close to everyday practices and media consumption as possible', for instance by using popular social media platforms, specific applications, and messaging services (Krona and Pennington, 2019: 2). This again demonstrates the need to consider the very media of dissemination when analysing the spread of enemy images. When war and conflict are mediatized to fit the format of smartphones, digital message-sharing services, and online audience engagement, something happens to the very depiction of enemies as such. As German states:

> Online participation has proven highly effective at mobilizing and directing anger at the enemy 'other.' The link is made vivid by Patrick Kingsley, who makes this comparison: 'In wars gone by, advancing armies smoothed their path with missiles. ISIS did it with tweets and a movie'.
>
> *(German, 2019: 137)*

One striking feature of the war in Ukraine is the use of social media messaging platforms such as Twitter and TikTok, with the Chechnyan contingent of the Russian side even being ridiculed as 'TikTok warriors'. While research into the phenomenon at the time of writing is not available, one standard format of news from the Ukrainian war theatre is heavily redacted (drone-)videos posted to Twitter: to the sound of heavy metal or Ukrainian folk music and pointing at the Russian adversaries as 'orchs' (in reference to fantasy author Tolkien), tanks or positions are blown up and sometimes scores reminiscent of video games are displayed. These short videos, around 1 minute in length, portray a seemingly realistic image of warfare while at the same time engaging in the dehumanization of the enemy as a visual strategy fit for the social media age with a close resemblance to realistic online war games. The increasing hybridity between virtual and physical reality, paired with the dynamics of hypermedia meaning-making and made fit for online dissemination, raises the question of the future construction of enemy images in the cognitive domain (Önnerfors, 2020: 178–193). Can we know or determine what is real and what is manipulated – or is the future hyperreal, one where the borders between reality and simulation are effectively blurred?

Media accountability

In the previous sections, it emerged that various types of media, from print to online, have contributed to the spread of enemy images, sometimes with catastrophic consequences. The relevant question arising, to be discussed below, is whether the producers of media can be held accountable for such content and on what grounds. A close reading of international tribunals reveals interesting arguments related to the accountability of media producers in this regard.

Since the days of the establishment of the Vatican *Index Librorum Prohibitorum* (List of Prohibited Books) in 1515, coinciding with the emergence of the printing press and the Reformation, there has been an acknowledgement that media content also carries certain responsibilities. The freedom of the press has been forced ever since to develop leeway between authoritarian censorship based on ideology/ religion or the preservation of political power. But in the earliest constitutional provisions for press freedom, those of Sweden in 1765 and Denmark in 1770, it already emerges that media content (like all liberties) has moral and legal limits when it infringes upon the liberties of others. Defamation, harassment, and libel are typical examples of criminal prosecution resulting from indiscriminate publication.

If this is true for individuals targeted by negative content, groups can also pursue their grievances. The famous Berne trial in 1933–1935 was a court case between Swiss Jewish congregations and the Swiss National Front (a far-right party), which had disseminated the *Protocols of the Elder of Zion*, a conspiratorial antisemitic tract about purported Jewish world dominance, portrayed as a factual account (see Chapter 1). The *Protocols* are a forgery and not an official document at all. The representatives from the Swiss National Front were fined for the dissemination of so-called *Schundlitteratur*, i.e. pulp fiction possibly instigating crimes by agitation against a minority (Hagemeister, 2022: 21–38). Vulgar antisemitism was inherent in the Nazi press in Germany. Julius Streicher (1885–1946, briefly mentioned in Chapter 2), publisher of the antisemitic weekly newspaper *Der Stürmer* from 1923 to 1945, was indicted on counts of 'crimes against peace' and 'crimes against humanity' at the International Military Tribunal (IMT) in Nuremberg in 1946 (The Avalon Project, 2008). On the last count, he was found guilty and sentenced to death.

In its ruling, the IMT pointed out that Streicher had over a very long time and in different ways 'infected the German mind with the virus of anti-Semitism and incited the German people to active persecution' and that each issue of *Der Stürmer*, which reached a circulation of 600,000 copies in 1935, was filled with articles inciting hatred. No fewer than 23 articles in the journal between 1938 and 1941 were identified in which the annihilation of the Jewish people was propagated. And, aware of the mass extermination of Jews, Streicher continued in another 26 articles between 1941 and 1944 with his calls to total annihilation, in what the IMT called 'propaganda of death'. The IMT also exposed Streicher's dehumanization, likening Jews to parasites, enemies, and evildoers, 'a disseminator of diseases who must be destroyed in the interest of mankind'.

In 1940, he published a letter to the editor 'which compared Jews with swarms of locusts which must be exterminated completely. Such was the poison Streicher injected into the minds of thousands of Germans which caused them to follow the National Socialist policy of Jewish persecution and extermination'. The IMT thus clearly connects Streicher's activities as publisher, editor, writer, and journalist with crimes against humanity. This indicates responsibility for the consequences of the content published.

In 2003, media scholar Renaud de la Brosse submitted a report to the Office of the Prosecutor of the International Criminal Tribunal for the Former Yugoslavia (ICTFY) about the use of propaganda in the Yugoslav wars in the 1990s (de la Brosse, 2003). The report not only covers topics related to the wars as such but also outlines more generally the weaponization of media in the conflict and the responsibility of media producers for the content disseminated. There seemed to be a clear nexus between the extreme nationalist discourse and the 'perpetration of horrible atrocities': media prepared the ground for war and crimes against humanity.

The weaponization of media developed along tighter control in the different territories and turned broadcasts in various formats into the 'regime's instruments of propaganda responsible for getting the population to subscribe to their political conceptions and actions' (de la Brosse, 2003 n p). De la Brosse demonstrates how news outlets consciously pushed lies 'to feed the hatred of the enemy', for instance by claiming that 'Muslim extremists' had thrown 'Serb children to the lions in the local zoo'. Propaganda campaigns like these were intended to sow divisions related to different ethnic identities and to undermine the cohesion of the various people across Yugoslavian space. De la Brosse also highlights how the technical development of media constituted a qualitative and quantitative break with the past: new techniques promoted 'emotion more than demonstration' and tended 'more towards suggestion rather than explanation'. In the context of aggressive Serbian nationalism, the desire to unite one people in one territory necessitated campaigns to justify the expulsion of other nationalities and ethnic and religious groups from 'Greater Serbia'. In line with what we have previously identified as the purpose of enemy images, De la Brosse notes that the entire press system was systematically geared towards inflammatory rhetoric pointing out dangers to the Serbian side and explicitly or implicitly threatening non-Serbs with reprisal. Serbian media were 'given the responsibility of distilling the venom of hatred and fear in the Serbian population', the existence of which according to the propaganda 'was directly threatened by the presence of the other minority ethnic groups'. In this process, 'the adversary or enemy has to be stigmatized using the most derogatory terms possible'. The ICTFY report finishes with a section on how disinformation triumphed and how false news was broadcast 'to stigmatise the enemy further'. Reading the proceedings of ICTFY provides more insights into how carefully the court investigated the question of guilt in relation to media producers, media content, and the audience effects of desensitization and mobilization against the constructed enemy.

In the same year, 2003, a similar argument was made during the Rwandan media case mentioned in the context of the 'broadcasting of hatred' above (ICTR, 2003). The accused trio from the Rwandan media industry, Nahimana, Barayagwiza, and Ngeze – a historian, lawyer, and journalist, respectively – were among other counts accused of direct and public incitement to commit genocide. The legal findings on this count amount to no fewer than 20 pages. Here it is noted that the UNGA in 1946 declared freedom of information a fundamental right, with the 'capacity to employ its privileges without abuse. It requires as a basic discipline the moral obligation to see the facts without prejudice and to spread knowledge without malicious intent' (ICTR, 2003: 317, paragraph 944). Additionally, it is stated that the case raised important principles concerning the role of the media which had not been addressed since the IMT in Nuremberg: 'The power of the media to create and destroy fundamental human values comes with great responsibility. Those who control such media are accountable for its consequences' (ICTR, 2003: 317, paragraph 945). The ICTR also found that

RTLM broadcasts engaged in ethnic stereotyping in a manner that promoted contempt and hatred for the Tutsi population and called on listeners to seek out and take up arms against the enemy […] defined to be the Tutsi ethnic group.

(ICTR, 2003: 318, paragraph 949)

The broadcasts called explicitly for their extermination. The court established a specific causal connection between the RTLM broadcasts and named individuals. In the case of Ngeze, who ran the newspaper *Kangura*, it was found that texts published therein 'conveyed contempt and hatred for the Tutsi ethnic group and for Tutsi women in particular as enemy agents' (ICTR, 2003: 318, paragraph 950). In the eyes of the court, 'the message of ethnic targeting for death was disseminated through RTLM and *Kangura*' (ICTR, 2003: 319, paragraph 953). As the court established, the accused were also directly involved in the planning and execution of killings, but of greater interest for our subject is that their genocidal intent was expressed in different radio broadcasts. From the quotes in the proceedings, it emerges clearly that the Tutsi were identified as enemies and legitimate targets of extermination: 'Kangura and RTLM explicitly and repeatedly, in fact relentlessly, targeted the Tutsi population for destruction. Demonizing the Tutsi as having inherent evil qualities, equating the ethnic group with "the enemy" and portraying its women as seductive enemy agents'. The accused even referred to their actions as a 'war of media, words, newspapers and radio stations' (ICTR, 2003: 320–321, paragraphs 963 and 966). Summing up, the tribunal stated that

the identification of Tutsi individuals as enemies of the state associated with political opposition, simply by virtue of their Tutsi ethnicity, underscores the fact that their membership in the ethnic group, as such, was the sole basis on which they were targeted.

(ICTR, 2003: 322, paragraph 971)

Nahimana, who had privileged knowledge of the Rwandan media sector, was said to be particularly responsible. He identified his establishment of RTLM as instrumental in the mobilization of hatred and violence 'to stand up against the Tutsi enemy' (ICTR, 2003: 323, paragraph 974).

The ICTR, however, did not only consider media content as such but also media programming and responsibilities inherent in ownership and institutional control over the media. The tribunal made explicit reference to the previous treatment of the issue at the IMT in Nuremberg. In the framework of international humanitarian law, freedom from discrimination must be balanced against freedom of expression (a negative, arguably stronger right, against a positive, arguably weaker right in the understanding of Isaiah Berlin and as outlined in his inaugural lecture in 1958). The International Covenant on Civil and Political Rights (ICCPR) provides that while everyone has the right to freedom of expression, the exercise of this right carries special duties and responsibilities and may therefore be subject to restrictions relating to individuals, national security, public order, or public health or morals. Moreover, the ICCPR states clearly that national, racial, or religious hatred inciting discrimination, hostility, or violence shall be prohibited by law. The ICTR reviewed available and relevant cases where this balance was tested at different courts to define 'elements of direct and public incitement to genocide as applied to mass media' (ICTR, 2003: 334, paragraph 1000).

These lengthy arguments merit a separate treatment. What matters to us is that the tribunal spelt out the modus operandi of the Rwandan media outlets in inciting violence. *Kangura*, for instance, published a list warning readers about 123 Tutsi and thus instilled fear in them, providing them with 'names to associate with this fear and mobilizing them to take independent proactive measures in an effort to protect themselves' (ICTR, 2003: 343, paragraph 1028), which is precisely consistent with how we have described the aims of an effective enemy image. According to the tribunal, the

> nature of radio transmission made RTLM particularly dangerous and harmful [...] Unlike print media, radio is immediately present and active. [...] Radio heightened the sense of fear, the sense of danger and the sense of urgency giving rise to the need for action by listeners, [... a] visceral scorn coming out of the airwaves.
>
> *(ICTR, 2003: 342–343, paragraph 1031)*

Here we can see an example of the court commenting on radio media and its qualities as such, with the message about the enemy reinforced by the 'urgency' of transmission over the airwaves.

All three accused were sentenced to life imprisonment; however, after an appeal in 2007, their sentences were reduced, and they were acquitted on some counts of the first chamber. The ICTR has nevertheless set important standards for the responsibility of the media in acting as mouthpieces of lethal enemy images. In the case of Russia's war of aggression in Ukraine, legal experts are already preparing the ground for holding propagandists to account in the future. In October 2022, a Russian TV journalist, for instance, suggested drowning or burning Ukrainian children (Moscow Times, 2022). The New York University School of Law gathers proof of 'Russia's eliminationist rhetoric against Ukraine' (NYU, 2023). And journalist Peter Pomerantsev (2022) has argued that 'Russia's genocidal propaganda must not be passed off as freedom of speech'. Time will tell if and how this case will develop. Technology is not neutral, and freedom of expression is not unlimited. Important issues concerning the accountability and responsibility of big tech platforms will also have to be solved in the future.

The imagination of the enemy in strategic battles of perception

In the last section of this chapter, we aim to capture contemporary challenges related to the expression of enemy images. The continuous digitization of media production requires specific attention to the way content is created, manipulated, and weaponized in malign foreign influence operations.

While we are moving fast into a future where synthetic, AI-generated/augmented media will be a considerable part of the information landscape, digital verification and fact-checking skills will grow in importance to defuse strategic narratives aimed at dominance in the cognitive domain of war, characterized as a 'battle of perceptions' (Zinzone and Cagnazzo, 2020). Such strategic narratives increasingly focus on the perception of geopolitical adversaries, something the war in Ukraine has forcefully demonstrated.

At the end of 2013, just before the illegal Russian annexation of Crimea, an image emerged on social media (see Figure 7.4). We see from behind a man with a traditional Ukrainian haircut (or *chupryna*) wearing a traditional Ukrainian shirt (or *vyshyvanka*), pondering his way forward – either to the angelic right, the Slavic East; or to the satanic left, the European West. It is a visual Manichean manipulation of public opinion, a vector of foreign influence effectively communicating disruptive strategic narratives, in this case about Ukraine and the purported existential choice it faces (Önnerfors, 2019: 13–20). The image operates at two levels of visual

FIGURE 7.4   Social media meme about Ukraine (ca. 2014).

Source: Artist Unknown and Uncredited. First known usage in November 14, 2013 in a now deleted post in the r/WTF subreddit on reddit.com. Within a few days, the image was reposted on multiple sites in rapid succession including several other subreddits, the Polish social media site www.sadistic.pl, (reposted at least 4 known times within a day of supposed original post) imgur, vk.com, and various other social media sites originating in Russia and various EU countries.

representation of abstract or inner states of conflict as frequently found in comics or caricatures. In the right field, coloured in reddish and golden tones, an angelic boy, dressed in Russian red, white, and blue, points to images of a glorious Slavic historical past and a radiant religious tradition coupled with traditional family values. But we also see representations of victory in Second World War, the race to space, and a modern fighter jet embodying military might. To the left, against a dark blue background, pot-bellied red Satan himself, openly displaying his genitalia and wearing stay-up stockings, demonstrates the alternative of the EU as a continuation of Nazi rule (Adolf Hitler is placed next to the EU and Pride flags), thrown into the deep decadence of Pride, homo- and transsexuality. A barely visible 'emo guy' represents the emasculation of Western manhood. What also waits in the West is drug addiction and tutelage under the whip of the euro.

If we analyse the image more closely, the following visual programme of existential and irreconcilable juxtapositions can be discerned (Table 7.1):

Since 2013, this image has morphed from a marginal meme in social media to a strategic matrix of contemporary warfare. The right to resort to war (or a 'special military operation', in Russian terms) was justified by frequent references to the Ukrainian state being populated by neo-Nazis. And the idea of liberating a people of shared Slavic origin and reintegrating them into a new Russian Orthodox empire was soon replaced by a more sinister trope, that the enemy population were in fact devil-worshippers or Satanists (EUvsDisinfo, 2022). By late February 2022, President Putin was calling the entire Ukrainian leadership 'a gang of drug addicts and Neo-Nazis' (Putin, 2022). Signing tougher legislation against LGBTQ rights in Russia has been taken to mean that homosexuality is now part of the war agenda in Ukraine. It was necessary to attack Ukraine because of the 'genocide against the Russian people, against Russian speakers, against those who don't accept LGBT, transgender-Nazi values' (Kucher, 2022). This falls into the general framing of

TABLE 7.1 Ukraine's choice between friends and foes as framed in pro-Russian propaganda

Satanic West	*Angelic East*
Colour scheme: dark blue/cold (*goluboi*, the colour blue in Russian, also denotes homosexuality)	Colour scheme: reddish, gold/warm (red and gold denoting resurrection in Orthodox iconography)
EU as continuation of Nazi rule	Glorious past of shared Slavic/national history
Pride as decadence of the West	Radiant religious tradition
EU implies homo-/transsexuality	Traditional family values
The 'emo guy' as a symbol of Western emasculation	Fighter jet: military might
Drug addiction as shorthand for decadence and decay	Victory in the race to space
Serfdom under foreign currency (euro)	Victory in Second World War

Europe as 'Gayropa', weakened by tolerance towards homosexuality (Önnerfors and Krouwel, 2021: 8).

In this case, it is obvious how images of the enemy and justification of warfare overlap. More subtly, the same iconographic strategy of Manichaean imagination was applied during the presidential campaigns in the Czech Republic and Slovakia in 2017–2018 (Önnerfors, 2019: 13–20). Here too, an increasingly dystopian existential dualism between a healthy national culture and the decadent and polluted West was evoked in social media campaigns. Czechs and Slovaks were framed in an existential choice between, on the left, the EU/NATO as a Babylonian, Satanist, and war-mongering Nazi entity orchestrating mass migration and engaging in homosexual emasculating perversion (the iconic 'emo boy' was also present in one of the images); and on the right, a paradise of clean nature, nuclear family, and national culture.

As Zinzone and Cagnazzo outline in their book *The Art of War in the Post-Modern Era* (2020), the battle of perceptions is of crucial importance to understanding the hybridity of contemporary warfare in multiple grey zones between hard/military and soft/civilian power. Consequently, it is no longer a question of only portraying the enemy during a war but preferably also already embedded in a larger geopolitical strategic narrative. Such a narrative outlines principal divides between allies and adversaries. It includes imagery that in peacetime explains and rationalizes political choices but in grey zones of hybrid warfare or open hostilities also provides pretexts to legitimize a just cause of war (*jus ad bellum*), the conduct during the war (*jus in bello*), or systematic breaches of international and humanitarian law. Visual representations and strategic narratives become intertwined. The cognitive and informational dimensions of warfare are increasingly important. Thus, the power of Foreign Information Manipulation and Interference (FIMI), its Tactics, Techniques, and Procedures (TTP), and the overarching aim of narrative strategic dominance are almost as relevant as the application of physical force in time and space.

Summary

In this chapter, we have argued that enemy images and the way they are expressed and disseminated in media are interrelated and that media and messages are intrinsically linked, ranging from traditional print media to posters, postcards, broadcasts, or social media postings. Enemy images adapt to evolving media logic and technique.

Our first example of the 'Yellow Peril' related to a widely circulated print from around 1900, evoking European unity in the face of vastly exaggerated external threats. Yet, during the actual war resulting from the increasing confrontation between Europe and Asia, the dehumanization achieved by the enemy image informed what today would be called crimes against humanity. We also outlined the afterlife and longevity of enemy images beyond the immediate context of their creation. This is particularly evident in the portrayal of the Jews as eternal enemies within. The blood libel, concocted during the Middle Ages, was immediately translated into a powerful visual narrative strategy, spread through woodcuts, encyclopaedias, statues, and interactive theatre plays. It survives today under the false flag of 'artistic freedom' on social media. As the example of radio broadcasts demonstrates, new technologies of mass communication transposed modes of enemy depiction to invisible radio waves, mostly employed in wartime propaganda and with lethal effect during the Rwanda genocide. The medium of moving images (paired with film music/music scores as an important mode of emotional mobilization) was also from its beginnings around 1900 prone to producing and reproducing representations of the enemy for various purposes. In recent decades, it can also be observed that feature films are employed to revise former enemy images and create reconciliation or to revise formerly inflexible schemes of perpetrator and victim.

Post-1945, warfare in televised news developed between journalistic freedom and excessive modes of governmental control. How far enemies (adversaries) were portrayed was not a matter of truthful or factual representation but of which images were allowed to be screened. The hegemony of reporting from the war theatre has, however, been challenged by other news outlets, spectacular leaks, and the most recent dynamics of IRL and online production and consumption of carefully crafted short videos for dissemination on social media in a considerable style of gamification. The hyperreality of synthetic media will challenge these trends further.

We finished the chapter by discussing the accountability of media producers for the violence instigated by the dissemination of toxic enemy images. Referring to the Nuremberg trials after the Second World War, the ICTFY (Yugoslavian wars), and the ICTR media case in 2003 (Rwandan genocide), it is highly worthy of note that international humanitarian law increasingly posits that the right to life enjoys greater protection than freedom of expression. These positions will most likely be tested once again in any future war trials after the war in Ukraine.

Finally, expressions of enemy images in various types of media demonstrate their salience in geopolitical 'battles of perception' and advanced information influence activities. The cognitive and informational dimensions of warfare open the way for a redefinition of enemy images as elements in achieving strategic narrative hegemony: they can be planted before a conflict has even started, mobilized during the grey area of hybrid warfare, and utilized as tools of open propaganda once hot conflict has commenced.

Desensitization can be viewed as a framing process that plays out over time and for instance leads to the acceptance of ever more extreme images in an interplay with more subtle insinuations. The likelihood of an enemy image mobilizing audiences across the threshold from mere ideation to (violent) action increases

- if it changes from a more complex to a more simplified representation
- from polychrome with nuances and a certain amount of fuzziness to monochrome with sharp contrasts

- from malleable to rigid
- from liquid and polysemic to solid and explicit.

A clear picture of the enemy underlines the dualist confrontation between friends and foes and intensifies the necessity of a resolution of the tension it creates. The final eruption of what is called hostilities relieves this tension. At the same time, it requires the enemy image to be upheld or even intensified across the hot conflict, after which it might decrease again in the processes of post-conflict peacebuilding.

Despite the wide variety of media and messages over the centuries since the invention of the printing press, moving from the solid Gutenberg galaxy to the dynamic global village of more liquid online dissemination, we believe it is possible to determine some common frames in the expressions of enemy images which resonate with their rhetoric and psychology. Some of these do overlap.

1 *Dichotomies.* Expressions of enemy images thrive on strong and existential contrasts, a dualism between 'us' and 'them'. The representation of the enemy is to a certain extent also a representation of self-design (see below; also Table 2.1). The repertoire of dichotomy is wide and has for instance following components:
   a humanization/dehumanization: the side of friends and allies is portrayed as civilized, gentle, and noble, and enemies as crude barbarians without ethical standards
   b trust/distrust, narratives of suspicion: the enemy and their collaborators are cunning and not to be trusted
   c reversed anthropomorphism: the association with animals (and fantasy creatures) serves either as a symbol of innocence or evil. Enemies are likened to monsters, beasts, and unwanted vermin
   d humour versus brutalization: the enemy is either ridiculed or brutalized
2 *Scapegoating and targeting.* The enemy is characterized as an inhumane collective of blame. They are all the same (see Chapter 2).
3 *External and internal threats.* Furthermore, enemies are portrayed as both external and internal. The threat against the community emanates from outside and within, where out-groups are referred to as agents of the external enemy. Moreover, any collaboration with or understanding of the enemy is vilified. This relates also to the consumption of enemy media, which a priori is regarded as contaminated.
4 *Stereotyping and stylized simplicity.* Enemies are portrayed according to preconceptions aligned with pre-existing identity images of 'the other', embedded in collective political mythologies. Thus, enemy images are constructed as simple representations in which these stereotypes are translated into messages and iconographic markers and easily decoded.
5 *Gendering.* Male characters are portrayed as heroes or villains, female characters either as national role models, passive victims of violence (frequently together with children as innocent targets), or as seductive femmes fatales.

6 *Transtemporal storytelling.* The actions of the enemy unfold along a predictable narrative string that establishes familiarity ('the enemy always acts like this'). Individual narratives are embedded in larger legendary cycles about 'the other' that can develop over centuries. Storytelling is reinforced by conspiratorial meaning-making.

7 *Religious references.* The portrayal of the enemy evokes religious references to concepts like evil (explanation of theodicy), Satanic deviance, decadence, and apocalypse.

8 *Reinforcement of self-designs.* All previous points serve the purpose of creating accounts of national/racial/religious might and superiority. Imagining the enemy serves the purpose of describing our actions as justifiable and noble. The portrayal of the enemy offers consolation, deflection of guilt, blame, and responsibility, and the prospect of future redemption.

Study questions

- Study the cartoons of Lancelot Speed and explain how the enemy is portrayed.
- Study the 'Serio-comic war map for 1877' and investigate how the image of the octopus has been used as a powerful representation of enemies across cultures and times (also make use of the article 'The octopuses of war: First World War propaganda maps in pictures' (The Guardian, 2014).
- Go through the ICTR judgement and sentence of 2003 and discuss the responsibility of media and journalists in portraying the enemy.
- Watch one of the movies mentioned in the section on feature films and analyse how enemies are portrayed.

Potential essay or thesis suggestions

- Select a social media outlet (YouTube, TikTok, Instagram, or similar) and see how the representation of enemies is framed in relation to the war in Ukraine. Analyse visuals, text, and music, and how they contribute to the construction of enemies.
- Explore the 'Yellow Peril' in various media in Europe around 1900 and try to reconstruct its meaning for enemy perceptions in this historical period. An additional perspective would be: do you see any parallels with any other culturally constructed representations of geopolitical adversaries in our own age?
- Carry out an analysis of *Zulu* (1964). How is this colonial conflict portrayed in terms of enemy representation? Why do you think that this feature film has experienced a revival and been adapted to the shorter format of social media through selected reels?

Recommended further reading

Sokołowska-Paryż, M. and Löschnigg, M. (eds.) (2018) *The Enemy in Contemporary Film.* Berlin/Boston: De Gruiter.

Somerville, K. (2012) *Radio Propaganda and the Broadcasting of Hatred.* London: Palgrave Macmillan.
Both books provide an excellent introduction to the topic of this chapter, how enemy images are expressed in different media. It not only is evident how the content promotes the communication of enemy images but also how the specific qualities of the medium as such impact modes of dissemination and audience engagement.

Bibliography

Alpert, J. (2005) Interview in "Enemy image" (2005) 1:11:35–1:11:50. www.youtube.com/watch?v=3VCWA2XNZgc, accessed 16 December 2022.

Astapova, A., Bergmann, E., Dyrendal, A., Önnerfors, A., Rabo, A., Grotle Rasmussen, K. and Þórisdóttir, H. (2021) *Conspiracy Theories and the Nordic Countries.* London: Routledge.

Aupers, S., Craciun, D. and Önnerfors, A. (2020) Introduction to Section 4.0 Media and Transmission. In Butter, M. and Knight, P. (eds.) *Handbook of Conspiracy Theories* (pp. 387–391). London: Routledge.

Baade, B. (2019) Fake news and international law. *The European Journal of International Law* 29(4): 1357–1376.

Bennett, W. L., Lawrence, R. G. and Livingston, S. (2007) *When the Press Fails: Political Power and the News Media from Iraq to Katrina.* Chicago, IL: The University of Chicago Press.

BFI (2022) Bully Boy (1914) | BFI National Archive. British Film Institute. https://youtu.be/HuYJk0Vr0NU, accessed 17 December 2022.

Bradshaw, P. (2023) Michael Caine might not like it, but Zulu shows cinema's power to rewrite history. *The Guardian*, 10 March 2023. www.theguardian.com/film/2023/mar/10/michael-caine-zulu-history-british-mythology, accessed 21 May 2023.

British Library (2014) Depicting the enemy. www.bl.uk/world-war-one/articles/depicting-the-enemy, accessed 16 December 2022.

British Pathé (2022) Britain's Effort (1918). https://youtu.be/x8flWqo7edY, accessed 16 December 2022.

Caumanns, U. and Önnerfors, A. (2020) Conspiracy Theories and Visual Culture. In Butter, M. and Knight, P. (eds.) *Routledge Handbook of Conspiracy Theories* (pp. 441–456). London: Routledge.

Caumanns, U. and Önnerfors, A. (2021) "Ritualmord" – konspiratorische Konstante antisemitischer Bildcodes vom Mittelalter bis zur Gegenwart. *Juden in Mitteleuropa* 2021: 12–18.

Cornell University (2015) Ungeziefer: Völker Europas, wahrt eure heiligsten Güter! https://digital.library.cornell.edu/catalog/ss:8245867, accessed 1 July 2024.

De la Brosse, R. (2003) *Report to the Office of the Prosecutor of the International Criminal Tribunal for the Former Yugoslavia (ICTFY).* The Hague: ICTFY.

Deaville, J. (2006) Selling war: Television news music and the shaping of American public opinion. *ECHO* 8(1): 735–741. https://musiconn.qucosa.de/api/qucosa%3A72045/attachment/ATT-0/?L=1

Der Spiegel (2013) Ein Ruf wie Donnerhall. 24 October 2013. www.spiegel.de/fotostrecke/soldatensender-calais-britischer-radiosender-gegen-hitler-fotostrecke-110493.html, accessed 5 November 2022.

Deutsches Historisches Museum (2022) Erzengel Michael mit dem Flammenschwert vor den Personifikationen der europäischen Nationen, darunter eigenhändige Aufschrift

Kaiser Wilhelms II. www.deutsche-digitale-bibliothek.de/item/CCXMA2KGWBVOD GK3RC3ANRPM4LHXHIEY, accessed 31 October 2022.

Doorn, M., von Duivestein, S. and Pepping, T. (2021) *Real Fake: Playing with Reality in the Age of AI, Deepfakes and the Metaverse*. Amsterdam: Ludibrium.

EU vs Disinfo (2022) Satan's little helpers. *EUvsDisnfo*. 8 December 2022. https://euvsdisinfo.eu/satans-little-helpers/, accessed 17 December 2022.

Films for Action (2022) 'Enemy image' (2005). www.filmsforaction.org/watch/enemy-image-2005/, accessed 6 November 2022.

Galtung, J. (1990) Cultural violence. *Journal of Peace Research* 27(3): 291–305. https://doi.org/10.1177/0022343390027003005

German, K. (2019) Video verité of ISIS. In Krona, M. and Pennington, R. (eds.) *The Media World of ISIS* (pp. 125–144). Bloomington, IN: Indiana University Press.

Gunning, T. (2004) What's the Point of an Index? Or, Faking Photographs. *Nordicom Review* 25: 39–49.

Hagemeister, M. (2022) *The Perennial Conspiracy Theory*. London and New York, NY: Routledge.

Hallin, D. (1986) *The Uncensored War: The Media and Vietnam*. New York, NY: Oxford University Press.

Harper's Weekly: Journal of Civilization (1898) A picture by Emperor William, No. 2144, 22 January 1898.

ICTR (2003) International Criminal Tribunal for Rwanda, Judgment and Sentence in the case Prosecutor v. Ferdinand Nahimana, Jean-Bosco Barayagwiza and Hassan Ngeze, ICTR-99-52-T. https://ucr.irmct.org/LegalRef/CMSDocStore/Public/English/Judgement/NotIndexable/ICTR-99-52/MSC26797R0000541998.PDF, accessed 6 November 2022.

Illustrirte Zeitung (1895) Völker Europas, wahret eure heiligsten Güter, No. 2733, 16 November 1895, 597.

IMDb (2022) 'Battle for Haditha' (2007). www.imdb.com/title/tt0870211/, accessed 6 November 2022.

Kendall, A. (2011) Freemasonry and the Second Ku Klux Klan in California, 1921–1925. *Journal for Research into Freemasonry and Fraternalism* 1: 123–143.

Klein, T. (2013) Die Hunnenrede. In Zimmerer, J. (ed.) *Kein Platz an der Sonne. Erinnerungsorte der deutschen Kolonialgeschichte* (pp. 160–172). Frankfurt am Main: Campus.

Knust, M. (2021) Fictionalizing populism: A music analysis of recent political journalist soundtracks. *Mobilis in Mobile: La revue des cultures populaires* 1(1): 1–11.

Krona, M. and Pennington, R. (2019) *The Media World of ISIS*. Bloomington, IN: Indiana University Press.

Kucher, S. (2022) Why Russia has made homophobia part of its anti-Ukraine propaganda. *Grid News*, 28 November 2022. www.grid.news/story/global/2022/11/21/why-russia-has-made-homophobia-part-of-its-anti-ukraine-propaganda/, accessed 17 December 2022.

May, O. (2016) *Europa und die "Gelbe Gefahr". Vom Boxer-Aufstand zum russisch-japanischen Krieg*. Geschichte im Postkartenbild (Band 7). Hildesheim: Franzbecker.

McLuhan, M. (1964) *Understanding Media. The Extensions of Man*. New York, NY: Signet Books.

Meier, A. C. (2018) An affordable radio brought Nazi propaganda home. *JSTOR Daily*, 30 August 2018. https://daily.jstor.org/an-affordable-radio-brought-nazi-propaganda-home/, accessed 5 November 2022.

MIGS (2022) *Rwanda Radio Transcripts: The Role of the Radio*. Montreal Institute for Genocide and Human Rights Studies. www.concordia.ca/research/migs/resources/rwa nda-radio-transcripts.html, 5 November 2022.

MIT (2022) Yellow Promise / Yellow Peril. Massachusetts Institute of Technology, Vizualizing Cultures. https://visualizingcultures.mit.edu/yellow_promise_yellow_peril/ yp_visnav07.html, n.d., accessed 30 October 2022.

Moscow Times (2022) RT Host Suspended for Calls to 'Drown, Burn' Ukrainian Children. 24 October 2022. www.themoscowtimes.com/2022/10/24/rt-host-suspended-for-calls-to-drown-burn-ukrainian-children-a79172, accessed 6 November 2022.

NYU (2023) *Russia's Eliminationist Rhetoric against Ukraine: A Collection*. New York University School of Law. www.justsecurity.org/81789/russias-eliminationist-rhetoric-against-ukraine-a-collection/, accessed 6 November 2022.

Önnerfors, A. (2017) Between Breivik and PEGIDA: The absence of ideologues and leaders on the contemporary European far right. *Patterns of Prejudice* 51(2): 159–175.

Önnerfors, A. (2019) Manichaean Manipulation – Europe between Apocalypse and Redemption in the Imaginary of the New Right. In Moberg A. (ed.) *European Disintegration (?)* (pp. 13–20). Forskning om Europafrågor No. 32. Gothenburg: CERGU.

Önnerfors, A. (2020) Researching Right-Wing Hypermedia Environments: A Case-Study of the German Online Platform einprozent.de. In Asche, S., Busher, J., Macklin, G. and Winter, A. (eds.) *Researching the Far Right: Theory, Method and Practice* (eds.) Routledge Studies in Fascism and the Far Right (pp. 178–193). London: Routledge.

Önnerfors, A. and Krouwel, A. (2021) Between Internal Enemies and External Threats: How Conspiracy Theories Have Shaped Europe. In Önnerfors, A. and Krouwel, A. (eds.) *A Continent of Conspiracies? Conspiracy Theories in and on Europe* (pp. 1–21). London: Routledge

Pomerantsev, P. (2022) Russia's genocidal propaganda must not be passed off as freedom of speech. *The Observer*, 16 October 2022. www.theguardian.com/commentisfree/2022/oct/16/propaganda-russia-ukraine-war-crimes-accountability, accessed 6 November 2022.

Potter, S. J. (2023) Broadcasting in the cause of peace: Regulating international radio propaganda in Europe, 1921–1939. *The International History Review* https://doi.org/10.1080/07075332.2023.2224352

Putin, V. (2022) Putin calls Ukraine government 'drug addicts and neo-Nazis'. *Agence France Presse*. https://youtu.be/rkos-aWbo7w?t=20, accessed 17 December 2022.

Ranstorp, M. and Ahlerup, L. (2023) *LVU-kampanjen. Desinformation, konspirationsteorier, och kopplingarna mellan det inhemska och det internationella i relation till informationspåverkan från icke-statliga aktörer*. Försvarshögskolan. http://fhs.diva-por tal.org/smash/get/diva2:1757636/FULLTEXT01.pdf

Sokołowska-Paryż, M. and Löschnigg, M. (2018) Introduction. In Sokołowska-Paryż, M. and Löschnigg, M. (eds.) *The Enemy in Contemporary Film*. Berlin/Boston, MA: De Gruiter.

Somerville, K. (2012) *Radio Propaganda and the Broadcasting of Hatred*. London: Palgrave Macmillan.

Sveriges Radio (2022) Online campaign spreading disinformation about Swedish social services. https://sverigesradio.se/artikel/online-campaign-spreading-disinformation-about-swedish-social-services, accessed 10 December 2022.

Taylor, P. (1992) *War and the Media, Propaganda and Persuasion in the Gulf War*. Manchester: Manchester University Press.

Teter, M. (2020) *Blood Libel: On the Trail of an Antisemitic Myth*. Cambridge, MA: Harvard University Press.

The Avalon Project (2008) Nuremberg Trial Proceedings, Volume 22, Two hundred and eighteenth day, in The Avalon Project. Documents in Law, History and Diplomacy, Yale University. https://avalon.law.yale.edu/imt/10-01-46.asp, accessed 6 November 2022.

The Blood Libel Trail (2022). https://thebloodlibeltrail.org, accessed 31 October 2022.

The Guardian (2014) The octopuses of war: WW1 propaganda maps in pictures. 3 June 2014. www.theguardian.com/books/gallery/2014/jun/03/war-ww1-propaganda-maps-in-pictures, accessed 18 December 2022.

von Hoensbroech, P. (1919) *Das englische Raubtier.* Leipzig: Breitkopf & Haertel.

Welch, D. (2014) Know your enemy: Images of the enemy in propaganda in the twentieth century. Freud Museum London, 31 October 2014. www.podbean.com/media/share/pb-j9s7c-51aeee?utm_campaign=embed_player_stop&utm_medium=dlink&utm_source=embed_player, accessed 17 December 2022.

Wikimedia (2018) German medal from 1920 about the so-called Black Horror on the Rhine. https://commons.wikimedia.org/wiki/File:Schwarze_Schande_Black_Shame.jpg, accessed 17 December 2022.

Zinzone, F. and Cagnazzo, M. (2020) *The Art of War in the Post-Modern Era: The Battle of Perceptions.* Milan: Zinzone & Cagnazzo.

INDEX

Printed and bound by CPI Group (UK) Ltd, Croydon, CR0 4YY

01/12/2024

01797774-0011